AMERICA'S FIRST RIVER:
THE HISTORY AND CULTURE OF THE HUDSON RIVER VALLEY

COLLECTED, AND WITH AN INTRODUCTION, BY

THOMAS S. WERMUTH, JAMES M. JOHNSON & CHRISTOPHER PRYSLOPSKI

A PROJECT OF THE

NEW YORK
HUDSON-FULTON-CHAMPLAIN QUADRICENTENNIAL
COMMISSION

2009

Published by
Hudson River Valley Institute
Marist College
3399 North Road
Poughkeepsie, New York 12601
and
State University of New York Press
State University Plaza
Albany, NY 12246

Distributed by
State University of New York Press

For information, contact State University of New York Press, Albany, NY
www.sunypress.edu

Library of Congress Cataloging-in-Publication Data

America's first river : the history and culture of the Hudson River Valley / collected by
Thomas S. Wermuth, James M. Johnson & Christopher Pryslopski.
    p. cm.
Includes bibliographical references.
ISBN 978-0-615-30829-6 (pbk. : alk. paper)
    1. Hudson River Valley (N.Y. and N.J.)—History. I. Wermuth, Thomas S., 1962– II.
Johnson, James M. (James Michael) III. Pryslopski, Christopher. IV. Hudson River Valley
Institute.
    F127.H8A514 2009
    974.7'3—dc22
    2009037463

10 9 8 7 6 5 4 3 2 1

CONTENTS

Natives & Newcomers

The American Revolution

Social and Economic Change: 1790–1850

Painters, Poets, and Writers

20th Century Leaders

On the Cover: Johann Hermann Carmienke's **The Hudson River at Hyde Park**, New York, 1856; Oil on canvas, 36 x 50 inches. Friends of American Art Purchase, 2005. Reproduction courtesy of The Orlando Museum of Art, which owns the painting. Photograph © The Orlando Museum of Art. A Project of the New York Hudson Fulton Champlain Quadricentennial Commission

Acknowledgments:

The editors would like to acknowledge the assistance of the following people, organizations and groups. At the Hudson River Valley Institute, Lindsay Moreau and Meredith Scott assisted with copy editing and Andrew Villani coordinated the business aspects of the project. Kate Donham read and offered valuable comments on "Four Hundred Years of Hudson River Valley History." In addition, special thanks to the following for sharing photographs and images: Kenneth F. Snodgrass, the Executive Director at Locust Grove; Patricia West, Curator at the Martin Van Buren National Historic Site; and Karen Casey Hines, at Vassar College's Frances Lehman Loeb Art Center. The New York State Office of Parks, Recreation, and Historic Preservation and Hudson River Valley Heritage assisted with images as well. The editors would like to recognize the founders of the *Hudson River Valley Review* (then the *Hudson Valley Regional Review* published by the Bard Center), Richard Wiles and the late William Wilson.

Thanks also go to the Hudson River Valley National Heritage Area for its continuing support of the Hudson River Valley Institute and the *Hudson River Valley Review*.

Preface

As New York and the world commemorate and celebrate the 400th Anniversaries of the historic explorations of Henry Hudson and Samuel de Champlain, as well as the bicentennial of Robert Fulton's historic voyage up the river, scholarly interest in the Hudson has renewed. New York's Hudson River Valley, America's first "melting pot," the only colony of the original thirteen not first settled by the English, has long intrigued historians. The region's unique landholding system in the colonial period, the many different ethnic and national groups that settled the region, its primary role in the American Revolution and the transportation and industrial developments of the nineteenth century and, more recently, the environmental movement, have made it a subject of great historical scrutiny. The region's contributions to the literary and visual arts have only enhanced its reputation further.

The Hudson-Fulton-Champlain Quadricentennial Commission and Office have been commemorating the region's history, dating to and preceding Henry Hudson's exploration of the river that now bears his name. With this collection of important articles and essays, the Hudson River Valley Institute has done the same. The following volume is a compilation of eighteen of the best articles written about the region's history, drawn from twenty-five years of publication of *The Hudson River Valley Review*. Originally published at Bard College under the editorial direction of Professor Richard Wiles, the journal has been published by Marist College's Hudson River Valley Institute since 2002. More than 200 articles and essays have been published since the journal's inception in 1984.

Join us as we celebrate the 400 years of New York's history.

Tara Sullivan
Executive Director
Hudson-Fulton-Champlain Quadricentennial

Four Hundred Years of Hudson River Valley History

Thomas S. Wermuth and James M. Johnson

In 1996, the United States Congress named the Hudson River Valley a "National Heritage Area," one of only thirteen in the nation at that time. The region was recognized for its role in the American Revolutionary War; its important contributions to American arts, letters, and architecture; its role in the economic development of the nation; and its significant and ongoing contributions to American culture and history that continue to this day. The essays that follow examine the many facets of the Hudson's rich history, distinctive regional culture, and important contributions to the development of modern America.

In many ways, the Hudson River Valley served as the symbol of America's identity and promise. Following Henry Hudson's 1609 exploration, the region became the nation's first "melting pot." Unlike the other areas of North America settled in the seventeenth century, such as New England and the Chesapeake, the valley was settled by many different national groups. While New England and Virginia witnessed the transplanting of English villagers, often from the very same villages and towns in England, to the "new" world, the Hudson River Valley was settled by several distinct ethnic and cultural groups. Dutch, English, French Huguenots, German Palatines, and slaves of African descent settled throughout the region. In 1646, the Jesuit missionary Isaac Jogues commented that he heard eighteen different languages spoken on the streets of Manhattan.[1] Several of the essays in this volume specifically examine the distinctive ethnic and national interactions that took place in the valley, the ways different groups attempted to maintain their unique heritages, and the various ways these ethnic cultures changed and evolved over time.

The North River Valley, as it was first known, was distinguished by its central role in the American Revolution, the region that George Washington referred to as the "Key to Victory." The region was prized by the British for its strategic and tactical advantages, its central role in communication and trade, and its primary role as the major agricultural producer in North America. For the same reasons, the American revolutionaries mustered all of their resources to retain and control the region. From 1776–1780, the region was the central battleground of the revolution, with major battles fought at Saratoga, Fort Montgomery, and Stony Point. It also witnessed some of the most dramatic and memorable aspects of the war, including Benedict Arnold's failed conspiracy at West Point, the burning of the New York capital at Kingston, the chaining of the river, and the almost 700-mile march of Rocheambeau and Washington's combined French-American army.

The Hudson River Valley has earned a place of historical distinctiveness because of its unique system of land ownership in the colonial and early national period—a manorial system in which a handful of landlords exerted an inordinate amount of power over the colony and, later, the state, as well as the thousands of tenants who tilled their land. While most families that lived in the Hudson River Valley did so

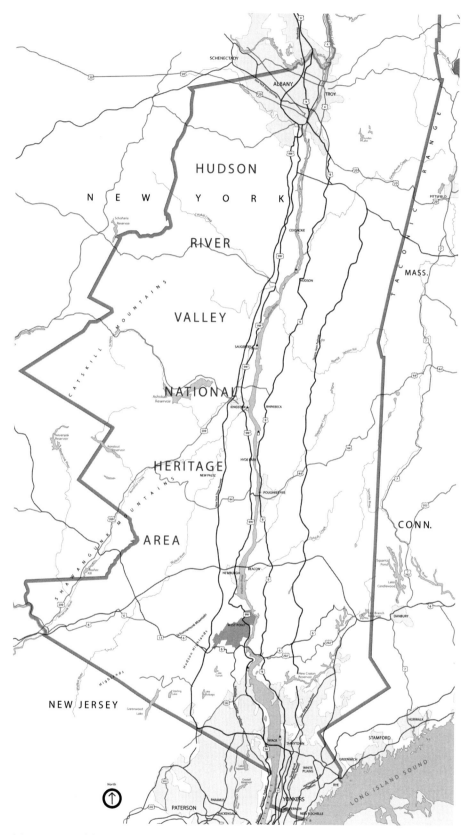

Map courtesy of the Hudson River Valley National Heritage Area

Thomas S. Wermuth and James M. Johnson

on free-hold farms, a significant minority of the population lived on one of the great landed estates owned by the Livingston, Van Renssalaer, Cortland, or Phillipse families. These manor lords possessed leases for several thousand tenant families, many of whom owed the lord traditional services and duties that were more characteristic of medieval England than eighteenth-century North America. Leases might run for several generations, demand that tenants grind their wheat at the landlord's mill or work several days a year for the lessor, or require symbolic payments of portions of rent in fowl and fruit.[2] Tensions existed within this system and tenant unease expressed itself in several different ways: the non-payment of rents, intimidation of the landlord's agents, and, at times, outright rebellion. In 1741, 1766, and of course during the great tenant revolt of 1839, fighting broke out between tenants and landlords on several of the manorial estates.[3]

In the nineteenth century, the Hudson River Valley emerged as the leader in American artistic and cultural life. The first recognized schools of American literature and art—the Hudson River writers and the Hudson River School of Landscape Painting—set out to define the valley as a unique progenitor of America's future, and imbued it with a past, sometimes mythic, to help give meaning to the region's, and by extension the nation's, promise. Painters such as Thomas Cole, Asher Durant, and Frederic Church painted the rich landscapes and imbued them with historic, mythical, and spiritual meanings. Authors like James Fenimore Cooper, Washington Irving, and William Cullen Bryant used real historical events, such as the French and Indian War or the American Revolution, in their writings, wrapping them in a fictionalized environment that metaphorically presented the region as a template for America's development. Naturalist John Burroughs, perhaps more than any other writer of the region, captured the details of his surroundings. As H. Daniel Peck has pointed out, the work of these painters and writers highlights the "manifold cultural meanings attached to the Hudson River Valley in the first half of the nineteenth century and exemplifies the process of national self definition."[4] Further, as Fran Dunwell has recently observed, "the river became the focus of a quest for national identity."[5]

The Hudson River Valley also emerged as the home of a distinctive architectural tradition. Architect Alexander Jackson Davis and landscape designer Andrew Jackson Downing designed their most memorable work in the valley and used the region as the model for new styles of architecture and landscape architecture. After developing successful separate careers, Davis and Downing worked together in the remodeling of the Annandale-on-Hudson estate, Montgomery Place. The new innovations in Hudson River architecture, the introduction of the "cottage" and the "villa" styles with their distinctive bracketed features, would help define not only the region's architecture, but America's nineteenth-century-living spaces.

The nineteenth century also witnessed the region's important and dynamic role in the rise of the "Empire State." New York City's emergence as a major commercial and industrial entrepôt took place in the early nineteenth century and was fueled, in part, by the economic growth of the valley. The region, long a leader in grain and other agricultural products, continued to play an important role in this transformation. Many farmers increased agricultural production to meet the needs of the growing urban markets in New York City and beyond. Other families in the Hudson River Valley altered their production and began to produce specialized market-oriented agricultural crops and manufactured goods. Others still turned away from farming and took jobs in the new mills that were springing up in Troy, Newburgh, and the vicinity of New York City.

The single largest factor in New York State's economic development was the so-called "transportation revolution"—the building of canals, turnpikes, and railroads across the state. Formerly isolated towns and villages throughout the northeastern United States were brought into an increasingly complex market system through the construction of turnpikes and canals. Between 1790 and 1820, 278 turnpike companies had built over 4,000 miles of road in New York and pulled fertile farmland from the rural interior into direct market competition with traditional agricultural producing regions like the Hudson River Valley. By the early 1830s, the construction of the Erie Canal and the Delaware and Hudson Canal had opened up the rich grain-producing hinterland of the western state to the New York City market, in direct competition with valley farm families.

With the changing economy, many valley residents also changed their work. In the early nineteenth century, some 80 percent or more of Hudson Valley residents were farmers or engaged in agriculture. By midcentury, the number of residents employed in the mills or warehouses along the river, or working for the canals or other transport industries, had swelled. The town of Kingston was emblematic of the larger trends. In 1825, almost 70 percent of the town's population were members of farm families. By midcentury, only 10 percent of Kingston residents made their living from farming.[6]

Through the first half of the nineteenth century, thousands of new immigrants, mostly Irish, swelled the population of the Hudson River Valley. They worked as unskilled laborers on the river's docks loading and unloading cargo, as well as on the canals shoveling coal and transferring goods for river shipment. Others worked as domestic servants or in construction. Long-time valley residents viewed these newcomers suspiciously, wary of their customs, traditions, and most notably their religion, primarily Catholicism. Nevertheless, these new residents slowly yet inexorably changed the social and cultural life of the valley. The power of the Empire State's industries and population would make it one of the leading suppliers of the manpower and finished goods, from horseshoes to textiles to iron plates, that would bring victory to the Union in the American Civil War.

The region emerged as a tourist attraction by the middle third of the nineteenth century. Writers like Cooper and Irving began to describe the region's beauty, painters like Cole and Durand highlighted the sublime and picturesque landscapes, and both painter and writer emphasized the valley's historical significance. Hotels like the Catskill Mountain House, among many others, emerged to meet the vacation needs of the growing New York City middle class. Travel authors wrote extensively about the beauty of the Palisades, the Highlands and West Point, the Catskills and Kaaterskill Falls, and the almost-spiritual experiences one could enjoy there. Thousands of tourists came up the Hudson by boat, some for a day tour and others for weeks at a time.[7]

By the end of the nineteenth century and continuing into the twentieth, America's moneyed elite built their castles along the river. New financial titans like the Rockefellers, Vanderbilts, and Morgans became neighbors of the landed gentry of Livingstons, Roosevelts, and Astors. The region continued as a tourist attraction, although on a far-reduced scale, and now focused on becoming the extended suburbs of New York City.

Thirteen of the essays in this volume originally appeared in *The Hudson Valley Regional Review*, now *The Hudson River Valley Review*, published by the Hudson River Valley Institute. We have chosen 18 articles, from the more than 160 published in these two regional journals, which we believe illustrate the richly textured history of this supremely important place. We hope that this anthology of representative pieces of writing about the Hudson River Valley will inspire you to enjoy many other editions of *The Hudson River Valley Review*.

The first group of essays examine the earliest periods of European contact and settlement. Charles Gehring and William Starna's "Dutch and Indians in the Hudson Valley: The Early Period," details the bonds of mutual interests forged between the Dutch and Mohawks in the early 17ᵗʰ century. The Mohawk served as "enforcers" of Dutch interests against other European and Indian groups and benefitted from the status as a privileged trading partner. The first half of the seventeenth century witnessed European groups parrying with each other and with the native peoples that knew, understood, and mastered the land the Europeans now coveted. These years witnessed both Europeans and Native Americans learning about each other and working out complex and, for a time, mutually beneficial relationships.

Vernon Benjamin examines the spiritual world of the native peoples of the river and the challenges forced upon this worldview due to European conquest. "The Algonquians in Context: The End of the Spirituality of the Natural World," investigates the sophisticated religious outlooks of the Valley Algonquians and their assimilation of the natural and spiritual worlds. Benjamin argues that the "integration of native life and spirituality with the ecosystem eventually proved so profound that survival as a people depended upon it." The European market system, most apparent in North America in the form of the pelt and fur trade, grew to threaten the natives' relationship to their material and spiritual world, thus undermining their worldview, economic culture, and social relations.

Firth Haring Fabend's "Pro-Leislerians Farmers in Early New York: A 'Mad Rabble' or 'Gentlemen Standing Up for their Rights'" examines early New York's role in the "Glorious Revolution." In England, the revolution led to the overthrow of James II and the installation of William and Mary. New York's role was more peripheral but certainly more violent. Fabend's essay explores who supported Jacob Leisler during the rebellion that bears his name, who opposed him, and "what was so threatening about Jacob Leisler that even his own relatives wanted him dead?" Over the years historians have posited many reasons for Leisler's Rebellion and the counter-actions afterward that led to his execution (by hanging and then, for good measure, beheading), ranging from political, religious, and socioeconomic. Fabend finds that the group of Leisler's followers that she has carefully traced were "respectable representatives of society's middling sort," and the reasons for opposition were fairly complex.

During the late seventeenth and early eighteenth centuries and the integration of English common law, women lost their identities as entrepreneurs and spousal partners, in Cynthia Kierner's judgment, and became ornaments focused on marriage, lavish decorum, fashion, education, and social standing. In her "From Entrepreneurs to Ornaments: The Livingston Women, 1679–1790," Kierner uses Alida Livingston as an example of the late-seventeenth-century wife who, under Roman-Dutch law, not only aided her husband in his political ventures but also oversaw their Albany County business. "Alida's entrepreneurial responsibilities had limited her leisure activities and social freedom. Her granddaughters, by contrast, enjoyed unprecedented social, cultural, and intellectual opportunities. . . ." Unfortunately they also lost the economic independence and equality that once allowed women the opportunity to play a significant role in the family's finances (56).

The second group of essays examines the revolutionary period. "The American Revolution in the Hudson River Valley" by James Johnson and Thomas Wermuth provides an overview of the region's important role in the Revolutionary War and the reasons that it was one of the most embattled areas in North America. Ultimately, it was the region's strategic importance, rich bounty, proximity to New York City, and leading role in trade that led both revolutionary and redcoat to prize the region.

Kenneth Shefsiek's "A Suspected Loyalist in the Rural Hudson Valley: The Revolutionary War Experience of Roeloff Josiah Eltinge" tells the story of New Paltz's Roeloff Josiah Eltinge, who was accused of being a tory by his neighbors and the conspiracy commissioners. His primary crime seems to have been disinterest in the revolutionary cause as revealed by his refusal to accept continental currency. As Edward Countryman has pointed out, Eltinge was by no means unique among people in the region and elsewhere, who chose no side in the conflict and preferred to watch the growing struggle from the sidelines.[8] The term "tory" was usually understood by generations following the revolution to mean someone who stayed loyal to the crown—a "loyalist." However, the term had much wider meaning during the war years and soon after. It connoted folks who were not "patriotic" enough or who simply seemed disinterested in the struggle. At times it referred to those who didn't seem to do their share to win the war, while other times it might be used to describe a local price-gouger. In the story of Roeloff Eltinge, we see the difficult world of the revolutionary Hudson and how a citizen could be driven into the loyalist camp by the harsh treatment of his neighbors.

Claire Brandt shows in "Robert R. Livingston, Jr.: The Reluctant Revolutionary" that Robert R. Livingston, Jr., might not deserve to be mentioned along the names of George Washington, Thomas Jefferson, George Clinton, and other prominent figures of the American Revolution. Nonetheless she gives him his due as she explores the numerous contributions that he made to the Whig cause in New York's Hudson River Valley. He was the chancellor of New York, a nominal member of the committee that drafted the Declaration of Independence, the Secretary of Foreign Affairs, and the Minister to France as the United States negotiated the acquisition of the Louisiana Purchase. For a leader of the democratic Whig cause in America's first civil war, he proved to be a reluctant revolutionary who regarded the masses "as irresponsible, immoderate, and injudicious" (82) and thus not to be trusted with political power. According to Brandt, Livingston hungered "for recognition, fame, and power" and in the end achieved only political ruination.

Thomas Wermuth's "'The women in this place have risen in a mob': Women Rioters and the American Revolution in the Hudson River Valley," tells the story of the popular disturbances and crowd actions that dominated valley towns and villages in the years during the revolution. While many crowd actions that occurred in the 1760s and 1770s were aimed at the British (Stamp Act Riots, Boston Massacre, etc.), it was far more common that eighteenth-century riots were aimed at local social and economic conditions. Boycotts of profiteering shopkeepers, "rough music" aimed at perceived social deviants, and riots against hoarding shopkeepers were not uncommon and in fact grew in number during the war years. These riots, often related to economic woes and shortages of basic foodstuffs, were dominated by women who exerted their public voice around these issues. Although women did not fight on the battlefield, they were involved in important social and economic activities central to the revolutionary process.

The third group of essays explores the dramatic social and economic development that occurred during the last part of the eighteenth century and the first part of the nineteenth century.

"The Struggle to Build a Free African-American Community in Dutchess County, 1790–1820," by Michael Groth, details the important changes taking place in African-American life in the years during their emancipation in New York. While some eighteenth-century-valley African Americans were free of slavery's bonds, they now faced an important new hurdle—developing independent households and constructing communities and lives from slavery's ashes. As Groth shows, this was no easy task, and the experience of former slaves in the mid-valley "cautions historians against romanticizing African-American life during the transitional period from slavery to freedom." Nevertheless, even while facing virtually insurmountable obstacles in the struggle to construct a free, independent existence, Groth argues that valley African Americans showed great courage and fortitude in their attempts.

Mark Carnes' article, "From Merchant to Manufacturer: The Economics of Localism in Newburgh, New York, 1845–1900," explores the changing nature of community and society during the period of market expansion. These years witnessed intense commercial and industrial growth, and these forces challenged many traditional ideas of family, community, and even a community's shared understanding of time and work. Communities that had once been organically tied to each other, woven together by bonds of mutual social and economic responsibilities, were transformed by the larger economic and market developments that were altering nineteenth-century America.

The railroad provided yet another transformative force to the physical, social, and economic landscape of America and the region. In 1849 the Hudson River Railroad created the village of Irvington in Westchester County out of Justus Dearman's farm. In his essay, "The Hudson River Railroad and the Development of Irvington, New York, 1849–1860" Rohit Aggarwala demonstrates how an innovation in transportation "altered the pattern of city growth" and turned rural regions "into extensions of a metropolitan region." Because of the Hudson River Railroad, prosperous members of the middle class could now enjoy the suburbs of Westchester County and commute to Manhattan every work day to increase their wealth.

Throughout the nineteenth century, new groups continued to enter the region, and many Germans and Brits, but mostly Irish immigrants, came to make the valley their home. Patricia West's essay, "Irish Immigrant Workers in Antebellum New York: The Experience of Domestic Servants at Van Buren's Lindenwald," examines some of the ways Irish immigrants intersected with the Hudson River aristocracies. The increasing social and economic wealth of many Hudson River Valley residents afforded the opportunity of domestic servants, a need met by the large influx of Irish to the northeastern United States in the early nineteenth century. West examines the important role these servants played in the domestic economy and the often contradictory and tense private life that occurred, using Lindenwald—the home of Martin Van Buren, eighth president of the United States and "the Sage of Kinderhook"—as a test case. West makes clear the contradiction of the ideology of the new republic, which emphasized independence and equality, with the reality of domestic servitude. Her research and analysis reveal much about the lives of laboring women in nineteenth-century New York and compel us to rethink the way we sometimes romanticize the historic sites we visit.

Susan Lewis's "Business Women in the 'Land of Opportunity': First- and Second-Generation Immigrant Proprietresses in Albany, New York, 1880," explores the role of immigrant women proprietors in the Albany economy in the mid-to-late-nineteenth century, a population that has been long overlooked by historians, who have tended to underestimate the numbers of women or ignore the important role they played in both the public market economy and private family economy. These grocers, saloon keepers, and boarding-house operators (among dozens of other vocations) chose proprietorship as a practical form of self-employment in their own homes and formed part of a business community where small family enterprises run by immigrant women and their relatives intersected regularly with male customers and suppliers. In order to understand how business functioned in the lives of these women and their families, Lewis proposes the model of a "family business economy," which both supplemented and complemented the wage labor of other family members.

The fourth group of essays examines the region's emergence as a literary, artistic, and cultural leader. America's first school of art, the Hudson River painters, and the first regional literary writers, the Hudson River authors, helped to shape the sensibilities of nineteenth-century Americans and define the possibilities of the young republic. Robert M. Toole's article "The 'Prophetic Eye of Taste': Samuel F. B. Morse at Locust Grove" traces the history and development of this Mid-Hudson site as well as the evolution of Morse's aesthetic and practice of landscape gardening there from 1847 to his death in 1872. In doing so, Toole also encapsulates much of the history of what Morse was first to describe in the United States as the fine art of landscape architecture, following its development in Europe and migration to the states. In reviewing the history and setting the context for Morse' entry, he provides a summary of the transition from wilderness to agriculture to Locust Grove's final state as a gentleman's farm, illustrating a pattern that recurred on estates throughout the region.

Authors like James Fenimore Cooper and Washington Irving, and painters like Thomas Cole, Asher Durand, and Frederick Church, were not only creating a historical and sublime Hudson River, they were also working in the very real world of the marketplace. Richard Wiles' "The Commerce of Art in the Nineteenth-Century Hudson Valley" reminds us of that all-important ingredient. Wiles seeks to determine the impact of the famous Hudson River School on its contemporaries. The Hudson River School has been recognized as America's first school of art and the originator of one of America's most enduring art forms. However, did average Hudson Valley folks have the opportunity to view these paintings, and how popular was this art form? What was its impact on social and cultural life? Wiles offers informative insights into these questions.

America's leading author of the first half of the nineteenth century chose the valley as his subject more than any other. Although James Fenimore Cooper set his stories throughout New York and North America—*The Pioneers* along Otsego Lake, *The Pathfinder* in upstate New York, and *The Prairie* in the Midwest—much of his work was set throughout the Hudson River Valley, such as *The Last of the Mohicans* in the area to the north of Albany, *Satanstoe* and *The Spy* in the lower valley, and his lesser known Wallingford novels in the mid-valley. Donald Ringe's "The Moral Geography of Cooper's *Miles Wallingford* Novels," examines Cooper's 1844 double novel *Afloat and Ashore* and *Miles Wallingford*. Wallingford travels far and wide on sea voyages and spends considerable time in New York City, a place of urban sophistication. However, as Ringe makes clear, Cooper believes that "permanent values," remain "on the land," specifically on Wallingford's Hudson Valley farm. This farm, Ringe points out, "represents the domestic values on which, in Cooper's view, the health of society depends" (218).

Thomas Casey's article "F.D.R., Father Divine, and the 'Krum Elbow' Flurry" reminds us how the Hudson River Valley was home to America's political, economic, and religious leadership in the twentieth century. These three traits came together during a curious little episode on the eve of World War II, when Franklin D. Roosevelt, Frederick Vanderbilt, and messianic leader "Fr. Divine" intersected around the purchase of a piece of property near F.D.R.'s Hyde Park home. Casey reveals the complex social, racial, and cultural issues involved in the story as well as the lengths F.D.R. may have been willing to go to control who his neighbors were.

Alfred Marks' appreciation of John Burroughs is an inspired introduction to this nineteenth century author and naturalist. A Roxbury native who later built a house and farm in West Park, Burroughs was a best-seller in his time, publishing essays in Harper's and other leading journals as well as twenty-five volumes of own. He was anthologized in educational readers, and befriended by Theodore Roosevelt, Henry Ford, Harvey Firestone, and other leading politicians and industrialists. As Marks emphatically states, Burroughs' legacy includes much more than just his books.

Notes

1. Russell Shorto, *The Island at the Center of the World,* (New York, N.Y.) p.107

2. Patricia Bonomi, *A Factious People: Politics and Society in Colonial New York,* (New York, N.Y; 1971), pp.180–96; Sung Bok Kim, *Landlord and Tenant in Colonial New York: Manorial Society, 1664–1775* (Chapel Hill, N.C., 1978), 235–80.

3. Kim, *Landlord and Tenant*, 39–40; Martin Bruegel, "Unrest: Manorial Society and the Market in the Hudson Valley, 1780–1850," *Journal of American History* 82 (1996):1393–1424.

4. H. Daniel Peck, *Hudson River Valley Images and Texts Brochure, NEH Summer Institute*, (Vassar College, 1993).

5. Frances Dunwell, *The Hudson: America's River*, (New York, 2008), p.69,

6. Thomas S. Wermuth, *Rip Van Winkle's Neighbors: The Transformation of the Rural Hudson River Valley* (Albany, 2002) pp.122–123

7. Dunwell, *The Hudson*

8. Edward Countryman, "The American Revolution: An Introduction," *Hudson River Valley Review* 20 (2003):.3

Natives & Newcomers

Dutch and Indians in the Hudson Valley: The Early Period

Charles T. Gehring and William A. Starna

The Rise of the United Provinces of the Netherlands, or How the Dutch Prepared Themselves to Face the New World

Sixteenth-century Europe was dominated by three major political and economic powers: Great Britain, the island kingdom that was developing into a unified economic force and would soon develop into a worldwide seafaring nation; France, whose expansionist drives threatened neighbors and influenced diplomacy from the Mediterranean to the North Sea; and the Hapsburg Empire, which stretched across Europe in a mosaic of possessions, determined by marriage and financed by the riches of the New World.[1] Among these powerful forces arose a nation that won its freedom from the Hapsburg Empire after an eighty-year struggle, successfully defended itself against the extra-territorial designs of France, and developed a seaborne empire that would compete with Great Britain in every corner of the world.[2]

The Low Countries or the Netherlands occupied the northwestern-most territory of the Hapsburg Empire's European possessions. They had come under the control of the Hapsburgs through a series of royal marriages designed as political alliances to strengthen and augment the empire. During the fifteenth century the seventeen provinces that constituted the Low Countries were acquired by the dukes of Burgundy through marriage, purchase, or bequest. The marriage of Mary, daughter of Charles the Bold, duke of Burgundy, to Maximilian von Hapsburg brought the Low Countries into an empire that sprawled across Europe. By the time Charles V abdicated his throne in favor of his son Philip and his brother Ferdinand in 1556, possessions of the Hapsburg Empire extended from Europe to the Americas to the Far East.[3] Although the Netherlands formed but a small corner of this vast empire, its location was ideal for warehousing goods from the Mediterranean, the Americas, and the Far East, and distributing them to the British Isles and the Baltic region. In addition to the Netherlands' pivotal position between Scandinavia, Great Britain, and the Mediterranean, three major river systems—the Rhine, the Maas (Meuse), and the Scheldt, which represent significant watersheds for France and Germany—converge there before emptying into the North Sea, creating a cultural and economic delta that steadily drew fresh human and financial resources from the interior of Europe. While subjected to the dynastic politics of the Hapsburgs, the Netherlands not only developed a merchant class that controlled most of the Baltic trade and a significant amount of the Mediterranean trade, but also provided seamen for service aboard Spanish ships throughout the world, which would serve the Dutch well in its Eighty Years' War against the empire.[4]

The Dutch revolt against the empire was caused by a complex set of social, religious, political, and economic issues. In simplified form the revolt was in reaction to two Hapsburg initiatives: an attempt to establish a central control and authority in the Netherlands to the detriment of local privileges, and the establishment of the Inquisition to suppress the Protestant heresy. The cerebral issue was perceived as an attack on the ancient rights and privileges of every political entity in the Netherlands. The emotional issue was seen as an attempt to suppress the religious threat to the Roman Catholic Church by the reformed religion of John Calvin. Both issues were ideal for Philip II to pursue. Unlike his father he had no affection for the Netherlands. He viewed these northern provinces merely as a fatted cow to be exploited. A centrally controlled Netherlands was to provide economic and human resources for Philip's political agenda.[5] As a devout Catholic he viewed the reformed movement in the North as a disease that had to be stamped out before it spread. Philip's inability to deal compassionately with these forces in the Netherlands and his view of the Dutch as nothing but hostile heretics led to the establishment of a new country, a new people, and a new world-trading power.[6]

The revolt began in 1568 more as an attempt to redress certain grievances than as an independence movement (as did our own American revolution). The Dutch side was led by a crafty member of the nobility, William the Silent of the House of Orange-Nassau.[7] For sixteen years he was the heart and soul of the revolt. During his leadership the northern provinces formed themselves into a political alliance. This 1579 Union of Utrecht was a defensive pact that still held the Spanish king as sovereign, although some proclaim it to be the foundation of the Dutch Republic. Prince William also promoted the Act of Abjuration in 1581, which has been called the Dutch declaration of independence. At the assembly in the Hague delegates from the United Provinces abjured their oath of allegiance to the king. The preamble read:

> Let all mankind know that a prince is appointed by God to cherish his subjects, even as a shepherd to guard his sheep. When he oppresses his subjects, destroys their ancient liberties, and treats them as slaves, he is to be considered, not a prince, but a tyrant. As such, the Estates of the land may lawfully and reasonably depose him, and elect another in his place.

Three years after this emotional scene in the Hague, at which the delegate from Friesland dropped dead from a heart attack, William of Orange fell victim to an assassin's bullet at his home in Delft.[8]

The first phase of the revolt lasted thirty-nine years, until the Truce of 1609. During this time thousands of Protestant refugees fled northward. When Antwerp, the major commercial center and port in the Low Countries, was captured and sacked by Spanish soldiers, there was a massive exodus of wealth, talent, and human energy. In 1585 the Dutch responded by blockading the Scheldt River, denying Antwerp its access to the sea. As Antwerp declined in importance and economic power, Amsterdam rose.

Although the Dutch were now fighting for independence, they were also struggling for economic survival. No longer a part of the Hapsburg commercial empire, the Dutch provinces were forced to seek their own markets, and secure and maintain their own trade routes. For years the Baltic trade or "mother trade," as the Dutch fondly and accurately called it, was the backbone of their commerce. Goods from all over the world were brought to the Netherlands, where they were warehoused, sometimes reprocessed, and shipped on to the Baltic in exchange for grain and timber. For example, Portugal imported spices from the Far East and salt from the Iberian peninsula. The exotic appeal of the former brought them into great demand in the Baltic, while the latter was necessary for the flourishing Dutch herring industry. After the herring spawning grounds shifted from the Baltic to the North Sea around 1400, the Dutch developed a preservation method that gave them an advantage over competitors. By immediately gutting the herring and pickling them in a brine solution, Dutch fishermen could keep their herring boats at sea longer in order to maximize their

Charles T. Gehring and William A. Starna

catches. However, this process required a steady supply of salt. When Portugal was united with Spain in 1580, Dutch access to both the spices of the Far East and the salt of Lusitania was threatened.[9]

Dutch merchants responded to the challenge by establishing their own markets in the Far East and finding new sources for salt. These new market ventures, however, brought the Dutch into direct conflict with the Portuguese for control of the spice trade. Similarly, in their search for salt, the Dutch were drawn into the Caribbean, where they found themselves competing with aggressive Spanish interests to control the numerous salt-producing islands. Companies were formed by merchants and commercial interests in various Dutch cities such as Amsterdam and Rotterdam to finance trading ventures to the Far East. In 1599 Jacob van Neck of the Far Lands Company returned with four ships loaded with spices. Investors received 100 percent return on their capital; when four more ships came into port the return increased to 400 percent. There was no lack of capital for such potentially dramatic returns on investment. Two years later fourteen fleets totaling sixty-five ships left for the Far East. The competition became so fierce that it was not only leading to bloodshed but also driving up prices—price fixing by monopolistic control of the product was basic to the mercantilistic system of maximizing profits. This fierce rivalry led to the formation of the Vereenigde Oostindische Compagnie (VOC), or East India Company, in 1602. Rather than having many private interests competing with one another to the detriment of all, one monopoly was formed in which all could participate as shareholders, and in which profit would not be diminished by competition."[10]

The VOC was formed as a joint-stock trading venture. Chartered by the States General of the Netherlands, the VOC had a trading monopoly from the Cape of Good Hope eastward to the Strait of Magellan—most of the world, except for the Atlantic region. It had the power to raise its own armies and navies, to make alliances with local sovereigns within its sphere of operations, and, if necessary, to make war and peace in defense of its interests. Company shares were traded on the Amsterdam stock exchange, where investors represented a broad spectrum of society—from prosperous merchants to barmaids. Within one month of announcing its intentions, the VOC was able to raise six and a half million guilders in operating capital. The company was governed by a board of directors, seventeen in number, who represented the interests of the six chambers centered at Amsterdam, Middelburg, Delft, Rotterdam, Hoorn, and Enkhuizen. The monopoly was granted for twenty-one years and was an immediate success. Portuguese colonies in the Far East were soon under intense pressure from VOC fleets. By mid-century Portuguese trading interests in the Spice Islands, the Indonesian Archipelago, Ceylon, Formosa, and Japan had been replaced by the VOC. Although the Dutch were enjoying great success acquiring Portuguese possessions and establishing a commercial empire in the Far East, the trading fleets still had to pass through hostile waters. Heavily armed ships reduced cargo space, decreasing profits, and the potential of losses to hostile forces increased marine insurance premiums.

All of these obstacles to successful trade drove both the English and the Dutch in the sixteenth century to find a northern route to the Far East. The lure of this theoretical route was driven by the ancient notion of symmetry in nature: if the world's land masses allowed for a southern route to China, there should also be a comparable northern route.[11] Attempts to find a northern passage by the Englishmen Sir Martin Frobisher, John Davis, et al., and by the Dutch mariners such as Willem Barentsz and Jacob van Heemskerck all failed.[12] It is in this context that Henry Hudson sailed west while searching for the legendary northern route to the east.[13]

In 1607 and 1608 Hudson had made two northern voyages for the English Moscovy Company. Both failed to discover the "passage to Cathay." His experience and enthusiasm, however, attracted the attention of the VOC. Hudson was given command of the Dutch-built pinnace *Halve Maen* (Half Moon). His instructions were to sail northeast, more or less in the wake of Willem Barentsz, in search of the elusive northern passage. After encountering adverse weather conditions and dangerous ice floes, his crew expressed a near-mutinous desire to sail in safer waters. Contrary to VOC instructions, Hudson turned his ship about, heading south by southwest.[14]

The year was 1609, a significant year for several reasons. In the Netherlands it saw the founding of the Bank of Amsterdam, and was the beginning of the Twelve Years' Truce with Spain. According to Barbara Tuchman: "[the bank was] the heart that pumped the bloodstream of Dutch commerce."[15] The truce, on the other hand, marked the end of the first phase of the revolt of the Netherlands. Stalemate in Spain's attempt to retake the seven northern provinces had caused exhaustion, which led to this tacit recognition of the existence of the United Provinces of the Netherlands. While the bank facilitated and regularized the exchange of foreign currencies, instilling trust in the security of loans and deposits, the truce allowed Dutch ships to leave port and range about the world, expanding and consolidating their commercial interests with little fear of opposition from their hereditary enemy. For New York 1609 is important for one event: the arrival of Henry Hudson. A half-century of Dutch contact with American Indians was about to begin.

The Encounter: The Dutch Enter the Hudson Valley

> Our countrymen who first explored this river . . . describe the wonderful size of the trees. . . . Wild grapes are abundant, and walnut trees. . . . This is also the case with other trees, shrubs, and plants that grow spontaneously. . . . So with various kinds of pulse, especially beans . . . pumpkins of the finest species, melons, and similar fruits of a useful character. . . . The forests everywhere contain a great variety of wild animals . . . . Innumerable birds are also found here . . . In winter superior turkey cocks are taken, very fat, and with flesh of the best quality. The rivers produce excellent fish, such as the salmon sturgeon, and many others. . . . . I am therefore of the opinion that scarcely any part of America is better adapted for the settlement of the colonies from our country. . . [16]

It took no time at all for the Dutch to recognize the enormous potential of what they first called the Mauritius Rivier, and soon the Noort Rivier or North River, later to become the Hudson. This magnificent waterway in the great ridge and valley province of the eastern United Stated offered an unobstructed opening into the interior and easy access to its fertile soils and the wealth of fur-bearing animals that would usher in Dutch mercantile dominance and riches unparalleled for the time.

Travel into the Hudson Valley also would bring the Dutch into contact with people very different from themselves, people who saw and understood the world in a fashion strikingly at odds with the European invaders. These were, of course, the American Indians, a diverse population whose ancestors had resided in the region for thousands of years. [17]

The first Europeans to see the Indians of the Hudson, as far as anyone knows, were not sent by the Dutch at all. On April 17, 1524, the ship *La Dauphine*, under the command of Giovanni de Verrazzano, an Italian mariner employed by the French crown, anchored in New York Bay at the Narrows. His observations of the Indians he saw there are disappointingly brief:

Charles T. Gehring and William A. Starna

The people are almost like unto the others, and clad with feathers of fowls of divers colors. They came towards us very cheerfully, making great shouts of admiration, showing us where we might come to land most safely with our boat.[18]

The same day, after having named this part of the country Angouleme, and the bay Santa Margarita, Verrazzano weighed anchor and sailed around Long Island on his way past Block Island to Narragansett Bay.[19] The next recorded encounter between Europeans and Indians in the Hudson Valley would not occur for another eighty-five years.

On the fourth of September of that year, the *Halve Maen* sailed into a "very good Harbour." Once at anchor, several of the ship's crew rowed a small boat to the nearby shore and netted some fish. They and the *Halve Maen* had not escaped the notice of the local Indians.

This day the people of the Countrey came aboored of us, seeming very glad of our comming, and brought greene Tabacco, and gave us of it for Knieces and Beads. They goe in Deere skins loose, well dressed. They have yellow Copper. They desire Cloathes, and are very civill. They have a great store of Maiz, or Indian Wheatem whereof they make good Bread.[20]

That night, the ship grounded itself before a stiff wind on "soft sand and Oze" in Sandy Hook Harbor. Two days later, in a less cordial meeting, the Indians killed one of Hudson's seamen "with and Arrow shot into his throat." The Dutch had arrived.[21]

The *Halve Maen* entered the Hudson River proper on the eleventh of September. Over the next several days Hudson sailed upriver, taking frequent soundings of the channel as he cautiously tacked around shoals and small islands. Indians in canoes visited the ship nearly every day, and carried out a brisk trade. They brought with them tobacco, beans, oysters, corn, and currants, exchanging with the sailors for knives, beads, hatchets, and other items. Reaching the vicinity of Albany, Hudson discovered that he could sail no farther, and on the twenty-third he began a return voyage to the river's mouth. There was no northwest passage.

Hudson and his men, although probably anxious and wary, do not seem to have been unduly surprised by the Indians they had come upon. Seamen of the day had undoubtedly heard many tales of the exotic New World from others who had sailed before them. Hudson, a skilled navigator, presumably had read the accounts of earlier voyages and discussed his journey with mapmakers and experienced mariners. Furthermore, Indian people were not entirely strangers in Europe. Gaspar Corte-Real and Estevan Gomes, both Portuguese navigators who had explored the Northeast coast in the first quarter of the sixteenth century, had returned with scores of kidnapped Indians to parade before their patrons.[22]

The Indians, in turn, were not in the least nonplussed by the appearance of the Dutch. The lack of fear displayed by the Indians, along with the apparent ease of which trade took place, suggests that they had had previous experience with Europeans and bore mixed feelings about them. The Indians seemed well prepared to barter with the Dutch, having on one hand "a supply of exactly the pelts that were in greatest demand," suggesting that they had done all of this before.[23] Moreover, their clashes with the Dutch, though decidedly one-sided, do not reflect the behavior of people easily intimidated by the strangely dressed white people, nor by the power of their guns.

The Indians of the Hudson Valley

During their 150-mile sojourn into the Hudson Valley, the Dutch had seen firsthand its natural beauty and the abundance of its forests and waters. Indeed, the few contemporary accounts that survive are replete with descriptions of the region's rich plant and animal life and the land's immeasurable potential for settlement.[24] Nonetheless, except for the visits Indians made to the *Halve Maen*, the Dutch learned virtually nothing about the thousands of other Indian people, living in countless settlements, who could be found in the valley.

The Carte Figurative, which may date to 1614, provides the earliest known enumeration of the Indian groups resident in the valley.[25] Recorded on this map are the Manhattes, Sangicans, Mechkentiwoom, Tappans, Wikagyl, Pachami, Woranecks, and Waronawanka, all located below Kingston, while the Mahicans are shown living in the northern reaches of the valley. De Laet, who may have had access to this document, repeats several of these tribal names.[26] Adriaen van der Donck adds the Wappingers on his map of 1656.[27]

The Indians of the Hudson Valley all spoke Algonquian languages. The Mahicans, situated on both sides of the valley from about the latitude of Catskill Creek and the city of Hudson north to above Albany, numbered something over five thousand people at contact. Their dispersed and thin distribution is consistent with conditions in many parts of northern New England.[28] The lower Hudson, however, was much more densely populated. Estimates of the numbers of Munsee-speaking people here in 1600 range between about fifteen and thirty-two thousand.[29]

The distinctions drawn between these groups of native people extend beyond language, numbers, and locations on a map. Van Meteren provides the first hint: "In the lower part of the river they [Hudson's crew] found strong and warlike people; but in the upper part they found friendly and polite people . . ."[30] Campisi suggests that this apparent cultural demarcation coincides with the geographical boundary between Mahican-speaking and Munsee-speaking Indians, thereby supporting the argument that only two ethnic groups were to be found in the Hudson Valley.[31] On the other hand, Indians living in the lower valley may have weathered more extensive and less congenial meetings with Europeans, given their proximity to New York Bay and the river's mouth, both objects of desire for those seeking a northwest passage. It was not until Hudson's voyage that there was any substantive contact with Indians living in the interior, thereby raising the eventuality of soured relations.

What is plain is that whatever the connection between the Mahicans, the Munsee-speakers, and the Dutch, there was considerable confusion regarding the names attributed to Indian groups; that is, the early documents leave one with the impression that the Hudson Valley was inhabited by "a bewildering assortment of ethnic entities" that seemed to have changed their designations from time to time.[32] As was frequently the case, Europeans often associated the name of the headman or "chief" in a village, or the place-name of a village, with a distinct ethnic group or "tribe"; hence the profusion of designations.

Goddard, however, has deciphered the puzzle surrounding the identities of the Indian groups mentioned in the documentary sources who include, from south to north: the Raritans on the lower Raritan River; the Navasinks near Sandy Hook Bay; the Hackensacks in the Hackensack and Passaic valleys, and south to the Kill Van Kull; the Canarsee in Brooklyn; the Rechgawawanks in the Bronx, Yonkers, and Manhattan; the Wiechquaeskecks in Tarrytown and Dobbs Ferry; the Sinsinks near Ossining; the Tappans of the Tappan Zee; the Haverstraw on Haverstraw Bay; the Kichtawanks in northern Westchester County; the Nochpeen in the Hudson Highlands; the Esopus and their sub-groups the Waoranecks, Warranawankongs, and others, who occupied the west side of the river from the Catskills and the highlands of West Point; and the Wappingers of Dutchess and Putnam counties.[33] Above these Munsee-speaking groups were the Mahicans.[34]

Brasser has argued that the way of life of the Mahican-speakers was similar to that of their several neighbors: the Mohawks, an Iroquoian-speaking people in the middle Mohawk Valley, with whom a devastating war would take place; the Wappingers and Esopus of the Hudson Valley; the Housatonics of eastern Massachusetts; and the Sokokis of Vermont. Yet there is little ethnographic evidence available on the Mahicans and the archaeological record is very spotty. As a result, the cultural reconstructions of Brasser and others rely primarily on unconfirmed or mistaken analogies drawn between the Mahicans and the Mohawks, and only incidentally with other Algonquian-speaking groups living to the north, east, and south.[35]

The Mahicans' way of life was a relatively balanced mix of farming, hunting, and fishing. They are said to have lived primarily in stockaded villages located on protected hilltops, each village containing a few oval or elongated bark-covered longhouses of varying lengths. The longhouse was home to several nuclear families. Chiefs' houses, which also served as ceremonial meeting places, are described as generally larger and decorated with paintings and carvings.

Ruttenber maintains that "at the time of discovery," there were three Mahican villages: Monemius' castle on Peebles Island in the Hudson below Cohoes falls; another on the east bank, south of the first village called Unuwat's castle; and Aepjin's castle, at or near Schodack.[36] None of these village locations, nor the location of any other stockaded village, have been located archaeologically.

Recently compiled archaeological data show that the palisaded village-type of settlement pattern, along with Iroquois-style longhouses, often associated with Mahican-speakers, is inaccurate for the proto-historic and early contact period.[37] Instead, settlement types and distributions were more like those of Indians living in central and southern New England and the Delaware Valley. In these regions, small, dispersed, semipermanent settlements or hamlets were the rule until sometime after contact, when large, fortified villages made their appearance.[38] Even so, the hamlet probably remained a customary form of settlement in the Mahican homeland after the arrival of the Dutch.

The same kind of settlement and subsistence pattern was present at earliest contact among Munsee-speakers in the lower reaches of the valley. Claims for the presence of stockaded villages and longhouses like those that have been made erroneously for the Mahican country cannot be substantiated.[39] There is, of course, a shortage of undisturbed archaeological sites, a result of the centuries of intensive development that has been part of the growth of the metropolitan New York-New Jersey area. It remains, however, that excavated sites consistently reaffirm a settlement pattern characterized by hamlets containing one oval house, or clusters of two or three, none of which are stockaded. Large groupings of people in fortified villages did not occur until well after contact.[40]

The three palisaded Mahican villages reported by Ruttenber were undoubtedly built in response to threats, especially those coming from the Mohawks. The earliest known map of the region, the Minuit map of circa 1630, shows two locations, one near the mouth of the Mohawk and the other on the east bank of the Hudson above Fort Orange, with the same notation: Vastigheid, "stronghold."[41] Both are sited in such a way as to secure the region around the fort, including the lower reaches of the Mahican Channel, from the Mohawks. The Map of Rensselaerswyck (c. 1632) identifies these strongholds as "Moenemin's Castle" and "Unuwat's Castle."[42]

Dutch and Indian Trade

Hudson's voyage into the valley may have been followed in 1610 or 1611 by that of the Dutch ship's captain Hendrick Christiaensz, although no documents survive of this alleged venture. There is more secure information that the St. Pieter was in the river in the late spring of 1611, chartered by the merchant Arnout Vogels in partnership with Leonard and Francoys Pelgrom. This voyage represents the first trading enterprise in the region.[43]

In 1612, the ship *Fortuyn* came to the Hudson, although nothing is known about this visit. Upon her return to Amsterdam, however, she was immediately refitted and sailed back to New Netherland under the command of Adriaen Block. For about two months, Block and his crew traded with the Indians, operating under the belief that they were the lone Europeans in the valley. The appearance of the ship *Jonge Tobias*, out of Monnikendam in the Netherlands, therefore, must have come as a shock.[44] Any monopoly Block thought he held on the river evaporated with the dropping of this interloper's anchor.

The *Fortuyn* returned again to the Hudson late in 1613 under the flag of the Lambert van Tweenhuysen company. Her captain was Hendrick Christianesz. Shortly thereafter, the ships *Tijger* and *Nachtegael* arrived in New York Bay, skippered by Block and Thijs Mossel respectively. Early in the summer of 1614, these vessels were followed by a second *Fortuyn* and the *Vos*.[45] The Hudson was becoming a very busy place indeed. Regrettably, however, there is no documentation of the interactions that assuredly took place between the Dutch and Indians at this time.

What Indians may have thought about the newly arrived Dutchmen and their behavior is impossible to assess directly. Hamell, however, suggests that Indians may have associated the appearance of Europeans with the return of culture heroes.[46] At the same time, they readily linked trade goods such as glass beads, copper and brass wares, and other so-called trifles with the ideologically valuable and prehistorically available stones, shell, quartz, and native copper, all "symbolically charged" items. As Hamell points out:

> Shell, crystal, and native copper were their owner's assurance and insurance of long life (immortality through resuscitation), well-being (the absence of ill-being), and success, particularly in the conceptually related activities of hunting and fishing, warfare, and courtship.[47]

Hamell's thesis is that Indians made perfect sense of the appearance of the Europeans and their trade by effecting a transference from their own worldview and its symbolic elements to that offered by these white men. It was this accommodation by Indians that made trade both possible and acceptable. In other instances, however, Indians must have assumed as jaundiced a view of the Europeans as the Europeans did of them, especially in terms of religious and social practices.[48]

The Dutch and Indians in the Hudson Valley undoubtedly sought to accommodate each other through various forms of agreements or ad hoc arrangements. For instance, in the early years of contact, it is likely that informal compacts were entered into by interested parties to facilitate trade. These, of course, were followed later by formal contracts or treaties, especially over the disposition of land and commercial ventures. Included here is the celebrated purchase of Manhattan in 1626, the trade agreement struck between the West India Company and the Iroquois in 1635, and land acquisitions negotiated with the Indians in and around Rensselaerswijck.[49]

A curious twist to this history was the report in 1968, by one L.G. van Loon, that a copy of the first "treaty" between the Dutch and the Iroquois had surfaced.[50] The "document" was dated 21 April 1613, and purported to spell out a compact made between two Dutch traders, Jacob Eelckens and Hendrick

Christiaensz, and four "chiefs of the Longhouse." Provisos of the treaty included the terms of a trade agreement; the purchase of Indian lands; mutual assistance in the event of food shortages; and a mechanism for the settlement of any future differences that might arise between the parties.

The publication of the "Tawagonshi Treaty," as it was called, caused no small amount of commotion in the academic community. Several historians and anthropologists accepted its validity without question, while others remained more chary. The chiefs of the Iroquois Confederacy, on the other hand, extolled the document as a confirmation of Indian oral tradition about the "Two-Row Wampum," which is said to define the important political relationship between two sovereigns—the United States and the Iroquois.

Van Loon must have enjoyed the furor his newly discovered "treaty" had caused, for, as it turns out, it is a fake. There was no 1613 treaty. Can Loon had conjured it. In fact, there is no evidence for any kind of formal agreement between the Dutch and the Iroquois until 1635, mentioned above, which was a renegotiation of a previous agreement made after the establishment of Fort Orange in 1624. No formal treaty was drawn up and signed until 1643.[51]

The Dutch Establish a Colony

The Dutch took their first steps toward a permanent presence in the valley with the building of Fort Nassau in 1614. This small, fortified trading post was on Castle Island at the mouth of the Normans Kill, a short distance south of the future site of Fort Orange at Albany. De Laet provides a description:

> The fort was built in the form of a redoubt, surrounded by a moat of eighteen feet wide; it was mounted with two pieces of cannon and eleven pedereros, and the garrison consisted of ten or twelve men. Hendrick Christaensz. first commanded here, and in his absence Jaques Elckens, on behalf of the [New Netherland] company which in 1614 received authority from their High Mightinesses, the States General.[52]

For three years business at the fort was brisk. The Dutch understood full well that the Mahicans dominated the region around Fort Nassau and, importantly, also controlled access to the lucrative fur trading of the St. Lawrence Valley though what Jennings has called the "Mahican Channel."[53] It is not surprising, then, that under these circumstances every effort was made to solicit Mahican cooperation and assistance to insure the free flows of furs.

The neighboring Mohawks evidently joined in the trade, although the extent of their involvement is unclear. Trigger has argued from negative evidence that the Mahicans did not monopolize the trade, nor did they prevent Mohawks from traveling freely through their territory.[54] Nevertheless, it is difficult to imagine that the Mahicans would have permitted the Mohawks unrestricted access to the Dutch traders in their territory, especially since there are suggestions that relations between these Indians were less than friendly. Simply put, the Mohawks were not in the best position to conduct free trade with the Dutch at Fort Nassau.[55]

There is no indication, however, of any difficulties between the Dutch and the Indian people who routinely brought their furs to the post to exchange for European trade goods. Business, successful business, was the order of the day. At the same time, the Dutch "armed traders" operating under licenses from the New Netherland Company may have understood the precariousness of their position and, uninterested in colonization or exploration, prudently stayed within the confines of their fort. The Indians, in turn do not appear to have sensed any threat from the Dutchmen, and participated in the trade willingly and apparently successfully. Once more there is no record of the intercultural interactions that took place. In 1617 the Dutch abandoned Fort Nassau because of frequent floods.[56]

In late spring of 1624, the ship *Nieu Nederlandt* arrived in New York Bay. Commanded by Cornelis Jacobsz May, it carried thirty Dutch families prepared to establish settlements for the West India Company.[57] The Dutch had decided to expand their mercantile hegemony, thereby challenging the English presence, by constructing trading posts on the three major rivers that led into the interior of New Netherland and the surrounding region. These were on High Island (Burlington Island) in the Delaware, Fort Hope (Hartford) on the Connecticut River, and at Fort Orange (Albany).

Eighteen families, probably some fifty people, disembarked from the *Nieu Nederlandt* at a place just north of the ill-fated site of Fort Nassau.[58] They were directed to construct a small redoubt there that would be christened Fort Orange. Once can only guess at what went through their minds as they stood alone on the river's bank in the midst of bundles and boxed containing their personal belongings equipment, and supplies. Neither can we begin to guess what the nearby Indians may have thought as they watched these white people stream off their ship.

The Dutch must have approached the Mahicans beforehand about building this trading post and their plans to bring in significantly more people than had inhabited Fort Nassau, apparently convincing the Indians that they would benefit greatly from the increased trade. The Mahicans, however, probably saw for themselves the advantages of controlling access others would assuredly seek to the fort and its trade goods, and may not have needed much coaxing. Whatever the case, the company's agents renewed their efforts to capitalize on the furs moving through the Mahican Channel.[59] For his part, May sailed for home to take on supplies and perhaps additional settlers for a planned return in the following year.

Cultural Conflicts and Accommodations

Between the abandonment of Fort Nassau and the building of Fort Orange, intermittent and informal trade continued between the Dutch and Indians in the upper valley.[60] In 1620–21, however, began one of the most disruptive and disturbing episodes known in Dutch-Indian relations.

The risk and uncertainty of exploring unknown regions in the seventeenth century did not always attract the idealist and pure of heart. The prospect of adventure, power, and wealth gained through exploitation of technologically disadvantaged peoples often brought out the dark side of human personality. That fringe area, no-man's land, or "frontier" where two cultures came into contact (in our case European and Indian) was frequently visited and inhabited by the most unpleasant representatives of both cultures. Consider Hernando Cortez, John Underhill, Kit Carson, or George Armstrong Custer. It was either the tension of the situation, the imagined need to exhibit a tough facade to discourage hostile actions, or inherent character flaws that led to needless violence, causing conflicts that often took years to resolve. A case in point is Hans Jorisz Hontom's confrontation with Indians in the Hudson Valley.

Hontom was born in Annverp around 1583 to Hans Jorisz Hontom and Elisabeth Rijckerts, and his family fled to Amsterdam soon after the capture of the city by the Spanish army in 1585.[61] Hontom's father earned a living as a fur trader—a trade to which his son would also be attracted. Hontom first appears in the Hudson River as supercargo aboard Mossel's ship the *Nachtegael* in 1613 and 1614.

We only indirectly know that he had a personality or disposition that attracted attention, sometimes evoking violent responses. During one such encounter, while supercargo aboard Mossel's ship, he was struck by Hendrick Christiaensz, skipper of the *Fortuyn*, "for no reason"; apparently unsatisfied, Christiaensz also threatened to shoot him. Unfortunately, the deposition does not record the cause for such anger.[62] Soon afterward, Christiaensz's gunner cut Hans Hontom on the cheek, again "for no reason." In yet another inci-

Charles T. Gehring and William A. Starna

dent Hontom was suspected to be the reason why the mulatto Jan Rodrigues refused to remain aboard the ship and was put ashore. Rodrigues had wintered over alone along the upper Hudson, where he was found and picked up by Christiaensz, who defended him from another attack by Hontom and his men.[63] Hans Hontom's unpleasant disposition is further revealed in an incident involving a Mohawk sachem—probably while serving as skipper aboard the ship *Duyff* (Jacob Eelkens, supercargo) in 1622.[64]

Following is the interrogatory of Bastiaen Jansz Crol,[65] sworn to before a notary in Amsterdam in June of 1634,[66] which sheds light on Hans Hontom's methods of dealing with the natives:

> Interrogatories or queries for the examination and interview of the person of Bastiaen Jansen Crol. Today the last day of the month of June in the year 1634, appeared in person before me, Joost van de Ven, appointed public notary by the court of Holland and registered by the highly esteemed and wise magistrates of the city of Amsterdam, residing in the same city, and the witnesses named below, the honorable Bastiaen Jansen Crol, about 38 years of age, produced as a witness, and examined and questioned on the following interrogatories or queries at the request of the honorable lords patroons of their colonies, which they have founded in New Netherland, residing in this aforesaid city; and, with true Christian words in place of an oath (which he offers if required), he deposes, declares and testifies to what is written below, namely:

> 1.) In what capacity and how long he, deposant, was in the service of the West India Company in N. Netherland. Firstly: He, deposant, declares that he shipped out as a comforter of the sick, and served there the first time for 7 and 12 months. For the second time he shipped out in the same capacity, and after he had been out 15 months he was given the directorship at Fort Orange on the North River, and he held the same for three years. The third time he went out again in the capacity as director of Fort Orange, which he again held, to the best of his recollection, for about two years. Whereupon he was selected as general director of N. Netherland at Fort Amsterdam on the island of Manhattan, located in the mouth of the North River, otherwise called Mauritius, and served 13 months.

> 2.) Whether he, deposant, while residing at Fort Orange did not understand from the chief of the Maquaas that previously a certain Hans Jorissen Hontom had been there, who traded with them, who first had Jacob Eelkens as his skipper, whom he, Hontorn, afterward employed as his commissary. Testifies: Yes.

> 3.) Whether afterward a misunderstanding did not arise between the aforesaid nation on the one side and the aforesaid Hans Jorissen on the other side. And whether he, Honthom, did not take a sachem or chief prisoner. Testifies: Yes.

> 4.) Also, whether Hontom afterward, at the request of the aforesaid sachem's subjects, did not agree to their ransom offer for the chief. Testifies: Yes.

> 5.) Whether after the ransom was delivered and paid, H. Hontom did not, in spite of his promise, cut out the male organs of the aforesaid chief, and hang them on the mast stay with rope, and thus killed the sachem. Testifies: Yes.[67]

There is no evidence that the Mohawks reacted immediately to this barbaric treatment of their chief; but neither was the act forgotten. In 1633, Hontom was appointed commissary to Fort Orange. Soon after his arrival, he was recognized by another Mohawk chief who had come to the fort to trade. Hontom's return was quickly reported to the Mohawks who swore that they would "strike . . . Hans Jorissen Hontom dead wherever they first would be able to find him alone."[68] More immediate acts of revenge resulted in the burning of the company's yacht, *De Bever*, and the killing of livestock in the vicinity of the fort. Hontom, however, survived this threat on his life only to be killed the following year in an argument with Cornelis van Voorst, the commissary of Pavonia, a Dutch post in New Jersey.

The establishment of Fort Orange coincided with the advent of the Mohawk-Mahican war of 1624–28. This conflict arose from the complications of Dutch-French competition in the fur trade and the enmity that existed between the Mohawks and Algonquian-speaking groups to their north and east. It ended with the defeat of the Mahicans and the Mohawks' gaining control of the trade at Fort Orange.

From the Mohawks' point of view, Fort Orange initially offered them only limited access to Dutch trade goods. Mohawk traders found it necessary to steal or purchase goods from the Mahicans.[69] At the same time, their relationship with the northern Algonquians and their French allies was one of mutual suspicion and belligerence, and did not provide an easy avenue for trade.

The Dutch chose to use their friendly working relationship with the Mahicans to further their efforts to gain access to the rich fur sources of the St. Lawrence Valley. They appeared much less concerned with the Mohawks or even Indians farther west. They believed that if the trade at the French settlements could be diverted to Fort Orange, their profits would increase significantly. The Mahicans stood much to gain by maintaining control of the region around Fort Orange and the critical Mahican Channel trade, acting as middlemen. And the Algonquian-speakers generally could benefit by playing off the French against the Dutch when it came to lowering the prices for trade goods. There was intrigue enough for all.[70]

The Mohawks, however, moved more quickly than the others to achieve their ambitions. In 1624 they finalized a treaty with the French and the northern Algonquians, making French-Iroquois trade possible and permitting the Algonquians to trap and trade in peace. The Mohawks' northern flank was secured.[71] Then, with the ink of the treaty barely dry, they attacked the Mahicans.

Little is known about the first year or so of this war. But by 1626 the Mohawks had lost their easternmost village to a Mahican attack and had managed to disrupt the trade at Fort Orange.[72] Neither the Mohawks nor the Mahicans were successful in gaining the upper hand, however, and following the instructions given to Willem Verhulst, the company's first director, to avoid any disputes between the Indians, the Dutch stayed out of the fray and continued their trade.

In April of 1626, however, Daniel van Crieckenbeeck, the commander at Fort Orange, chose to ignore company policy. He and a contingent of Dutch soldiers accompanied a Mahican war party against the Mohawks. Van Crieckenbeeck's reasons for disobeying orders are not entirely known, although Trelease has suggested that his actions might have been part of a larger plan to guarantee Canadian tribes a right of way through the Mahican Channel.[73] It is also possible that Van Crieckenbeeck and the Mahicans had struck a deal for land to be used by the families stationed at Fort Orange, and that his agreement to help the Indians militarily was part of the bargain. In any case, the outcome of the Dutch-Mahican campaign against the Mohawks was disastrous. Van Crieckenbeeck and several of his men, along with an unknown number of Mahicans, were killed, and the survivors fled back to the fort.[74]

The Van Crieckenbeeck incident had repercussions throughout New Netherland. The families and garrison at Fort Orange had every reason to believe that the Mohawks would choose to press their advantage and they would be overrun. Heavily outnumbering the Dutch, these Indians could threaten trading posts on the Connecticut River and elsewhere in the colony.

The Mohawks, in turn, were evidently more concerned with having broken their trust with the Dutch, however informal it may have been, than pressing their military advantage. Several days after the Van

Charles T. Gehring and William A. Starna

Crieckenbeeck defeat, Pieter Barentsen, who may have arrived at Fort Orange with Petrus (Peter) Minuit, the new director of the company, paid these Indians a visit. His charge was to avert any further actions against the Dutch because of Van Crieckenbeeck's recklessness. His task became much easier when, upon his arrival in Mohawk country, he discovered that:

> . . . they [the Mohawks] wished to excuse their act, on the plea that they had never set themselves against the whites, and asked the reason why the latter had meddled with them; otherwise they would not have shot them.[75]

The question whether or not the Mohawks were sincere in their apparent distress, or were simply maneuvering the Dutch into maintaining the peace, cannot be answered. What is true is that they continued to wage war against the Mahicans, now with the Dutch out of the picture. In 1628, they launched a major offensive in the region around Fort Orange, defeating the Mahicans and driving the survivors into the Connecticut Valley.[76]

Following the Van Crieckenbeeck affair, and despite having made amends with the Mohawks, Minuit ordered the families living at Fort Orange to withdraw to Manhattan Island, which the Dutch had recently purchased. A garrison of sixteen men was left to maintain a presence and also to continue the trade with the Indians. The same orders were given to the commanders of the Dutch posts on the Connecticut and Delaware rivers. Fort Orange would remain essentially an isolated outpost for the next several years.

The Mohawk victory was not altogether beneficial for the Dutch, although Van Rensselaer reported that the Indians around the fort were so exhausted from the fighting that they readily sold their land to Dutch agents in 1630 and 1631.[77] Still, the Mahican Channel trade was cut off, forcing the northern Algonquians to deal exclusively with the French on the St. Lawrence. In later years, however, the Mohawks in control of the region around Fort Orange, along with other Iroquois groups to the west, would reestablish good relations with the French, playing the Europeans against one another to drive down the price for trade goods.[78]

Conclusion

In spite of intermittent conflicts, the mutual interests of the Dutch and Mohawks resulted in the forging of a bond of friendship that was never broken. Indeed, Dutch dependency on the Mohawk became so strong that they were often called upon to mediate Indian disputes on the periphery of New Netherland, and not infrequently they served as enforcers of Dutch interests against other tribes. At the same time, the presence of the Mohawks in the Fort Orange region discouraged potential enemies, Indian or white, who might think of raiding the isolated and undermanned trading post.

Dutch settlers did not return to the area around Fort Orange until the formation of the patroonship of Kiliaen van Rensselaer, an Amsterdam diamond merchant, in 1631. Fort Orange would serve the Dutch West India Company as a military and administrative center and trading post until the English takeover. The Mohawks would take part in the destructive Beaver Wars against the Hurons and maintain their control of the region around the fort and the important trading route through their valley. And the French would continue to press their trading interests in Iroquois country, much to the consternation of the Dutch.[79] The early years of contact—characterized by economic venture and cultural conflict and accommodation were over, and a new period of Dutch-Indian interaction was beginning.

Notes

1. The Hapsburg Empire was a geographical mosaic of alliances sanctified and perpetuated by royal marriages, as demonstrated by the contemporary Latin aphorism: "Bella gerant fortes, Tu, felix Aurtria, nube. Namquae Marsaliis, dzt tibi regna Venur. (Let the strong wage war. You, lucky Austria, do you marry.)" For details of the various marriages and Burgundy's connection with the Netherlands see Christopher Cope's *The Lost Kingdom of Burgundy: A Phoenix Frustrated* (New York: Dodd, Mead & Co., 1986).

2. Another force in European affairs worth considering is, of course, the Ottoman Empire. It was the capture of Constantinople in 1453 by the Turks that disrupted the overland trade routes to Asia, making it necessary to find alternate routes by sea. The major preoccupation of the Hapsburg Empire during the revolt of the Netherlands was an attempt to prevent the Turks from capturing Vienna, an event that would have had disastrous consequences for the Hapsburg Empire as well as all of Europe. These distractions in the East contributed to Dutch successes in the West. The famous Dutch "sea beggars," who harassed the enemy at sea and succeeded in 1572 in capturing the city of Den Briel, mocked the Hapsburgs by wearing a half-moon medallion, which carried the inscription "Liever Turm dzn Pars (Better Turk than Catholic)."

3. The so-called father of the Hapsburg dynasty was Charles I, king of Spain, and Charles V, Holy Roman Emperor. When ailing health forced him to abdicate his throne in 1656, Charles V chose William the Silent, prince of Orange-Nassau, to support him during his farewell address. To his son Philip went the Spanish crown, holdings in Italy, and the Netherlands. To his brother Ferdinand went the imperial office of emperor and the Hapsburg lands in Central Europe.

4. For the Netherlands' place in sixteenth- and seventeenth-century Europe see especially Fernand Braudel, The Mediterranean and the Mediterranean World in the Age of Philip II 2 vols. (New York: Harper & Row, 1972). A significant factor in the extraordinary Dutch success at sea was the development of the $uyt ship, sometimes called a flyboat or flute. It was sturdily built and had a large cargo capacity. A simplified rigging allowed it to be sailed by a crew 20 percent smaller than crews for ships of equal tonnage. Interchangeable parts allowed them to be turned out quickly and economically by an assembly-line procedure. These parts could also be stockpiled at various repair facilities around the world.

5. Charles was born in Ghent and educated among the Flemish nobility. He spoke Dutch and had a native affection for the land and its people. When he assumed the crown of Spain as Charles I, he arrived with a large Flemish retinue who had little esteem for the Spaniards. Charles's son Philip, on the other hand, was born in Spain and totally devoted to Catholicism. His obsession with stamping out Protestantism led him to regard the Netherlands as conquered provinces rather than constitutional entities, and to regard the Dutch as enemies rather than dissatisfied subjects.

6. A popular quote proclaims, "God created the heavens and earth, and the Dutch created the Netherlands." It can also be said that the Dutch created themselves as a distinct entity. The distinctive Dutch character was forged in the crucible of common purpose and struggle caused by the Eighty Years' War with Spain. See Simon Schama's The Embarrassment of Riches: An Interpretation of Dutch Culture in the Golden Age (New York: Alfred A. Knopf, 1987) for an analysis of the common elements that constitute Dutch culture. See also William Sherter's The Pillars of Society: Six Centuries of Civilization in the Netherland (The Hague: Martinus Nijhoff, 1971).

7. The house of Orange derived its name from a small principality in France just north of Avignon. The family also owned extensive property in Hesse-Nassau and in the Netherlands. William was born in 1533 in Dillenburg. He was raised a Lutheran, but at the age of eleven converted to Catholicism in order to inherit lands from a Catholic cousin; he later reconverted to the Reformed religion. Religion among the nobility was often driven more by political forces than by conscience. William's standing with Charles V is evident by his position of chief attendant at the emperor's abdication. As chief negotiator at the peace of Cateau-Cambreses, he handled himself with such a guarded tongue that the French called him It taciturnc hence the appellation William the Silent. See C. V. Wedgwood's William the Siht: William of Nassau. Prince of Orange 1533–1584 (London: Jonathan Cape Ltd., 1944) for a concise biography of this central figure in the Dutch revolt.

8. For works on the Dutch revolt see Pieter Geyl, *The Revolt of the Netherlandr 1555–1609* (London: W'iliams & Northgate Ltd, 1932; paperback by Cassell History, 1988); Geoffrey Parker, *The Dutch Revolt* (Ithaca: Cornell University Press, 1977).

9. See Charles R Boxer, *The Dutch Seaborne Empire: 1600–1800* (London: Hutchinson & Co. Ltd., 1965); D. W. Davies, *A Primer of Dutch Seventeenth Century Oversem Trade* (The Hague: Martinus Nijhoff, 1961); also Charles Wilson's *Profit and Power: A Study of England and the Dutch Wars* (London: Longmans, 1957); and Jonathan I. Israel's *Dutch Primacy in World Trade, 1585–1740* (Oxford: Oxford University Press, 1989).

10. For a discussion of the rise of the trading companies see Fernand Braudel's *Civilization & Capitalism 15th-18th Century*, 3 vols. (New York: Harper & Row, 1979).

11. For a discussion of the classical concept of the shape of the world see A. Torayah Sharaf's *A Short History of Geographical Discovery* (London: George G. Harrap & Co. Ltd., 1967); see especially 32pp. for Aristotle's influence on geography.

12. Explorers were attracted to the idea of a northwest passage by such legends as "Fretum triumfiatrum, per quod Lusitani ad

Orientem et ad Inah et ad Moluccm navigare conati sunt" (Strait of the Three brothers through which Portuguese attempted to sail to the Orient and the Indies and the Moluccas), which enticed navigators with the promise of a passage from the Atlantic to the Pacific at 40 degrees. See Samuel Eliot Morison's *The European Discovery of America: The Northern Voyages* (Oxford: Oxford University Press, 1971) for a discussion of the various searches for and tales surrounding the northwest passage. Willem Barentsz (after whom the Barents Sea is named) accompanied an expedition in 1596 to discover a passage along the northern coast of Siberia to the Far East. When the Dutch ship was frozen in the ice at Nova Zembla, Barentsz and his crew were forced to spend the winter there under extreme hardship. Barentsz died as he and the remainder of the crew were preparing to attempt a return to Europe. After more incredible adventures and hardship the crew eventually made its way back to Amsterdam to tell the tale. See *Reiun van Willem Barents, Jacob van Heemskerck, Jan Cornelisz Rijp en anderen naar het noorden* (159 &157), ed. S. P. L'Honork Naber ('s-Gravenhage: Maninus Nijhoff, 1917), for the journal kept by Gerrit de Veer, a survivor of Barentsz's crew.

13. See Daniel J. Boorstin's *The Discoverers: A History of Man's Search to Know His World and Himself* (New York: Random House, 1983) for an interpretation of the age of exploration.

14. See *Henry Hudson's Voyages from Purchm His Pilgrmes Samuel Purchm* (originally printed in London, 1625; reprinted in facsimile form by Readex Microprint Corp., 1966) for the accounts of Hudson's four voyages. For a thorough analysis of Hudson's service with the VOC see Henry Hudson's *Reiu on& Nehlandrche vhg van Amsterkm naar Nova Zembla, Amerika en temg naar Dartmouth in England, 1609*, ed. S. P. L'Honoré Naber ('s-Gravenhage: Martinus Nijhoff, 1921).

15. Barbara W. Tuchman, *The Fint Salute: A View of the American Revolution* (New York: Alfred A. Knopf, 1988), 28.

16. "From the 'New World,' by Johan De Laet, 1625, 1630, 1633, 1640," in *Narratives of New Netherland, 160+1664*, ed. J. Franklin Jameson (New York: Charles Scribner's Sons, 1909), 54–56.

17. Robert E. Funk, *Recent Contributions to Hudson Valley Prehistory*, New York State Museum, Memoir 22 (1976).

18. Giovanni da Verrazzano, cited in Morison, *The European Discovery*, 301.

19. Ibid., 302–3.

20. "From 'The Third Voyage of Master Henty Hudson,' by Robert Juet, 1610," in Jameson, ed., *Narratives of New Netherland*, 18.

21. *Ibid.*, 18–19.

22. Morison, *The European Discovery*, 215, 331; Jack Campisi, "The Hudson Valley Indians Through Dutch Eyes," in *Neighbors and Intruders: An Ethnohistorical Exploration of the Indians of Hudson's River*, ed. Laurence M. Hauprman and Jack Campisi, Canadian Ethnological Service, Paper No. 39 (1978):164.

23. Donald Lenig, "Of Dutchmen, Beaver Hats and Iroquois," in *Current Perspectives in Northeastern Archeology: Essays in Honor of William A. Ritchie*, ed. Robert E. Funk and Charles F. Hayes 111, Researches and Transactions of New York State Archeological Association 17 (1977): 73; William A. Starna, "Seventeenth Cenmty Dutch-Indian Trade: A perspective from Iroquoia," *De Halve Maen* 59 (1986): 5–8,21.

24. Emanuel van Meteren, "On Hudson's Voyage, by Emanuel van Meteren," in Jameson, ed., *Narratives of New Netherland*; Juet, "From 'The Third Voyage'"; De Laet, "From the 'New World.'"

25. E. B. O'CaUaghan, ed., *Documents Relative to the Colonial History of the State of New York* (Albany, New York: Weed, Parsons and Company, 1856), I. The terms "tribe" and "bandn may or may not be applicable to named Indian groups living in the Hudson Valley. We have opted to avoid them. See William C. Sturtevant, "Tribe and State in the Sixteenth and Twentieth Centuries," in *The Development of Political Organization in Native North America*, ed. Elisabeth Tooker, 1979 *Proceedings of the American Ethnological Society*, 3–16; Eleanor Leacock, "Ethnohistorical Investigation of Egalitarian Politics in Eastern North America," ibid., 17–31; William N. Fenton, "Leadership in the Northeastern Woodlands of North America," *The American Indian Quarterly 10* (1986): 21–45.

26. De Laet, "From the 'New World,'" 45–47, 52–53.

27. Adriaen van der Donck, *A Description of the New Netherlands* [1656], Thomas F. O'Connell, ed. (Syracuse: Syracuse University Press, 1968).

28. Dean R. Snow, *The Archaeology of New England* (New York: Academic Press, 1980), 33–34, 88.

29. Ibid., 33–34, 96; cf. Ives Goddard, "Delaware," in *Handbook of North American Indians, vol. 15, Northeast*, Bruce G. Trigger, ed. (Washington: Smithsonian Institution, 1978), 213. See also Francis Jennings, *The Ambiguous Iroquois Empire* (New York: W. W. Norton, 1984), 48.

30. Van Meteren, "On Hudson's Voyage," 7; cf. Juet, "From 'The Third Voyage,'" 20, 24; De Laet, "From the 'New World,'" 45.

31. Campisi, "The Hudson Valley Indians," 169.

32. *Ibid.*, 170.

33. Goddard, "Delaware," 213–14.

34. T. J. Brasser, "Mahican," in Trigger, ed., *Handbook of North American Indians, vol. 15*, Northeast, 198–212.

35. Ted J. Brasser, *Riding on the Frontier's Crest: Mahican Indian Culture and Culture Change*, National Museum of Man *Mercury Series, Ethnology Division, Paper No. 13* (1974); Brasser, "Mahican," 198–200; and Snow, *The Archaeology of New England*, 88–90.

36. E. M. Ruttenber, *History of the Indian Tribes of Huchooni River; Their Origin, Manner,. and Customs; Tribal and Sub-Tribal Organizations; Wars, Treaties, Etc., Etc.* [I872] (Port Washington: Kennikat Press, 1971), 85–86.

37. Susan J. Bender and Edward V. Curtin, *A Prehistoric Context for the Upper Hudson Valley: Report of the Survey and Planning Project*, Prepared for the New York State Office of Parks, Recreation, and Historic Preservation (1990), 4–12; Funk, Recent Contributions, 303–4.

38. Ibid.; see William A. Starna, "The Pequots in the Early Seventeenth Century," in *The Pequon in Southern New England. The Fall and Rise of an American Indian Nation*, ed. Laurence M. Hauptman and James D. Wherry (Norman: University of Oklahoma Press, 1990), 34, 36; and Kevin A. McBride, "The Historical Archaeology of the Mashantucket Pequots, 1637–1990: A Preliminary Analysis," ibid., 101, along with the materials cited therein.

39. Goddard, "Delaware," 216.

40. Herbert C. Kraft, "The Northern Lenape in Prehistoric and Early Colonial Times," in *The Lenape Indians: A Symposium*, ed. Herbert C. Kraft, *Archaeological Research Center, Seton Hall University, Publication No. 7* (1984): 5–6; *The Lenape: Archaeology, History, and Ethnography* (Newark: New Jersey Historical Society, 1986); Robert S. Grummet, "The Minisink Settlements: Native American Identity and Society in the Munsee Heartland, 1650–1778," in *The People of Minisink: Papers from the 1989 Delaware Water Gap Symposium*, ed. David G. Orr and Douglas V. Campana (Philadelphia: National Park Service, 1991), 181–82.

41. I. N. Phelps Stokes, *The Iconography of Manhattan Island, 1498–1909* (New York: Robert H. Dodd, 1916), 2, color plate 40.

42. "Map of Rensselaers ck, 1632" in *Van Rensselaer Bowier Manusrripts*, trans. and ed. A. J. F. van Laer (Albany: University of the State of New York, 1908), 33–36 and map pocket.

43. Oliver A. Rink, *Holland on the Hudson: An Economic and Social History of Dutch New York* (Ithaca: Cornell University Press, 1986), 32–33.

44. Ibid., 33–34.

45. Ibid., 42–45; see also Stokes, *The Iconography of Manhattan* (1922), 4,3742.

46. George R. Hamell, "Trading in Metaphors: The Magic of Beads," in *Proceedings of the 1982 Ghs Bead Conference*, ed. Charles F. Hayes III, Rochester Museum and Science Center, Research Records No. 16 (1983), 5–28.

47. *Ibid.*, 25; cf. Starna, "Seventeenth Century."

48. See, for example, William A. Starna, "Indian-Dutch Frontiers," *De Halve Maen 64* (1991): 21–25.

49. Rink, *Holland on the Hudson*, 86–87; Charles T. Gehring and William A. Starna, eds., *A Journey into Mohawk and Oneida County, 1634–1635: The Journal of Harmen Meyndertsz van de Bogaert* (Syracuse: Syracuse University Press, 1988); Shirley W. Dunn, "Enlarging Rensselaerswyck: 17th Century Land Acquisition on the East Side of the River," *A Beautiful and Fruitful Place: Selected in Dutch and Indians in the Hudson Valley: The Early Period Rensselamwijrk Seminar Papers*, ed. Nancy Anne McClure Zeller (Albany, N.Y.: New Netherland Publishing, 1991), 13–21.

50. L. G. Van Loon, "Tawagonshi, the Beginning of the Treaty Era," *The Indian Historian 1* (Summer 1968): 22.

51. Charles T. Gehring, William A. Starna, and William N. Fenton, "The Tawagonshi Treaty of 1613: The Final Chapter," *New York History 68* (October 1987): 373–93. De Laet, "From the 'New World,'" 47.

52. DeLaet, "From the 'New World,'" 47.

53. Jennings, *The Ambiguous Iroquois*, 30–31.

54. Bruce G. Trigger, "The Mohawk-Mahican War (1624–1628): The Establishment of a Pattern," *Canadian Historical Review 52* (September 1971): 277.

55. Cf. De Laet, "From the 'New World,'" 47; Allen W. Trelease, *Indian Affairs in Colonial New York: The Seventeenth Century* (Ithaca: Cornell University Press, 1960), 34; Bruce G. Trigger, *Natives and Newcomers: Canada's "Heroic Age" Reconsidered* (Kingston and Montreal: McGill-Queen's University Press, 1985), 177; Paul R. Huey, "The Dutch at Fort Orange," in *Historical Archaeology in Global Perspective*, ed. Lisa Falk (Washington, D.C.: Smithsonian Institution Press, 1991), 29.

56. Trelease, *Indian Affairs*, 32–34.

57. Rink, *Holland on the Hudson*, 79–80.

58. E. B. O'Callaghan, *The Documentary History of the State of New York* (Albany, N.Y.: Weed, Parsons & Co., 1850), 1: 32.

59. Jennings, *The Ambipus Iroquois*, 49.

60. Trelease, *Indian Affairs*, 34.

61. See Simon Hm's *The Prehistory of the New Netherland Company: Amsterdam Notarial Record of the first Dutch voyager to the Hudson* (Amsterdam: City of Amsterdam Press, 1959), 60, for biographical sketch of Hontom and other Dutch traders on the Hudson.

62. See ibid., 83–86, for a translation of the complete deposition of the crew of Mossel's ship, the *Nachtegael* dated 23 July 1614.

63. See ibid., 80–82, for a translation of the complete deposition of the crew of Christiaensz's ship the *Fomyn* dated 23 July 1614.

64. Deposition in the Notarial Archives of Amsterdam, 5471304, dated 16 November 1621, which states that this ship, owned by Hendrick Eeles, Hans Joris Hontom, et al., was about to leave for New Netherland.

65. Bastiaen Jansz Crol served as comforter of the sick—a non-ordained substitute for a domine—at Fort Orange. When Van Crieckenbeeck was killed in 1626, an event described at note 72, Crol was appointed commander and commissary of the fort. He also served as director of the colony for nine months in 1631–32 before the arrival of Wouter van Twiller.

66. The Dutch text was taken from A. Eekhofs BastiaenJanszKrol ('s-Gravenhage, 1910).Another, less extensive version of this interrogatory appears in *Oud Holland, viii* (1890), 287–89; this shorter text was translated in Van her, Van Rensselaer Bowier, 302–4. The following excerpt from the longer version appears translated here for the first time.

67. The remaining nineteen questions and responses in this interrogatory have been omitted here because they relate to events more than a decade later. A complete transcription and translation of this longer version of Crol's interrogatory will appear later this year in the *Nieu Nederlanse Marcurius*, a newsletter of the New Netherland Project in Albany, NewYork.

68. Ibid.

69. Trigger, *Natives and Newcomers*, 177.

70. Jennings, *The Ambiguous Iroquois*, 49; Trigger, "The Mohawk-Mahican War," 278–79.

71. Trigger, "The Mohawk-Mahican War," 279.

72. Gehring and Starna, eds., *A Journey into Mohawk and Oneida Country*, 22; Trelease, *Indian Affairs*, 46.

73. Trelease, *Indian Affairs*, 47.

74. Nicholaes van Wassenaer, "From the 'Historisch Verhael,' by Nicholas van Wassenaer, 1624–1630," in Jameson, ed., *Narratives of New Netherland*, 84–85.

75. Wassenaer, "From the 'Historisch Verhael,'" 85.

76. Ibid., 89; Trelease, *Indian Affairs*, 48;Trigger, "The Mohawk-Mahican War," 281.

77. Rink, *Holland on the Hudson*, 86, n. 35.

78. Trigger, "The Mohawk-Mahican War," 282.

79. Gehring and Starna, eds., *A Journey, Into Mohawk and Oneida Country*, xix.

This article originally appeared in the *Hudson Valley Regional Review*, Volume 9.2.

The Algonquians in Context
The End of the Spirituality of the Natural World

Vernon Benjamin

"When we have a sermon, sometimes ten or twelve of them, more or less, will attend, each having a long tobacco pipe, made by himself, in his mouth, and will stand awhile and look, and afterwards ask me what I was doing. . . . I tell them that I admonish the Christians, that they must not steal, nor commit lewdness, nor get drunk, nor commit murder, and that they too ought not to do these things. . . . They say I do well to teach the Christians; but immediately add, *Diatennon jawij Assyreoni, hagiowisk*, that is, 'Why do so many Christians do these things?'"

—Dominie Johannes Megapölensis
Rensselaerswyck, 1644

". . .the chronic practice of describing man as a tool-using animal conceals some of the very facts that must be exposed and revaluated. Why, for example, if tools were so important to human development, did it take man at least half a million years. . .to shape anything but the crudest stone tools? Why is it that the lowest existing peoples. . .have elaborate ceremonials, a complicated kinship organization, and a finely differentiated language, capable of expressing every aspect of their experience?"

—Lewis Mumford, 1966

"An ecosystem is a discrete community of plants and animals, together with the nonliving environment, occupying a certain space and time, having a flow-through of energy and raw materials in its operation, and composed of subsystems. For convenience of analysis, an ecosystem can be separated into its physical and biological components, although one should bear in mind that in nature the two are completely intermeshed in complex interactions. And from the standpoint of cultural ecology, there is a third component: the metaphysical or spiritual."

—Calvin Martin, 1974

The intricate details of the first European steps in the Hudson Valley were momentous, fearsome, audacious, and even heroically comic in some of the telling. Yet, large though their ambitions were, little did these few dozen men from a small country far away know that the handsome harbor they entered and the valley behind it lay on the edge of a continent vaster and more resourceful than anything heretofore known to civilized man. The *St. Pieter, Fortuyn, Tijger, Nachtegael,* and other immediate successors to Henry Hudson's *Halve Maen*[1] crossed the Upper Bay to Manhattan Island as if entering the very maw of *Tchi Manito,* the Indian godhead or Great Spirit, a force of nature so ubiquitous its spirituality was everywhere in this vast new land.

Details of Olin Dows' WPA murals in the Rhinebeck Post Office

Vernon Benjamin

The fierce competition between Adriaen Block, the first of the Dutch traders and also the region's principal cartographer, and Thijs Mossel, a trader for a rival group of Amsterdam merchants, operatic in its Old World blusterings, was made all the more humorous by the fact that they were arguing over a store thousands of miles wide filled with millions of animals worth harvesting. There was more, vastly more than enough for all, despite the arguing, and still some disgruntled players rose up and stole a ship for themselves, sailing off to the West Indies after leaving enough trinkets for their countrymen to trade. One ship burned accidentally at its Manhattan mooring, another was built virtually on the spot from the immense bounty of natural resources at hand; traders came and were killed in misunderstandings with the Indians, and still the trade continued unaffected by these little dramas.[2] Yet for all their intensity in pursuit of the pelts given up by the Indians for mere trinkets, the details of this New World, like the trees of the forest, hid an even larger reality that diminished these men and the grand ego of a world they came from. Huddled with their flagons of warm beer in the crude enclaves they created, first at Manhattan and later at Fort Orange, the Europeans who were so intensely focused on the profits of the pelt trade did not see the integrated, natural reality that loomed all around them. They walked through their roughly hewn doorways into a landscape of trees the Indians had scorched and burned to make maizefields, or that they themselves had hacked at and felled with crude and inefficient axes.[3] The entire fractured landscape was served up as a fitting metaphor for the broken world they were creating. They were not "discovering" a New World; they were dismembering an old one.

There was little sense of sanctity for the land to the European of Galileo's time. They arrived with the trappings of a history that was centuries in the making, their appearance in America coinciding with the dissolution of the medieval world view brought about by the Reformation. Now was a time for man to willingly embrace the mysteries of an unknown world with the new tools of science, time, and capitalism, each of them aspects of practical utility in the new Protestant ethos. The Dutch in particular were masters of the utile, having forged a nation literally from the sea. The original sense of geopiety that characterized man's relationship to the land under the old order was now gone, its origins abstracted into practicality, and in this foreign context the land was reduced to mere troublesome scenery. Adriaen van der Donck (1620–1655), of all the Dutch the most intellectual and learned, could remark at how the great falls at Cohoes might have inspired a Roman or a Greek in inspirational verse, but he could never evoke that poetry himself. Perhaps they had had it in an earlier time, but for now the Europeans lacked an essential innocence of spirit by which the Indians had assimilated with the natural world. They were in a completely alien landscape; an amazing one, remarkable at times, yet ultimately nothing more than a background for the larger drama of their own ego presence, a background to be altered, mangled or ignored at will. All became abstracted in the headstrong pursuit of the *guilder*, and the ultimate abstraction was of the people themselves, into *wilden menschen*, "wild men," not like the "Turks, Mamelukes, and Barbarians" of the Old World, whom the Dutch called "Heathen," but further removed from the human reality; a part of the landscape was all. More sympathetic than most, van der Donck justified the name *wilden* for those "who are not born of Christian parents" because of their strange religion, marriage practices, and laws "so singular as to deserve the name of wild regulations."[4] Given such a worldview and context, it is not surprising that the process of dehumanization that unfolded constituted not simply a sad and inevitable commentary on the meaning (and meanness) of European colonialism, but on the morality of the men who drove the process as well. Why did so many "Christians" do these things? The question never occurred to them.

The lifestyle patterns of both Munsee and Mahican Indians living in the Hudson Valley at the time of contact (1609) reflected characteristics far more advanced than any earlier cultures. The needs of these two Algonquian cultures were as basic as their predecessors', but by now they had manifested spiritual as well as material aspects. Exactly when a teleological dimension came to exist, or how, is unknown, but the process must have developed slowly over centuries.[5] As with the Paleo-Indian, awe, wonder, and fear toward aspects of the natural world had to have been common to later cultures, and were gradually translated, however crudely at first, into spiritual dimensions and religious forms, although the evidence of such manifestations in the Hudson Valley is poor prior to Late Woodland time.[6]

By the time of Columbus' discovery of America, the religious outlooks of the Hudson Valley Algonquians were relatively sophisticated. Mahicans believed that the soul went westward upon leaving the body, where black otter and bearskins were worn and the souls of their forebears were there to joyously greet them. They felt death was evil, "the offspring of the Devil," and could not understand the odd Western notion that God had control over death as well as life.[7] Advanced societal organization evolved with population growth and the needs of people living closer together and sharing common expectations and anxieties. A richer array of natural resources reduced the time needed for subsistence activities.[8] The people's store of common events, stories, heroic actions, and tragedies grew naturally and enriched the fabric of their lives and heritage. Eventually collective knowledge was memorized and periodic conferences evolved for those charged as keepers of the memory to recite the stories and expose the heritage to the youth, who were expected to remember it and pass it along in their day. The strung beads kept by the headman was used as mnemonic devices to recall and relate this oral tradition;[9] it is ironic as well as significant that these beads, very early in the Dutch period, became abstracted into *sewan*, a new form of currency.[10]

The transformation of the practical and immediate into the spiritual and imaginative lay ultimately in the native's relationship to the ecosystem and its creatures and forces,[11] for the spiritual world of the Algonquian cultures was identical with the world around them. Such was not the case for these new arrivals. The European stepped into a physical world that was mute, incapable of dialogue or communication, but the same world to the native American was vibrant with an active spirituality in which the cognizance of humans was shared by bears, turtles, wolves, even the rocks around them. Trees had thought, language, magic powers. The sun was our "elder brother," the earth, moon, wind, and other aspects of nature cherished also as relatives.[12] The beaver was the mythical earth brother who lived in a separate nation and could not be taken by hunters without its own amiable consent. This was religion, a pantheism perhaps, but unknown to the Western world.[13] Natives knew the difference between man and animal:

> "...they were not fuzzy in their systematic thought. However, they were capable of more than systematizing. They also conceived of a world in which plants, animals, pictures, words, actions, as well as humans, storms, and sunlight had the potential of power and life. All entities in the Indian world view were potentially equivalent. A word could stand for the thing it spoke of; a human in animal skin could be the animal."[14]

Native perceptions of reality included an array of supernatural beings of varying benefit or danger whose existence was essential to native survival in the ecosystem. Nanahboozho, the son of the West Wind (*Mudjekeewis*), was the Mahican legendary hero (Gluscap to the Micmacs) and "first" Algonquian in the mythic sense. A *Tchi Manito* was common to all Algonquian cultures, as was an evil spirit (*Mahtantu* to the Lenape, *Windigo* to other Algonquians) that put the thorns on bushes and made flies, mosquitoes, reptiles, and useless plants.[15] Munsees called their beneficent godhead *Kishelëmukong* ("Our Creator"), placed him in the twelfth layer of the heavenly realm, and had an array of *manëtuwàk* ("spirits") or lesser gods that served as spirit helpers. *Manëtuwàk* "grandfathers" and "grandmothers" guarded the four directions and the seasons. The *Mësingw* or Living Solid Face (always depicted with a face painted half black and half red, signifying the opposite nature of things) took care of animals, provided hunters with food, and rode the forest on the back of a deer; this deity was extremely important in Minisink rituals and burials.[16] Some deities held both good and bad functions, a sophisticated concept that reflected a dual nature of reality. Thunder beings (*Pèthakhuweyok*), which looked like huge birds with animal heads, were responsible for watering the crops but were also unpredictable and dangerous. The *manëtutëtak* (or *wèmahtèkënis*), "little people" like the Mahican *pukwujininee*, stood a foot tall, helped those lost in the woods (especially children), and had the power to grant great stamina or longevity to any who saw them, but could also injure those who did wrong. Snow Boy endangered children with frostbite but also gave hunters the means to track animals and cross water in winter. Doll Beings (*Ohtas*) were important manitous for some Munsee families (not all), who had to dance with or "feed" their Doll once a year or face dire consequences. Munsees also had *Wehixamukes*, a trickster hero known to the English as Crazy Jack or "the Delaware Sampson," who was substantially the same legendary figure as the Mahican *Moskim* or *Tschimammus*: foolishness was an aspect of his personality.[17]

As this abbreviated assemblage of minor Munsee deities suggests, the average Indian in the Hudson Valley before contact faced a complex array of mental choices, many of them potentially life-threatening, in reconciling their lives with the natural environment. A psychologist might ponder theories on the origin of modern consciousness in the right- and left-brain activities these choices might engender, yet in reality the complexity was simplified by communal familiarity with the mythologies, basic beliefs in dreams and visions, and by the existence of personal guardians who assisted the natives. "The vision," C. A. Weslager noted, "was the point of contact, a line of communication between the supernatural world and the sphere of everyday life."[18] For some, these visions were singular, epiphanic, and life-defining; for others, they were matters of a particular moment, yet all were intuitive perceptions of sympathetic relationships that existed between the physical and the metaphysical worlds.

Communal integrations of these mythological aspects of Native American culture with the ecosystem occurred in various rituals that coincided with the planting of corn, summer growth, the fall harvest, winter hunts, and the like. The rituals might be expressed as a dance ceremony lasting from one to a dozen days. Among Munsees, special occasions called for a buffalo dance, bread dance, woman dance, and others; a war dance was called *kinte-kaying* (according to Ruttenber). The August corn celebration seized the men as, one Dutchman observed, in "a universal torment," in which they "run like men possessed, regarding neither hedges nor ditches, and like mad dogs resting no where except from sheer inability." The most important ritual was occasioned by the fall harvest, in Munsee culture a *Gamwing*, or "Big House" ceremony, in which the universe and the earth were depicted over a twelve-day duration. (Twelve was a special number for the Munsee and corresponded with the twelve carapaces of the turtle's shell. It was the age at which a boy became a man or, if it was his fate, had the vision that defined his future course; the shaman or *kitzinacka*, for example, was determined at this age.) The Big House ceremony began with ceremonial attendants (*ash-kah-suk*), who swept the floor twelve times with turkey wings, to clear the path to heaven. They also painted the carved faces (*Mesingw*), passed the twelve prayer sticks, kept fires going and otherwise assisted the ceremony participants. The ceremonial hut contained twelve faces carved on posts, not to be worshipped as the idols of pagans or revered as in Christian rituals, but as witnesses who carried the prayers to the Creator. Men and women participated, all painted for the occasion, but they were segregated and remained silent; a tortoise shell rattle was used by those reciting a vision. The twelfth night, called *ah-tay-hoom-ween*, was reserved for women to recite their visions.[19]

One common myth that helps to explain the sympathetic attitude natives had toward animals has all these creatures identical in ancient time, looking and speaking like humans. Another states that with the advent of hunting man diverted from nature and began killing too many animals, who retaliated by sending the flies and mosquitoes to create diseases—but the plants took pity on the humans and provided them with remedies.[20] (This myth is particularly relevant in our context because the mass harvesting of beaver pelts signaled the demise of the Indian spiritual world.) Now, whenever a man faced an animal, the process of subduing the animal's spirit was more important than the taking of the carcass: an apology was made, or the animal might even be berated for allowing the man to position himself for the kill.[21] The actions of groups and individuals on the hunt, the aspect of the native alone in the woods, the various harvest festivals that brought bands together in seasonal sharing and thanksgivings, and the most rudimentary aspects of daily life were all ways of acting in consort with the fellow (mythic as well as physical) creatures of the wild.[22]

This familiarity made the natives acute observers of the environment. Their traps, for example, were highly effective because they were based on detailed observation of animal habits. The average Algonquian woman was expert on the astronomical world[23] and integrated that world into the community mythos, where (in Mahican myth) a treasure-box of storms and sunshine was presided over by an old squaw, Minnewawa, who made the day and night and cut up the old moons to make the stars. She gave light to the fireflies to help the little men of the woods (*pukwujininee*) raise Morning Star into the sky. She also climbed the *Ontiora* to hang the moons, and when hunting was over, she let her people know by tipping the crescent moon up "so that a bow could be hung upon it."[24]

Native perspicacity extended to all aspects of the natural world in ways that are frequently marvels of detail. A common Algonquian tale about the origin of tobacco pits Nanahboozho against a giant who guarded tobacco in one of the mountain cloves.[25] Nanahboozho steals the tobacco and in the ensuing struggle pushes the giant off the mountain, transforms him into a grasshopper, and derisively names him *Pukaneh*, after the "dirty" saliva of both the chewed tobacco and a grasshopper's defensive mechanism of expectorating a sticky brown substance that smells like nicotine.[26] An attention to detail also allows the native temperament to view the world's broader perspectives in intimate terms, as in the Indian summer legend. Nanahboozho gives us those hazy days of late autumn when he returns each year to see how things are going, slumps across a few mountains, and has a big smoke.[27]

This integration of native life and spirituality with the ecosystem eventually proved so profound that survival as a people depended upon it. The decimation of the local beaver population within a few decades after Henry Hudson's arrival graphically demonstrated the symbiotic relationship between man, his spiritual world, and the environment. When the mythical earth brother gave "amiable consent" to its own virtual extinction, the virtual extinction of the original people was the logical and unforgivable corollary. This was a process of abstraction similar to that which the Europeans themselves had undergone in the Reformation, yet in the New World, because the choice was not conscious, the results were calamitous. Indians literally became apostates in the practice of the pelt trade, displacing their traditional respect for an animal brother in a blind embrace of shiny replacements. With the loss of the old worldview went the old taboos. The interior *wilden* landscape, like the bogs and ponds of the real world left uncompleted in their evolutionary process by the loss of an essential component (the beaver), was now transformed into the ghastly wreck of a collapsed mythology. A bizarre new reality rendered the old native ways and cures ineffective,[28] affirming the destruction of the natural world in the destruction of the people themselves. Huge mortalities from sickness and epidemic added a symbolic and palpable horror to the situation. When the mythical earth brother became as commonplace a commodity as a skinned, scraped, smelly pelt, an essential moral relationship between man and beast was destroyed. The native universe, like Galileo's at the same time, was irrevocably changed: a terrible beauty was born.[29]

Endnotes

1. The first demonstrable effort to explore the Hudson Valley for merchantable commodities began in May of 1611 when the *St. Pieter* under skipper Cornelis Rijser was chartered by Arnout Vogels (1580–1620), an Amsterdam merchant with an interest in furs, and two merchant brothers, Leonard and Francoys Pelgrom. Simon Hart, *The Prehistory of the New Netherland Company: Amsterdam Notarial Records of the First Dutch Voyages to the Hudson*, Amsterdam, Holland (1959), tr. Sibrandina Geertruid Hart-Runeman, 20. On January 17, 1612, also apparently under Vogel's authority, Adriaen Block purchased in Amsterdam a 55-last *spiegelschip* called the *Fortuyn* (with a "long beak head, high rising aft, and flat stern"), sailed to "Virginia," and returned "a better voyage even than last year." (Virginia and "Terneuff" were Dutch euphemisms for New Netherland.) Francoys Pelgrom (1574–1616) to his wife in Brno (Prague), July 20, 1612, quoted in Hart, 21, 73–74; Van Cleaf Bachman, *Peltries or Plantations: The Economic Policies of the Dutch West India Company in New Netherland, 1623–1639*, Baltimore (1969), 6, n. 15. Bachman, 6, n. 13, says that Vogels was "likely" part of the group in 1612. Johannes de Laet (1582–1649), a respected historian and director of the West India Company, asserted that a ship sponsored by Amsterdam merchants did visit in 1610. This might have been the 100-last *Hoope*, which sailed to the West Indies and traded along the coast under Vogels' authority, but Vogels also traded in Canada with French partners and no direct evidence places the *Hoope* in Hudson Valley waters. Laet, "From the 'New World,'" in J. Franklin Jameson, ed., *Narratives of New Netherland*, New York (1909), 28; this was repeated in Holland's 1660 "Deduction" on its disputes with the English, *DCHSNY*, II, 133; see Bachman, 4; Hart, 15–17. The *Tijger*, under Block's command, and the *Nachtengal* under Mossel sailed here in the fall of 1613; Hart, 25, Bachman, 7; Oliver A. Rink, *Holland on the Hudson: An Economic and Social History of Dutch New York*, Ithaca (1986), 40–41.

2. The *Tijger* burned one night at its mooring at Manhattan, so Block had a small *yacht*, the *Onrust*, built from the plentiful forest resources. Meanwhile, crew members from the *Tijger*, disgruntled that Block was trying to resolve his bitter differences with Mossel, took the *Nachtegael* in a bloodless coup. Pieter Franssen (or Fransz) came over with the Vos ("Fox") in early 1614 but was killed in an unknown trading incident; Jan de Wit succeeded him as skipper and simply continued the trade. Hart, 29–30, 97–98.

3. The axes used by the early Dutch weighed more than four pounds each, had brittle iron heads that frequently cracked in the cold, and were fitted with a thin steel blade in need of frequent sharpening. A smaller, lighter felling ax was not introduced until the 18th century. See Charles F. Carroll, "The Forest Society of New England," in Brooke Hindle, ed., *America's Wooden Age: Aspects of its Early Technology*, Tarrytown (1975), 18–19.

4. Adriaen van der Donck, *A Description of the New Netherlands*, ed. Thomas F. O'Donnell, Syracuse (1968; originally published in 1655), 20. On the distinction between pagan, heathen, and savage, see Christopher Vecsey, "American Indian Environmental Religions," in Christopher Vecsey and Robert W. Venables, eds., *American Indian Environments: Ecological Issues in Native American History*, Syracuse (1980), 37. Although Robert Juet, an Englishman, had used the word, the term "Indian" was not common in the Dutch Hudson Valley. The French called the original native inhabitants *sauvages, peaux-rouges* ("redskins") or, when polite, *indigènes* ("natives"). The Dutch called the natives *wilden menschen* ("wild men"), shortened to the *wilden*. The English called the Virginians "savages" and translated the Dutch term the same. Samuel Eliot Morison, *The European Discovery of American: The Northern Voyages A.D. 500–1600*, New York (1971), 428; Mrs. John King Van Rensselaer, *The Goede Vrouw of Mana-ha-ta: At Home and in Society 1609–1760*, New York (1898), 2; Alice P. Kenney, *Stubborn for Liberty: The Dutch in New York*, Syracuse (1975), 25; *A Description of the New Netherlands*, 73–74; Francis Jennings, *The Ambiguous Iroquois Empire: The Covenant Chain Confederation of Indian Tribes with English Colonies from its Beginnings to the Lancaster Treaty of 1744*, New York (1984), 49 (n. 6), 50.

5. New York Algonquian artifactual remains are sparse on this subject, but the lesson of Owasco spiritual development may provide a clue. James A. Tuck has suggested that the presence of miniature pots and pipes at Owasco sites prefigure later Iroquois "dream-guessing," a soul-enriching practice; Owasco face and antler carvings also may anticipate the Iroquois False Face Society or other social or curing organizations within that culture. Their lack in pre-Owasco archaeology suggests that more sophisticated Iroquois spiritual development began during the Owasco period. See Matthew Dennis, *Cultivating a Landscape of Peace: Iroquois-European Encounters in Seventeenth-Century America*, Ithaca (1993), 49–50.

6. On the antiquity of Munsee myths, see John Bierhorst, *Mythology of the Lenape: Guide and Texts*, Tucson (1995), 8, 30, 39; C. A. Weslager, *The Delaware Indians: A History*, New Brunswick, N. J. (1972), 92–93, 97. A turtle creation myth finds one of its oldest expressions in Munsee myth (Bierhorst, 28–29, 71, 12) and was among the earliest recorded by Europeans; see Jameson, ed., *Narratives of New Netherland*, 77–78.

7. Nicolaes van Wassenaer, "First Settlement of New-York by the Dutch," in E. B. O'Callaghan, M.D., ed., *A Documentary History of the State of New York*, Albany (1850), III, 45–46.

8. "One estimate of subsistence activity per day is two to four hours for primitive hunters." Christopher Vecsey, "American Indian Environmental Religions," 8.

9. Shirley Dunn, *The Mohicans and Their Land 1609–1730*, Fleischmanns, N.Y. (1994), 32–36.

10. Lewis Mumford considered the creation of money (and by extension the rise of capitalism) in the same historic context as the "abstraction" of reality that emanated from the Reformation—"and in money they achieved a calculus for all human activity"; *The Golden Day: A Study in American Literature and Culture*, New York (1968; 1926), 9. *Sewan* (which the English, borrowing from Narragansett Indians, called "wampum" after introduced to the currency by the Dutch) soon became that calculus in the Hudson Valley.

11. Calvin Martin's definition of "ecosystem" introduces this section. "The European Impact on the Culture of a Northeastern Algonquian Tribe: An Ecological Interpretation," in *William and Mary Quarterly*, 31 (January 1974), 5.

12. "According to Lenape [Munsee] Indian belief, all things had spirits: animals, insects, trees, air, even rocks; therefore, everything had to be respected and cherished." Herbert C. Kraft and John T. Kraft, *The Indians of Lenapehoking*, South Orange, N. J. (1991), 30.

13. Weslager, *The Delaware Indians*, 66, calls the native application of spiritual facets "a pantheistic concept in which the entire world was under the control of invisible beings." All aspects of the environment were equally endowed with spirituality by native Americans, but each aspect had its own characteristics that were unique in their various manifestations and quite specific to the natural world they represented.

14. Vecsey, "American Indian Environmental Religions," 36, 16.

15. E. M. Ruttenber, *History of the Indian Tribes of Hudson's River*, Albany (1872), II, 362–363, tells a tale about the origin of the Steppingstone Islands that once stretched from the bottom of the Hudson Valley and were used by the evil spirit to escape Indians who drove him from Long Island; furious, he stood at Cold Spring and hurled rocks all over Connecticut. In Ruttenber's time, one of those little islands was still called "Satan's Toe," a name used by James Fenimore Cooper in the title of his best novel depicting a Hudson Valley setting. See also Theodore Kazimiroff, *The Last Algonquin*, New York (1982), 179.

16. One found in a Minisink burial site dated to A.D. 1380±55. Herbert C. Kraft, "Late Woodland Settlement Patterns in the Upper Delaware Valley," in Jay F. Custer, ed., *Late Woodland Cultures of the Middle Atlantic Region*, Cranbury, N. J. (1986), 115.

17. See Bierhorst, *Mythology of the Lenape*, 8–10, 21–27; Nora Thompson Dean, "The Spiritual World of the Lenape or Delaware Indians," in Catherine Coleman Brawer, ed., *Many Trails: Indians of the Lower Hudson Valley*, Katonah (1983), 36; Kraft and Kraft, *The Indians of Lenapehoking*, 29–30; Herbert C. Kraft, *The Lenape or Delaware Indians*, South Orange, N. J. (1991), 46; Nicholas Shoumatoff, "The Algonkian Spirit," in Brawer, *Many Trails*, 37. *Manëtu* is a Unami (or southern) Delaware word; the *-ou* form was a New France contribution. Alexander F. Chamberlain, "Algonkian Words in American English: A Study in the Contact of the White Man and the Indian," in *Journal of American Folklore*, 15 (1992), 247.

18. *The Delaware Indians*, 68.

19. Richard C. Adams, *The Delaware Indians: A Brief History*, Saugerties (1995; 1906), 8; Ruttenber, I, 28–29, n. 2; Weslager, *The Delaware Indians*, 66, 69–71; Kraft and Kraft, *The Indians of Lenapehoking*, 31; Julian Harris Salomon, *Indians of the Lower Hudson Region: The Munsee*, New City (1982), 24, 27; Ives Goddard, "Delaware," in Bruce G. Trigger, ed. (William C. Sturtevant, gen. ed.) *Handbook of North American Indians: Volume 15 Northeast*, Washington (1978), 220. Weslager's Figure 11 (p. 70) is a diagram of the places taken up by the participants and some of the ceremonial properties of the Big House Ceremony. On the *kitzinacka*, see Wassenaer, "From the 'Historisch Verhael,'" in Jameson, ed., *Narratives of New Netherland*, 68.

20. Dorothy M. Reid, *Tales of Nanabozho*, New York (1963), 85–88.

21. See, e.g., Reid, *Tales of Nanabozho*, 48. A missionary among the Delawares watched a native deliver a "curious invective" to a bear before dispatching it; the missionary asked if the bear understood his words, and the native responded, of course: "did you not observe how *ashamed* he looked while I was upbraiding him?" *The Poems of Henry Wadsworth Longfellow*, New York (n.d.), 126, n. 1. (Longfellow was quoting Rev. John Heckewelder, *Transactions of the American Philosophical Society*, I, 240.)

22. In anthropological terms, Vescey, 10–11, distinguishes three ways in which native Americans "integrated" their spiritual world into the real one: primary integration such as talking to animals they hunted or coinciding agricultural festivals with stages of plant growth; secondary integration, such as atomistic shamanism in hunting; and morphological or symbolic inte-

gration by referencing natural phenomenon into myths or rituals.

23. Vescey, "American Indian Environmental Religions," 9. "The women there are the most skillful star-gazers; there is scarcely one of them but can name all the stars; their rising, setting; the position of the Arctos, that is the Wain, is as well known to them as to us, and they name them by other names." Wassenaer, "From the 'Historisch Verhael,'" in Jameson, ed., *Narratives of New Netherland*, 69.

24. See Charles Hayes, ed., *From the Hudson to the World: Voices of the River*, n.p. (1978), 22, 31; Emelyn Elizabeth Gardner, *Folklore from the Schoharie Hills, New York*, New York (1977; 1937), 18. Minnewawa spoke in thunderclaps.

25. Reid, *Tales of Nanabozho*, 83. Tobacco was used in sacred rites and blessings as well as for consumption; Delawares occasionally mixed it with sumac in a concoction called *kinnikinnick*. See Weslager, *The Delaware Indian*, 58.

26. This was an Ojibway tale, but common to all Algonquians. Egerton R. Young, *Algonquin Indian Tales*, New York (1903), 240–242. Naturalist Spider Barbour, who had a fascination with grasshoppers while growing up in Ohio, recalled the admonishments of adults: "Don't pick up those grasshoppers—they'll spit tobacco juice at you!" (Personal communication.)

27. Young, 255–256.

28. In all northeastern cultures, the principle health treatment was sweating, in a lodge or bath (*pimëwakàn* in Munsee) built near a stream out of saplings covered with clay and heated with rocks carried in from a communal fire—literally an earthen oven. In another telling irony, the *pimëwakàn* proved entirely the wrong remedy when the European smallpox struck, because the sweating prevented the pox pustules from drying. A description of the sweat lodge is found in Kraft, *The Lenape or Delaware Indians*, 14. See also Kraft and Kraft, *The Indians of Lenapehoking*, 33; Goddard, "Delaware," 219; Weslager, *The Delaware Indians*, 51; and Charles Wolley, *A Two Years' Journal in New York and Part of its Territories in America*, Harrison (1973; 1701), 54.

29. See Vecsey, "American Indian Environmental Religions," in Vecsey and Venables, eds., 29; Calvin Martin (to whom I am indebted for the apostasy concept), "The European Impact on the Culture of a Northeastern Algonquian Tribe: An Ecological Interpretation," *William and Mary Quarterly*, (January 1974), 25. William MacLeish sees the ruined beaver ponds as "the first signs of European corporate power." *The Day Before America*, New York (1994), 188.

This article originally appeared in *The Hudson River Valley Review*, Volume 20.2.

Pro-Leislerian Farmers in Early New York: A "Mad Rabble" or "Gentlemen Standing Up for Their Rights"?

Firth Haring Fabend

"It is a singular and melancholy fact, and one from which we may learn wisdom, that in the heat of those days, Leisler's connexions were his bitterest enemies. [Nicholas] Bayard and [Stephanus] van Cortland, who were of the Council that urged his execution, were his wife's nephews."[1]

So observed E. B. O'Callaghan, the nineteenth-century editor of documents relating to the extraordinary late seventeenth-century upheaval known as Leisler's Rebellion. What wisdom was it that O'Callaghan thought we might learn from the "singular and melancholy fact" that Leisler's own relatives condemned him to the gallows in 1691? What was so dangerous about Jacob Leisler, or his supporters, that his execution was necessary to satisfy his enemies?

The danger, I will suggest here, was that in Leisler's uprising, a new elite that had begun to emerge after the second English takeover of New Netherland in the 1670s heard the rumblings of an egalitarianism that they foresaw would change their world. In the complex nexus of religious, political, and socioeconomic factors that underlay the uprising, it may have been the latter that generated the most heat and the most fear among those with the most to lose.

In Jacob Leisler's mind, socioeconomic factors were hardly in the forefront. Leisler protested to his dying moments on the gallows that his "maine end, totall Intent & endeavors . . . [were only] to maintaine against popery or any Schism or heresy . . . the interest of our Sovereign[s] . . . and the reformed Protestant Churches in those parts." What he had done, he insisted, "was for king William & Queen Mary, for the defence of the protestant religion & the Good of the Country."[2]

This begs the question, however. Leisler's enemies, for the most part, were also Protestants with no fondness for Roman Catholicism. In fact, despite conflicts over points of doctrine and differing styles of worship, both factions were affiliated with the Reformed Protestant Dutch Church, the French Reformed Church (Huguenot), or English Dissenting churches, all with common origins in Reformation Europe. And despite all the rhetoric and mutual name-calling, there is no doubt that both sides shared an allegiance to William and Mary and valued their constitutional rights and liberties as English subjects. The Dutch also retained a clear memory of and appreciation for Dutch political institutions, Dutch historical models, Dutch tolerance, and Dutch liberties and rights going back to the fourteenth century at least. (The Huguenots, in their turn, remembered the Edict of Nantes, lately revoked.) Moreover, Nicholas Bayard, the main spokesman for those who opposed Jacob Leisler so strenuously, hardly ever referred to religion as the issue that divided them. Leisler was, in Bayard's words, a drunkard, the chief malefactor of the rebellion, a tyrant, a rough rascal, a traitor, a rebel, a usurper "Lording and domineering in all Causes"—epithets that have political and socioeconomic connotations, but not religious ones.[3]

Bayard's language became even more vitriolic when he focused on Leisler's followers—or rather on his "abettors" and "accomplices," his "crew" and his "creatures"—as this master of invective called them. Leisler's supporters were, in Bayard's terms, "all men of meane birth sordid educacon & desperate ffortunes." The "lesser & meaner part of the people," they were disorderly, malicious, of "mad and franticq humor," a "mad Rabble" of "byassed & Disaffected men" whose "Religion . . . was as unaccomptable & obscure as their birth & fortunes." Bayard also chose the language and imagery of economics, rather than of religion or politics, to characterize himself and his anti-Leislerian friends. They were the "strictest Protestants," to be sure, but they were also "men of sence, Reputation and Estate," "men of greatest probity & best figure amongst us." "Their majesties' most affectionate subjects," they were men of the "best sort," "some of the most Considerable persons of the Province," "gentlemen" all.

Yet it is—and was then—no secret that most of these elegant, proud, and wealthy anti-Leislerians were but a generation removed, if that, from the middling ranks of society. Nor was it a secret that some had attained their high estate in part through advantageous marriages to wealthy Dutch women, and in part by seeking the favor and patronage of English governors. That the anti-Leislerians attacked Leisler and his supporters with rhetoric so heavily laced with economic and class slurs suggests a vulnerability—as if those opposed to Leisler felt their newfound economic position was threatened in some way by his adherents. Just as Leisler, for whom the situation was "about" religion, almost always used religious epithets to attack his opponents, so Bayard reviled Leisler's supporters with economic invective, suggesting that, for Bayard, the situation was "about" economic issues. Leisler thundered and fumed at Papist devils, Papist dogs, Papist murderers, false Protestants, Popish trumpets, false Priests of Baal, and false Popish grandees. Bayard and company cast stones of another type at "poor, ignorant, and senseless folk," a "hotheaded and meane sort of people," a "rude crew," the "meanest and most abject Common people" in the province of New York.

Historians have sometimes taken this language at face value and assumed that the Leislerians really were the "meanest Sort" around. But were they of such "Desperate fortune" that they hoped "to make up their Wants by the ruin & Plunder of his Majesties' Loyal Subjects?" Was their Religion "as unaccomptable & obscure as their birth & fortunes?" Indeed, were their birth and fortunes unaccountable and obscure?

The public record is a rich source of information about any number of obscure Leislerians. We will look here at several who were linked to one another by family ties, Protestantism (Dutch, French, and English), economic position, political inclinations, and the intellectual underpinnings of those inclinations. Furthermore, all in this group were linked to Orange County, an area west of the Hudson River whose seventeenth-century history has received scant attention. Yet the religious and political proclivities of its residents in the seventeenth century, as well as their socioeconomic status, may provide a clue to the question asked above: What was so threatening about Jacob Leisler that even his relatives wanted him dead?

The men we will look at are Daniel De Clark, a member of the Committee of Safety that, on June 8, 1689, appointed Leisler captain of the fort in New York and on August 16 appointed him commander in chief of New York Province; De Clark's stepson, Peter Haring; Guiliam Bertholf, the Pietist *voorlezer* (lay reader) and then minister who was to organize in 1694 the Reformed Church where De Clark and Haring were members and officers in Tappan, New York; Teunis Roelofsen van Houten, also a member of the Committee of Safety; and Cornelius Cooper, captain of the Orange County militia company that occupied the New York fort from 1689 to 1691.

Daniel De Clark had emigrated from Oostburg in Zeeland, where, judging from his refined handwriting, he appears to have received an education beyond the ordinary. His last name, meaning scribe, clerk, or accountant, suggests that he may even have come from a line of educated men. In 1685, De Clark, a widower, married Margrietje Haring, *nee* Cosyns, daughter of Cosyn Gerritsen van Putten, a New Amsterdam farmer and wheelwright. When she married De Clark, Margrietie was the widow of Jan Pietersen Haring, a schepen (magistrate) in New Amsterdam and the leader of a group of families who had obtained a grant in 1683 for 16,000 acres in the Hackensack Valley (known as the Tappan Patent).

Tax records for the last decades of the seventeenth century indicate that De Clark owned a house and land in the Out Ward in Manhattan; other records show that both he and Margrietie were members of the New York Reformed Dutch Church. De Clark was solvent enough to continue to maintain his New York property long after he became the leader, as Pietersen's widow's husband, of the enterprising settlers who had cooperatively purchased the Tappan Patent, 16,000 acres in today's Rockland County, New York, and Bergen County, New Jersey. Settled in Tappan, De Clark was licensed as a brewer and served as an elder in the church, as justice of the peace for Orange County, and as a captain in the militia. Of the forty-odd householders in Orange County in 1702, he was among the three best off, owning (besides his share of the patent lands) four slaves and a fine brick house, which is still standing.[4]

Peter Haring, De Clark's stepson, was also one of the original Tappan patentees, having become so by inheritance when his father died shortly before settlement. Both Haring and his wife, Margaret Bogert, had been born in the 1660s into prospering farming families. Like his stepfather, Haring continued to own his New York lands until his death in 1750; also like De Clark, he was appointed a justice of the peace in Orange County. Beginning in 1701, Haring (whose patent share entitled him to nearly 1,000 acres in Tappan) was the county's representative to the New York Provincial Assembly. Here he and his brother, Cornelius, served over the course of thirty-six years. A colonel in the Orange County militia, Peter Haring was for decades the largest contributor to the church in Tappan, a fact suggesting his relative economic standing in the community.[5]

Guiliam Bertholf also came to America from Zeeland, in his day the heartland of Dutch Pietism, where he had been in the thick of the religious controversies of that time and place and a disciple of the fiery Pietist preacher and writer Jacobus Koelman. By occupation a baker, Bertholf was employed soon after arriving in New York in 1684 as *voorlezer* in Harlem and then as *voorlezer* and schoolmaster for two communities, Hackensack and Acquackanonk (Passaic), in Bergen County, New Jersey. Records reveal that Bertholf was an ardent supporter of Leisler. Indeed, anti-Leislerian New York Domine Rudolfus Varick complained to the Classis of Amsterdam that Bertholf had "violently urged [Leisler] on." This adverb was an inappropriate one, as all other sources reveal Bertholf to have had a calm, irenic spirit. Varick's choice of the word "violently" underlines the anxiety felt by the ruling powers at the prospect of the opposition rising in their midst. Two years after Leisler's Rebellion ended, Bertholf returned to the Netherlands to be examined and ordained in the Reformed Church, a step that suggests he was no violent instigator, but a man with a calling who must have had facility in Latin, Greek, and Hebrew, and training in Reformed theology, doctrine, church history, homiletics, and oratory. Back in America, Bertholf organized a dozen or more Pietist congregations in the hinterland and has been called the "itinerating apostle" of New Jersey.[6]

The backgrounds of De Clark, Haring, and Bertholf were similar to that of Teunis Roelofsen van Houten and Cornelius Cooper: Both born in New Netherland in the 1650s, they were landowners, solid citizens, and elders in the church. A merchant in Tappan, Roelofsen was elected to the Committee of Safety that elevated Leisler in 1689. For his support, Leisler named him that same year as justice of the peace in Orange County. In 1703 he became a justice of the Court of Common Pleas in the county.[7]

Born in Manhattan in 1659, Cooper was a shareholder in the Tappan Patent, which entitled him to about 1,000 acres of land. He also owned other lands, some inherited and some purchased, in Bergen County; in the Kakiat Patent in Orange County; in Haverstraw (the De Hart Patent); and in New Castle, Delaware. High sheriff of Orange County, he was also a justice of the peace, a judge of the Court of Common Pleas, and later a member of the New York General Assembly. In Leisler's Rebellion, Cornelius Cooper was captain of the troops that occupied the fort in 1689.

How representative were such men in the age of Leisler? They were far from unique. Hundreds of Leisler's supporters throughout New York and New Jersey shared a similar background, and as this brief glimpse indicates, such men were no abject mob. Some of them were by 1689 already third-generation Americans. They were landowners, their housing stock was excellent, their families large, their life expectancy long. They were prospering in America in a steady and satisfactory way, worshiping in churches they themselves had founded, serving as officers in their militias, and shouldering the main burden of administering their town and county governments. Some of them participated in a significant way in province-level political affairs. In a nutshell, they were respectable representatives of society's middling sort; they were, indeed, model citizens. In "Loyalty Vindicated," the anonymous pamphlet published in New York in 1698 (note 3), such men described themselves as having behaved in 1689 not as a mad rabble, but as "Gentlemen" standing up for "all bounds, and Laws of English Right and Government."[8]

If the harsh and defamatory language of Nicholas Bayard does not, then, accurately describe the actual socioeconomic characteristics of the Leislerians, we might explore the idea that it reveals the anxiety of a small and recently established elite confronted by the political energy, intellectual ideas, and moral force of the numerous, discontented, and eager-to-advance class beneath it.

Historians with a social-class model in mind have attributed the Dutch farmers' motives in supporting Leisler in 1689 to a vague resentment at having been passed over in the new order that developed in New York after the English takeover. Randall Balmer has specifically attributed "class antagonisms" among the Dutch in the Leislerian period to the "emerging alliance" between upwardly mobile Dutch clergy and English merchants. But the internecine tension in the Dutch community at this time had little to do with New York politics per se. Rather, it was related to long-standing theological disputes that were in turn related to the Arminian controversies of the early decades of the seventeenth century in Reformation Europe. It also echoed the political situation in the Netherlands between the States Party and the Orange Party, and it was exacerbated by the differing worship styles of the strict Calvinists in the Netherlands and the more liberal Calvinists.[9] Nevertheless, if they were discontented in 1689, the Dutch farmers bore grievances were that were real and particular—and they were not limited to the clergymen among them, or to the clergy's specific complaints. The important irritant was economic.

If economics was the battlefield, that field had real metes and bounds. We have only to recall how men acquired land in seventeenth-century New York and New Jersey to understand this. Good land was becoming expensive by 1680, and small-to-middling farmers had to pool their resources to acquire even relatively small parcels, like the Tappan Patent. The newly arriving Huguenots had to rely on Jacob Leisler, who himself purchased 6,000 acres in today's New Rochelle and sold them to the fairly penurious settlers. But these farmers had reason to suspect that others would receive huge grants of land from the royal governors, much in the way that King Charles in 1664 bestowed New Jersey on the Duke of York, with the duke in turn giving the land to his favorites, Sir George Carteret and Lord John Berkeley, a year later. When Governor Richard Nichols ruled that Dutch land claims be renewed under the so-called Duke's Laws in 1665, Dutch suspicions regarding the patterns of land tenure evolving around them were heightened. And time would prove their fears well grounded. In 1683, Robert Livingston—who had a talent for knowing what royal governors needed or wanted—paid $600 in trade goods for 2,000 acres on the Hudson River in today's Columbia County. In 1685, he purchased an additional 600 acres twenty miles away, with Governor Thomas Dongan throwing in for no clear reason the intervening 160,000 acres. The van Rensselaers' claims were confirmed in 1685 for what eventually grew to be the one million acres of Rensselaerswyck. In 1686, Philipe Philipse, a son of Frederick Philipse, received a patent for what is today all of Putnam County in the Hudson Valley. In the post-Leislerian period, Anglicizers received—often as outright gifts from British governors—tracts of valuable wilderness so vast as to stagger the imagination. These huge grants, basically political favors, were a cause for resentment among men who had to scrimp and save for their plot of earth, and had to band together in groups, at that, to acquire it. As one historian of colonial New York put it, the "tremendous concentration of landed estates in the hands of a few boded ill for the future of a society whose many yeomen had come to view these great landlords with grave suspicions."[10]

Despite all of the name-calling, daily economic concerns, forming class interests, and social standing were not in themselves the final battlefield. The ultimate source of anxiety for Nicholas Bayard and the anti-Leislerians was a set of intellectual ideas undergirding the Leislerians' resentment at inequity and injustice. As Bayard put it in 1691, "many of the people of this province have been debauched with strange principles and tenetts Concerning government . . . [which] are not easily to be rooted out. [M]any here of Considerable fortune and knowne integrity to the Crown of england whose lives and fortunes have almost been Ship wracht ware uneasy thinking it [w]ill never afterwards be safe for them to live in this province [n]or can their lives or fortunes ever be secure if such men doe survive to head an ignorant Mobile."[11]

The strange principles and tenets concerning government that bound the farmers of New York and New Jersey to Leisler's cause were not so strange after all. They were the very ideas circulating in Europe in the 1680s concerning liberty of conscience, power and prerogatives, and natural rights—including the right of property. It has long been known that Guiliam Bertholf and his fellow Pietists conveyed the religious basis for these ideas to the people of New Netherland. But since this paper was first published in 1990, research indicates that a number of prominent New York Leislerians were part of the hive of political activity known as the Protestant International in Rotterdam in the 1680s, when that port city was a Voetian-Orangist stronghold.[12] Among the men who met in the salon of Quaker merchant Benjamin Furley (along with John Locke) were none other than Jacob Milborne, Leisler's main supporter and future son in law, and Samuel Edsall, Milborne's father in law.

The Samuel Edsall connection provides food for thought in the context of the Orange County Leislerians discussed above, for they had long been associated with him. It is suggested here that he is the figure who links them with the political events of 1689, just as Bertholf is the religious link. Born in 1633/4 in Reading, England, Edsall was a hatter. He became a burgher of New Amsterdam in 1657; rose to affluence as a trader, merchant, and landed proprietor; and enjoyed a long career as magistrate and adviser to a number of administrations both in New York and New Jersey. He owned vast tracts of land, among which were 2,000 choice acres between the Hudson and Hackensack rivers (just a few miles south of the Tappan Patent). In 1680, he accompanied Jan Pietersen Haring, his exact contemporary in age, into the wilderness as translator in the negotiations with the Tappan Indians; the following year, he was a signatory on the deed to the land the Tappan patentees acquired.[13] Also that year, while sitting on the council of East Jersey Proprietary Governor Philip Carteret, Edsall angered the delegates to the General Assembly by siding with the Governor's attempts to whittle away at their traditional rights and privileges under the Concessions of 1665.[14] Prudent after this experience, Edsall was not to be on the wrong side of popular will again.

Considered by one historian who investigated his career as having a "better acquaintance with matters of government than was possessed by any of his colleagues [at the time of Leisler's Rebellion] or by Leisler himself," Edsall exercised, according to this writer, a "leading influence in the affairs of the Colony during that period."[15] He was a member of the Committee of Safety that chose Leisler captain of the fort in New York on June 8, 1689—the same committee on which Daniel De Clark and Teunis Roelofsen van Houten sat. Also on this committee were Jean Demarest and William Laurence, both with Orange County connections. (Demarest, of a Huguenot family, was a Haring in-law.) These same five men were among the ten who signed a "Commission to Capt. Leisler to be Commander in Chief" on August 16, 1689. Abraham Gouverneur, later to marry Leisler's daughter, was Clerk of the Committee of Safety, and had Orange County connections as well. Johannes Blauvelt, Teunis Talman, and Peter Bogert—all Dutch farmers related by ties of blood and marriage with the above Orange County families—were among those who captured the fort and served there under Leisler. All knew Edsall.

It has been assumed that these obscure men were isolated in their Orange County wilderness from the main intellectual ideas of the times. To the contrary, they were quite abreast of them. The farmers of Tappan, like hundreds of their fellow Leislerians all over New York and New Jersey who listened on Sundays to the views of Guiliam Bertholf and his Pietist colleagues, were, through this religious connection, privy to the ideas that anticipated the Glorious Revolution in England, when the Dutch stadtholder William took over the throne of James II. Now it appears that through their connection to Samuel Edsall and Jacob Milborne (and perhaps to other New York Leislerian merchants with business in the port city of Rotterdam) they were part of a transatlantic community of ideas that demanded, in the New World as well as in the Old, the triumph of Protestantism over Papism (if not toleration over persecution) and their traditional rights and privileges over royal tyranny.

The Glorious Revolution's immediate outcome in New York was not so glorious for Leisler, who was hanged and then for good measure beheaded, his property confiscated, and his family left nearly destitute. But his cause did not end there. It was carried over into the New York Assembly, where for thirty years his supporters clamored for redress of his wrongs and theirs—as we might expect on economic, and not religious, grounds. Property was the basis of it. And in the matter of property, the Leislerians had the last word. Leisler's estate was restored to his heirs, and even the sore thumb of royal land grants was eventually salved, though it would take a century.[16]

The Leislerians have been discounted by some historians because they were not "for English liberties" per se. But many of them, like Samuel Edsall, were English and thoroughly acquainted with the liberties of the "ancient constitution." The Dutch among them were men steeped in an understanding of Dutch liberties going back at least to the so-called "Joyous Entry of Brabant" in 1356, which established the right to overthrow a tyrant. And as mentioned, the Huguenots remembered all too well their recent liberties under the now-revoked Edict of Nantes. Further, through their connection to Bertholf and men like Edsall and Milborne, the farmers, artisans, and merchants of New York were acquainted, we know now, with the heady ideas circulating in Rotterdam in the 1680s, including the ideas of John Locke, who wrote his *Two Treatises of Government* in Holland during his expatriate years there (1683–1689) "to make good [King William's] title in the consent of the people . . . and to justify to the world the people of England, whose love of their just and natural rights . . . saved the nation when it was on the very brink of slavery and ruin." In other words, they were conversant with the notions that all men are equal and independent, that government emanates from the people and must seek the popular welfare, and that revolution against a tyrant, especially in the case of religious oppression, *vide* James II, is justified.[17]

Locke's views on the natural right of property, which built on those of the Dutch jurist Hugo Grotius, must also have been known to them. "I ask," Locke mused as he theorized on the value added to land by labor, "whether in the wild woods and uncultivated waste of America, left to nature, without any improvement, tillage, or husbandry, a thousand acres yield the needy and wretched inhabitants as many conveniences of life as ten acres of equally fertile land do in Devonshire, where they are well cultivated."[18] The farmers of New York and New Jersey in 1690 already knew that it was only a matter of time and sweat before the question was an academic one. In such ways, these Leislerian farmers were not merely backwoods hearers of ideas filtered down to them through men like Bertholf and Edsall. Rather, in their progressive hopefulness, they were already acting on them—and on a continuum with the more successful revolutionaries who would be informed by Locke's ideas in later American history.

No wonder the ruling elite in New York feared the "strange principles and tenetts Concerning government" of these troublesome men, and no wonder they wanted their leader dead, even if he was, for some, their relative.

End Notes

1. E. B. O'Callaghan, ed., "Introductory," *The Documentary History of the State of New York*, 4 vols. (Albany, N.Y., 1849-1851), 2: n.p.; hereafter <u>Docs. Rel. N.Y.</u>

2. Ibid., 378, 379.

3. Attributed to Nicholas Bayard, "A Modest and Impartial Narrative of several Grievances and Great Oppressions That the Peaceable and most Considerable Inhabitants of . . . New-York . . . Lye Under, By the Extravagant and Arbitrary Proceedings of Jacob Leysler and his Accomplices," in *Narratives of the Insurrections, 1675-1690*, ed. Charles M. Andrews (New York, 1915), pp. 319-354, passim. Andrews notes that the account was neither modest nor impartial. See also "A Letter from a Gentleman of the City of New York, 1698," in ibid., 360-372, a letter thought to have been written at the request of Bayard and other anti-Leislerian members of the Privy Council; and "Loyalty Vindicated, 1698," ibid., 375–401, where the other side of the issues dividing New York in the rebellion are clarified.

4. *Marriages from 1639 to 1801 in the Reformed Dutch Church: New Amsterdam, New York City*, Collections of the New York Genealogical and Biographical Society, 15 vols. (New York, 1940), vol. 9, 56. They married on February 7, 1685. A census of the New York Reformed Dutch Church membership in 1686 places them in the Out-ward for that year. George o. Zabriskie, "Daniel De Clark (De Klerck) of Tappan and His Descendants," *The New York Genealogical and Biographical Record*, 96:4 (October 1965), 195. In all, twenty-two men sat on the Committee of Safety, with seven constituting a quorum. Correspondence with David W. Voorhees, July 19, 1999.

5. Information about Peter Haring is found in the records of the New York Reformed Dutch Church and the Tappan Reformed Church; the "Notes and Proceedings of the New York Legislative Assembly"; the Orange County Census of 1702; the records of the Board of Supervisors of Orange County (located in the George Budke Collection, New York Public Library); and documents relating to the Tappan Patent. For a fuller discussion of the Leislerian farmers of Tappan, see Firth Haring Fabend, *A Dutch Family in the Middle Colonies, 1660-1800* (New Brunswick, 1991).

6. Primary source materials on Bertholf (also spelled Bartholf) are the *Ecclesiastical Records of the State of New York*, 7 vols., ed. E. T. Corwin (Albany, N.Y., 1901-1914). (See Volume 7, index, for page references.) See also Joseph Anthony Loux, trans. and ed., *Boel's "Complaint" Against Frelinghuysen* (Rensselaer, N.Y., 1979). Secondary sources include James R. Tanis, *Dutch Calvinistic Pietism in the Middle Colonies: A Study in the Life and Theology of Theodorus Jacobus Frelinghuysen* (The Hague, 1967); James R. Tanis, "Reformed Pietism in Colonial America," in *Continental Pietism and Early American Christianity*, ed. F. Ernest Stoeffler (Grand Rapids, Mich., 1976); James R. Tanis, "The American Dutch, Their Church, and the Revolution," in *A Bilateral Bicentennial: A History of Dutch-American Relations, 1782-1982*, J. W. Shulte Nordholt and Robert T. Swierenga, eds. (New York and Amsterdam, 1982); Howard G. Hageman, "William Bertholf: Pioneer Domine of New

Jersey," *Reformed Review*, 29 (Winter 1976), 73-80; Howard G. Hageman, "Colonial New Jersey's First Domine: I and II," *de Halve Maen* (October 1969, January 1970); Adrian Leiby, *The United Churches of Hackensack and Schraalenburgh, New Jersey, 1686-1822* (River Edge, N.J., 1976); David Cole, *History of the Reformed Church of Tappan, New York* (New York, 1894), 7-20; and Fabend, *A Dutch Family in the Middle Colonies*, chap. 7.

George O. Zabriskie obtained transcripts and translations of some of Bertholf's correspondence with the Classis of Walcheren that adds new information about him and corrects some older accounts, including that he was a baker, not a cooper. These papers can be found in the Bertholf folders at the New Jersey Historical Society and in the archives of the Gardner A. Sage Library, New Brunswick Theological Seminary.

7. For Teunis R. van Houten and Cornelius Cooper, see the sources in note 5 above and George H. Budke, comp., *Patents Granted for Lands in the Present County of Rockland, New York, with Biographical Notices of the Patentees*, 1928 (BC-67 of the Budke Collection, New York Public Library).

8. One historian who has looked closely at Leislerians describes them as "well integrated into the structure and culture of New York's civic, community, and family life." Ruth Piwonka, "Old Pewter/Bright Brass: A Suggested Explanation for Conservativism in Dutch Colonial Culture," *de Halve Maen* , 68 (Summer 1995), 43. Leisler's active supporters in New York, she goes on, "were leading members of their own merchant or craftsmen classes" and were probably more prosperous than the 1695 tax rolls indicate. This is because much of their property had been attainted in 1691, not to be restored until 1699 and after.

9. Randall H. Balmer, "The Social Roots of Dutch Pietism in the Middle Colonies," *Church History*, 53:2 (June 1984), 187, 188. See also Randall H. Balmer, "From Rebellion to Revivalism: The Fortunes of the Dutch Reformed Church in Colonial New York, 1689-1715," *de Halve Maen*, 56:2 (Fall 1981), and 57:2 (Winter 1982). For background on Pietism, Voetians, and Cocceians, see the sources in note 6 above.

10. Irving Mark, *Agrarian Conflicts in Colonial New York, 1711-1775* (New York, 1940), chap. 1, passim. Stephanus van Cortland received an 86,000-acre manor in northern Westchester in 1697. On the west side of the Hudson in Orange and Ulster counties were the huge Evans' Patent (800 square miles, secured for twenty shillings quitrent per year and 500 pounds sterling to Governor Fletcher), and the Hardenburg Patent (two million acres). As noted, even anti-Leislerian clergymen got into the act. The Reverend Godfriedus Dellius of the Reformed Dutch Church claimed 840 square miles on the Mohawk River with four partners in 1696.

11. O'Callaghan, *Docs. Rel. N.Y.*, 2:392–393.

12. David William Voorhees, "'All Authority turned upside downe': The Ideological Origins of Leislerian Political Thought," paper presented at the regional meeting of the Omohundro Institute of Early American History and Culture, Worcester, MA., June 1998. See also David William Voorhees, "The Milborne Family in the Seventeenth-Century Atlantic World," *The New York Genealogical and Biographical Record* 129:3 (July 1998). For Protestant International, also called International Calvinism and Protestant Capitalist International, see M. Prestwick, ed., *International Calvinism, 1541–1565* (Oxford, 1985).

13. For Samuel Edsall, see Thomas Henry Edsall, "Something about Fish, Fisheries, and Fishermen, in New York in the Seventeenth Century," *The New York Genealogical and Biographical Record* 13:4 (October 1882), 181–200; and George E. McCracken, "Samuel Edsall of Reading, Berk, and Some Early Descendants," *The New York Genealogical and Biographical Record* 89:3 (July 1958), 129–145; and 89:4 (October 1958), 216–220.

14. John E. Pomfret, *The Province of East New Jersey, 1609–1702, The Rebellious Proprietary* (Princeton, 1962), esp. chap. 6; and Richard P. McCormick, *New Jersey from Colony to State, 1609–1789*, rev. ed. (Newark, 1981), 28–29.

15. Thomas Henry Edsall, "Something about Fish, Fisheries, and Fishermen," 194.

16. In 1783, Cornelius Haring—Peter Haring's grandson and newly appointed Commissioner of Seized Estates in Bergen County—no doubt appreciated an historical irony when he confiscated for the state of New Jersey the extensive properties of William Bayard—a descendant of Nicholas Bayard. And in 1784, descendants of Leisler's Orange County supporters no doubt took satisfaction in seeing the Tappan lands of Frederick Philipse's descendants confiscated by the new government.

17. The role of ancient Dutch liberties is spelled out in Martin van Gelderen, *The Political Thought of the Dutch Revolt, 1555–1590* (Cambridge, 1992), where the author estimates that there are more than 2,000 extant political treatises and pamphlets dealing with the historical justification for the Revolt. John Locke, The Second Treatise of Government, ed. Thomas P. Peardon (New York, 1952), x. See also Jonathan I. Israel, "William III and Toleration," in Ole Peter Grell, Jonathan I. Israel, and Nicholas Tyacke, eds., *From Persecution to Toleration: The Glorious Revolution and Religion in England* (Oxford, 1991), chap. 6.

18. Pearden, ed., *Second Treatise*, 23. For a recent reassessment of the influence of Locke's ideas on the Declaration of Independence, see Michael P. Zuckert, _The Natural Rights Republic (Notre Dame, 1996), passim.

This article originally appeared in *The Hudson River Valley Review* Volume 22.2.

From Entrepreneurs to Ornaments: The Livingston Women, 1679–1790

Cynthia Kierner

Alida Schuyler Livingston (1656–1726) would have been ill at ease in the world of her granddaughters. Alida was one of early New York's extraordinary female entrepreneurs. She traded at Albany, supervised industrial and agricultural operations at Livingston Manor and, in equal partnership with her husband Robert, established a family business that would grow to magnificent proportions in subsequent generations. By the Revolutionary era, however, dynamic and assertive businesswomen, such as Alida, were anomalous in provincial New York. She had been a shrewd and industrious entrepreneur, but her granddaughters were genteel ladies and aspiring belles.

Changes in the lives of the Livingston women and their social peers mirrored the transformation of provincial society as a whole during the eighteenth century. Two factors, in particular, made women's world increasingly distinct from that of their fathers, husbands, and brothers. First—and more important for the Livingston women—was the gradual development of stable and extensive family networks, replete with male relatives to whom authority could be delegated. While the first lord of the manor had relied heavily on his wife's energy and business acumen, his son Philip used his brothers, and later his sons, as partners and commercial agents. Second, the replacement of Roman-Dutch law by the English common law, after the conquest of New Netherland in 1664, deprived married women of their legal identities and thus, theoretically, restricted their economic activities. While scholars generally overestimate the immediate impact of this legal transformation, the English doctrine of the *femme covert* did gradually gain widespread acceptance.

As demographic development and legal change gradually deprived New York's women of their formal economic authority, the wives and daughters of the elite acquired a new social authority befitting their families' lofty position at the apex of provincial society. By 1750, economic growth and prosperity in both New York and England encouraged wealthy provincials, like the Livingstons, to imitate the pleasures and rituals of London's high society, which, of course, included women. New Yorkers' increased emphasis on gentility and sociability, in turn, was transforming wealthy women from entrepreneurs to ornaments; women's new social responsibilities as the arbiters of taste and decorum in an increasingly cosmopolitan society were reflected in new modes of female education and dress, as well as in innovations in interior decoration that accentuated the home's growing importance as a place for display and polite entertainment. Sociability encouraged women to broaden their intellectual horizons, to take an interest in fashion, and to cultivate polite accomplishments.

The effects of this transformation were ambiguous. While Alida Livingston had worked diligently and enjoyed few luxuries or diversions, she was an independent entrepreneur with authority equal to that of her husband. Although the activities that her descendants pursued certainly were more enjoyable than tending shops or supervising mills and tenants, when Alida's granddaughters read poetry, learned music, or ventured political opinions, they did so—at least according to popular notions of a woman's sphere—in order to attract and to entertain men.

When Lawrence H. Leder published his biography of the first Robert Livingston in 1961, the development and maintenance of Livingston Manor received scant attention in his otherwise exhaustive study. Leder felt justified in omitting a detailed analysis of the manor's daily operations because, as he correctly noted, such details were more appropriate to a biography of Robert's wife, Alida, who, during most of the couple's married life, conducted the family's business in Albany County while her husband attended to their New York interests. While it would be wrong to argue that Alida alone was responsible for Robert's great success, their marriage in 1679 was a crucial turning point in what would eventually become a remarkable political and entrepreneurial career. As a member of the most prominent family in seventeenth-century Albany, Alida supplied Robert with political and commercial connections which, as a recent immigrant without family in New York, he otherwise would have taken years to cultivate. By virtue of her prior marriage to Nicholas Van Rensselaer, Alida also claimed a share of the vast patroonship of Rensselaerswyck. Robert's exploitation of his wife's highly questionable claims resulted in a protracted feud with the proprietary family that, in the long run, probably won Livingston his own manorial estate. In 1686, Governor Thomas issued a patent for the 160,000-acre Livingston Manor, possibly with the understanding that Robert would drop his case against Alida's former in-laws.[1]

Although Dongan issued the patent to Robert alone, the manor became Alida's bailiwick. Robert's political connections furnished them with military provisioning contracts and, in 1710, a corps of Palatine refugees to be settled and maintained. Nevertheless, it was Alida who filled these contracts, supervised the milling of grain and baking of bread, and traded in Albany County while her husband handled their business in the provincial capital. Typically, she sent Robert furs and surplus flour, bread, and lumber, and he returned the family sloop to her laden with imported goods for home consumption or, more frequently, for sale in their stores at Albany and the manor. Alida's letters suggest that business absorbed much of her time and that she took her business very seriously. Indeed, several surviving letters indicate that while Robert sometimes let his political ambitions detract from their commercial interests, his wife was the shrewder entrepreneur who was not above chastising him for his occasional imprudence. Robert apparently accepted his wife's intermittent criticism, and he most certainly respected her business judgement.[2]

Alida Livingston was an extraordinary woman, but her entrepreneurial activities and achievements were not unique among the women of early New York. Indeed, Alida had probably received her commercial education from her own mother, Margareta Van Schlectenhorst, who traded as an independent Albany fur merchant at least as late as 1686.[3] Linda Briggs Biemer's engaging monograph, *Women and Property in Colonial New York,* describes the business dealings of other equally successful female entrepreneurs. Maria Van Cortlandt's commercial experience began when, as a young woman, she was charged by her father with the management of a family brewery. After her marriage to Jeremias Van Rensselaer in 1662, Maria shared with her husband the administration of Rensselaerswyck, and when Jeremias died in 1674, she became the *de facto* director of the patroonship. Margaret Hardenbroeck, who also came from a trading family, was among New York's most successful transatlantic merchants; she owned ships and traded independently, as well as in partnership with her husband, Frederick Philipse. Martha Tunstall Smith, the wife of William "Tangier" Smith, ran a successful whaling business on Long Island until her death in 1708. Although these women

Cynthia Kierner

were hardly typical New Yorkers, their careers suggest that Alida Livingston was part of a rich tradition of female entrepreneurs in early colonial New York.[4]

Biemer maintains that the Dutch legal tradition, which gave men and women equal economic rights, made New Netherland uniquely tolerant of female entrepreneurs, while the English conquest of 1664, and the subsequent imposition of the far more restrictive common law, made such women an endangered species. By itself, this thesis is not persuasive. Biemer's own research shows that these extraordinary women continued trading for decades after 1664. To be sure, the common law doctrine of coverture did deprive married women of their legal identity and, in so doing, prohibited them from owning property and signing binding that certainly hindered the effective prosecution of trade. Indeed, the strictures of coverture, if enforced, did force women traders to rely on their husbands or sons in certain instances, but such obstacles were surmountable for the enterprising and ambitious. Marriages like Robert's and Alida's were partnerships, in both the business and emotional sense. Decades after 1664, Robert continued to consign cargoes to his wife, and she continued to act as his attorney and to provision local troops, even if Robert's signature was required on the actual victualing contract.[5] Likewise, in the mid-eighteenth century, Mary Spratt Provoost Alexander was still one of New York's leading merchants, even if the formalities of English law forced her to depend upon men to act as figureheads or assistants in the actual conduct of her business. Mary's success was exceptional, but her occupation was not unique. Drawing upon newspaper advertisements, customs records, and other sources, Jean P. Jordan found that at least 106 women engaged in overseas trade in colonial New York. As late as 1770, New York had no fewer than fifteen female merchants. Many of these women, like Margaret Livingston Vetch, were widows, but others, like Mary Alexander, traded as married women. Some traded only intermittently, but others had long and illustrious careers. The merchant occupied a lofty position in New York's social hierarchy; many more women were employed in trade as shopkeepers and artisans.[6]

While it would be wrong to trivialize the common law's extreme sexual bias, research on other colonies indicates that legal strictures alone did not determine the roles and functions of women in colonial America. Female colonists fulfilled vital economic functions even in colonies lacking a liberal Dutch tradition. Particularly in sparsely settled or demographically unstable regions, women performed many economic or entrepreneurial tasks that were normally reserved for men. For example, Edmund S. Morgan has described early Virginia as a "widowarchy" in which women, because of high mortality rates and a severely skewed sex ratio, exercised economic power far beyond the limits allowed under English common law. Lois Green Carr and Lorena S. Walsh found a similar situation in seventeenth-century Maryland, and Laurel Thatcher Ulrich has argued persuasively that wives in northern New England acted as their husbands' "deputies" in business affairs throughout the colonial era.[7]

Ulrich's emphasis upon the lack of uniformity in women's lives could well be applied to other colonies. In New York, even during the Dutch period, most women were neither as assertive nor as autonomous as those that Biemer has chosen to study. Most of the obscure *huis vrouws* of New Netherland undoubtedly led more traditional lives, as junior partners in very limited family enterprises. Although the liberal tradition of the Dutch trading towns may have made the women of New York more autonomous than their counterparts elsewhere, female participation in family economic concerns was indispensable in new societies where relatives of either gender were scarce. In their comparative study of the legal status of women in New York and Virginia, Joan R. Gundersen and Gwen Victor Gampel found that demographic and economic growth gradually undermined women's economic roles in both colonies. In the early eighteenth century, married women in both New York and Virginia exercised their informal rights to control property and to act as their husbands' attorneys, despite the colonies' formal adherence to the common law. By mid-century, however, these informal rights were increasingly disregarded by courts, lawyers, and husbands alike. Gundersen and Gampel suggest that economic development enabled the emerging colonial gentry to accept the English notion of the ornamental gentlewoman. At the same time, sons and brothers could fill women's vacated positions in the family business, and a rising class of professional lawyers could render unnecessary the wife's power of attorney.[8]

In the Livingston family, as in many other wealthy families through-out the colonies, family structure and overall demographic development were the most significant constraints on women's economic activities. Robert and Alida had four sons whom they expected to continue their entrepreneurial tradition, while they assumed that their daughters, Margaret and Joanna, would marry and, if necessary, help their husbands with their work. Although the elder Livingstons probably did not foresee mercantile careers for their daughters, Margaret and Joanna learned the rudiments of commerce so that they could engage in trade if the interest of their family required it. Surviving letters indicate that the Livingston daughters fully understood the business of trade, and Margaret actually turned merchant during the frequent absences of her husband, Samuel Vetch, and continued trading after his death in 1732. Between 1707 and 1748, Margaret Livingston Vetch intermittently imported and exported assorted goods. Her commercial activities were neither condemned nor applauded by her family and trading partners but, rather, mentioned casually to indicate that she did nothing especially unusual.[9] Married women whose husbands remained at home were generally less autonomous, but most understood their husbands' businesses and occasionally offered them advice or performed certain essential services. Since Philip Livingston, the second lord of the manor, rarely left Albany, there are no surviving accounts of the daily duties of his wife, Catrina Van Brugh. Nevertheless, Philip respected Catrina's judgment, and her advice was instrumental in persuading him to erect an iron forge at the manor in the early 1740s. "I am doing all I can to Satisfy your good mother about the building of this forge," wrote Philip to his eldest son, "and [I] am persuaded you will do any reasonable act to Satisfy her [as well]."[10]

In the Livingston family, Catrina's generation was a transitional one in which wives were neither autonomous entrepreneurs like Alida nor genteel ladies of high society like their daughters. Gradually, however, a myriad of new social responsibilities filled the void created by the diminution of women's economic functions. For example, because Alida Livingston was charged with operating the family's growing enterprises at Livingston Manor, she could justifiably scold her husband for sending her unannounced guests. When Robert sent an unexpected visitor to Alida in 1722, she sought lodging elsewhere for her guest and carried on her business.[11] As later generations delegated their commercial and industrial responsibilities to willing sons and brothers, hospitality and sociability became increasingly important feminine attributes. Mary Stevens Livingston, for instance, was by all accounts an exemplary wife to Chancellor Robert R. Livingston, one of the most prominent men in Revolutionary New York. Yet all that is known of Mary is that she was a "polite, wellbred, sensible woman, of one of the best families in the State, and who brought a great property into the family." She was widely admired for her unassuming devotion as wife and mother, as well as for her "grace in polite society."[12] Similarly, Henry Beekman Livingston rejoiced in the marriage of his cousin, Robert Cambridge Livingston, to Alice Swift in 1778 because the bride was "an amiable young Lady who will be an ornament to our Neighborhood."[13]

Turning daughters into ornamental young ladies and genteel wives required the expansion of both the quality and quantity of female education. Just as young gentlemen increasingly attended college to acquire the requisite social skills and a veneer of polite learning, the education of colonial gentlewomen came to include disciplines that were far beyond the pale of homely practicality. Early colonial education had been a thoroughly practical matter. Alida Livingston had taught her sons and daughters to write both Dutch and English, though the quality of their letters reveals that her sons received the more rigorous training in the use of both languages. Children of both sexes also received religious and moral instruction, as well as a basic knowledge of arithmetic, an accomplishment that was essential both for trade and for efficient household management. Throughout the colonial period, daughters also learned cooking and needlework. Although the daughters of the gentry could expect to have servants in their homes, they needed to be proficient in the domestic arts in order to assign and supervise the tasks of their house-hold staffs. Furthermore, even if they had servants, women often performed traditional domestic duties. Decorative and functional needlework were standard pastimes among colonial women, and, though the wealthy employed professional tailors as early as the seventeenth century, Robert and Alida's daughters were expected to sew some articles of clothing for family use.[14] In 1750, even the wife of the third lord of Livingston Manor occasionally prepared a sumptuous meal. Robert Livingston, grandson of the first Robert, boasted that his wife prepared a splendid turtle dinner, adding that "she wishes to have frequent opportunity to make herself perfect in this piece of Couckery."[15]

By the middle of the eighteenth century, however, the education of the daughters of the wealthy was expanding to allow them to become gentlewomen who could be accepted and appreciated in an increasingly sophisticated and cosmopolitan society. The letters of the late colonial Livingston women indicate that they received rigorous instruction in grammar, syntax, and penmanship; while Alida Livingston had written hurried letters simply to communicate the latest business or family news, her great-granddaughters wrote elegant missives sometimes purely for purposes of entertainment. Furthermore, although the Livingston daughters continued to learn traditional domestic skills, lessons in French, music, and dancing now were considered equally useful. Parents regarded their daughters' education as a matter of especial importance. Philip Livingston made a provision in his will for educating his unmarried daughters, Alida and Catharine, aged twenty-one and sixteen, respectively, when he died in 1749. Thirty years later, not even the ravages of war and revolution disrupted the dancing lessons of the Livingston girls at Clermont. While most daughters learned their lessons from hired tutors in their homes, some went elsewhere to acquire the requisite social skills. Judge Robert R. Livingston's daughter Margaret studied French at New Rochelle, and her cousin Alida spent a winter in New York City with a married sister. Alida's sojourn in the provincial capital was not a mere vacation; her father, the third lord of the manor, had sent her to Manhattan to "improve" herself, warning that she "must not Spend her time Idlely." Likewise, James Duane sent his daughter to Philadelphia in 1781 because "she wanted this opportunity of polite Company to give her the Accomplishments which tho' inferior to those of the Mind are essential to her Rank."[16]

This new genteel code of feminine behavior did not automatically debase women or deprive them of personal fulfillment. Indeed, as Duane noted, most parents hoped that their daughters would improve their minds, and the understanding of a gentlewoman's proper demeanor gave some young women opportunities for bona fide intellectual growth. If the Livingstons were typical, New York's young gentlewomen were far more bookish than those surveyed in Mary Beth Norton's dreary portrait of pre-Revolutionary female education.[17] The province's economic and social development created a demand for books, and they, like other luxury items, were increasingly available to eighteenth-century New Yorkers. In 1740 the provincial capital had only one bookshop, and that establishment sold only news-papers, almanacs, and a few common school texts; on the eve of the Revolution, however, the city boasted ten booksellers offering far more diverse selections.[18] The increased accessibility of books, coupled with a desire to excel in polite conversation, encouraged young women to read far more than had their mothers and grandmothers. Such serious tomes as Smollett's *History of England* and Alexander Pope's *Works* accompanied the daughters of Judge Robert R. Livingston on a summer visit to Clermont. William Livingston's daughters were familiar with his political writings and wrote and received letters that revealed a detailed understanding of contemporary politics. Susannah Livingston, who served as her father's personal secretary when he was governor of New Jersey, enjoyed *Don Quixote*, *Robinson Crusoe*, and Noel Antoine Pluche's *Nature Delineated* which, with the Bible, were some of her basic texts when she tutored nephew Peter Jay. Nancy Livingston was an equally avid reader, whose favorites included Milton's poetry and Goethe's *Sorrows of Werter*.[19] As Linda Kerber notes, some of these well-informed women added disclaimers to their letters, apologizing for their interest in and knowledge of traditionally male-dominated matters. On the other hand, the fact that they had this knowledge at all indicates significant changes in the education of New York's colonial gentlewomen.[20]

Nevertheless, if the intellectual attainments of some young women did expand perceptibly by the Revolutionary era, they did so, at least partly, to make women more agreeable companions for men. Both William Livingston and William Smith, Jr. complained that frivolous and insipid women made bad company; they applauded female education as a means to promote virtue, good conversation, and pleasant society. Similarly, Colonel Alexander Hamilton enjoined his fiancée Elizabeth Schuyler, to spend all her leisure time reading because, as her husband, he would take pride in her accomplishment and "it will be a fund too, to diversify our enjoyments and amusements and fill all our moments to advantage."[21] The prescriptive literature of the period echoed these sentiments, arguing that women should cultivate their minds in order to attract and entertain men, the best of whom admired "simplicity, softness, a sedate carriage, and rational conversation." Contemporary moralists upheld virtue and graciousness as the feminine ideal: women should be accomplished but not assertive, ornamental not in vain.[22]

By contrast, a seventeenth-century moralist would have stressed the importance of *private* feminine virtue, while neglecting to discuss proper *public* feminine conduct. Even active and assertive women led extraordinarily circumscribed public lives in the early colonial period when social functions revolved largely around political events-the convening of the assembly, the arrival of a governor, the sitting of a court-and thus the changes in the education of young women to enable them to fulfill their new public and social functions were symptomatic of a more general cultural transformation that swept the colonies in the middle decades of the eighteenth century. Prosperity and the cumulative effects of decades of economic growth gradually enabled wealthy New Yorkers to live genteelly while, at the same time, a rapidly expanding English economy supplied desirous provincials with the stuff of which gentility was made.[23]

Beginning among the elite in the 1690's, but spreading to the middle classes in the next century, the English had become a nation of consumers. The consumer revolution of the eighteenth century begot such venerable commodities as fashion plates, Wedgwood pottery, and Chippendale furniture; English producers scrambled to satisfy the demands of a prosperous and growing population who came to view the quality and quantity of consumer goods they could amass as emblems of their own social standing. Leisure also became commercialized as Englishmen increasingly preferred shows and exhibitions to older and more spontaneous forms of amusement. In eighteenth-century England, prosperity and social competition gave rise to a culture that valued fashion over function. As elites spent vast sums to enjoy the best that their society had to offer, others were swept into the new consumer culture by their desire to emulate their social betters.[24]

England's consumer culture was exportable, and most provincials found its allure irresistible. Per capita colonial consumption of English imports rose markedly in the second half of the eighteenth century, and New York imported more English goods than any other colony in the decades prior to the Revolution.[25] Contemporaries noticed this rising tide of anglicized consumerism, and they attributed the increasing demand for English products to general colonial prosperity and to the great profits that New Yorkers had made from provisioning and privateering during King George's War (1744–1748). Observers also noted that luxury items seemed to account for most of New York's increased trade in English imports. As early as 1744, Cadwallader Colden noted that his countrymen had "made great progress in aping the luxury of the mother country." Likewise, in 1753, William Livingston reported that "Our extraordinary Success in the late War, has given Rise to a Method of living unknown to our frugal Ancestors." By 1757, William Smith declared confidently that New York City was "one of the most social Places on the continent" of North America.[26]

Ornamental, sociable, and accomplished women were part of an increasingly distinct elite culture that looked to England for its standards of gentility and general excellence. As London's social season came to be the model cultural agenda for growing colonial cities, women acquired unprecedented importance in the social life of the colonies. For instance, the first Robert Livingston had journeyed to New York City unaccompanied and solely to attend to his affairs. In 1744, however, his son Philip, the second lord of the manor, broke that tradition by bringing his entire family to Manhattan to enjoy the novelties of city life while he attended the meetings of the provincial council.[27] Such family outings, virtually unheard of in the early colonial period, became common in the decades preceding the Revolution.

Increased means, increased leisure, and a predisposition to imitate England's privileged classes encouraged wealthy New Yorkers to frequent theatres, operas, and educational exhibitions, all of which acquired great popularity in the closing decades of the colonial era.[28] Far more elegant, however, were the public gardens that opened in New York's rural Out-Ward in the 1760s. Raneleigh and Vauxhall gardens were exclusive resorts after the fashion of their famous London name-sakes. Both establishments featured spacious formal gardens "laid out, at a great Expence, in a very genteel, pleasing Manner," as well as stylish entertainments to please the most discriminating patrons. Raneleigh Gardens offered summer band concerts, gracious dining, premium wines, and a large hall suitable for evening dances. Vauxhall was renowned for its waxworks and its fashionable breakfasts and evening teas.[29]

In New York City, in particular, the affluent also began to form exclusive clubs to plan their social calendars. In the 1740's, the province's most fashionable citizens formed the New-York Dancing Assembly, an organization that sponsored fortnightly balls during the fall and winter social season. The New York Harmonic Society, at about the same time, began to organize regularly scheduled concerts and other musical entertainments. Although the elected officers of these clubs were always men, the amusements they sponsored also included women. Perhaps a similar organization was responsible for planning the turtle barbecues, for which the New York gentry acquired great notoriety. As one eighteenth-century visitor reported, "There are several houses, pleasantly situated on the East river, where it is common to have turtle-feasts: these happen once or twice in a week. Thirty or forty gentlemen and ladies meet and dine together, drink tea in the afternoon, fish and amuse themselves till evening, and then return home in Italian chaises . . . a gentleman and a lady in each chaise."[30]

Daniel Blake Smith has argued that in rural Virginia the training of genteel women was overwhelmingly oriented toward improving the quality of family life inside the planters' homes.[31] In provincial New York, however, an urban and cosmopolitan society gave women's accomplishments a decidedly public application.

Certainly, New York's wealthy women—even those who lived in New York City—were expected to preside over efficient and pleasant households, but as elites came to value gentility and sociability, even private residences acquired public significance. Rhys Isaac has shown that the century Virginia gentry used their hospitality to set themselves apart from their social inferiors. These Virginians built elegant homes with huge areas designated solely for dining, entertaining guests, and staging gala public occasions. During the eighteenth century, this increased emphasis on display, gentility, and a distinct "high-style" domestic culture transformed affluent homes throughout the colonies from mere residences to grand show places.[32] James Alexander's Manhattan home, for example, had two ceremonial dining rooms—one large and one small—at least two parlors for receiving guests, and other "apartments innumerable, sumptuously furnished in all the pomp of [the] period.[33] Generally, the entire first floor of both the town and country homes of the elite were reserved solely for public entertainments. Such elaborate homes were uncommon in the early colonial period. In 1704, Sarah Knight found New York homes remarkable only for their cleanliness. Forty years later, however, Peter Kalm—who found little to admire in New York—conceded that the provincial capital was an opulent city, graced by many fine buildings. In 1775, John Adams found the homes of the province's leading citizens to be splendid beyond his wildest expectations.[34]

Elaborate interiors may have made New York's late colonial homes more pleasing to their residents, but elegant domestic displays were also intended to impress visitors with the status and gentility of their hosts. Portraits, looking glasses, and cupboards decked with silver, china, and other ornaments graced the ceremonial rooms of the elite, whose private living quarters were often rather simple by comparison. The upstairs furnishings at Clermont, for example, were worth $2500 when Chancellor Robert R. Livingston died in 1813, but the china and plate displayed downstairs were valued at nearly three times that sum.[35]

As always, household management continued to fall within woman's sphere, but overseeing the affairs of an affluent residence increasingly entailed organizing elaborate dinner parties, balls, social teas, and other polite entertainments. By the middle of the eighteenth century, entertaining guests at home was such an integral part of upper-class life that William Livingston imagined that the inability to be suitably hospitable to one's friends was the most onerous burden of "poverty".[36] Affluent New Yorkers took pride in their homes and appreciated due praise for the hospitality they offered. When Governor William and his wife toured the Hudson Valley in 1772, the proprietor of Livingston Manor boasted that they "were highly delighted with . . . the kind of reception they had met with where Ever they came ashore, and particularly at my House." The Livingstons appreciated their visitors' compliments "for in truth we did all we could to make them welcome as I Suppose Everyone Else did; but all great folks do not Chuse to acknowledge when they are treated in the best manner the house affords." Ten years later, when George and Martha Washington visited Clermont, they found its mistress's hospitality equally to their liking. As Margaret Beekman Livingston re-ported happily to her son, "He admired the place and Mrs. Washington seemed pleased" with the few days they spent at her riverfront mansion.[37]

Women's increasing social prominence both at home and in society was perhaps best illustrated by the revolution in fashion that began in America around mid-century. In the closing decades of the colonial period, women's personal attire, like the homes they presided over, revealed a new regard for display, elegance, and current English fashions. Alida Livingston and her daughters had owned clothing reflecting the wealth and position of their family, but unlike their descendants, they were not obsessed with fashion. Indeed, seventeenth- and early eighteenth-century correspondence mentions men's clothing far more frequently than women's because men were more likely to appear socially and, consequently, their apparel was more often subjected to public scrutiny. When Sarah Knight visited New York in 1704, she did scrutinize the attire of the city's women, and found the quality of their dress more distinguishable by ethnicity than by wealth. While she admired the clothes of English New Yorkers, Knight found the Dutch styles gaudy and unrefined. Forty years later, however, Dr. Alexander Hamilton of Annapolis found Manhattan's affluent women uniformly stylish, comparing them favorably to the "women of fashion" in contemporary Philadelphia.[38]

By the time Hamilton visited New York, timely fashions, not time-less functions or customs, had begun to dictate the dress of wealthy provincials. Neil McKendrick has shown that the eighteenth-century commercial revolution gave rise to a concept of annually changing fashions that catapulted the Anglo-American garment industry to unprecedented prestige and prosperity. McKendrick, however, neglects to mention that the consumer revolution in apparel resulted in another equally significant cultural change: the feminization of clothing and fashion. By the middle of the eighteenth century, for the first time, clothing was seen as an overwhelmingly feminine concern both because women had more occasion to display their finery and because the fashion industry saw them as a readily exploitable market. As a result, innovations in fashion advertising appealed almost exclusively to a feminine audience. Life-sized, three-dimensional fashion dolls, dressed in the latest style, arrived in Boston as early as 1733 and made their way to New York by the 1750s. Equally popular, however, were the flat cardboard dolls, printed by the thousands in England to cater to a mass market. These dolls were easily exportable, and the fashions they promoted changed annually to stimulate consumption. Although men continued to purchase and wear fine clothing, an entire new industry had appeared to provide increasingly fashion-conscious colonial women with the latest London style.[39]

By the 1750's, imported fashion dolls and local advertising prescribed an all-encompassing code of proper feminine attire. Hats imported from England or made in New York by milliners trained in London sat atop hair piled high on "Tatematongues and Towers, after the Manner that is now worn at Court."[40] Elaborate hair designs were held in place by ivory, horn, or tortoiseshell combs fashioned by local craftsmen who had learned their trades in Europe. In the 1760's, New York had at least two shops specializing in the manufacture and sale of ornamental combs, and one comb-maker, Thomas Dunn, claimed to have "had the Honour to serve most of [Dublin's] Nobility" before he removed to America.[41] Torsos, like hair, were molded and contorted to fit the demands of current fashions. Stays made of bone, buckram, or steel "in the very newest Fashion, directly from London" minimized busts and relocated hips to accommodate the creations of tailors promising to reproduce the costumes of the imported fashion dolls.[42] Two New York seamstresses began their business in 1757 by assuring their prospective clients that they had "fixed a correspondence so as to have from . . . London, the earliest fashions in miniature." The advertisers further guaranteed that "Ladies and gentlewomen . . . may depend on being expeditiously and reasonably served, in the making of . . . Sacks, negligees, negligee-night-gowns, plain-night-gowns, pattanlears, shepherdesses, roman-cloaks, cardinal, capuchins, dauphinesses, shades, lorrains, bonnets, and hives."[43] In short, women could choose from an unprecedented array of clothing and accessories suitable for various social occasions.

Literally and figuratively constraining fashions, like the general transformation of women's lives, had both drawbacks and advantages. By the Revolutionary era, increased means and increased leisure enabled the Livingston women and their social peers to concern themselves with fashion's fickle dictates, but, like the clothing itself, their status as gentlewomen restricted their activities in accordance with contemporary notions of genteel propriety.

Affluent New Yorkers of both sexes became gentlefolk during the closing decades of the colonial era, but changes to women's lives were the more substantial because, over four generations, economic, demographic, and legal circumstances more profoundly affected the roles and responsibilities of the wives and daughters of the elite. The net result of these changes was not a simple matter of improving or debasing the status of colonial women. It is worth remembering that Alida Livingston did not have a career, but rather an imposing agenda of economic duties that were essential to the welfare of her family. In her granddaughters' time, women's social duties and cultural accomplishments were equally essential to their family's reputation. Alida's entrepreneurial responsibilities had limited her leisure activities and social freedom. Her granddaughters, by contrast, enjoyed unprecedented social, cultural, and intellectual opportunities, but they did so only after losing the economic independence that had allowed Alida to play an integral role in the foundation of their family's fortune.

Notes

1. Lawrence H. Leder, *Robert Livingston, 1654–1728, and the Politics of Colonial New York* (Chapel Hill: University of North Caroline Press, 1961), p. vii, chs. 1–2.

2. For a translated selection of Alida's letters to her husband, see Linda Biemer, ed., "Business Letters of Alida Livingston, *New York History*, 63 (1982): pp. 183–207. The original correspondence of Robert and Alida Livingston is in the Livingston Redmond Manuscripts, Franklin D. Roosevelt Library, Hyde Park, New York, reels 4 and 6 in the microfilm collection.

3. See, for example, John to Robert Livingston, Jan. 1686, Livingston-Redmond mss., reel 1, in which the writer, a London merchant, thanks Livingston for persuading his mother-in-law to send him a case of beaver.

4. Linda Briggs Biemer, *Women and Property in Colonial New York: The from Dutch lo English Law, 1643–1727* (Ann Arbor: UMI Research Press, 1983). See Biemer's fifth chapter for an admirable biographical sketch of Alida Livingston.

5. Livingston gave his wife power of attorney when he went to England in 1694 and 1703, and again in 1710 when the arrival of the Palatine refugees necessitated that Alida be given full authority of over-manor and its resources (Powers of attorney to Alida Livingston, 12 Oct. 1694, 30 Apr. 1703, Livingston-Redmond mss., reel 1 and 2; Robert Livingston to Alida Livingston, 11 Apr. 1611, ibid., reel 1; James Weems to Alida Livingston, 9 Apr. 1692, ibid., reel 3). For Alida's activities as a victualer, see, for example, Robert Livingston to Alida Livingston, 9 Apr. 1692, ibid., reel 1; James Weems to Alida Livingston, 23 Oct., 21, 30 Nov. 1700, ibid., reel 6. Invoices for cargoes that Robert, while in England, consigned to his wife, dated 30 Mar., 12 July 1704, 31 Mar., 20 Apr., 30 Apr. 1705, and 10 Apr., 1706, appear in ibid., reel 2.

6. Jean P. Jordan, "Women Merchants in Colonial New York," *New York History*, 58 (1977): pp. 412–39. On Mary Alexander, see also Livingston Rutherfurd, comp., *Family Record and Events, compiled Originally from the Original MSS in the Collection* (New York: De Vinne Press, p. 36.

7. Edmund S. Morgan, *American Slavery, American Freedom: The Ordeal of Colonial Virginia* (New York: W.W. Norton, 1975), pp. 164–70; Lois Green Carr and Lorena S. Walsh, "The Planter's Wife: The Experience of White Women in Seventeenth-Century Maryland," *William and Mary Quarterly*, 3rd ser., 34 (1977): 542–71; Laurel Thatcher Ulrich, *Good Wives: Image and Reality in the Lives of Women in Northern New England, 1650–1750* (New York: Oxford University Press, ch. 2.

8. Joan R. Gundersen and Gwen Victor Gampel, "Married Women's Legal in Eighteenth-Century New York and Virginia," *William and Mary Quarterly*, 3rd ser., 39 (1982): pp. 114–34.

9. Merchants," p. 420: Henry Douglas to Philip Livingston, 27 May, 1709, Livingston-Redmond mss., reel 6; Henry Livingston to Robert 11 Oct. 1742, ibid., reel 7. *See also*, Joanna Livingston Van Horne to Robert Livingston, 8 July 1725, ibid., reel 4.

10. Philip Livingston to Robert Livingston (1708–1790), 30 Jan. 1745, ibid., reel 7.

11. Alida Livingston to Robert Livingston, 23 July 1722, in Biemer, ed., "Business Letters," p. 205.

12. William Strickland, *Journal of a Tour in the United States of America*, J.E. Strickland, ed. (New York: New-York Historical Society, 1971), p. 119 See also, Alonzo Potter's manuscript biography of Chancellor Robert R. Livingston, Robert R. Livingston Papers, New-York Historical Society (hereafter NYHS), reel 15.

13. Henry Beekman Livingston to Robert R. Livingston, Jr., 20 Nov. 1778, ibid., reel 1.

14. Alida Livingston to Robert Livingston, 8 Apr. 1698, 3 Aug. 1717, in Biemer, ed., "Business Letters," pp. 192, 202; Robert Livingston, Jr., (1688–1775) to Joanna Livingston 8 Oct. 1717, Livingston-Redmond mss., reel 3. *See also*, Mary Beth Norton, Liberty's *Daughters: The Revolutionary Experience of American Women, 1750–1800* (Boston: Little, Brown and Company, 1980) pp. 23–25, 28, and May King Van Rensselaer, *The Goede Vrouw of Mana-ha-ta at Home and in Society* (New York: Charles Scribners' Sons, 1898), pp. 10–13, 185.

15. Robert Livingston (1708–1790) to Peter Van Brugh Livingston, 22 May 1750, Welch-Livingston mss., NYHS.

16. Will of Philip Livingston, 15 July 1748, Livingston-Redmond rnss., reel Margaret Beekman Livingston to Robert R. Livingston, Jr., 4 June 1782, Robert R. Livingston Papers, NYHS, reel 2; Margaret Livingston to Robert Livingston 27 Oct. 1761, ibid., reel 1; Robert Livingston (1708–1790) to James Duane, 16 Oct. 1762, MSS, Robert Livingston (1708–1790), NYHS; James Duane to Mary Livingston Duane, 20 Feb. [1781]. Duane Papers, NYHS. box 4; Julia *of Francis and Morgan Lewis* (New York: D.F. Randolph &Company, 1877) p. 155.

17. Norton, *Liberty's Daughters*, pp. 257–63.

18. Edwin D. Hoffman, "The Bookshops of New York City," *New York History*, 30 (1949): pp. 53–54.

19. Robert R. Livingston to Robert Livingston 24 Aug. 1765, Robert R. Livingston Papers, NYHS, reel 1; Catharine Livingston to Sarah Livingston Jay, 21 Nov. 1777, in Richard B. Morris, ed., *John Jay: The Making of a Revolutionary*, Unpublished Papers, 1745–1780 (New York: Harper & Row, 1975), pp. 448–449; Sarah Livingston Jay to Catherine Livingston, 1 Dec.1780, in Richard B. Morris, ed. *John Jay: Winning of the Peace, Unpublished Papers,1780–1784* (New York: Harper & Row, 1980). p. 171; Catharine Livingston to John Jay, 30 Dec.1783, ibid., p. 671; William Livingston to Sarah Livingston Jay, 21 Aug. 1781, ibid., pp. 199–200; William Livingston to Catharine Livingston, 16 Nov. 1779, quoted in Theodore Jr., *A Memoir of the Life of William Livingston* (New York: Harper, 1833) p. 340; Ethel Armes, ed., *Nancy Shippen, Her Journal Book. . .* (Philadelphia: J.B. Lippincott, 1935) pp. 141, 185. See also the many letters exchanged by Matthew and his future wife, Catharine Livingston (Matthew Ridley Papers, Massachusetts Historical Society).

20. Linda K. Kerber, *Women of the Republic: Intellect and Ideology in Revolutionary America* (Chapel Hill: University of North Carolina Press, 1980), pp. 35, 76–79.

21. William Livingston to [Susannah French], 4 Oct. 1744, William Livingston Papers, Mass. Hist. Soc., reel 2; William Smith, Jr., *The History of the Province* 2 vols., Michael G. Kammen, ed. (Cambridge, Mass.: Belknap Press of Harvard University Press, 1972), 1:227; Alexander Hamilton to Elizabeth Schuyler, [2–4 July 1780] in *The of Alexander Hamilton,* 26 vols., Harold C. Syrett and Jacob E. Cooke, eds. (New York: Columbia University Press, 1960–1979), 2:351.

22. James Fordyce, *Character and Conduct of the Female Sex, and the Advantages to be Derived by Young Men from the Society of Virtuous Women*, 3rd ed. (Boston: Gill, 1781) pp. 11, 27–28, 39–43; John Gregory, *A Father's Legacy to his Daughters* (New York: Shober Loudoun, 1775), pp. 8, 14–24

23. The best overview of colonial economic growth and the resulting revolution in consumption, particularly of English goods, in John J. and Russell R. *The Economy of British America, 1607–1789* (Chapel Hill: University of North Carolina Press, 1607–1789 (Chapel Hill: University of North Carolina Press, 1982).

24. This phenomenon is examined in the essays in Neil McKendrick et. al., *The Birth of a Consumer Society: The Commercialization of Eighteenth-Century England* (London: Europa Publications, 1982).

Note: Footnote #25 is missing in original.

26. Cadwallader to Peter Collinson, June 1744, in *The Letters and Papers of Cadwallader Colden*, New-York Historical Society *Collections*, 50–56 (1917–1923), 52:61; William Livingston, et al., *The Independent Reflector, or Weekly Essays on Sundry Important Subjects More particularly adapted to the Province of New-York*, Milton M. Klein, ed. (Cambridge, Mass.: Belknap Press of Harvard University Press, 1963), pp. 257–58; Smith, History 1:226.

27. Philip Livingston to Jacob Wendell, 4 Sept. 1744, Livingston Papers, Museum of the City of New York, box 2.

28. Dixon Ryan Fox, "The Development of the American Theatre," *New York History*, 17 1936): 24; Joseph Borome, "The Origins of Grand Opera in New York," ibid., 27 (1946): 169–72. For a selection of advertisements for public entertainments in eighteenth-century New York, see Rita Gottesman, comp., *The Arts and Crafts in New York, 1726–1776: Advertisements and New Items from New York City newspapers* (New York: New-York Historical Society, 1938): pp. 374–94.

29. *New-York Post-Boy*, 6 June 1765, 3 June 1766; *New-York Mercury*, 5 July 1768, 17 Aug. 1772, 17 May 1773.

30. Smith, *History, 1:226*; Morris, ed., *John Jay: The Making of a Revolutionary*, p. 116n; Esther Singleton *Social New York Under the Georges, 776* (New York: D. Appleton and Company, 1902). pp. 291–92, 301–5; *New-York Mercury*, 24 Oct. 1774. On the turtle feasts, see Alexander Hamilton, *Itinerarium . . .*, Albert Bushnell Hart, ed. (St. Louis: William K. Bixby, 1907), pp. 107–8 and Andrew Barnaby, *Travels through the Middle Settlements in North America, in A General Collection of the Best and Most Interesting Voyages and Travels in All Parts of the World*, John Pinkerton, ed. (London: pp. 738–39.

31. Daniel Blake Smith, *Inside the Great House: Planter Family Life in Eighteenth-Century Chesapeake Society* (Ithaca, N.Y.: University Press, 1980), pp. 62–68.

32. Rhys Isaac, *The Transformation of Virginia, 1740–1790* (Chapel Hill: University of North Carolina Press, 1982), pp. 70–79; Richard L. Bushman, "High-Style and Vernacular Cultures," in Jack P. Greene and J.R. Pole, eds., *British Colonial America: Essays in the New History of the Early Modern Era* (Baltimore: Johns Hopkins University Press, 349–52.

33. Rutherfurd, *Family Record and Events,* p. 42.

34. Sarah Knight, *The Private Journal kept by Madam Knight on a Journey from Boston to New-York in the Year* 1704 (Boston: Small, Maynard & Co., 1920), pp. 52–53; Adolph B. Benson, ed., *The American of 1750: Peter Kalm's Travels in America,* 2 vols. (New York: Wilson-Erickson Inc., 1937), 1:130–32; L.H. Butterfield, ed., *Diary and Autobiography* 4 vols. (New York: Atheneum, 1964), 2:105–11.

35. Inventory of the estate of Robert R. Livingston, 30 Sept. 1813, Robert R. Livingston Papers, NYHS, reel 11.

36. William Livingston to Noah Wells, 7 Nov. 1747, Johnson Family Papers, Correspondence, Yale University.

37. Robert Livingston (1708–1790) to James Duane, 28 Aug. 1772, Duane Papers, NYHS, box 2; Margaret Beekman Livingston to Robert R. Livingston, Jr., 4 June 1782, Robert R. Livingston Papers, NYHS, reel 2.

38. Knight, *Journal,* p. 54; Hamilton, pp. 52, 108.

39. Neil "The Commercialization of Fashion," in McKendrick, et al., Birth of a Consumer Society, pp. 40–54.

40. *See* for example, *New-York Post-Boy,* 8 May 1749, 7, 21 May 1750; *New-York Mercury,* 19 Apr. 1754, Jan. Aug. 1773; *New-York Journal,* 26 Mar. 1767.

41. *New-York Post-Boy,* 11 Sept. 1766; *New-York Mercury,* 3 July 1769.

42. *New-York Gazette,* 28 Jan. 1735, 24 Feb. 1766; *New-York Mercury,* 30 June 1760, 11 Jan. 1773. On women's fashions, in general, *see* Singleton, *Social New York Under the* pt. V.

43. *New-York Mercury,* 3 Jan. 1757.

This article originally appeared in the *Hudson Valley Regional Review,* Volume 4.1.

This souvenir postcard from the 1909 celebration details the native-Americans greeting Hudson in slightly more exuberant tone than the contemporary sources describe.

"Hudson Landing from the Half Moon," 1909 souvenir postcard from the collection of Vivian Yess Wadlin, courtesy of Hudson River Valley Heritage.

This contemporary reproduction depicts the storming of the North Redoubt.

"The Battle of Fort Montgomery," painting by Jack Mead. Courtesy of the New York Office of Parks, Recreation, and Historic Preservation.

George Boughton's "Rainy Day at West Point" is characteristic of the later Hudson River landscape painters that emphasized more subjective and psychological connotations to their work.

George H. Boughton, American (1833-1905), "Rainy Day at West Point," Oil on canvas, 9 7/8 x 15," The Frances Lehman Loeb Art Center, Vassar College, Poughkeepsie, New York, Gift of Matthew Vassar, 1864.0001.0009.00.

Charles Moore's 1861 painting is characteristic of Hudson River school paintings that tended to portray a romanticized vision of the past. Although the paintings routinely pictured a serene, quiet Hudson, they did so after commerce and industry began to dominate the River and its valley.

Charles Herbert Moore, American (1840-1930), "Down the Hudson to West Point," 1861, Oil on Canvas, 19 ½ x 29 ¾," The Frances Lehman Loeb Art Center, Vassar College, Poughkeepsie, New York, Gift of Matthew Vassar,1864.1.59

Newburgh at the turn of the century was the bustling town portrayed in Mark Carnes' article and this image.

Clarence Kerr Chatterton, American 1880-1973, "Clinton Square, Newburgh," 1917, Oil on canvas, 27 1/2 x 35 ¼," The Frances Lehman Loeb Art Center, Vassar College, Poughkeepsie, New York, Bequest of Leila Cook Barber, 1985.11.1

Lindenwald's façade, Formal Parlor, and Dining Room.

Martin Van Buren National Historic Site, photos by the National Park Service.

Locust Grove's eastern façade and porte-cochère was the formal entrance from the Post Road, (New York State Route 9 today), and a view of the Italianate tower from the southwest lawn.

Photos courtesy of the Locust Grove Estate.

W. H. Bartlett.

R. Brandard.

This hand-tinted lithograph was typical of the nineteenth-century travel publications discussed in Richard Wiles' article. The subject of this lithograph, the Catskill Mountain House, was also subject of many Hudson River artists' creative efforts.

Hand-tinted engraving of the Catskill Mountain House, after W.H. Bartlett's "View from the Mountain House," 1836, Private collection.

"Slab Sides" (Home of John Burroughs), Poughkeepsie, N.Y.

John Burroughs, the "Sage of Slabsides," on the steps of his writing retreat, overlooking his celery farm.

Colorized postcard of John Burroughs on the steps of Slabsides, in West Park, New York. From the collection of Vivian Yess Wadlin, courtesy of Hudson River Valley Heritage.

The American Revolution

The American Revolution in the Hudson Valley: An Overview

James M. Johnson and Thomas S. Wermuth

Although the "shot heard 'round the world" that ignited the American Revolution occurred a few miles outside of Boston and the campaign that ended it took place in Virginia, the nexus of the conflict was New York's Hudson River Valley. Throughout the war, officers on both sides made it their top priority to gain control of the river—and to keep hold of it—at any cost.

As a result, the Hudson Valley—the virtual center of the colonies—hosted many key figures, battles, and political events throughout the eight years of war, and its final drama was played out here with the British evacuation of New York City on November 25, 1783. In the years leading up to the Revolution, the Sons of Liberty, as active in New York as they were in Massachusetts, printed broadsides, encouraged boycotts, rallied, rioted, and dumped British tea into New York Harbor. Patriot housewives throughout the Valley threw their own "tea parties" at the expense of merchants and Loyalist neighbors. The region's social fabric was ripped apart, first by the struggle between the powerful coalitions of DeLanceys and Livingstons, and then by the clash between the Loyalists and Whigs (or Patriots).

The New York Provincial Congress established itself at the courthouse in White Plains in July 1776 and created the State of New York with its acceptance of the Declaration of Independence on July 9. New York adopted its constitution in Kingston on April 20, 1777, and on February 6, 1778, it ratified the Articles of Confederation, tying its fate to the rest of the United States of America.

Prelude to War

On the eve of the American Revolution, the Hudson River Valley was among the most fertile and productive regions in North America. Its grain, flour, and dairy products were sent all over the world. The port towns of Albany, Poughkeepsie, and Kingston were thriving commercial entrepots that served as regional hubs in the vibrant agricultural trade with New York City.

The Hudson Valley had been settled primarily by the Dutch in the mid-seventeenth century, and the English soon thereafter, with some French Huguenots and Germans following. Much of the Hudson's west bank was still ethnically and culturally Dutch, perhaps three generations removed from leaving Europe. Dutch customs prevailed, the Dutch Reformed Church dominated, and while the Second Continental Congress was approving the Declaration of Independence, Dutch was spoken more regularly in many Hudson Valley towns than English. Indeed, through 1774 the Ulster town of Kingston (a mere two years away from being the state capital) kept its official records in Dutch.

As late as 1763, residents of the Hudson Valley still felt strong bonds to the King of England and his empire. A typical outpouring of this affection was the celebration in Kingston of George III's ascension to the throne in 1761. Hundreds of residents paraded through the streets and offered toasts and cannonades to "His most Royal and Sacred Majesty."[1] Similar celebrations were held throughout the region.

Nevertheless, relations between England and the colonies began to sour. Following the French and Indian War, the British government levied new taxes on the American colonies that were intended to defray its large war debt. The Stamp Act of 1765, which imposed a tax on a variety of goods and services, was viewed suspiciously by Valley inhabitants, as well as other colonists. In towns throughout the region, residents resisted the implementation of the act, and in Albany and New York City riots broke out in order to prevent the tax from going into effect.[2]

TIMELINE

1763	Treaty of Paris concludes French and Indian War
1765	Stamp Act Riots in New York, Albany, and Boston
1766	Stamp Act Repealed
1770	Boston Massacre
1773	Boston Tea Party
1774	Coercive (or Intolerable) Acts
1775	Battle of Lexington (April); Battle of Bunker Hill (June)
1776	British Invasion of New York City
1777	Campaign for the Hudson River Valley
1778	Washington's Encampment at Pawling (Fredricksburg)
1779	Battle of Stony Point
1780	Fortress West Point opened
1781	Battle of Yorktown
1782	Washington's army encamped at New Windsor
1783	Evacuation Day (November)

Calm returned to North America following the Stamp Act's repeal in 1766, and over the next several years there was a rapprochement of sorts between England and her colonies. Nevertheless, the quartering of British troops in Boston and New York inflamed tensions in both cities, leading to sporadic outbursts of violence. The Boston Massacre further ignited anti-British sentiment.

The primary debate in the 1770s continued to be over Britain's authority to tax the colonists. Britain asserted this right as essential to the process of governance. Although the colonial argument varied, in essence it recognized the empire's right to tax to regulate imperial relations, but not to raise revenue. Colonists generally agreed with Patrick Henry's famous declaration of "no taxation without representation." Such sentiment led to a variety of responses from British officials, one of the most interesting being the distinction between "actual" and "virtual" representation: The colonists were not physically represented in Parliament (and neither were many English subjects). However, the colonists *were* represented, so the argument ran, in the sense that Parliament represented the interests of all subjects of the realm.[3]

From 1770 through 1773, relations between the colonies and Britain were relatively stable, but events in late 1773 changed that. The newly enacted Tea Act, offering East Indian tea at reduced prices (and including a tax), inspired "tea parties" throughout the colonies, including the Hudson Valley. The most famous, of

James M. Johnson and Thomas S. Wermuth

course, occurred in Boston, where members of the Sons of Liberty dressed as Mohawk Indians and dumped British tea overboard.[4]

The Coercive Acts of 1774, implemented to punish Boston following its Tea Party, ignited resistance throughout the colonies. New Yorkers had their own tea party on April 22, when "Mohawks" dumped tea from the ship *Hook* into the harbor, forcing another ship, the *Nancy*, to return to England. In communities up and down the Hudson, committees of safety, observation, and inspection sprang into action to challenge recent British policies.[5]

Characteristic of this resistance was the Kingston Committee of Safety's anger over Parliament's attempt to establish "the Romish Religion in America," a feature of the Quebec Act of 1774. The Kingston committee was equally shocked by the "avowed design of the [British] ministry to raise a revenue in America." The New Windsor Committee of Observation articulated its fear of Parliament's desire to levy taxes "on us without our consent" and for asserting absolute legislative authority over the colonies. The committee resolved that such powers were "subversive of our natural and legal rights as British subjects, and that we would be deficient in point of duty to our King and the British Constitution were we to yield in tame submission to them."[6]

As war began in New England in 1775, the people of the Hudson Valley began to choose sides. Throughout the war, there were pockets of loyalism in the region, but devotion to the revolutionary cause remained strong. The Valley was able to muster several Continental and militia regiments.

The Campaigns for the Hudson River Valley

Control of the Hudson Valley was one of the primary strategic objectives of the British high command. The Valley's defense was equally important to General George Washington, whose army was to spend more than a third of the war in (or in close proximity to) the region. In 1776, Washington stated that "the importance of the river in the present contest and the necessity of defending it, are so well understood that it is unnecessary to enlarge upon them." Whereupon he proceeded to enlarge upon those reasons, citing its strategic transportation and communications significance, as well as the importance of its agricultural production.[7]

That July, the largest armada the British Empire had ever sent abroad entered New York Harbor. Five hundred ships carrying more than 34,000 British Regulars, sailors, and German mercenaries under the joint command of the brothers Howe, Admiral Richard and General Sir William, landed at the southern tip of Manhattan Island. Facing them across the East River, atop Brooklyn Heights, were some 20,000 Continentals and militia under Washington's command.[8]

In late August, Howe's army slipped around Washington and attacked from the rear. The Americans were driven across the river to Manhattan. In mid-September the two armies clashed again near Kip's Bay, sending Washington's army reeling northward up the island. In early October, the British again seized the advantage, striking Washington at Pell's Point; later that month, the two armies battled to a draw at White Plains. In just three months, the Continental Army had been pushed out of New York City and into the lower Hudson Valley.[9]

The British engaged in several small raids in the mid-Valley in 1776 and early 1777. Its subsequent campaign to control the region consisted of an elaborate three-pronged invasion.

The main force, under General John Burgoyne, was to depart from Canada and push its way south through the Adirondacks to Albany, where it was to meet up with a combined British-Indian force pushing

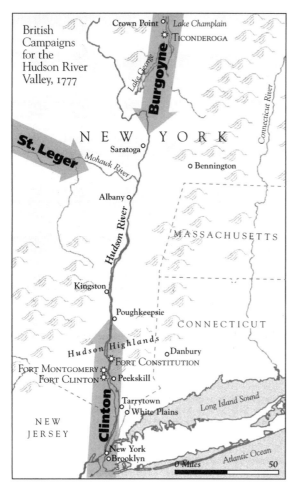

British Campaigns for the Hudson River Valley, 1777.

eastward along the Mohawk Valley. The third force was to be an expeditionary unit under the command of Sir Henry Clinton, who had been left in command of New York City when General Howe unexpectedly sailed south to Philadelphia in July 1777. Clinton's push up the Hudson aimed at either meeting with, or giving support to, Burgoyne's forces. Military scholars have often noted the lack of proper planning and coordination of this major invasion, whose failure led directly to the British defeat at Saratoga, "the turning point of the war."[10]

As Clinton's army made its way up the Hudson, about 2,000 Continental soldiers from the 5th New York Regiment and Lamb's Artillery (along with elements of the Ulster and Orange county militia) garrisoned forts Montgomery and Clinton. The state's new governor, Brigadier General George Clinton, commanded the posts. His brother, James, commanded the troops at Fort Clinton. On the morning of October 6, after a day of fierce fighting, British troops captured both forts and spent the next several days destroying them, along with an iron chain that had been stretched across the Hudson there. The main part of the American force was able to escape.[11]

Despite the British victory, Henry Clinton's troops suffered almost 200 casualties and were delayed by the action. They resumed their movement upriver and stopped at several points along the way, landing small units for limited forays against local militia units. British forces reached Kingston, the state capital, ten days later.

Advance British units approached Kingston before dawn on October 16. Many residents had already escaped in the days before the British arrival, and local militia were prepared to conduct a delaying action if large numbers of troops came ashore. Major General John Vaughn led a British raiding party of several hundred men that quickly drove local militia units west from the town in pre-dawn fighting on the banks of Rondout Creek. Determined to punish the region, British troops burned large portions of the town before departing later that afternoon. Henry Clinton pushed another ten miles upriver over the next few days, dropping landing parties at various points (including the Livingston estate at Clermont, which, with the nearby Belvediere, was burned to the ground) before heading back to New York City. By this time, Burgoyne had surrendered and Clinton's northward movement had been made irrelevant.[12]

Although there was limited military action in the mid-Valley in 1778, the Hudson remained the primary target of both British and American strategists. In May 1779, Henry Clinton attempted a second invasion, seizing Stony Point. However, Washington kept his army between Clinton and the northern stretches of the Valley, and on July 15 he sent a force under General "Mad" Anthony Wayne to drive the British from

James M. Johnson and Thomas S. Wermuth

Stony Point. The surprise nighttime attack was a huge success, and all British troops in the vicinity retreated downriver in the fall.[13]

It was the importance of maintaining control of the Hudson that had led Washington, in 1778, to order construction of fortress West Point—a complex of forts and redoubts that he dubbed "the key of America." A feature of the fortress was a new iron chain, which was laid across the river to prevent any future British naval incursion upriver. In 1780, the British made one more attempt on the Hudson, when Henry Clinton opened secret negotiations with General Benedict Arnold, recently appointed commander of West Point, to gain control of the fort. Arnold's plans were discovered when Clinton's aide-de-camp, Major John Andre, was captured. He was hanged as a spy in Tappan; Arnold escaped to safety in New York City.[14]

In the last years of the war, the mid-Valley remained central to Washington's plans. After the British were defeated at Yorktown, they continued to occupy New York City for two more years, and their continued threat to the Valley kept Washington and his army stationed nearby. The Continental Army encamped in southern Ulster County, in and around the town of New Windsor, while Washington himself took up headquarters a few miles north, at Newburgh. In the summer of 1781, the French commander, the comte de Rochambeau, marched his 5,000-man army from Rhode Island to Philipsburg, in Westchester, to join the Continental Army, first in the siege of New York and then in the pivotal Yorktown Campaign in Virginia.

War and the Home Front

With the gradual collapse of New York's colonial government, the committees of safety, observation, and inspection emerged to fill the vacuum of power. In most towns, these developed alongside existing town boards and governments. In many communities, they maintained a strong presence by exerting their influence not only in the political sphere, but also in the economic arena. The committees regulated prices, controlled the importation and exportation of goods, and set maximum- and minimum-wage rates for local labor.

Often the powers invested in the committees were greater than those that town officials possessed. In 1776, the Provincial Congress gave the committees the authority to tax and appoint tax collectors and assessors. During the war, the committees gradually gained additional powers and became the de facto governing authority in many valley towns. Besides control over local taxation and legislation, they also assumed judicial and police powers. The committees could use their authority over local militia units to enforce their rulings.[15]

Usually, the committees did not have to resort to displays of power; they were able to employ community pressures against those suspected of unpatriotic actions or of any activity seen as threatening. These punishments included public denunciations of those who were considered to be enemies of the cause, symbolic burnings of effigies, or boycotts of shopkeepers and tradesmen who seemed lukewarm to the Revolution. Committees instructed residents not to patronize businesses whose patriotism was suspect because "every shilling of property we put in their hands . . . enable them to purchase the chains to bind us in slavery."[16]

The issues upon which committees expended the most energy tended to be economic. Food shortages, inflated prices, currency of questionable value, rising taxes, and, on the Hudson's east bank, tenants demanding land redistribution all helped to shape some of the most revolutionary aspects of the Revolution. On the eve of the war, the local committees of observation supervised economic activities in their counties and towns. Initially, the role of the committees was to promote non-importation and the boycott of British goods. Once the war began and shortages and inflation became rampant, the local committees started to scrutinize and regulate the trade and economic activities of local shopkeepers to ensure that they engaged in business practices that promoted the war effort and supported a vibrant local economy.[17]

The End of the War

Following the American victory at Stony Point, the British never directly threatened the Hudson Valley again. (The last engagement in the region occurred in the summer of 1779, when Chief Joseph Brant, leading a mixed band of Mohawks and Loyalists, conducted a raid on Minisink.) Following their dramatic victory at Yorktown, Washington and the Continental Army spent the last two years of the war encamped at New Windsor and Newburgh. On November 25, 1783, Governor George Clinton led the Americans into New York City after the British evacuation. And on December 4, the commander in chief bid a tearful farewell to his officers of the Continental Army at Fraunces Tavern in Manhattan. The war that started in Massachusetts and had centered in New York at last ended there.

Notes

1. *New York Gazette*, February 1761

2. Edward Countryman, *A People in Revolution: Political Society and the American Revolution in New York, 1760–1790*, (Baltimore, 1981), 37–39; Joseph Tiedemann, *Reluctant Revolutionaries: New York City and the Road to Independence, 1763–1776* (Ithaca, 1997).

3. Bernard Bailyn, *Ideological Origins of the American Revolution* (Cambridge, 1967), 166–71; Edmund S. Morgan, *The Birth of the Republic, 1763–89* (Chicago, 1967), 23–24.

4. Alfred Young, *The Shoemaker and the Tea Party: Memory and the American Revolution* (Boston, 1999), 99–107.

5. Countryman, 137–43.

6. "Resolves of the New Windsor Committee" in Peter Force, *American Archives* (Washington, D.C.: 1837–1853), 2:131–33.

7. Washington's comments are cited in Louis V. Mills, "Attack in the Highlands, the Battle of Fort Montgomery," *Hudson Valley Regional Review* (Sept. 2000), 39–40.

8. Bernard Schecter, *Battle for New York: City at the Heart of the American Revolution* (New York, 2002), 112–16.

9. William Polf, *Garrison Town: The British Occupation of New York City* (Albany, 1976), 5–7.

10. Mark Lender & James Kirby Martin, *A Respectable Army: The Military Origins of the Republic* (New York, 1981), 83–7.

11. Robert Venables, *The Hudson Valley in the American Revolution*, (New York, 1975) 12–13.

12. Schecter, 286–299.

13. Venables, 18.

14. Willard Sterne Randall, *Benedict Arnold: Patriot and Traitor* (New York, 1990), 526–37.

15. Countryman, 137–40.

16. "Minutes of Committee of Ulster, May 11, 1775" in Force, 2:833.

17. Thomas S. Wermuth, "The Central Hudson Valley and the American Revolution," in Joseph Tiedemann and Eugene Fingerhut, *The Other New York: The Revolution Outside New York City* (forthcoming, SUNY Press).

This article originally appeared in *The Hudson River Valley Review*, Volume 20.1.

A Suspected Loyalist in the Rural Hudson Valley: The Revolutionary War Experience of Roeloff Josiah Eltinge

Kenneth Shefsiek

In the years leading up to the War of Independence, battle lines were being drawn not only between the British government and its American colonies, but also among the colonial citizenry itself. For the radical revolutionaries who believed in the existence of a British governmental conspiracy to deprive the colonists of their liberty, as well as for those whose strong conservative stance enabled them to accept British authority in whatever form it was foisted upon them, matters of allegiance were fairly clear. But these two positions were the extremes, and the opinions of many resided in "the twilight zone between wholehearted support of the American cause and overt identification with the British."[1] Most of the populace, whether or not they eventually became Patriot or Tory, were thoroughly uncomfortable with the innovative methods Parliament had enacted to raise a revenue directly from the colonies. As William Nelson states, in regard to taxation the Tories "were as indignant as other Americans as to what seemed an unjust and arbitrary exercise of British authority."[2] What separated the revolutionaries from the Tories was not the belief that the British government was overstepping its bounds. Where they differed was in their opinion of the role of the British Crown and Parliament in relation to the elected governments of the colonies and the means open to them for resolving the controversy. There were, of course, Loyalists who actively fought on the side of the British. However, there were also many who considered themselves Loyalists because they felt negotiation and read-justment within the current imperial system was the proper approach to resolution. Then there were those who opposed the radical revolutionaries because "they were alarmed at the prospect of strife between Britain and the colonies;" however, it took years for the "the issue of allegiance [to] crystallize."[3]

The issue of allegiance was particularly complicated in New York, where the heterogeneity of the population in terms of ethnicity, religion, and wealth resulted in a similar heterogeneity in political beliefs. Whereas the greater homogeneity of society and political belief in New England and Virginia resulted in a greater clarity of political divisions, the heterogeneity of New York resulted in a greater distribution throughout the possible range, from left to right.[4] Additionally, New York's extensive experience in dealing with political and social division resulted in a culture of negotiation and moderation.[5] The way of moderation was also followed in New York as a means of preventing a renewed outbreak of violence, like that experienced during the Stamp Act Riots of 1765.[6]

Once the war began, the situation became increasingly difficult for those who were unable to support the Patriot cause fully, and even for those "who have affected to observe . . . a dangerous and equivocal neutrality."[7] To a revolutionary, there was no middle ground: moderates were considered potential Tories.

The Roeloff Josiah Eltinge House in New Paltz.

It was these moderates who faced some of the greatest personal challenges of conscience during the war. Since the revolutionaries, who held the reins of government and the law, would accept nothing less than full, unequivocal support, the moderates were forced to compromise their principles by choosing either the far left or the far right, or simply lying and stating that they supported the Patriots.[8] Those of questionable allegiance were particularly vulnerable in New York because the state was wedged between the British forces occupying New York City and the threat of invasion from the north. Both the British and the Americans believed that silent Tories would be encouraged to declare their true allegiance and threaten the state from within if the British forces were able to advance into the interior.

It was therefore incumbent upon the authorities in New York to find a method to deal with the Loyalist threat, whether real or phantom.[9] The government imprisoned suspected Tories, often in extremely substandard facilities and without due process of law. Particularly feared Tories were exiled, others were put to hard labor (although many authorities denounced such punishment). The property of some Loyalists was confiscated; Patriot vigilantes occasionally tarred and feathered their opponents. Alexander Flick contends the treatment was "firm but comparatively moderate,"[10] and other historians also declare it "moderate and fair, all things taken into consideration."[11] Robert Calhoon is generally forgiving of the governmental organization charged with suppressing Loyalist activity; he notes that it was "more concerned with identifying persons of doubtful loyalty than with punishment or harassment." Tories, Calhoon adds, were given the opportunity either to take an oath of allegiance or "move to New York City." (By "move," he means exile.)[12] Although exile is neither punishment nor harassment, it was rather harsh, especially when forced upon those who did not pose any real threat, even if they did have Tory leanings. Calhoon also states that in New England, county committees provided suspected Loyalists with the opportunity to end their "estrangement from the community through a recanting of any loyalistic statements," and thus "served to define the moral and inclusive character of a community in crisis."[3] The same was true in New York. Being given the chance to recant before a committee that had the power to punish hardly suggests the "inclusiveness" of a community in regard to political opinions. Philip Ranlett is not so forgiving, stating that the treatment of suspected Loyalists "was not kind."[4]

Many of the recent investigations into New York Toryism focus on sophisticated political ideology. The high-minded constitutional principles that were the basis for discussion and dispute were primarily the domain of the politicians and gentry. However, they were not the only Tories of the day: they were found in all ranks of society. It is more difficult to investigate the issue of allegiance for people of the middle and lower ranks of society because suspected Loyalists who were neither nonbelligerent nor socially prominent were handled by local committees, and few of their records survive.[15] Jonathan Clark has attempted to define allegiance for residents of all walks of life in Poughkeepsie, but he categorizes so many as "occasional loyalist" or "occasional patriot" that it is apparent that the issue of allegiance is often unclear.[16] It is also difficult to investigate fully how such suspects were treated by the revolutionary authorities. In the archives of the Huguenot Historical Society in New Paltz, a town of modest size during the eighteenth century, there survives a collection of documents relating to the wartime experience of one resident, Roeloff Josiah Eltinge (1737–1795), which substantially documents his treatment at the hands of the revolutionaries. His story provides insight into both the mind of a man who was neither an avowed Patriot nor a staunch Loyalist and the methods and motives of Patriot authorities during the early years of the conflict.

Roeloff Josiah Eltinge was a third-generation resident of New Paltz, which had been founded by French Huguenot refugees in 1678 on a patent of nearly 40,000 acres. The first Eltinge who moved to New Paltz was Roeloff Josiah's grandfather, a man of Dutch descent also named Roeloff (1689–1746/7), who married Sara DuBois (1682–c.1746), the daughter of New Paltz Patentee Abraham DuBois (1657–1731). According to tradition, the first Roeloff's son, Josiah, began to operate a general store in New Paltz around 1740 and was considered the wealthiest man of the town.[17] Roeloff Josiah took over the business from his father and was involved in many entrepreneurial endeavors.[18] He was one of New Paltz's most prominent citizens, but his influence did not extend outside the town. Although it is difficult to say where Roeloff Josiah fit in the overall social structure of his time and region, New Paltz was a small, isolated, relatively unimportant town in the eighteenth century, thus his social position would have been restricted. His small house, with three above-ground rooms, still survives, and it attests to his modest social standing.

Eltinge's Revolutionary War experience begins with his signing of the Articles of Association in May 1775. The articles had been prepared by the Committee of New York City on April 29, 1775, ten days after the battles at Lexington and Concord, and they had been transmitted to the counties of New York for signing in every town. The purpose of the association was to create a "firm union of its inhabitants in a vigorous prosecution of the measures necessary for safety (because) of the necessity of preventing the anarchy and confusion which attend a dissolution of the powers of government." It was a response both to Britain's taxation of the colonies and its subsequent aggression in Massachusetts. The association was an early statement of the independence movement, so many future revolutionaries signed it. So, too, did many future Loyalists. This sometimes occurred because of pressure by the local committees and other townspeople, but moderates would have generally felt comfortable signing because it also stated that "we most ardently desire . . . a reconciliation between Great Britain and America on Constitutional Principles."

Whether or not Eltinge willingly signed the articles is unknown, but his signature ensured his continued safety for the following eighteen months. This was to change on October 26, 1776, when he was brought before the Ulster County Committee meeting at the home of his kinsman, Abraham DuBois.[19] The extra-legal governmental committee of Ulster County had been in existence since January 6, 1775, when five town committees had met in Hurley, near the county seat of Kingston. County, town, and district committees, some of which had been formed as early as 1774, were becoming increasingly central to the war effort and served to fill the function of regional and local government with the collapse of the colonial government. After the Declaration of Independence, they became the local governments in a free state until the new government was set up under the state constitution of 1777. Whether or not these committees were truly representative of the people is questionable. As Hugh Flick states, "In speaking for the people (in 1774–1775), active minorities were usurping the functions of local governments and, for the most part, without hindrance by the more passive conservative(s),"[20] and as Samuel Seabury noted at the time, "It is notorious that in some districts only three or four met and chose themselves to be a committee . . ."[21] By the time Eltinge came before the Ulster committee in 1776, it probably was more representative of the public voice than in earlier years because sentiment against the British had been growing, especially since the struggles began in Massachusetts. Nevertheless, there was still a question in the eyes of many, particularly those with conservative tendencies, whether the committees had the right to assume governmental functions. Thus Eltinge might have approached his examination with severe misgivings.

The county committees were essentially the regional representatives of the New York Provincial Congress, and it was their responsibility to assist the Congress in its revolutionary efforts. One of these activities was to confront the internal threat posed by those who were loyal to the British crown—the "disaffected." This became an increasing concern with the close proximity of British forces after the occupation of New York City in the fall of 1776, as well as the ongoing possibility of attack from the north. This effort to apprehend Tories had begun in May 1776, and it was stepped up with the creation of the Committee for Defeating and Detecting Conspiracies (to which the county committees were subordinate) on September 21, 1776. It was in its capacity as locator of Tories that Eltinge was brought before the Ulster County Committee.

Eltinge was forced to appear because he refused to take Continental currency in his store. According to his statement to the committee, he never entirely trusted the value of the currency, and although he initially received it, his trust in it subsequently eroded further. After the withdrawal of Continental forces from Long Island and a "general rumor amongst the people of [his] neighborhood that in a little time Congress money would be good for nothing as the King was likely to overcome," others came to his store to purchase goods with the currency, but he believed they did so simply because they also considered it would soon to be worthless. Although he refused the currency, he told the customers that he would allow purchases on credit. According to the New York Provincial Congress, such actions were unacceptable according to their resolves passed on June 5, 1776, which indicated that those who prevented the circulation of paper money "were to be imprisoned, put under bond for good behavior, or removed from their localities on parole."[22] This local statement reflected the policy of the Continental Congress promulgated on January 11, 1776: those who did not accept currency should be treated as enemies. Although activities such as Eltinge's were nonbelligerent in nature, such an extreme position was taken because the acceptance of Continental money was absolutely necessary to fund the war effort, and the revolutionaries feared that "Tories" such as Eltinge might influence others, directly and by example. The Committee chose to take the most extreme action they could under the Provincial Congress' resolves, and Eltinge was sentenced to the prison in Fishkill, Dutchess County.[23]

While Eltinge's refusal to take Continental currency was in itself unacceptable to the authorities, the fact that he was brought before the committee and soundly punished might also have been reflective of personal animosities in both New Paltz and nearby Kingston. Tradition has it that there was an ongoing feud between the Eltinges and another prominent local family, the Hasbroucks, whose progenitors—the brothers Jean and Abraham—had been founding members of New Paltz, along with Abraham DuBois. According to Ralph LeFevre, the disagreement between the families resulted from a dispute over a land grant received by Eltinge's uncle, Noah, which some landowners in New Paltz protested because they claimed that part of the land was contained in the New Paltz patent.[24] Jacob Hasbrouck, Jr. (grandson of Jean Hasbrouck), and Abraham Hasbrouck (grandson of patentee Abraham Hasbrouck) instigated proceedings over this dispute in 1748. Unfortunately for Eltinge, the woman from whom he first refused to take the currency was Esther Hasbrouck Wirtz, the daughter of Jacob Jr. Both Jacob Jr. and Abraham were active Patriots. Jacob Jr. (of New Paltz) was a member of the Ulster County Committee and a major in the militia, while Abraham (of Kingston) was a colonel, and a rather petulant one at that.[25] Thus, Eltinge's run-in with the authorities might have had an extremely personal side to it, as small-town politics often do.

From that point until after the signing of the peace treaty in 1784, Eltinge's freedom was circumscribed by the authorities. After a stay of more than a month at the jail in Fishkill, he was sent to New Hampshire for confinement.[26] He and others were exiled from New York, according to John Jay, a member of the Committee for Conspiracies, because it was "indispensably necessary to remove a number of dangerous and disaffected persons, some of whom have been taken in arms against America, to one of the neighboring states."[27] The committee's prime concern was the men's proximity to the British stronghold of New York City. The Council of New Hampshire was willing to take them. Leaving Fishkill on December 4, 1776, Eltinge arrived in Atkinson, New Hampshire, on December 13. He was confined at the home of a Lieutenant Belknap for several days before being moved to the home of Lieutenant Colonel Joseph Welch until February 3, 1777, when he was placed in prison at Exeter.[28] Even though Eltinge and the other prisoners had been confined against their will, they remained responsible for their own "expenses and diet"[29], a policy made necessary because of the limited financial resources of the provincial government.

While officials in New Hampshire were willing to take the prisoners, the New Hampshire Council had some misgivings about their guilt. "Their clamours of being sent here without an examination at home and consciousness of their innocence which they assert, has had considerable influence among the people . . . And as a great number of them make such protestations of their not being sensible of their having ever given occasion for any person to suppose them unfriendly to the American cause, we wish an impartial inquiry might be made into their characters," wrote council President Meshach Weare.[30]

Eltinge remained in jail in Exeter until March 25, when he was released back to New York in response to a March 13, 1777, request by the Commissioners for Conspiracies to return all prisoners except those who were "closely confined in Goal (sic)"[31], to administer an oath of allegiance. If the prisoners refused, they were to be forced to remove themselves behind enemy lines. Eltinge arrived in Poughkeepsie to see the commissioners on May 13, but there is no evidence that he was asked to take an oath at that point. Nevertheless, he was given an order on May 21 to report to the Fleet prison in Kingston in six days. Opened on May 2, 1777, the prison originally consisted of two former privateer vessels anchored off Kingston, but as the need arose, other boats were added. Initially intended to house prisoners whom the commissioners feared might lead rumored uprisings in Dutchess County, Westchester County, and Livingston Manor, the prison later swelled with detainees from Albany and Orange counties, as well as with those, like Eltinge, who had been recalled from New England. Eltinge remained on board until June 18, when he was paroled to the home in Hurley of Jacobus Hardenburgh, his brother-in-law, who had petitioned for his release. This was the first time in almost eight months that Eltinge was able to enjoy a modicum of freedom and be with family. It was to be short-lived.

In his diary, Eltinge does not record any dealings with the authorities for the subsequent four months, but on October 6, 1777, after being accused of breaking his parole, he was taken back to Kingston to appear before the Commissioners for Conspiracies. He proved that he was innocent of the charge, and he was again paroled back to Hardenburgh's, although his parole was to last only a few more days. Forts Clinton and Montgomery, about forty miles south of Kingston, had been taken on October 6 by British forces under General Sir Henry Clinton; General John Burgoyne's forces were eighty miles north of town, at Saratoga. Meeting on October 8 in Kingston, the Council of Safety was not yet aware that Burgoyne's forces had been defeated on October 7, and in its eyes, the northern and southern armies were too close for comfort. Fearing that inactive Loyalists would be emboldened to act if British forces pushed into the region, the council felt it was necessary to remove all prisoners in and around Kingston to Hartford, Connecticut. Within hours, the militia was at the home of Jacobus Hardenburgh, where it again took Eltinge into custody. It also detained Eltinge's luncheon companion, Cadwallader Colden, Jr., who was on parole to the Van Deusen House in Hurley. From that moment on, the wartime fates of these two men would be bound together.[32]

Colden was the son of Cadwallader Colden, Sr. (1688–1776), of Coldengham, near Newburgh. The elder Colden had been a member of the Governor's Council from 1721 through 1776 and lieutenant governor from 1761 until his death. During several periods—most importantly throughout the Stamp Act crisis of 1765–1766—he filled the position of acting governor. He was the owner of a great deal of land, although not to the extent of families such as the DeLanceys or Livingstons. He was a thorough supporter of royal authority and prerogative, and as a high-ranking royal official, he made considerable use of the power of his office in furthering the interests of both himself and his family. The Colden name was synonymous with the colonial royal government, and the family was soon to be considered the enemy of the Revolution, which they were.

David Colden, Cadwallader Jr.'s younger brother, was a resident of Long Island who "actively supported royal government, and as a leader of the loyalists who outnumbered whigs in Flushing, prevented the creation of local protest committees in 1775 and '76."[33] Also, as leader of 1,293 freeholders and inhabitants of Queens County who had "steadfastly maintained their royal principles"[34], he petitioned the governor for the reinstitution of royal government when the British took New York City. After the war, David Colden was denied admission to the State of New York (as an active Loyalist, he had been forced to flee when the British evacuated New York City), and his property was confiscated after his death in 1784.

The Loyalist activities of Cadwallader Colden, Jr., were not as forward as those of his brother, possibly because the smaller number of Tories in Ulster County made it extremely difficult and dangerous to be so blatant. Nonetheless, his sympathies were identical. On April 14, 1775, he, Walter DuBois, and Peter DuBois[35] published a protest in response to the election of delegates from Ulster County to the Provincial Congress. They stated that the election was bogus because it had been executed by a group that in no way represented the eligible voters, and that the only legal governmental body was the Assembly. (Both were common Loyalist complaints.) They also declared that they would remain loyal "to our Parent State and British Constitution."[36] Although Colden signed the Articles of Association in April because of pressure from the local committee, he continued to espouse his Loyalist rhetoric. He was arrested by the committee in June 1776 so they could disarm him. (Because he was considered an active Loyalist, he was assumed to have a large cache of guns at his home. Only a broken gun and his son-in-law's fowling piece were found.) On July 4, he was asked to sign an oath stating that he would abide by the Association. He refused to sign when a codicil was added stating that, if necessary, he would bear arms against the British army. As a result, he was sentenced to jail as a Loyalist. On August 22, 1776, his case was given to the state Committee for Conspiracies. His troubles with the authorities would last throughout the war, as would Roeloff Eltinge's. Although Colden consistently claimed that he would obey the rules of the state and remain neutral throughout the struggle, he later stated that he could never swear an oath to the state in God's name, since his oath to the king was completely binding and could not be superseded. During the Revolutionary War, however, neutrals in New York were believed to be "cowardly tor(ies)"[37] and could not be countenanced. While Eltinge's condemnation as a Loyalist was not based on any overt support of the power of the king and Parliament, keeping company with an avowed Loyalist—especially one from such a hated family—was extremely compromising.

After the militia burst in on the luncheon at the Hardenburghs, it took Colden and Eltinge to Kingston along with other parolees it picked up along the way. Meeting in the Ulster County Courthouse in Kingston, the Committee for Conspiracies issued a list of those who were to be sent out of state, but for some unrecorded reason Colden and Eltinge had been left off. They were ordered by the "officer of the guard to come out of the ranks and (were) left on the street."[38] Not knowing what to do, both returned to Hurley, obeying their parole.[39]

Eltinge was taken by guard back to Kingston on October 12 and confined to "close goal by the Council of Safety till further orders."[40] He remained there for only a short time, as he and the other prisoners were removed on October 16, and "As soon as we got out of town it was in flames."[41] The British forces under Major General John Vaughan arrived in Kingston on October 15, having been sent by Sir Henry Clinton in the Highlands to meet up with Burgoyne at Saratoga. Burgoyne had already asked for surrender terms on the 13th, but Clinton had been unaware of this when he dispatched Vaughan. On the 16th, the residents of Kingston had fled, and Vaughan's forces burned the town nearly to the ground.

Colden was still under parole in nearby Hurley at the time of the burning, and he was subsequently sent to appear before the State Council of Safety meeting in Marbletown. He stated before the council a few days later that he was bound by oath to the king, but would remain neutral and subject to the laws of the state. The council responded that he must remain a prisoner if he was a subject of the king, and it paroled him to the Hardenburghs'. Eltinge had been held as a "close prisoner" at the house of Johannes Tack, in Marbletown, since the burning of Kingston.[42] On November 5, an order was issued by the Council of Safety that both men were to be sent away to a remote district of Dutchess County called the Nine Partners. There were so few Tories in that region, it was felt, that the two would have little opportunity to influence others.

Although they petitioned the council for a reprieve or postponement, Colden and Eltinge did not receive a response and arrived in Nine Partners, near the Connecticut border, on December 9. On January 27, 1778, they went to Poughkeepsie to confront the state legislature. Since their arrival in Nine Partners, Colden had been campaigning to be allowed to return home. He had approached the council, spoken with and written letters to Governor George Clinton (his former lawyer), and contacted many others, including his "old friend Coll [Levi] Pawling," an important Patriot. His entreaties were apparently of no avail.[43] With the reorganization of the state government under the new Constitution of 1777, there was a question of jurisdiction regarding the cases of the men. Colden attempted to use the influence that he thought he possessed with Clinton and others to have the state legislature decide their case, but that body decided that their fates should be under the purview of the reorganized Commission for Conspiracies, which had not yet met. Colden and Eltinge contacted the two available members of the old commission, who agreed to a two-week parole to their own homes until the new commission met. Eltinge left for New Paltz on January 30.

During the period of Eltinge's incarceration, which had begun back in October when he was initially to be sent to Connecticut, it is obvious that various governing bodies were unsure about how to deal with him, as well as with Colden. While the two did not pose any direct threat to the war effort, their being designated Loyalists required that their influence on others be contained. Furthermore, the jurisdiction that was to deal with their situation—whether local, county, or state—was unclear, and there was no defined protocol to be followed on any level. Thus the two were in a state of legal limbo that would last a few months longer.

As directed, Eltinge returned to Poughkeepsie on February 13, but he was not accompanied by Colden, who had received a one-month extension because he anticipated he would not be able to cross the Hudson due to ice. This was probably a ploy to remain home longer, as Eltinge had been able to make the crossing. Eltinge was also given an additional month at home, quite possibly because the commission considered the two cases to be a single issue. Colden arrived in Poughkeepsie on March 15, Eltinge on the 18th. According to Eltinge, he was "detained"[44] until March 23, but Eugene Fingerhut states that "For four days Colden parked himself outside the Assembly door, awaiting his fate"[45], so the status of their level of freedom is unclear. Colden was told that he could return home until further orders, while Eltinge "was . . . permitted to remain at my place of abode . . .till I could be exhanged for some well-affected citizen or prisoner with the enemy."[46] While Colden's status was still uncertain, Eltinge's situation was apparently coming to a head.

On June 30, the legislature passed "An Act More Effectively to Prevent the Mischieffs ariseing from the Influence and Example of Persons of Equivocal and Suspected Character in this State." No longer would the state accept neutral persons in its midst; with British forces so close, it felt the risk was too great. While people like Eltinge and Colden never aided British forces or bore arms against the revolutionaries, the state thought it would be better to be rid of them. However, they were given one last chance to regain their freedom and stay: Loyalists were given a final opportunity to take an oath of allegiance to the laws of New York. If they refused, they would be banished. This oath would also require the person to declare that the state had a right to be free and independent. Colden was the first person to be dealt with under the new law, and on July 4 he declined to take the oath. Although he could abide by the state laws, his oath to the king could not be superseded. On July 6, Eltinge also refused to take it.

Following Eltinge's refusal, he was paroled back to New Paltz, but on July 26 he received a notice from the Commission for Conspiracies. "Pursuant to the act of the Legislature," he was to appear at Fishkill on August 3 "in order to effect his removal within the Enemy's lines, that he be permitted to take with him his family (males capable of bearing arms excepted) one week's provisions and as much of his effects as together with his family and provisions as would be transported in two wagons."[47] Colden also was to appear on August 3 for the same purpose. Eltinge met up with him at Coldengham, and when they arrived in Fishkill they remained there for two days because no one knew how their transport would be effected. It was decided that they would travel to New York City on a sloop that had been obtained by another banished Loyalist, William Smith, Jr., under the guard of Colonel Aaron Burr.[48] Even though Eltinge had been permitted to take his family, they remained in New Paltz, and he arrived in New York City on August 11. On September 8, 1778, he indicated that he "took (his) boarding at Anthony van Noorstrandt in Wolves Hollow on Long Island in Queens County," where it appears from his diary that he primarily remained throughout the war, although he made trips into the city every few months.

Kenneth Shefsiek

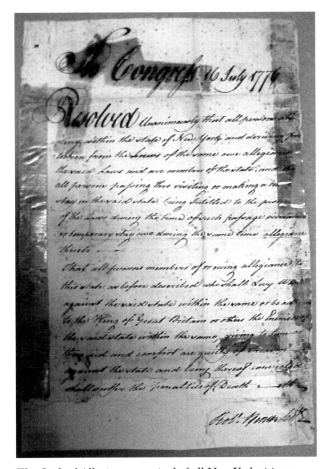
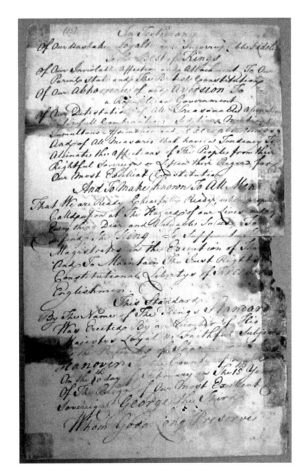

The Oath of Allegiance required of all New York citizens.
Courtesy of NYS Office of Parks, Recreation and Historic Preservation. Senate House Historic Site.

Also living in New York was Eltinge's younger brother Solomon (1742–1809). He, too, had been in trouble with the authorities. On November 8, 1776, he had been sent by the Committee for Conspiracies to Exeter, New Hampshire, for being "notoriously disaffected to the American cause, which [he has] evinced by refusing to receive in payment the Continental currency, and endeavouring to depreciate the same"—the same charge originally levied against his brother.[49] Solomon followed Roeloff in his refusal to take the oath of allegiance on August 1, 1778, and he, too, was banished. Records indicate that the brothers were in close contact during their exile.[50]

Although some account information concerning Roeloff Eltinge's financial situation during his exile survives, no descriptive information about his day-to-day life exists. His financial situation must have been precarious, since it would have been impossible for him to perform his livelihood as a merchant. To earn money, it appears that he turned to crafts such as "patching shoes" and "making a slay." Additionally, from January 1780 through March 1783 he left a considerable amount of "stoves," pails, piggins, "koolers," sugar boxes and "canteens" to be sold at various locations. This provided him with a steady, albeit small, income.[51] Food, other essential goods, and housing were difficult to come by because of a significant surge in Loyalist refugees and the large garrison of British troops. Making matters worse, inflation rates were dramatic. However, Eltinge appears to have survived reasonably well. The last entry in his wartime diary and account book indicates that in 1784 (presumably at the conclusion of his exile) he had amassed £26.2.8.

Provisional articles of peace between the Britain and the United States were signed at Paris on November 30, 1782, thus beginning the process for Loyalists either to emigrate or reconcile with and remain in the new nation. Article Five provided for "the restitution of . . . the estates, rights, and properties of persons resident in districts in the possession of his Majesty's arms and who have not borne arms against the said United States," but this provision was only to be "earnestly recommended . . . to the legislatures of the respective states." The provisional articles were included in the final treaty, which was signed by representatives of both countries in Paris on September 3, 1783. Because the agreement concerning the appropriate treatment of Loyalists was not binding on any state, Roeloff Eltinge's position in relation to New York remained unaltered at the conclusion of the war. In other words, he remained banished. Thus, when the British army began the process of evacuating New York City in the spring of 1783, it was necessary for him to leave the state. A letter from Eltinge to his son (probably his eldest, Ezekiel) dated September 29, 1783, indicates that he and Solomon had moved to Achquechkononck, New Jersey (now Passaic). In this letter, he informed his son that "if any of my friends want to see me [they] may come here, because I see no probability as yet to come to see them with Safety."[52] He and Solomon were still there on January 11, 1784, as indicated in a letter Roeloff wrote to his wife. He stated that "I [will] not be able to come home as soon as I had expected on account of the definitive triety [sic] not being published . . . and not knowing yet . . . whether [the state government] will or can do anything for us."[53]

The peace treaty was ratified by Congress on January 14, 1784, but New York refused to consider its recommendations regarding the treatment of Loyalists. On February 12, 1784, Roeloff and Solomon petitioned the state legislature to be "released from the disagreeable situation to which they have been so long exposed and humbly pray the Honorable Legislature to make such order in their behalf as may remove the effect of the law under which they suffer and enable your Petitioners to return with safety to their families."[54] Several other banished Loyalists, including Cadwallader Colden, Jr., also submitted petitions. The Assembly voted to reject them all, and the Senate voted to postpone consideration. According to Alexander Flick, "In early 1784 the wartime policy of the state legislature was still clear and certain." It had no intention of revoking the banishment of Loyalists.[55]

On May 12, however, Roeloff, Solomon, and 25 others were permitted to return to their homes. This permission was passed in conjunction with an antiloyalist act that upheld the banishment of those Loyalists who actively took part in the war on the side of the British. Only 36 loyalists had their banishments revoked in 1784. It was not until 1792 that all of those who had been exiled were allowed to return.

The exact date of Roeloff Eltinge's return to New Paltz is unknown, but it is likely that he returned forthwith. Few records survive that indicate the process of his reintegration into society. Because he never took an active part on the side of the British, his property was never confiscated, nor he did face persecution extreme enough for him to emigrate from his native land. According to Alexander Flick, "Those whose worst crime was open loyalty, who had been arrested, imprisoned, exiled, or paroled, but never charged with treason, were found in every community, and, although subjected to more or less abuse, were for the most part allowed to remain after the war was over, and to keep their property. While never fully forgiven, in time they came to be looked upon as true Americans, and were given full political rights."[56] Roeloff Eltinge's experience in New Paltz supports Flick's assertion. Within a few years he was respected enough to serve in several elected government positions, first as overseer of the poor in 1790 and then "as one of the New Paltz Twelve Men for the share of Louis DuBois from 1791 until his death in 1795."[57] He also returned to his mercantile activities in partnership with his son Ezekiel.

It is clear that the revolutionary authorities believed that Eltinge was a Tory, but were they accurate in their perception? His refusal to take the oath of allegiance clearly indicates that he did not embrace the Patriot cause, but in and of itself that might not indicate that he harbored pro-British sentiments. Before the issue of Eltinge's allegiance is considered in depth, his involvement in an earlier dispute concerning the relation between the colonies and Europe must be considered.

Eltinge was a lifelong member of the Dutch Reformed Church, having joined the Kingston congregation in 1762, at the age of 25. In 1737, the same year as Eltinge's birth, a controversy began to develop in the Dutch Reformed congregations in the colonies. The governing organization of the church, which was responsible for doctrine, ordination, dispute resolution, and all general ecclesiastical business, was the Classis of Amsterdam. Because of its distance from the colonies, a movement began in the 1730s to establish an organization in America to conduct church business, but this organization—the Coetus—would remain subordinate to the Classis. When the Coetus was formed in 1737, several congregations refused to send representatives because they believed that some congregations had obfuscated their true intention of ultimate independence from the Netherlands. Indeed, in 1754 the Coetus expressed its belief that it should serve as an independent, American Classis. The result was a schism in the colonial churches, with those that desired maintaining ties with Amsterdam forming a separate, smaller body of congregations called the Conferentie, meaning "conference." The schism was not mended until 1772, when the Articles of Union (which resulted in virtual independence of Dutch Reformed congregations in America) was signed by the American congregations with the approval of the Classis.

The New Paltz congregation sided with the Coetus, but there were residents who wished to remain subordinate to the Classis, and this resulted in the formation of a new, Conferentie congregation on August 29, 1766. Ten of the original 15 members of this new church had never been official members of the New Paltz church, but rather were congregants in the Dutch Church in Kingston. (However, it appears likely that these Kingston members attended services in New Paltz on a regular basis.) The other five were members of the New Paltz congregation, although four of them had previously been members in Kingston. Although there was a great deal of strife in the Kingston congregation, it officially remained in the Conferentie party. Interestingly enough, one of the protagonists in the dispute within the Kingston congregation was Colonel Abraham Hasbrouck (of the reputed Eltinge-Hasbrouck feud), who was attempting to force the church in the direction of the Coetus. This would have placed the Eltinges in opposition to the Hasbroucks once again.[58] The founding members from the Kingston church had been granted a dismissal by the Kingston consistory in order to form the new church, as "they [were] living too far away from the church of Kingston to dutifully and stately attend divine worship there . . . in the pure doctrine of the truth, and to lead them to the communion of a Reformed (and to the Reverend Classis of Amsterdam subordinated) congregation."[59]

A leading member of the new congregation was Roeloff Josiah Eltinge's father, Josiah Eltinge, who provided a large portion of the funds for construction of a house of worship. Roeloff Josiah (who was a member of the Kingston congregation) and his three brothers joined the church the year after its creation. Roeloff Josiah was active in his new congregation, serving as both elder and deacon at various times. The last elections for elder and deacon of the second church in New Paltz for which evidence survives is dated December 16, 1776, four years after the Articles of Union had been signed, but the churches did not unite until May 25, 1783.[60]

The fundamental question in this dispute was whether or not the colonial church should remain subordinate and dependent on the mother country or should it, as a result of growth and maturation and the need to manage its own affairs, become independent. That these issues were being faced in the Dutch church at the same time that the political independence movement was gaining momentum was not coincidental. American society in many ways was considering its position in relation to Europe, with many in America leaning towards separation. That Roeloff Josiah Eltinge sided with the Conferentie party suggests a conservative mindset, and when faced with the issue of political independence the implication is that he would have possessed more of a Loyalist mentality.

While it is true that members of the Conferentie faction were cultural conservatives, those who were opposed to the Coetus party were not necessarily *political* conservatives as well. The controversy concerning religious independence did develop at the same time as the political independence movement, and both movements were guided by similar principles regarding American and European relationships. But it also occurred at a time when Dutch culture and language was being diminished by the dominating English influence, and those who expressed a desire to remain subordinate to Amsterdam might have been led by an equal desire to retain their cultural identity. Additionally, there were many in the Coetus who tended toward evangelical style of worship, thus encouraging those "uncomfortable with the vagaries of revivalism" to join the Conferentie opposition.[61] Thus, all members of the Dutch conservative faction, including Eltinge, were not necessarily antirevolutionaries by definition since they were also being influenced by other cultural and spiritual concerns.

What, then, is the evidence that sheds light on Eltinge's allegiance? His involvement in the conservative faction of the Dutch church suggests that even before the American political independence movement began he was a proponent of continued cultural connections with Europe. However, the incident that marked him as a Loyalist in the eyes of the Patriots—and by the definition of the Continental Congress—was his refusal to take Continental currency. At his trial, he never stated any support for the British government other than indicating that he did not feel that the Patriots would prevail. His decision not to take the currency was based on economic pragmatism and his belief that he was being taken advantage of. If he was truly a Loyalist, at that point it is likely that he would have made statements to that effect; both his involvement in the less-powerful Conferentie faction and his future refusal to take the oath suggest that he was a man of principle who was willing to declare publicly his ideology, whether it was popular or not. It must also be remembered that in the fall of 1776, even though independence had been declared, Loyalist and Patriot ideologies had not yet polarized the people into two camps. It is likely that, given his conservative mindset, Eltinge leaned toward the Loyalist side without fully committing to it—at least in 1776.

When he refused to take the oath in 1778, however, the situation had changed. By that time, a person had to be either a Loyalist or a Patriot because it had become a matter of one party against another, rather than an issue of a somewhat fluid ideology. Refusing to take the oath in itself was not a clear statement of pro-British sympathies; it could also have been an *antirevolutionary* declaration. During the previous two years, Eltinge had been shuttled around from place to place, confined in prisons, and in general treated poorly by authorities whose right to punish was questionable, particularly in the early years before the state had been officially formed. If we keep in mind that he did not declare pro-British opinions (if he in fact possessed them) when he would likely have done so, it is quite possible that his treatment at the hands of the Patriots hardened his heart against them and made it too galling for him to take the oath. *Thus, it is likely that he was a conservative forced into the Loyalist camp by the harsh treatment to which he was subjected for a perceived offense that was simply a matter of financial self-preservation.*

Kenneth Shefsiek

The other piece of evidence that might suggest a Loyalist stance was Eltinge's relationship with Cadwallader Colden, Jr. Although the two were at least acquainted with each other before the war, their close interaction did not begin until both had difficulties with the Patriot committees. While it appears that the committees treated the two almost as a unit, suggesting that they believed the men shared a common ideology, there is no evidence to suggest that Eltinge held the same staunch Loyalist outlook that Colden did. Their relationship, then, was substantially a matter of circumstance. Finally, Eltinge's lack of involvement in the Patriot movement might have been a response to the active part played by such influential Ulster County leaders as Major Jacob Hasbrouck, Jr. , and Colonel Abraham Hasbrouck. If indeed there was a feud between the two families, it is possible that Eltinge was loath to support the Patriots in Ulster County due to personal conflicts.

Eltinge's political ideology will, unfortunately, never be known. During the Revolution itself, it is quite likely that his position was equally unclear in the eyes of his community, and his treatment was a direct result of this ambiguousness. To the authorities, his actions would have marked him as a suspicious person, but because he did not pose any clear threat, they were at a loss to determine an appropriate method of containing him. Had he taken up arms against the Patriots, or otherwise blatantly assisted the British, the appropriate punishment would have been clear. But Eltinge's suspiciousness placed him in limbo, and his resulting treatment might have influenced his inability to sign an oath that would have resolved his predicament and allowed him to return home.

It is also clear that Eltinge's ambiguousness was considered a substantial threat; otherwise, he would not have been removed from the area whenever the possibility of British invasion increased. This highlights a different dimension of the activities of committees in relation to the Loyalists from that suggested by Jonathan Clark, who states that their primary goal was "to enforce a patriotic consensus" within the community by requiring that suspicious individuals "choose between acting like Patriots and silent acquiescence."[62] Unfortunately, pretending to be a revolutionary and/or keeping one's mouth shut would not have been sufficient to satisfy the Patriots. Even if oaths were taken by those whose actions suggested a Loyalist mentality, "Many participants remarked upon the difficulty of knowing who had sworn the oath with conviction, and who was simply being pragmatic in order to save his property or his skin."[63] Because those of ambiguous allegiance—many of whom did take an oath of allegiance—were still feared as potentially active Tories, the committees were additionally required to deal with the silent threat that they posed.

It is difficult to compare Eltinge's experience with that of others whose political allegiance was unclear, as there is little modern research on the subject other than that which concerns key figures, or the experience of Tories in general. But certainly Eltinge would not have been alone. In Poughkeepsie, Clark contends that 130 out of the 239 residents whose allegiance can be sufficiently determined were not fully supportive of the Patriot cause, although the level of their support (or lack thereof) varied.[64] He also states that "Perhaps the most unjustly treated victims of patriotic justice were men who belonged . . . in one of the 'occasional' categories."[65] This is likely because they were seen as unknown quantities and therefore unpredictable. As to the experience of Loyalists, or suspected Loyalists, after the war, Alexander Flick contends that nonbelligerents were generally accepted back into their communities, although not always fully forgiven.[66] Clark's investigation suggests a similar postwar treatment in Poughkeepsie, possibly because "Ties to family, to farms, and to the community . . . proved to a surprising extent stronger than political causes," although they were excluded from political affairs.[67] Eltinge was apparently successfully reintegrated, possibly more so than many in similar circumstances in Poughkeepsie, but this might have been because the affairs of New Paltz were heavily influenced by the original founding families through the organization known as "The Twelve Men," and Eltinge was the dominant member of the line of patentee Abraham DuBois. As long as his family accepted him, he would retain a position in the community.

Even though Eltinge's experience was far from unique, his story is rare for its completeness given his social standing. It demonstrates the sticky issue of allegiance, both in its time and in retrospect, as well as the motivations of a suspicious community in an anxious time. While those in the higher ranks of society were involved in an ideological struggle to understand how, and if, the colonies should remain attached to Great Britain, there were many in the middle ranks whose allegiance—although not always without philosophical foundations—was also determined by small-town politics, familial animosities, suspicion, and pride.

Notes

1. Robert M. Calhoon, *The Loyalists in Revolutionary America, 1760–1781* (New York: Harcourt Brace Jovanovich, 1973), 300.

2. William H. Nelson, *The American Tory* (Oxford: Oxford University Press, 1961), 5.

3. Calhoon, xii.

4. Nelson, 41.

5. Nelson, 43–45; Philip Ranlett, *The New York Loyalists* (Knoxville: University of Tennessee Press, 1986), 10–25.

6. Ranlett, 26–51.

7. Robert Benson, "To Aaron Burr," 2 Aug. 1778, Matthew L. Davis, ed. *Memoirs of Aaron Burr* (New York: Da Capo, 1971), 131.

8. Michael Kammen, "The American Revolution as a *Crise de Conscience:* The Case of New York," in Richard M. Jellison, ed., *Society, Freedom, and Conscience: The Coming of the Revolution in Virginia, Massachusetts, and New York* (New York: Norton, 1976), 125–89.

9. Both British and American authorities of the period felt that New York was rife with Loyalist sympathizers. Most modern histories follow the lead of A. Flick who contended that half of all New Yorkers were against the Patriot cause [*Loyalism in New York During the American Revolution* (1901; New York: Arno Press, 1969), 180–182]. Most historians who followed Flick accepted his analysis until Ranlett questioned this accepted view in his 1986 reevaluation of the issue [*The New York Loyalists*]. He suggests that "New York was probably similar to the other revolutionary states in its degree of loyalism" (186–7). The issue of Tory strength in New York is sticky at best and irresolvable at worst, since it would have been almost impossible to determine allegiance of many at the time, let alone hundreds of years hence.

10. Alexander Flick, *Loyalism in New York During the American Revolution*, 71.

11. University of the State of New York, Division of Archives and History, *The American Revolution in New York: its Political, Social and Economic Significance* (Albany: The University of the State of New York, 1926), 225.

12. Calhoon, 410.

13. Calhoon, 304–5.

14. Ranlett, 162.

15. The only extensive group of documents related to a local committee are those of the Albany Committee.

16. Jonathan Clark, "The Problem of Allegiance in Revolutionary Poughkeepsie," in David D. Hall, John M. Murrin, and Thad W. Tate, eds., *Saints & Revolutionaries: Essays on Early American History* (New York: Norton, 1984), 285–317.

17. Ralph LeFevre, *History of New Paltz and its Old Families* (Albany: Fort Orange Press, 1903), 487.

18. The archives of the Huguenot Historical Society and Senate House (Kingston, New York) contain a great deal of information about Roeloff Josiah's financial activities, but these have yet to be fully studied.

19. Roeloff Eltinge's paternal grandmother was Sara DuBois, daughter of Abraham DuBois (1657–1731), one of the holders of the patent of New Paltz. Also, his mother was Magdalena DuBois, his father's first cousin. As there were several men with the name of Abraham DuBois alive in 1776, the familial relationship between Eltinge and this Abraham DuBois is unclear.

20. Hugh Flick, "The Rise of the Revolutionary Committee System," in *History of the State of New York"* (New York: Columbia University Press, 1933) III, 232.

21. Quoted in H. Flick, 230. However, Seabury's analysis cannot be entirely trusted because his staunch loyalism might have clouded his perceptions. Additionally, in his desire to discredit the revolutionaries, he might have overstated his case.

Kenneth Shefsiek

22. A. Flick, 67.

23. According to his parole of June 17, 1777, he had been "confined since last Fall." Additionally, his diary attests to his leaving Fishkill on December 3, 1776. *Roeloff and Ezekiel Eltinge Family Papers*, Huguenot Historical Society, New Paltz, N.Y.

24. LeFevre, 485. While this supposed feud is a matter of folklore, it is said in New Paltz today that animosity extended well into the twentieth century.

25. Abraham Hasbrouck resigned his position as commander of the Ulster Fourth Regiment because he had been passed over for generalship in favor of George Clinton. The return of his commission was described as "childish" by the provincial government [quoted in Marius Schoonmaker, *The History of Kingston, New York* (New York: Burr Printing House, 1888), 175].

26. Prisoners were also sent to Connecticut, Massachusetts, and Pennsylvania.

27. New York State, Commission for Detecting and Defeating Conspiracies, 1777–78. *Minutes of the Committee and of the First Commission for Detecting and Defeating Conspiracies in the State of New York* Minutes of Committee, October 13, 1776, The New-York Historical Society, *Collections* (New York, 1918), 414.

28. Lt. Col. Welch was an officer of New Hampshire who had been assigned to New York by Washington and was made responsible for removing the prisoners to New Hampshire. It is not clear from the Minutes exactly to whom Welch had been assigned, but he had a great deal of interaction with the Committee of Conspiracies in 1776–7.

29. Receipt of February 15, 1777 from Roeloff Eltinge to Joseph Stacy of the Exeter Gaol. *Eltinge Papers*.

30. Meshach Weare, President of the Council of New Hampshire, "To William Duer, Chairman of the Committee for Conspiracies," December 27, 1776, *Minutes of the Committee . . . Defeating Conspiracies*, 417–418.

31. Commissioners for Conspiracies, "To the Honourable Committee of Safety of New Hampshire." March 13, 1777, *Minutes of the Committeee . . . for Defeating Conspiracies*, 433–5.

32. Eugene Fingerhut suggests in *Survivor: Cadwallader Colden II in Revolutionary America* (Washington, University Press of America, 1983), 27, that the two might have become acquainted while involved in court cases in Kingston in the previous years, when Colden served as a judge. Their first recorded meeting of a personal nature occurred on June 18, 1777, when Eltinge was paroled and left several items, including eating and cooking utensils, in the care of Colden, who remained incarcerated on the prison ships. *Eltinge Papers*.

33. Fingerhut, 40.

34. Quoted in A. Flick, 97.

35. Peter DuBois was Roeloff Josiah Eltinge's third cousin. Walter DuBois is not identified in the published DuBois family genealogy.

36. Cited in Fingerhut, 44.

37. Fingerhut, 92.

38. *Eltinge Papers*.

39. It is not clear if Eltinge returned to Van Deusen's house in Hurley with Colden or if he returned to Hardenburgh's, also in Hurley. His diary simply states "went to Hurley again."

40. *Eltinge Papers*.

41. *Eltinge Papers*.

42. *Eltinge Papers*.

43. Quoted in Fingerhut, 88.

44. *Eltinge Papers*.

45. Fingerhut, 92.

46. *Eltinge Papers*.

47. In his diary, he recorded that he was to report on July 30. *Eltinge Papers*.

48. William Smith, Jr. (1728–1793) was a prominent lawyer and historian who had been appointed to his father's seat in the Governor's Council in 1767 and subsequently served as Chief Justice of the Province of New York (appointed in 1780 by the royal governor during the British occupation of New York). He left for Canada after the British evacuation of New York City and was appointed Chief Justice of Quebec in 1786. While Smith was also banished from the State of New York for refusing to take the oath of allegiance, and while he was adamantly against independence, he was also staunchly opposed to parliamentary taxation and was for the "cause of truth and liberty," as he stated in the first issue of his 1752 weekly, *The Independent Reflector* [as quoted in William Sabine, introduction, *Historical Memoirs of William Smith from 12 July 1776 to 25 July 1778* (Hollis, N.Y.: Colburn & Tegg, 1958), 2–3]. He was a close colleague of many other patriot radicals, including

John Morin Scott, the Livingstons (to whom his wife belonged), and Alexander McDougall.

49. *Minutes of the Committee . . . Defeating Conspiracies,* 11.

50. Eltinge's diary indicates that he loaned Solomon six half guineas in April 1781, and two letters written from New Jersey in September 1783 and January 1784 state that they were together there pending the decision regarding their being allowed to return to New York. Roeloff had additional contact with his family during his exile; his wife, Maria, visited him in the company of Mrs. Colden, who was given permission to visit her husband in April 1781 for a total of 11 days. Eltinge's eldest son, Ezekiel, who was eighteen years of age, began the journey with his mother but was sent home when the American General William Heath detained their sloop at West Point. Additionally, when the general found "a quantity of provisions . . . over and above what appeared necessary to support the families on their way to the enemy," he seized the goods and put them in the public stores [New York State. *Public Papers of George Clinton,* (New York and Albany: State of New York, 1899–1914) VI, 756].

51. A piggin, or pipkin, is a small wooden vessel with a handle. A "stove" probably refers to a footstove or footwarmer. A "kooler" might refer to a wooden vessel for cooling wine, and a canteen is a type of wooden keg. While Eltinge's account book does not definitively state that he made these objects himself, it is quite likely that he did; if he was serving as a middleman, he would probably have dealt in a greater variety of objects.

52. *Eltinge Papers.*

53. *Eltinge Papers.*

54. *Eltinge Papers.*

55. Fingerhut, 125.

56. A. Flick, 165.

57. Eric Roth, "Finding Aid, Elting Family Papers," Huguenot Historical Society Archives. The Twelve Men was a quasi-governmental organization in New Paltz that was charged with the administration of the land patent received in 1678 by the twelve founders of the town. Organized in 1728, the Twelve Men were primarily involved in dividing land in the early years, but by the 1790s they were generally only responsible for resolving disputes concerning land titles. They were elected by the freeholders of the town, with each man serving as the representative of the share of one of the original twelve patentees. Only a person descending from an original patentee could represent the share of his ancestor, in this case, Louis DuBois, Roeloff Eltinge's great-great-grandfather.

58. Abraham Hasbrouck, a supporter of the Coetus, forced the domine (the minister) of the Kingston church to take an oath of allegiance to the King, which he felt would nullify any connection between the American churches and the Classis since the oathtaker would be forced to declare "that no foreign prince, person, prelate, State or potentate had, or ought to have, any jurisdiction, power, superiority, dominion or authority ecclesiastical or spiritual within this realm" (quoted in Schoonmaker, 216). It was later determined that Abraham Hasbrouck had no right to administer an oath.

59. D. Veersteeg, *Records of the Reformed Dutch Church of New Paltz, N.Y.* (New York: Knickerbocker Press, 1896) 9. If they felt that they were too far from Kingston to worship, that would have been the case even prior to the internal disputes, thus suggesting that they had been previously attending the New Paltz church without becoming official members.

60. The last two elections are recorded on a single sheet of paper, rather than in a book or other such longer document, suggesting haphazard record keeping. It is possible that there were additional elections for which no records survive.

61. Randall Balmer, *A Perfect Babel of Confusion: Dutch Religion and English Culture in the Middle Colonies* (New York: Oxford University Press, 1989), 147.

62. Clark, 306.

63. Kammen, *Crise,* 156.

64. Clark, 296. Clark created four categories of allegiance: Patriot, Loyalist, Occasional Patriot, and Occasional Loyalist. He states that "While another investigator might, in a very few instances, decide to assign to an individual an allegiance slightly different from the one I assigned, the general conclusions regarding allegiance would, I am confident, still stand" (310). Clark probably would have categorized Eltinge as a Loyalist, considering that he refused an oath. But as we have seen, Eltinge's allegiance is questionable. Using Clark's categories, I would define him as an "Occasional Loyalist."

65. Clark, 306.

66. A. Flick, 165.

67. Clark, 309.

This article originally appeared in *The Hudson River Valley Review* Volume 20.1, Summer 2003.

Robert R. Livingston, Jr.:
The Reluctant Revolutionary

Claire Brandt

Robert R. Livingston, Jr. was a member of an extraordinary generation of American statesmen, a generation which included, among others, Thomas Jefferson, John Adams, James Madison, George Washington, and John Jay. It is to their breadth of mind, erudition, foresightedness, dedication, and courage that the success of the American Revolution may be largely ascribed.

Most of these political and military midwives, who supervised the delivery of our infant nation during a long and hazardous labor, were very young at the onset. Thomas Jefferson turned thirty-three the year he wrote the Declaration of Independence; and that same year, 1776, Madison turned twenty-five, John Jay thirty-one, and Robert R. Livingston, Jr., of New York, thirty.

The name of Robert R. Livingston, Jr. does not, of course, usually appear with these others on the standard list of America's founding fathers. Anywhere outside the Hudson Valley, the inclusion of his name is generally greeted with "Robert Who?" But here today, in the Hudson Valley, and in the process of examining the Livingston family's role in American history, we may choose to ask a different about Robert: Why did this man, so eminently qualified, so strategically positioned, and so highly motivated, fail to gain a place in his country's pantheon of revolutionary demigods?

Chancellor Livingston was unquestionably a man of accomplishment, and the present inquiry is intended neither to deny nor to diminish those accomplishments. In fact, our investigation may result in a better appreciation of his real achievements—a clearer vision of what the Chancellor was by delineating what he was not.

Unfortunately, these are very muddy waters—due, in part, to a bad habit we all have of answering the question "Robert Who?" by citing, first and foremost, Robert's membership on the committee that drafted the Declaration of Independence. We do that, of course, because the committee is instantly recognizable; it is an efficient way to put Robert on the historical map. The trouble is that we are also, at least by implication, claiming a distinction for Robert that does not belong to him. We all know that Robert neither wrote nor edited a word of the document. Most modern historians have concluded that he was appointed to the committee simply in order to get the name of a prominent New Yorker attached to the Declaration, thereby forcing the faction-torn New York Provincial Assembly into a firm commitment to independence. Robert was a pawn in a political maneuver, and he served on the committee not because of his eloquence and erudition (which he had in good measure), but because he was a delegate from a colony that could not make up its mind. Yet his membership on that committee has come to be his principal claim to fame. He is best known, even in his own family, for something he did not really do.

This is both ironic and emblematic. It is ironic because in the process of magnifying Robert's national historical significance, we often minimize his real accomplishments—or at least put them badly out of focus. It is emblematic because this tendency to overinflate Robert—to try to turn him into something he wasn't—is a tendency to which he himself consistently yielded.

Robert R. Livingston, Jr. was unlucky enough to be born into what the old Chinese curse calls "interesting' times." He graduated from King's College in June of 1765, only a few weeks after the promulgation of the Stamp Act, and his commencement oration was aptly entitled "On Liberty." But what he and most of the rest of his family, including his father, Judge Robert R. Livingston, Sr., meant by liberty in 1765 was not independence for the American colonies but rather a return to the *status quo ante*, before traditional colonial rights had been usurped by the terms of the Stamp, Currency, and Sugar Acts. These conservative Whigs stood firm against independence at this stage not just because of its short-term dangers, but, much more important, because they firmly believed it was contrary to the best long-term interests of the thirteen colonies. Instead, they sought—and fought for, in a whole series of extra-legal congresses and committees during the decade leading up to the war—the restoration of their traditional rights as British citizens.

As late as May 1775, a month *after* colonial lives had been lost at Lexington and Concord, Judge Robert R. Livingston wrote to his son at the Second Continental Congress in Philadelphia, "Every good man wishes that America might *remain* free [emphasis added]: in this I join heartily; at the same time I do not desire, she should be wholly independent of the mother country. How to reconcile their jarring principles, I profess I am altogether at a loss."[1] For the judge, as for many patriotic colonials, the notion of an independent America was never the greater good, only the lesser evil. They were extremely reluctant revolutionaries.

What disquieted them as much as the act of insurrection itself was the stated political goal of the American revolt: the establishment of a democratic republic. Democracy was not a congenial concept to Judge Robert R. Livingston, Sr. or to his son. They did not share the faith of Thomas Jefferson in the virtue and educability of the people. Quite the contrary, they regarded the masses as irresponsible, immoderate, and injudicious—an attitude which they and other members of their family came by quite naturally, after three generations of exercising political power in the Province of New York and social and economic power in the manorial world of the Hudson Valley.

New York had been founded in the mid-seventeenth century as a commercial colony. From the outset, its goals and values were commercial and its politics, quite unabashedly, were the politics of self-interest. During the Leisler interlude of the 1680s and New York's political picture was further disfigured by the stain of social snobbery. By 1765, when the first pre-revolutionary crisis hit the colony, New York was politically divided into two passionately opposed parties: the so-called "merchant faction," led by the powerful family of New York City, and the party of the upriver landed aristocracy, dominated by the Livingstons. These parties disagreed not so much on policy, or even goals, as they did on pedigree. The DeLanceys were descended from a supporter of New York's one-time self-appointed Lieutenant Governor, Jacob Leisler, a man whom Robert Livingston, the first manor proprietor, had called "ye vulgar sort."[2] Because the parties' differences were social and personal rather than ideological, members of both were perfectly capable of shifting ground when the occasion demanded. (As Philip Livingston, the second manor proprietor, put it, "We Change Sides as Serves our Interest best.")[3] In addition, the parties themselves veered from one end of the ideological spectrum to the other in the interest of expedience—a phenomenon amply demonstrated by the following capsule summary of the political events of the late 1760s.

Claire Brandt

In 1765, concurrent with the Stamp Act riots in New York City, there occurred a tenant uprising in the Hudson Valley which directly threatened both the life and property of Robert Livingston, the third manor proprietor. The proprietor's Clermont cousin, Judge Robert R. Livingston, was appalled not only by the affrontery of the insurgents but also by the fact that, after the uprising was quelled by British troops and its leader, William Prendergast, convicted and sentenced to death, he was granted a full pardon by His Majesty George King of England. This, coming so soon after the contretemps with His Majesty over the Stamp Act, was naturally received by the Livingstons and their fellow landed conservatives as a humiliating royal slap in the face. Their sovereign, whom they had always regarded as their natural ally against the forces of domestic radicalism, had finally, publicly, slammed the door in their faces. When they turned to look for new allies among their own countrymen, they discovered an unpleasant truth. While they had been preoccupied with the tenant uprising and with the Stamp Act congresses, their committees and their moderate addresses to the king, the political opposition had been busy in the streets. The DeLancey party, recognizing the potential of the newly aroused populace of New York, had successfully wooed the radical leadership and manipulated its followers in order to control votes. It was all quite cynical: the DeLanceys were no more dedicated to the radical cause than were the Livingston (even less, as it turned out). But they did recognize an electoral bonanza when they saw one, and they mined it with ruthless ingenuity.

In a series of stunning electoral victories between 1767 and 1770, the DeLancey party assumed political control of the Province of New York, and in the process confirmed all the conservatives' fears about the baseness of popular politics. In pursuit of votes, they employed all the time-honored political techniques: oversimplification of issues, concoction of scapegoats, and inflammatory catchwords, not to mention intimidation, bribery, and titillation. Exploiting their party's merchant origins and urban orientation, they depicted the Livingstons as aloof highbrows and would-be intellectuals lolling on their vast country acres. In one election, they attacked the entire legal profession, largely because of the prominence and popularity of Judge Livingston and his cousin William. In another they exploited the issue of religion, depicting all Anglicans as snobs and royalists, in contrast to the Presbyterians as men of the people. They even tried to defame a Livingston political ally, John Morin Scott, as a homosexual; one of their political broadsides read: "[He] dances with, and *kisses (filthy beast!)* those of his own sex."[4]

The Livingstons and their allies naturally fought back, indulging in a little mud slinging of their own. But they didn't have their hearts in it; and by the end of the campaign of 1770, the DeLanceys and their allies were firmly established as the political darlings of the crowd and undisputed masters of the Provincial Assembly. It was from this unassailable position that they were able to unseat from the assembly both the popular Judge Livingston and his powerful cousin Philip, leaving the family unrepresented in the assembly for the first time since Livingston Manor had been given its seat, fifty-four years before. The judge, deprived of his voice and vote at a time when his country's fate was hanging in the balance, suffered what he called "melancholy and dejection;" and he concluded sorrowfully, "This country appears to have seen its best days."[5]

Within a few years, however, the situation had reversed itself, in a preposterous sequence that went roughly as follows. After the death of Governor Sir Henry Moore in 1769, the new acting governor, Cadwallader in an attempt to ape his sovereign, withdrew gubernatorial support from the upriver landlords—the Livingston party—and in the process perforce allied himself with the opposition. This meant that the DeLanceys, in order to capitalize on his support, had to endorse his measures in the assembly, even unpopular legislation such as a 2,000 appropriation bill for the provisioning of British troops in New York City. The Livingstons naturally exploited these issues to wean the populace away from the DeLancey party but then, in order to solidify their gains with the voters, found themselves toeing the popular line on almost every issue.

This is, of course, an oversimplified description of a very complex shift. Suffice it to say that after the political seesaw tilted once again, the Livingston and DeLancey parties found themselves at the opposite ends of the political spectrum from where they had started, with the Livingstons, perhaps to their own surprise as much as anyone else's, holding down the left. If this seems unlikely, just remember that this was New York, where politics was practiced with mirrors, and logic, loyalty, and principle stood regularly on end in obeisance to power.

It was in this political tradition that Robert R. Livingston, Jr. was raised, so perhaps it is understandable that he should instinctively distrust the people as a political force. He shared the desire of his colleague, Thomas Jefferson, for the people, but good government by the people was, to him, a self-contradiction. He was not alone in this; many of his contemporaries—including some of our more eminent founding fathers—distrusted the people. What set Robert apart—and what finally prevented him from achieving preeminence in the political democracy his colleagues created—was that he lacked not only the head for democracy but also the stomach. His disdain for the people was both intellectual and visceral. He harbored a deeply felt, personal aversion to the people—an aversion that was a strong element of Livingston family tradition, bred into the family's collective subconscious as part of the manorial experience.

The Hudson Valley society into which Robert was born had almost as much in common with European fifteenth-century medieval society as it did with the eighteenth-century European Enlightenment. His perception of the character of the people was inevitably colored by his family's traditional perception of the tenants of Livingston Manor—a perception which had gotten off to a bad start, three generations before the Chancellor was born, when the relationship between his great-grandfather, the manor's founder, and a group of Palatine refugees ran on the rocks of greed, wishful thinking, and ineptitude. Their story has been told elsewhere in all its heartrending detail, and I will not repeat it here. By the end of it, the first proprietor of the manor had reached the conclusion that his Palatine tenants were, to a man and woman, nothing more than shiftless parasites, out to bleed the Livingston family and its resources to death. He called them (among other things) "worse than northern savages"[6]—which, in the context of the bloody French and Indian Wars, was probably the worst thing he could think to say about them.

This profound suspicion of the tenantry, laced with fervent contempt, was inevitably passed along to the next generation of Livingstons, and the next, until in the family vocabulary tenant came to mean parasite, and the people became synonymous with scoundrels. An examination of Livingston descriptive language over several generations leaves little doubt of the validity of this conclusion. One good example is the second manor proprietor's injunction to his son: "Our people are hoggish and brutish [;] they must be humbld."[7] And in the next generation, Walter Livingston simply categorized the tenantry as "Pests of Society."[8]

Naturally, the feeling was mutual. One of the third manor proprietor's tenants, escaping capture by his lordship's constables during a tenant uprising, yelled over his shoulder as he ran into the woods, "Robert Livingston: Kiss his ass!"[9]

In this context, Robert R. Livingston, assessment a few years later seems quite moderate. In 1779 he wrote, "From habit & passion I love and pity my fellow creatures would to God I could esteem them."[10]

The Chancellor's misgivings about his fellow men were not alleviated by the demeanor of the Livingston tenantry during the Revolutionary War. In 1775, when the Articles of Association were circulated, Robert informed his friend, John Jay, that "many of our Tenants here refused to sign . . . and [have] resolved to stand

Claire Brandt

by the King . . . . [But] since troops have been raised changed their battery."[11] Later in the war, bands of Tory tenants roamed the valley; and Robert's mother, Margaret Beekman Livingston, reported, "Some say their number is 4000 . . . . They have taken a Congress Member. . . and carried him off to no one knows where, they have three boxes of gun powder that has been sent to them by some as bad as themselves."[12]

That letter was written on July 6, 1776, two days after the final draft of the Declaration of Independence had been sent to the printer in Philadelphia. Robert R. Livingston, Jr. was already on his way back to New York to steer ratification of the declaration through the torn Provincial Assembly. The assembly managed without him, however. Acting expeditiously for perhaps the first and only time, it approved the declaration after one morning of debate; and Robert, arriving days later, was permitted to contribute nothing, not even his vote. Having thus forfeited this mark of distinction in the history books of his home state, he proceeded to lose his rightful place on his country's most exclusive roll of honor. Becoming engrossed in urgent business at home, he was unable to return to Philadelphia in time to sign the declaration, a ceremony which took place (popular legend notwithstanding) on August 2. His cousin Philip was there to give the seal of approval, and he is known in the family to this day as "Philip the signer." Robert's posterity, on the other hand, has had to be content with the inadvertent, but devastatingly accurate, designation on a plaque in the town of Rhinebeck, where he is memorialized as

Robert R. Livingston
Draftee of the Declaration of Independence

Despite his increasing concern, even abhorrence, at the democratic complexion of his newly independent country, Robert R. Livingston, Jr. served both the nation and his state with great steadfastness and personal courage throughout the war. During late 1776 and early 1777 he labored unceasingly, at considerable personal risk, to secure the defenses of New York State, particularly of the Hudson Valley, the military key to the war. (He was rewarded by having his magnificent new Hudson River mansion burned to the ground in October 1777, during the British army's only successful foray into the valley.) Concurrently, he served on the committee to draft New York State's first constitution. A predictably conservative document—penned largely by John Jay, with Robert's assistance—it was accepted by the constitutional convention at Poughkeepsie only after considerable amendment from the floor, engineered by a large group of delegates from the new political class: mechanics, small farmers, and country lawyers. Observing the process, Robert complained to his friend Edward Rutledge,

> "In this state we are to form a government under which we are to spend the remainder of our lives, without that influence that is derived from respect to old families wealth age are to contend with the envy of some, the love of power in others who would debase the government as the only means of exalting themselves and above all with that mixture of jealousy and cunning into which Genius long occupied in trifles generally degenerates when unimproved by education and unrefined by honor. . . . I am sick of politics and power, I long for more refined pleasures, conversation and friendship. I am weary of crowds and pine for solitude nor would in my present humor give one scene of Shakespeare for one thousand . . . Lockes, Sidneys and Adams to boot. If without injuring my country I could once return to my own farm and fireside, I aver, I would not change any situation to be Great Mogul or President of the Congress."[3]

Unfortunately for Robert's peace of mind, the latter was not true. He hungered for recognition, fame, and power; so despite his revulsion, he stayed on.

To Robert's horror, the winner of the New York gubernatorial election a few months later, over the patrician Philip Schuyler, was George Clinton, a country lawyer and the son of a farmer. Meanwhile, the tenants of the Hudson Valley had staged an uprising in support of the British army which, although easily quashed, nonetheless confirmed the Livingstons' perception of their tenants as ungrateful, un-reliable, and shortsighted. Robert's mother may have summed up the family attitude best when, in a New Year's greeting to her son, she prayed for "Peace and Independence and deliverance from the persecutions of the Lower Class."[4]

Robert R. Livingston, Jr. became his country's first Secretary for Foreign Affairs in 1781; but within a year of taking office he had reached the conclusion that the position was not commensurate with his political abilities and social standing, so he resigned. The implications of this action, as well as the motives behind it, did not escape his political colleagues—men such as George Washington, John Adams, and Thomas Jefferson, who would become the first three presidents of the United States of America. Robert's now firmly established reputation for pride, disdain, and ambivalence probably cost him the high positions in their administrations which he felt he deserved. Robert was not only unprepared to share power with the *hoi polloi*, he was even more squeamish about submitting himself to their political judgment as a candidate for public office. Yet at the same time, he hungered for eminence at the national level. Torn between ambition and repugnance, poor Robert never satisfactorily sorted out his muddled set of goals, motives, and loyalties. It was perhaps nature's little joke to have given him one blue eye and one brown.

Robert's inevitable frustration at not receiving the recognition he thought he deserved soon began to express itself in behavior that was petty, foolish, transparent, and utterly self-defeating. For example, shortly after administering the oath of office to George Washington at the first presidential inauguration in April 1789, Robert conceived a burning notion that a major post in Washington's first cabinet was his due. During the early weeks of the new administration, he and his sister, Janet Montgomery, waged a strenuous behind-the-scenes campaign to secure one of the coveted places. But although President Washington solicited Robert's advice on a variety of matters, the expected offer of a cabinet post did not ensue. Finally, Robert swallowed his pride and applied to Washington directly, letting it be known that he preferred one of two offices: Secretary of the Treasury or Chief Justice of the Supreme Court. The president's reply to his letter was swift, tactful, and devastating:

> "When I accepted of the important trust committed to my charge by my Country, I gave up every idea of personal gratification that I did not think was compatible with the public good. . . . However strong my personal attachment might be to anyone—however desirous I might be of giving a proof of my friendship— and whatever might be his expectations, grounded upon the amity, which had subsisted between us, I was fully determined to keep myself free from every engagement that could embarrass me in discharging this part of my administration."[5]

The depths of Robert's disappointment and humiliation are easily measured. Within a year he had launched a vicious public attack on the man who had received the job of Chief Justice, his one-time bosom friend, John Jay; and he had taken himself and the entire Clermont branch of the Livingston family out of the Federalist party and into an alliance with its political foes. This put him in the ridiculous position a few years later of supporting George Clinton for governor of New York, not because of any personal enthusiasm for the farmer's son but because his opponent, the Federalist candidate, was John Jay. A sixteen-page diatribe entitled "John Jay Exposed for What He Is" appeared over Robert's name. The Clinton victory (a highly questionable one, after the votes from two large Federalist districts were invalidated on a technicality) must have been a bittersweet triumph for Chancellor Robert R. Livingston.

During the next decade, as Jay went from triumph to triumph at the national level, Robert continued to serve as chancellor of New York State. He refused President Washington's invitation to become minister to France in 1794; and five years later, when he was nominated to run for governor of New York against Jay, he waged only the most perfunctory of campaigns and lost by the largest majority in the state's history.

Throughout this period, he professed to find entirely satisfactory the life of an enlightened eighteenth-century gentleman. In 1793 he began construction of a new and elegant mansion at Clermont. He read the classics. He studied mechanics, particularly steam propulsion, and formed a partnership with his brother-in-law to build a prototype steam vessel in the North Bay near Tivoli. He studied botany and conducted experiments in agriculture, horticulture, and animal husbandry. He wrote public papers and corresponded extensively with other members of an elite transatlantic fraternity of like-minded intellectuals, including Arthur Young and William Strickland. His literary output during this period is remarkable for both its volume and variety, as demonstrated by the following representative titles: "Reflections on Peace, War and Trade;" "Thoughts on Lime and Gypsum;" "Reflections on the Site of the National Capital;" "Complaint on the Postal Service;" "The Use of Ashes and Pyrite as Manure;" "Reflections on Monarchy" (written in 1793 in response to the guillotining of Louis XVI); "Notes on Alkali;" "Thoughts on Coinage and the Establishment of a Mint;" "On the Fine Arts;" a plan regarding "the discovery of the Interior parts of this Continent establishing the Indian trade in that Quarter;" "Notes on Winds;" and many, many others. His name was known and esteemed in the fraternity of learned men as well as in judicial and legal circles, where his performance on the bench drew continued regard.

It was not enough, of course—not for a spirit in which inner contentment was so dependent on outward acclaim. Living the private life that he professed to find ideal, Robert burned when others' public lives outshone it.

In 1801, Robert accepted President Thomas Jefferson's appointment as minister to France. His primary diplomatic objective—negotiating United States purchase of West Florida and the Port of New Orleans—quickly bogged down in French bureaucratic red tape and the whims of First Consul Napoleon Bonaparte (whom Janet Montgomery dubbed "the Wary Corsican.")[16] None of this was Robert's fault. Nevertheless, in 1803, President Jefferson dispatched James Monroe to Paris as a special envoy to get the negotiations back on track. Within forty-eight hours of Monroe's arrival in the capital, Napoleon summoned the two American diplomats to his presence and stunned them with an offer to sell not only New Orleans but the whole of the Louisiana Territory, a tract of some 825,000 square miles, whose acquisition would double the size of the United States. Livingston and Monroe, with no instructions from home, took a deep breath and accepted, and the formal agreement was drafted and signed within a fortnight.

It was a diplomatic coup of major dimensions—a political jewel to fit nicely into Robert Livingston's well-earned crown—except that his cursed, battered pride rose up and knocked it away. After all his months of patient toil behind the scenes, Robert obviously felt up-staged by Monroe's dramatic entrance just before the end so he altered the dates in his official record book to indicate that Napoleon had offered to sell Louisiana three days earlier than he actually did, the morning before Monroe's arrival in Paris. To drive the point home, Robert leaked a "secret" memorandum to the same effect to the New York press.

The State Department in Washington issued a vigorous denial and then made public Robert's own official correspondence, which revealed the true timetable in his own handwriting. Public outrage was intense and long-lived. Robert's bungled lie cost him the credit he rightly deserved for negotiating the Louisiana Purchase, and it gave the coup de grace to his political reputation. It also cost him the position that he had ardently desired for years, the governorship of the State of New York. A few weeks before the scandal broke, his party, virtually assured of victory in the approaching election, had promised the nomination to Robert. Now the offer was withdrawn for good, and a few months later Robert learned that the post had gone to a man of distinctly inferior intellect and attainments, his own brother-in-law, Morgan Lewis.

When Robert returned to Clermont in the summer of 1805, it was easy for him to become embroiled in domestic details: his handsome house had to be enlarged to accommodate the new furniture and fittings he had purchased in France; he spent hours supervising the care of the merino sheep he had imported from the famous flock at Rambouillet; and he worked enthusiastically with Robert Fulton on the final stages of their steamboat, which made its triumphant maiden voyage in 1807, the year of Robert's sixtieth birthday. Two years later he published the charming "Essay on Sheep." He suffered a series of strokes in late 1812 and died at Clermont in February of 1813.

Back in 1768, when Robert was twenty-two years old, his father had written a letter to his mother as follows: "My son Robert must not live in the country, he has talents, if he will use them, to make a figure at the head of his profession, a farm would ruin him."[7]

In a way the farm did ruin him, although perhaps in ways that even his wise father had not imagined. It ruined him, in the first place, by elevating his expectations. Robert always assumed that, as a Livingston of Clermont, he would automatically achieve primacy in every undertaking. At the same time, "the farm"— Clermont effectively saw to that these dazzling prospects could never be fulfilled, by instilling in him a manorial attitude that was utterly out of place in the new republican America.

"The farm" also provided him with a refuge from disappointment. Clermont's attraction for Robert went far beyond its pastoral serenity and much deeper than the satisfaction he received from its socially redeeming intellectual activities—husbandry, botany, mechanics, etc. At Clermont he was utterly secure: his status there was guaranteed by his name. On "the farm," the lower orders kept their places, and nobody dared to visit on him the humiliations he experienced in the outside world. Because of "the farm," Robert expected perhaps more than was his due, but he ended by settling for less. The son of the manor was also its victim.

Notes

1   Robert R. Livingston to Robert R. Livingston, Jr., May 5, 1775. Livingston-Bancroft Transcriptions, Broadside Collection, Astor, Lenox and Tilden Foundations, The New York Public Library.

2   Letter from Robert Livingston, November 27, 1690. Livingston-Redmond Papers, F.D.R. Library, Hyde Park, New York.

3   Philip Livingston to Jacob Wendell, October 17, 1737. Livingston Papers, Museum of the City of New York.

4   Broadside Collection, New York Public Library.

5   Judge Robert R. Livingston to Robert R. Livingston, Jr., September 18, 1767, Livingston-Bancroft, op. cit.

6   Robert Livingston to Alida Livingston, May 3 1, 17 13. Lieurance Translation, Livingston-Redmond, op. cit.

7   Philip Livingston to Robert Livingston, Jr., June 1, 1745, Livingston-Redmond, op. cit.

8   Walter Livingston to Robert Livingston, December 29, 1766, Livingston-Redmond, op. cit.

9   E.B. O'Callaghan, *The Documentary History of the State of New-York* (Albany, N.Y.: Weed, Parson & Co., 1849–1851, 4vols.), Vol. III, p. 753

10   Robert R. Livingston, Jr. to John Jay, February 2, 1779. Robert R. Livingston Papers, New-York Historical Society.

11   Robert R. Livingston, Jr. to John Jay, quoted in Staughton Lynd, "The Tenant Rising at Livingston Manor, May 1777," *The New-York Historical Quarterly*, XLVIII, No. 2, April 1964, p. 167.

12 Margaret Beekman Livingston to Robert R. Livingston, Jr., July 6, 1776. Living-Family Papers, Broadside Collection, New York Public Library.

13 Robert R. Livingston, Jr. to Edward Rutledge, October 10, 1776. Bancroft, op. cit.

14 Margaret Beekman Livingston to Robert R. Livingston, Jr., December 30, 1779. Robert R. Livingston Papers, op. cit.

15 George Washington to Robert R. Livingston, Jr., May 31, 1789. Robert R. Livingston Papers, op. cit.

16 Janet Montgomery to General Horatio Gates, December 4, 1803. Collection, New York Public Library.

17 Robert R. Livingston to Margaret Beekman Livingston, January 11, 1768, quoted in E.B. Livingston, *of Manor* Supplement, handwritten manuscript, Clermont State Historic Site.

This article originally appeared in the *Hudson Valley Regional Review*, Volume 4.1, March, 1987.

"The women in this place have risen in a mob": Women Rioters and the American Revolution in the Hudson River Valley

Thomas S. Wermuth

Historians have long assessed the role of women as participants in pre-industrial riots. One of the most famous of these, of course, was the 1789 "March of the Fishwives" at the beginning of the French Revolution. The 1863 Confederate Bread Riots are another example. Less attention has been given to the role of women in American Revolutionary riots.[1] This essay examines the important role of Hudson Valley women in the crowd actions that characterized that era.

From the beginning of the war through the late 1770s, popular disturbances and crowd actions became a part of the social landscape in the Hudson Valley. Usually aimed at Tories, many of these actions were sanctioned, or at least tolerated, by the local governments or the popular committees that directed revolutionary activities.

Crowd actions were not peculiar to the Revolutionary period, nor were they specific to this region. Indeed, as historians like Natalie Davis, George Rude, and E.P. Thompson have pointed out, mass disturbances and riots were seen as acceptable resolutions to a community's social or economic problems in the early modern period.[2] Throughout the eighteenth century, crowds engaged in popular action served as quasi-official forces, sometimes with authority delegated by local governments, sometimes without. For example, in 1740 a Kingston "delegation" investigating an ongoing boundary dispute between Johannis Wynkoop and Christian Nedick was given the authority to "pull down his Fence" if "Wynkoop did not comply w/ the proposition they make to him." Others who threatened community standards, such as monopolizers or prostitutes, were threatened with "skimmington rides" and "charivaris" in Poughkeepsie, while residents representing more dangerous threats in Kingston and Saugerties witnessed the destruction of their property.[3]

These actions conform to the model described by historians of popular protest: A group of community residents act with "quasi-official" authority to address and redress a problem threatening their town or village. Classic examples of this in early America include crowds harassing price-gouging merchants, press gangs, or prostitutes.[4]

The number of such crowd actions increased substantially during the American Revolutionary period. This was true for several reasons. First, the official government was in disarray, leading townsfolk to take matters into their own hands more frequently than would have been the case under normal conditions. Second, the Revolution created a series of problems and threats—political, social, and economic—that had not existed earlier and that needed speedy resolution, and which official authorities seemed unable to resolve.

Some of the crowd actions were clearly political, as with the arrest of Loyalist Cadwallader Colden, Jr., son of the former acting governor, at his home near Newburgh. Acting on the authority of the local

William Hogarth's depiction of a riot in eighteenth-century England.

committee of safety, a "delegation" stormed his estate at midnight on June 21, 1776. The group searched and ransacked his house and ordered him arrested. Although the raiding party threatened him with the humiliating possibility that he would "be rode upon a rail" to the local jail if he did not accompany them willingly (a punishment traditionally reserved for prostitutes, wife abusers, or other community miscreants), he was ultimately arrested far less dramatically. Nevertheless, the threat to one of the most substantial men in the mid-Valley of such a fate—and Colden's apparent belief that the committee would make good on its threat—reveal the extent of the challenge to the existing social and political order.[5]

Shortly before the British invasion of New York City, crowds there seized Tories, rode them on rails, and stripped them of their clothes. In Albany, crowds made suspected Loyalists run a gauntlet, beating them as they ran.[6] Riots of this nature, aimed primarily at Tories, continued throughout the war.

Many other popular disturbances were not so well coordinated with local authorities and were aimed not at Loyalists but at resolving social and economic threats to the community. It is important to keep in mind the social and economic context in which these riots occurred. The day-to-day workings of village economies in the Hudson Valley were not left to the vagaries of the free market. Local town governments, as well as New York provincial authorities, enforced formal legislation or exerted informal community pressures that sought to encourage neighborly behavior and discourage any economic actions that might threaten the corporate body of the community. Old medieval injunctions against forestalling (withholding goods from the market in order to drive up prices) and engrossment (the monopolization of products destined for markets) remained on the law books throughout New York, although before the American Revolution they were irregularly enforced.[7]

Regulation of the local economy relied heavily on the force of community tradition. Where informal means proved insufficient, responsibility for balancing competing economic interests fell to the local gov-

Thomas S. Wermuth

erning boards. These policies generally reflected the communities' consensus of the primary importance of fostering a healthy agricultural trade. Nevertheless, local regulations—whether of prices, trading practices, or quality standards—were shaped as much by broad community concerns as by a desire to protect the interests of producers.

The government regulation that began with the original acts of incorporation in the seventeenth century carried into the early nineteenth. The charter of Kingston called for a public market, eventually located at Hendrick Sleght's, where the weights and measures were inspected, sellers and butchers licensed, financial exchanges supervised, flour and meat routinely inspected, and prices on various goods capped.[8] The towns of New Paltz and New Windsor set maximum prices on bread and salt, among other goods, and scrutinized wages as well. The regulation of prices and quality of goods continued well into the early nineteenth century in Kingston and Rochester, where the "assize of bread" was regularly posted. The assize listed the price and size of the normal loaf, and set these prices according to the price of local flour. It also ordered that "each loaf shall be marked with the initials of the Christian and surname of the baker."[9]

The Corporation of Kingston also kept wheat on hand in the common store for local use, with limits on the amount one could purchase, a ceiling on prices, and instructions for its use. This wheat, rye, and "indian corn" was sold at a further reduced rate to poorer residents, so long as it was to be used "for Bread" and not sold.[10] The trustees also regulated interest rates for money put out on loan, with six percent the maximum allowed to be charged within the town. Additionally, no more than five percent could be charged to the town's poor or to freeholders, but seven percent could be "Lett out upon Interest out of the Corporation." The trustees also lent money, usually to the poor or freeholders. However, the corporation mandated that "such persons as are able to let money out themselves, shall not have it unless they pay 8%."[11]

Thus social settings, personal relations, family and personal reputation, and even economic needs and demands that could not be met through commercial markets helped determine proper economic behavior.

During the economic crisis of the Revolution, shortages of necessary items (particularly bread and salt) were blamed on "ingrossing jockies," and high prices were believed to be the work of price-gouging merchants. As early as 1776, residents of Kingston and New Windsor took matters into their own hands when they felt that their elected officials were not going far enough in regulating the economy and prosecuting monopolizers.[12] The Ulster Committee reported in 1776 that "we are daily alarmed, and our streets filled with mobs." According to the committee, the situation had grown so desperate in Ulster that if the legislature could not solve the economic woes affecting the central valley, local committees would have to assume authority in the name "of the People at Large."[13] Kingston's Johannes Sleght appealed to the Provincial Congress for help, declaring that "mobs" were "breaking of doors, and committing of outrages."[14]

The years 1776 through 1779 witnessed regular boycotts, forced sales of necessary products, and riots in the mid-Hudson Valley. Many of the participants in these riots were women. The first of these occurred in Kingston in November 1776, when a crowd raided warehouses and stores, seizing tea. Two weeks later, one of Orange county's first families, the Ellisons of New Windsor, were the victims of a riot. A large crowd, composed of both men and women, came to William Ellison's store and, after accusing him of price-gouging and engrossment, it seized all the salt "except one bushel," which it left for the use of his family.[15]

Poughkeepsie-area shopkeeper Peter Messier suffered a crowd action in early 1777. Claiming that he was selling tea above the Poughkeepsie Committee's imposed price-cap, a crowd of women used their own weights and measures to weigh and distribute the tea among themselves. The women, accompanied by two Continental soldiers, offered Messier "their own price," which was considerably lower than his selling price.[16] The women returned twice more over the next several days to repeat these actions.

Two Albany merchants who had purchased tea in Philadelphia had the misfortune of sending it overland through New Windsor in 1777. A crowd of both "men and women" besieged the transporters and seized the load, asserting that it was being marketed at a higher price than the six-shilling limit set by the local committee. They then sold it to themselves at that price.

The New Windsor and Poughkeepsie riots reveal that the rioters drew upon the legitimacy of the local government in order to explain their own activities. The rioters at Ellison's store reminded the shopkeeper of the committee's price regulations, which he was allegedly breaking. The women who confiscated Messier's tea specifically stated that "they had orders from the Committee to search his house." However, it is important to point out that in each of these actions, the rioters exceeded the committee's dictates. Neither riot was authorized by the local authorities.[17]

The actions of the rioters in seizing foodstuffs reveal traditional economic beliefs that denied the role of an unregulated market during times of economic crisis. Further, these rioters questioned the very essence of private property when they seized goods, making clear their belief that a shopkeeper was not the only person who could decide what to do with his or her merchandise, and that the community had a legitimate voice in its distribution. What is remarkable is that during the Revolutionary War, these beliefs and activities became associated, even synonymous, with patriotic behavior. Those who participated in the riots claimed that by their actions they were revealing their loyalty to the cause, while their targets, such as William Ellison, were exhibiting signs of toryism.[18]

Also remarkable is that many of the rioters were women, who had no public or political role in the mid-Valley at this time, for voting, jury duty, and even unlimited control over property were denied to them. However, during the Revolution, women often took the lead in Hudson Valley riots. It was a crowd of women, for example, who first confronted New Windsor shopkeeper Mrs. Lawrence in 1777 for price gouging, and by so doing forced the committee to act. At another riot in New Windsor, a local observer complained to a tea merchant that "the women! in this place have risen in a mob, and are now selling a box of tea of yours [the owner] at 6s per lb." A store in Fishkill was raided by female relatives of the owner.[19]

The action of women in relation to economic controls was not limited only to seizures and crowd action. Women also made it clear that they would use their power as wives and mothers to halt the war effort if certain measures were not taken to regulate the economy. In August 1776, the women of Kingston surrounded the chambers of the committee of safety and demanded that if the food shortages were not resolved, "their husbands and sons shall fight no more."[20] In this way, these riots were not only protests against the economy; they had clear political implications as well. The site of the women's action was not the Kingston public market, nor a shopkeeper's warehouse, but the meeting house of the town's political authorities. It was not simply a symbolic location for the women to make their statement: it was the place where policy-makers met. And far from making threats of boycotts or disruptions, these women were warning of political action if their demands were not met.

Women tended to exert a public voice around those issues in which the needs of the domestic sphere crossed those of the public. The ability to get salt, tea, or flour at good prices fell firmly within the socially and culturally constructed gender roles of eighteenth-century America. Like their counterparts in the French Revolution, women's political action usually formed around issues of family and domestic concerns, particularly food and supplies.[21]

Generally, historians have agreed that women's participation in bread and food riots was based on their socially constructed gender roles as being responsible for providing food for their children. Also, as Natalie Davis has suggested for early modern France, women's participation could be excused by the fact that they were not viewed as responsible for their actions, and therefore could not be held accountable for their behavior. Since a riot was, at best, of questionable legality, those with limited legal and political roles could not be held fully responsible. English officials complained during the 1605 enclosure riots that women were "hiding behind their sex."[22]

Nevertheless, as E.P. Thompson has pointed out, women were primarily responsible for marketing, most sensitive to price fluctuations, and more likely to detect irregularities in sales or inferior products.[23] Women, therefore, would probably detect subtle price changes or questionable marketing practices and were more likely to act on them.

Notes

1. For a useful corrective, see Barbara Clark Smith, "Food Riots and the American Revolution," *William & Mary Quarterly* (1994), 3–30.

2. Natalie Davis, *Society and Culture in Early Modern France* (Stanord, 1975), 102–5; George Rude, *Ideology and Popular Protest* (New York, 1980), 27–37; E. P. Thompson, *Customs in Common* (New York 1993), 845–89.

3. "Kingston Trustees Minutes," May 14, 1740; 1721.

4. Gary Nash, *The Urban Crucible: Social Change, Political Consciousness, and the Origins of the American Revolution* (Cambridge, Mass., 1979), 77–78; Edward Countryman, *A People in Revolution: Political Society and the American Revolution in New York, 1760–1790*, (Baltimore, 1981), 37–45.

5. Cadwallader Colden Jr. to Ulster County Committee, June 27, 1776, in Force, *American Archives* 6:1112

6. Countryman, 170.

7. *Ibid*, 56–59.

8. "Kingston Trustee Minutes" July 27, 1753, describes the market at Hendrick Sleght's. Petrus Smedes was appointed the "first manager of the market." See "Kingston Trustees Minutes" Oct. 19, 1753, January 29, 1790, Ulster County Clerk's Office, for various aspects of market supervision.

9. "Kingston Trustees Minutes," April 12, 1779, U.C.C.O., "Kingston Directors Minutes," April 20, 1807, May 14, 1819, Kingston City Hall; Edmund Platt, *The Eagle's History of Poughkeepsie, 1683–1905* (Republished by Dutchess County Historical Society, Poughkeepsie, NY, 1987), 75.

10. For price ceilings on Corporation wheat see "Kingston Trustees Minutes," March 22, 1772, Feb. 6, 1785, Jan. 29, 1790. For restrictions on its use, see Feb, 19, 1790, U.C.C.O.

11. For regulation of usury see "Kingston Trustees Minutes," March 2, 1728, New York Historical Society. This rate was reduced to five percent in 1750, but raised back to six percent in 1752. "Kingston Trustees Minutes," Dec. 10, 1750, Nov. 8, 1752, U.C.C.O.; "Trustees Minutes," March 2, 1728, NYHS.

12. "Henry Ludington to New York Council of Safety, Dec. 3, 1776," *Journals of the Provincial Congress*, 2:355.

13. "Ulster County Committee to New York Convention," Nov. 18, 1776, *Journals of the Provincial Congress*, 2:229–230;

14. Clark Smith, "Food Riots and the American Revolution," *William & Mary Quarterly*, 15.

15. *Ibid*.

16. Correspondence of John Hathorn, Dec. 2, 1776 in Ruttenber, *History of New Windsor*, 67–68; Countryman, *People in Revolution*, 183.

17. Correspondence of John Hathorn, Dec. 2, 1776 in Ruttenber, *History of New Windsor*, 67.

18. For a discussion of the political implications of Revolutionary rioting, see Clark Smith, 5–12. For suspicions that Ellison was unpatriotic because of his economic dealings see "Boyd to Clinton, July 3, 1776," *Public Papers of George Clinton*, 10 vols. (Albany, 1899–1914), 1:244–47.

19. "James H. Kip to James Caldwell, New Windsor, July 14, 1777," *Journals of the Provincial Congress*, 506.; Clark Smith

20. New York Convention Proceedings, August 1776, in *American Archives*, 5th Series, 1:1542–43.

21. Linda Kerber, *Women of the Republic: Intellect and Ideology in Revolutionary America*, (New York, 1980), 44.

22. Davis, p.146

23. E.P. Thompson p. 234

This article originally appeared in *The Hudson River Valley Review*, Volume 20.1, Summer 2003.

Social and Economic Change: 1790–1850

The Struggle to Build a Free African-American Community in Dutchess County, 1790–1820

Michael Groth

Historians have traditionally regarded the Revolutionary and Early National periods as a watershed in African-American history and culture. The Great Awakening, the ideology of Revolution, and the experience of war struck a powerful blow against the institution of slavery, and the states of the North adopted measures which abolished slavery outright or set the institution on a course of extinction. Free men and women in the North and Upper South migrated to urban centers like Boston, New York, and Philadelphia in search of social and economic opportunity. The urban environment allowed African-Americans to reconstitute families, organize independent churches, establish benevolent societies, and achieve a modicum of economic success. Freedpersons not only survived but forged a vibrant community life which afforded them protection against the most debilitating effects of racial hostility and economic adversity.[1]

Such a broad interpretation of the national experience, however, obscures the particularly difficult challenges African-Americans faced in Dutchess County. The nature of slavery in the North and the gradual means by which abolition was realized in New York fragmented family life and presented serious obstacles for African-Americans in their efforts to build autonomous community institutions. It was in rural regions like the Hudson Valley, however, where slavery and the conservatism of emancipation were most debilitating. Dispersed settlement and geographic distance restricted opportunities for friends and family to gather, and the lack of economic opportunity in the countryside threatened to reduce emancipated slaves to destitution. African-Americans in Dutchess County led more isolated lives than their counterparts in cities, and their experience cautions historians against romanticizing African-American life during the transitional period from slavery to freedom.

An institution which formed personal identity and provided a bulwark against a hostile world, the family was the fundamental building block of community life. The slave family in rural New York, however, was a fragile institution. The threat of separation by sale was particularly salient in the Hudson Valley, where the seasonal nature of labor and the frequency of hiring meant that African-Americans frequently served several different masters during their lifetimes. Since children born of slave women presented added financial burdens for masters without providing an immediate return, parents were particularly fearful that children could be torn from them. Advertisements for women and their children appeared frequently in Dutchess County newspapers in the decades following the Revolution, and while slaveholders commonly offered to sell their bondswomen and children together, other masters were less concerned with keeping families intact. Abraham Teller offered to sell an eighteen-year-old woman with or without her one-year-old child as would "best suit the purchaser."[2]

The small size of slaveholdings in the Hudson Valley fragmented African-American families by separating husbands from wives and parents from children. The typical holding in Dutchess County at the end of the eighteenth century numbered fewer than three slaves. Almost half of all African-Americans in white households in 1790 resided in homes with three or fewer blacks. More than one third of those men, women, and children lived only with whites, and the proportion of African-Americans living alone in white households actually increased in the decades after 1790. It is not unreasonable to estimate that as many as three-quarters of African-Americans in the Hudson Valley at the end of the eighteenth century did not reside with family members.[3]

While clustering allowed African-Americans in urban centers opportunities to maintain kin networks, dispersed settlement in the countryside and geographic distance made contact between family members in the Hudson Valley difficult. Many African-Americans might have traveled only to neighboring farms to visit loved ones, but others undoubtedly had to traverse greater distances. Even when family members did live together, the intimacy of slaveholding in the Hudson Valley and the accommodation of slaves under the same roof as their owners denied families privacy. The slaveholder also undermined the position of African-American husbands and parents as protectors and providers. Whatever his standing as a moral guardian, and however deep the bonds of personal affection between husbands and wives and parents and children, the black husband and father competed with his family's owner for loyalty and obedience.[4]

However debilitating the impact of slavery on the African-American family, it did not destroy it. Enslaved men and women took advantage of the very institution which held them in bondage by exploiting the familial nature of slavery to their own advantage. Their economic worth and bonds of personal affection between slaves and masters permitted some African-Americans to gain concessions from their owners. One twenty-two-year-old woman was offered for sale in 1812 supposedly for no other reason than her desire to live near her husband in Poughkeepsie. Henry Livingston was also willing to sell a twenty-year-old male slave to a local purchaser when the bondsman refused to remove with Livingston to New York City. When another young woman similarly refused to relocate with her master's family to Albany, her master acceded to her demands not only by offering to sell her but also by noting that the woman's free black husband was willing to hire himself as a laborer in the family that purchased her.[5]

Enslaved African-Americans separated from family members risked punishment to be reunited with them. Almost half of runaways appearing in Dutchess County newspapers after the Revolution whose owners surmised their motivations for fleeing allegedly did so either to visit loved ones or to return to places of previous residence. Stephen, a nineteen-year-old mulatto who purportedly ran away to Shawangunk in neighboring Ulster County, and Tom, whose master suspected him of fleeing across the river to Goshen in Orange County, absconded to where they had been brought up. Others were willing to take greater risks; despite the dangers of being a black woman traveling alone, William Ryder's slave Sukey was willing to flee to Boston to be reunited with her husband.[6]

If the willingness of enslaved men and women like Stephen, Tom, and Sukey to run away attests to the refusal of African-Americans to allow slavery to separate them from family members, efforts of freed slaves to purchase the liberty of loved ones held in bondage testify to the determination of African-Americans to build independent households. The price for enslaved family members could be sizable, but some African-Americans were able to negotiate with sellers to make payments in installments. Moses Hallem contracted to pay as much as one hundred dollars for the freedom of Jane, his future wife.[7]

Michael Groth

The slow means by which slavery was abolished in New York presented a serious impediment to Moses Hallem and other African-Americans seeking to create or reconstitute families (see table 1). New York approved an abolition law almost two decades after her neighboring states had adopted measures to eliminate slavery, and opponents of the institution achieved their long awaited victory only after making significant concessions to the state's slaveowners. The statute of 1799 freed only children born of slave women after July 4, 1799 and required them to serve their mother's owners until female children reached the age of twenty-five and male children attained the age of twenty-eight. Almost twenty years later, the state in 1817 provided for the emancipation of all slaves in the state effective July 4, 1827 but conceded to slaveholders a provision which required children of slaves to serve their mother's masters until the age of twenty-one.[8]

The 1799 law only codified common practice. Slaveholders in Dutchess County were reluctant to surrender their slave property, and although the frequency of manumission gradually increased during the Early National era, slaveowners typically postponed manumission until slaves reached adulthood. Husbands eager to provide for their wives during their widowhood commonly bequeathed freedom only after their spouse's death. Masters considered manumission a reward for loyal and obedient service, and manumission remained an individual act. Slaveowners commonly freed some but not all of their slaves. Adolph Myers, a Fishkill farmer, ordered the manumission of a man and a woman, willed one slave to each of his three children, and directed the sale of a fourth, the money from the transaction to be put "at interest" for his grandchildren.[9]

Once freed, many African-Americans in Dutchess County continued to reside in white households, working for their former owners or other white employers as free laborers. Although the slave population gradually but steadily declined after 1790, the number and proportion of white households with black members remained constant, and the proportion of all African-Americans residing in such homes declined only gradually. At the beginning of the final decade of the eighteenth century, almost nine of ten African-Americans in Dutchess County lived in white households. Although fewer than one-third of African-Americans in the county remained in bondage thirty years later, more than half of all black residents continued to reside with whites (see table 2). The number of free African-American households more than doubled between 1790 and 1810, but proportionally as many free blacks resided in white homes in 1810 as did twenty years earlier. African-Americans persevered in establishing separate households during the 1810's, as both the number of black households and the number of African-Americans in black families increased markedly. As late as 1820, however, almost three of every ten free blacks in the county continued to live with whites (see table 3). Although free, many African-Americans in the Hudson Valley led lives not unlike those they had led under slavery.

The gradualism of abolition in Dutchess County was only one reason for the persistence of African-Americans in white households. Emancipation brought not only joy but also anxiety and uncertainty. Like other laboring people in America, free African-American men and women found the economic world of the late eighteenth and early nineteenth centuries an unstable and impersonal one. As wealth became increasingly maldistributed in a market-oriented economy and as traditional paternalistic relationships between masters and their workmen deteriorated, laborers experienced a deterioration of skills and found earning basic subsistence increasingly difficult. A series of articles and letters in the Dutchess Observer in 1817 addressed dwindling opportunities for workers in the Hudson Valley and elsewhere in the eastern states. Drawing parallels to the oppression of ancient Israel under Pharaoh, a letter by "Freedom" lamented the plight of the "poor, honest, and industrious citizen" and warned of the enslavement of the nation's workers by "money interests."[10]

TABLE 1
African American Population of Dutchess County
1790–1820

Year	Slaves	Proportion of African American	Freepersons	Proportion of African American
1790	1,856	80.8	440	19.2
1800	1,609	63.3	932	36.7
1810	1,244	52.1	1,146	47.9
1820	772	31.3	1,697	68.7

Source: *Heads of Families at the First Census of the United States Taken in the Year 1790* New York (Baltimore, MD: Fenealogical Publishing Co., 1976); "Population Schedules of the First Census of the United States, 1790, "Microcopy 637, Roll 6, New York, vol. 2, (Washington, D.C., 1965); "Population Schedules of the Second Census of the United States, 1800," Microcopy 32, Roll 21, New York (Washington, D.C., 1959); "Population Schedules of the Third Census of the United States, 1810," Roll 31, New York (Washington, D.C., 1968); "Population Schedules of the Fourth Census of the United States, 1820," Roll 71, New York, vol. 10 (Washington, D.C., 1959).

TABLE 2
Proportions of African-Americans in White Households
1790–1820

Year	Proportion of African-Americans in Slavery	Proportion of African-Americans in White Households	Total African-American Population
1790	80.8	440	19.2
1800	63.3	932	36.7
1810	52.1	1,146	47.9
1820	31.3	1,697	68.7

Source: See Table 1

TABLE 3
African-American Households in Dutchess County
1790–1820

Year	Number of Households	Number of Persons in African-American Households	Proportion of African-Americans in Black Households
1790	59	262	59.5
1800	100	484	51.9
1810	142	675	58.9
1820	272	1,191	70.2

Source: See Table 1

Michael Groth

African-Americans in Dutchess County began their lives as free men and women in a hostile environment with few resources of their own. Few were as fortunate as Michael Vincent's slaves; Sambo, Pompey, Jane, and Sarah, who, in addition to sharing 135 pounds in cash, each received a bed, bedding, and a chest filled with clothing upon their manumission.[11] However, even with cash, tools, and livestock, opportunities for independent land ownership were few in a region where real estate had been traditionally held by a privileged elite and where tenancy was common. Charles Freeman, who purchased approximately three acres of land in the town of Beekman for the sum of $312 in 1818 was exceptional.[12] The vast majority of African-Americans who remained in the countryside after emancipation labored as hired hands or as tenants not unlike their counterparts in rural New Jersey, Pennsylvania, and Maryland.[13]

The many African-Americans in Dutchess County like Anthony Murphy, who struggled to support himself and his family as a common laborer, found work in the Hudson Valley to be seasonal and often temporary.[14] Largely propertyless, former slaves in Dutchess County migrated from place to place in pursuit of employment. For men and women in eastern portions of the county like Freelove Marsh, a mulatto who moved to Poughkeepsie from Amenia after the completion of her indenture, and Robert and Sarah Churchill, who migrated to the county seat from their home in the Oblong, the more populous western region of the county along the Hudson River offered more economic and social opportunities.[15] Others moved about without any clear destination. After serving as a printer's apprentice in New York City, Benjamin Furman resided in Horesneck, Greenfield, and Newtown before moving with his family to Dutchess. Once in the county, the Furmans moved from Amenia to Poughkeepsie to Beekman and back to Poughkeepsie again within the span of approximately two years.[16] Of course, local residents found the presence of such migrants disconcerting. Fears of such a transient population and confusion about the legal status of some of the black men and women who came before them compelled the Poughkeepsie overseers of the poor in 1810 to commission a census of the town's free African-American population to delineate those who were residents and those who were likely to become public charges.[17]

Economic security could be fleeting for free African-Americans during the late eighteenth and early nineteenth centuries. Flora Francis's mother was sincere when she "thanked God" that she was in good health and able to support herself, disease and injury daily threatened to reduce laboring people from bare subsistence to destitution.[18] The Bloom family discovered the precariousness of life in the aftermath of emancipation. Permete Bloom was more fortunate than most when he began his life as a freeman. With the thirty dollars he received upon his manumission, Bloom purchased his wife's freedom, and the couple worked in the Town of Beekman until they were able to rent a house and eight acres for thirty dollars in produce. After renting two other places in the town, the Blooms and those of their children who lived with them migrated to Poughkeepsie, where Permete was able to purchase a house and a plot. However, Bloom evidently overextended himself. The family found it difficult to make their mortgage payments and faced destitution when both Permete and his wife became ill.[19]

The Blooms were not alone when they applied for public assistance. Although comprising only seven percent of Poughkeepsie's population at the beginning of the nineteenth century, the forty-nine cases of African-Americans appearing in the town poor record accounted for almost one of every five examinations conducted by the overseers of the poor between 1807 and 1815.[20] That number is even more significant taking into account the proportion of black residents residing in white households. Sickness or injury most frequently brought African-Americans before the overseers of the poor; ill and debilitated men and women comprised three of every five African-Americans appearing before the authorities. Typical were the experiences of Hagar Davis, a sixty-year-old woman "fatigued" by a "female complaint," and forty-year-old Amy Lewis, who appeared before the overseers in 1811 afflicted by the "King's Evil."[21]

Women comprised almost three of every five African-Americans in the poor record, and the clear majority of them (twelve of the nineteen women whose marital status was specified) were either single, separated from their spouses, or widowed. Lucy Anderson, who supported herself as a spinner while her husband was at sea, and Simantha Lewis, a cook in the employ of the Jewett family in Poughkeepsie, found opportunities for employment limited and low-paying. Although the rural economy of the Hudson Valley sometimes required women to labor on the farm and in the field, women had few realistic options outside of domestic service.[22] The, presence of children exacerbated the burdens placed upon female wage earners. The mother of a two-year-old boy, Diana Jackson appeared before the overseers of the poor sick and destitute six days after giving birth to her second child.[23]

Older women and men traditionally found themselves on relief rolls. The abandonment of old and decrepit slaves was a persistent cause for concern for public authorities. Provincial law imposed fines on slaveowners who allowed their slaves to beg or who fraudulently sold incapacitated slaves under the pretense of freeing them, and slaveholders desirous of manumitting their human chattel had to demonstrate that their freed slaves would not become public charges.[24] Such legislation was only partially successful. At age seventy-five, Cuff Low appeared before the overseers of the poor in 1811 after his mistress's second husband simply refused to support him. After a lifetime of service, some men and women expected their owners to provide for them in their later years. Low's wife, Rachel Pride, told the overseers of the poor in Poughkeepsie that Moses Downing had given her permission to work for herself but had promised to assist her whenever she found herself in need. When Downing himself testified that he had fully discharged the woman and was not liable for her support, the overseers awarded Rachel temporary relief.[25]

Rachel was more fortunate than many. Anyone seeking assistance from the overseers of the poor found the state's poor laws unforgiving. Residency, not race, was the principal criteria in dispensing relief. To meet the growing challenge of poverty and to address rising public fears of the rapidly growing transient population, the state passed stringent laws which empowered overseers of the poor not only to deny relief to nonresidents but also to remove them from the community.[26] Peter Harrison had been in Poughkeepsie for barely eight weeks when the overseers of the poor ordered his removal. The overseers were undoubtedly eager to remove Cary Stevenson, an unmarried mother of six children who was eight months pregnant with her seventh child when she appeared before them in July 1809.[27]

Despite their numbers in the poor record, African-Americans turned to public assistance only as a last resort. Recently freed from slavery or servitude, African-Americans did whatever they could to avoid the stigma of dependency.[28] The fact that African-Americans were more than twice as likely than native-born whites to appear in the poor records for sickness or injury suggests that many black residents sought relief only when debility prevented them from laboring. Phebe Lewis managed to provide for herself and her two young daughters for two years after being abandoned by her husband and applied for relief only when illness incapacitated her in 1814. Smallpox had so debilitated Abraham Foe by the time he appeared before the overseers that he was unable to sign his mark.[29]

Even when incapacitated by disease or injury, men and women in need turned to others before seeking public assistance. Robert Rutgers found that his former master was willing to assume liability for his care, but former owners were not always so compassionate.[30] Although a few needy men and women looked to those who had traditionally provided for their material needs under slavery, many more turned to kin. Mary

Cary's mother and stepfather were willing to support their pregnant eighteen-year-old single daughter until she gave birth and was able to provide for herself. Although poor and afflicted with rheumatism, Jane Thom claimed that she could support herself at her sister's place in Pleasant Valley.[31] Bonds of kinship, however, were not always strong and frequent mobility and transiency meant that not all of those in need had family or friends upon whom they could rely. A widower, Robert Newkirk, who evidently did not have a close relationship with his family (he could not name all of his grandchildren), turned to his former master only to be remanded to the overseers of the poor.[32]

Poverty limited the ability of even families bound by powerful emotional ties to provide for their own members. Many parents frequently bound out their children, and the experience of Jenny Van Brunt, the daughter of free parents who spent most of her childhood as a servant in white homes, was hardly atypical.[33] Ill or dependent kin could overburden families that depended upon the income of all members to eke out a bare subsistence. Dick Francis of Poughkeepsie managed to care for his seriously ill brother John for four months but appealed to the overseers of the poor in April 1811 when he found himself unable to support him any longer. Two years later, Dick's wife, Flora, claimed that she could provide for herself and her family during her husband's absence as long as her mother and lame father moved elsewhere.[34]

While it is dangerous to generalize from the experience of the Francis family or those of the other men, women, and children in the poor record, the document serves to illuminate the specific challenges African-Americans encountered in the aftermath of slavery. The tribulations of the Tabor family put the struggle of freedpersons in Dutchess County into perspective. The daughter of free mulattos, Sarah Tabor worked for several families throughout Dutchess County after her father's death. While residing in Dover, she met Jacob Tabor, a slave from Pawling. The couple married and eventually raised a family of six children. Sarah's brother, Absalom Titus, purchased Jacob's freedom, and in 1805 the Tabors migrated to Poughkeepsie to begin life anew. Jacob Tabor, however, found life as a freeman a difficult one. Although renting several different tenements in Poughkeepsie, the Tabors failed to establish a permanent residence, and, perhaps unable to find work, Jacob turned to less than legitimate means to support his family. In August 1809, Maria Herrick, a prostitute, testified to having been "induced" to Tabor's home and forced to flee after an "altercation" with several men. The town justices convicted another woman at Tabor's residence of being a "disorderly person" and fined Jacob for keeping a "disorderly house." Shortly afterwards, Jacob was imprisoned for an unspecified offense, and his wife and children were left dependent upon public relief. Tabor died less than two years after being released from prison, and the justices of the peace eventually ordered the indenture of the Tabor children.[35]

The ordeal of the Tabor family illustrates the tragedy of the African-American experience in the Hudson Valley during the transitional period from slavery to freedom. The relative isolation of the countryside, the gradualism of abolition, and economic dependency upon their former owners constrained the ability of African-Americans in Dutchess County to create independent households. Those who were unwilling or unable to labor for their former masters found economic opportunities limited, and poverty forced some African-Americans to seek public relief. Perhaps it was out of desperation that Jacob turned to crime, but his incarceration ultimately deprived his family of a husband and father, and his death meant the indenture of his children and the dissolution of his family. Emancipation brought insecurity to former slaves in Dutchess County. While African-Americans in urban centers were able to forge separate households, build churches, and establish other community institutions, freedpersons in Dutchess County struggled simply to survive.

The Tabors' struggle, however, also testifies to the fortitude of African-Americans in Dutchess County, and the adversity of life after slavery only casts what African-Americans did achieve into greater relief. Jacob and Sarah's marriage, Absalom Titus's purchase of his brother-in-law's freedom, and the Tabors' migration to Poughkeepsie to establish new lives for themselves attest to the aggressiveness and determination of African-Americans in Dutchess County to procure their freedom and forge free and economically independent families. By exploiting the intimate nature of Hudson Valley slavery to gain concessions from their owners, by absconding to be with loved ones, and by purchasing the liberty of spouses and children, African-Americans challenged the institution of slavery. Despite the constraints of rural poverty, free men and women gradually established independent households, and kin networks provided a valuable safety net for needy relatives and friends who refused to seek public relief. The African-American experience in Dutchess County during the late eighteenth and early nineteenth centuries ultimately forces historians to reexamine the meaning of "freedom" and "community" in Hudson Valley life and culture.

Notes

1. The vast scholarship on the African-American experience during the Revolutionary and Early National periods includes Ira Berlin, "The Revolution in Black Life," in Alfred Young, ed., *The American Revolution: Explorations in American Radicalism* (DeKalb, IL: Northern Illinois University Press, 1976), 349–82; Ira Berlin and Ronald Hoffman, eds., *Slavery and Freedom in the Age of the American Revolution* (Charlottesville, VA: University Press of Virginia, 1983); Leonard P. Curry, *The Free Black in Urban America, 1800–1850: The Shadow of a Dream* (Chicago, IL: University of Chicago Press, 1981); Sylvia Frey, *Water from the Rock: Black Resistance in a Revolutionary Age* (Princeton, NJ: Princeton University Press, 1991); Graham Russell Hodges, *Slavery and Freedom in the Rural North: African-Americans in Monmouth County, New Jersey, 1665–1865* (Madison, WI: Madison House, 1997); James Oliver Horton and Lois E. Horton, *In Hope Liberty: Culture, Community, and Protest Among Northern Free Blacks, 1700–1860* (New York, NY: Oxford Univer[si]ty Press, 1997); Gary Nash, *Forging Freedom: The Formation of Philadelphia's Black Community, 1720–1840* (Cambridge, MA: Harvard University Press, 1988); Nash, *Race and Revolution* (Madison, WI: Madison House, 1990); Gary Nash and Jean Soderlund, *Freedom by Degrees: Emancipation in Pennsylvania and Its Aftermath* (New York, NY: Oxford University Press, 1991); Benjamin Quarles, "The Revolutionary War as a Black Declaration of Independence," and "Antebellum Free Blacks and the 'Spirit of '76'," in Quarles, *Black Mosaic: Essays in Afro-American History and Historiography* (Amherst, MA: University of Massachusetts, 1988); Billy G. Smith, "Black Family Life in Philadelphia from Slavery to Freedom," in Catherine E. Hutchins, ed., *Shaping a National Culture: The Philadelphia Experience, 1750–1800* (Winterthur, DE: Henry Francis du Pont Winterthur Museum, 1994), 77–97; Shane White, *Somewhat More Independant: The End of Slavery in New York City, 1770–1810* (Athens, GA: University of Georgia Press, 1991); Donald Wright, *African-Americans in the Colonial Era: From African Origins Through American Revolution* (Arlington Heights, IL: Harland Davidson, 1990); Wright, *African-Americans in the Early Republic, 1789–1831* (Arlington Heights, IL: Harland Davidson, 1993).

2. *Poughkeepsie Journal*, 27 March 1798. For similar examples, see 1 March 1792, 14 August 1798, and 18 February 1800. Billy G. Smith has observed that slaveowners from the "middling sort" who were unable to weather downturns in the economy regularly purchased and sold slaves according to fluctuating economic cycles. Smith, "Black Family Life," p. 86. The northern slave family is examined in Horton, *In Hope of Liberty*, pp. 24–27; Vivienne Kruger, "Born to Run: The Slave Family in Early New York, 1626–1827," (Ph.D. dissertation, Columbia University, 1985); William D. Piersen, *Black Yankees: The Development of an Afro-American Subculture in Eighteenth-Century New England* (Amherst, MA: University of Massachusetts, 1988), chap. 3; Smith, "Black Family Life;" White, *Somewhat More Independant*, pp. 89–92.

3. *Heads of Families at the First Census of the United States Taken in the Year 1790: New York* (Baltimore, MD: Genealogical Publishing Company, 1976); "Population Schedules of the First Census of the United States, 1790," Microcopy 637, Roll 6, New York, vol. 2 (Washington, D.C., 1965); "Population Schedules of the Second Census of the United States, 1800," Microcopy 32, Roll 21, New York (Washington, D.C., 1959); "Population Schedules of the Third Census of the United States, 1810," Roll 30, New York," (Washington, D.C., 1968); "Population Schedules of the Fourth Census of the United States, 1820," Roll 71, New York, vol. 10 (Washington D.C., 1959). Kruger, "Born to Run," pp. 167–76; Smith, "Black Family Life," pp. 86–87; Jean R. Soderlund, *Quakers and Slavery: A Divided Spirit* (Princeton, NJ: Princeton University Press, 1985), p. 81.

4. Piersen, *Black Yankees*, pp. 35–36, 93–95.

5. *Poughkeepsie Journal*, 8 January 1812; *Poughkeepsie Journal*, 30 November 1802; *Political Barometer*, 22 November 1803.

6. *Poughkeepsie Journal*, 29 November 1803; *American Farmer and Dutchess County Advertiser*, 3 September 1799; *Poughkeepsie*

Michael Groth

Journal, 20 August 1799. Twelve of twenty-five fugitives in Dutchess County newspapers between 1785 and 1827 whose masters surmised their destinations allegedly absconded to visit loved ones or to return to places of previous residence. The desire of fugitives to be with loved ones attests to the strength of the African-American family. Smith, "Black Family Life," pp. 80–81.

7. "Record of the Overseers of the Poor, Poughkeepsie, New York, 1807–1815," Adriance Memorial Library, Poughkeepsie, New York, p. 162.

8. *Laws of New York*, 22d Sess., Chap. 62.; 40th Sess., Chap. 137.

9. Michael Groth, "Slaveholders and Manumission in Dutchess County, New York," *New York History*, 78 (1) (January 1997), 33–50; Will Book C, Dutchess County Surrogate's Court Poughkeepsie, New York, pp. 29–30.

10. *Dutchess Observer*, 19 and 26 March, 2 April, 25 June, and 17 September 1817. The plight of America's working people during the late colonial and Early National periods is examined in John K. Alexander, *Render Them Submissive: Responses to Poverty in Philadelphia, 1760–1800* (Amherst, MA: University of Massachusetts Press, 1980); Robert E. Cray, Jr., *Paupers and Poor Relief in New York City and Its Rural Environs, 1700–1830* (Philadelphia, PA: Temple University Press, 1988); Priscilla Ferguson Clement, *Welfare and the Poor in the Nineteenth-Century: City Philadelphia, 1800–1854* (Rutherford, NJ: Farleigh Dickinson University, 1985); Gary Nash, "Poverty and Poor Relief in Pre-Revolutionary Philadelphia," William and Mary Quarterly, 3rd series, 33 (January 1976), 3–30; Nash, *The Urban Crucible: Social Change, Political Consciousness, and the Origins of the American Revolution* (Cambridge, MA: Harvard University Press, 1979); Nash, "Urban Wealth and Poverty in Pre-Revolutionary America," Journal of Interdisciplinary History VI (4) (Spring 1976), 545–84; Billy G. Smith, *"The Lower Sort": Philadelphia's Laboring People, 1750–1800* (Ithaca: Cornell University Press, 1990); Smith, "Poverty and Economic Marginality in Eighteenth-Century America," *Proceedings of the American Philosophical Society*, 132 (1) (1988), 85–118.

11. Sambo also received a horse and bridle. Will Book C, pp. 232–33. Only 18 of the 55 Dutchess County slaveholders (32.7 percent) who manumitted slaves in their wills between 1744 and 1820 provided money or property for their former slaves. Bequests most commonly comprised merely the slave's own clothing; in only seven cases did the slaveowner offer cash, and in six cases the testator provided tools, a cow, or a horse. In no instance did the testator bequeath any real estate.

12. "Dutchess County Deeds, Liber 26," p. 580. Freeman's property provided a nucleus for the African-American neighborhood of "Guinea Town," or "Freemanville," during the antebellum period. Philip H. Smith, General History of Dutchess County (Pawling, NY, 1877), p. 135; A.J. Williams-Myers, "The Arduous Journey: The African-American Presence in the Hudson-Mohawk Region," in Monroe Fordham, ed., *The African-American Presence in New York, State History: Four Regional History Surveys* (Albany, NY: State University of New York Press, 1990), p. 29.

13. Richard S. Dunn, "Black Society in the Chesapeake, 1776–1810," in Berlin and Hoffman, *Slavery and Freedom*, pp. 77–79; Hodges, *Slavery and Freedom*, pp. 130–33, 161–65, 178–81; Nash and Soderlund, *Freedom by Degrees*, pp. 188–91.

14. "Overseers of the Poor," pp. 399400.

15. "Overseers of the Poor," pp. 81–82, 164–65, 192.

16. "Overseers of the Poor," p. 1.

17. "Overseers of the Poor," P. 167. Transiency in the colonial and early national periods is explored in Cray, *Paupers and Poor Relief*, chapter 5; Douglas Lamar Jones, "The Strolling Poor: Transiency in Eighteenth-Century Massachusetts," *Journal of Social History*, 8 (1975), 28–54; Carl Oblinger, "Alms for Oblivion: The Making of a Black Underclass in Southeastern Pennsylvania, 1780–1860," in John E. Bodnar, ed., *The Ethnic Experience in Pennsylvania* (Lewisburg, PA: Bucknell University Press, 1973), 94–119; Smith, *"The Lower Sort,"* chapter 6; Smith, "Poverty and Economic Marginality," 85–118.

18. "Overseers of the Poor," pp. 292–93.

19. "Overseers of the Poor," p. 184.

20. Robert Cray calculated similar figures for New York City's rural environs. Cray, *Paupers and Poor Relief*, pp. 148–52.

21. "Overseers of the Poor," pp. 150–51, 212.

22. "Overseers of the Poor," pp. 137, 282. Gary Nash, "Forging Freedom: The Emancipation Experience in Northern Seaport Cities, 1775–1820," in Berlin and Hoffman, *Slavery and . . . . Freedom*, p. 19; Cray, *Paupers and Poor Relief*, pp. 138–40,157–58; Clement, *Welfare and the Poor*, pp. 30–32; Grigg, *The Dependent Poor of Newburyport: Studies in Social History, 1800–1830* (Ann Arbor, MI: UMI Research Press, 1984), chap. 6; Smith, "Poverty and Economic Marginality," pp. 106, 112.

23. "Overseers of the Poor," p. 396.

24. *Colonial Laws of New York from the Year 1664 to the Revolution* (Albany, NY: James B. Lyon, 1894), 5:533–34; *Laws of the State of New York*, 8th Sess., Chap. 68; 11th Sess., Chap. 40; Robert E. Cray, Jr., "White Welfare and Black Strategies: The Dynamics of Race and Poor Relief in New York, 1700–1825," *Slavery and Abolition* 7 (December 1986), 277–78, 283; Kruger, "Born to Run," chap. IX.

25. "Overseers of the Poor," pp. 207, 222, 233–34, 327–29, 362.

26. *Laws of New York*, 7th Sess., Chap. 35; 11th Sess., Chap. 62; 24th Sess., Chap. 184. Scholarship on poverty and poor relief during the late eighteenth and early nineteenth centuries includes Alexander, *Render Them Submissive*; Cray, *Paupers and Poor Relief*; Clement, *Welfare and the Poor*; Grigg, *The Dependent Poor of Newburyport*; Jones, "The Strolling Poor"; Michael Katz, *In the Shadow of the Poorhouse: A Social History of Welfare in America* (New York, NY: Basic Books, 1986); Katz, *Poverty and Public Policy in American History* (New York, NY: Academic Press, 1983); Raymond Mohl, *Poverty in New York, 1763–1825* (New York, NY: Oxford University Press, 1971); Nash, *The Urban Crucible*; Nash, "Urban Wealth and Poverty"; Stephen J. Ross, "Objects of Charity: Poor Relief, Poverty, and the Rise of the Almshouse in Early Eighteenth-Century New York City," in William Pencak and Edick Wright, eds., *Authority and Resistance in Early New York* (New York, NY. New York Historical Society, 1988), 138–72; David J. Rothman, *The Discovery of the Asylum: Social Order and Disorder in the New Republic* (Boston, MA: Little and Brown, 1971); Smith, "The Lower Sort"; Conrad Edick Wright, *The Transformation of Charity in Postrevolutionary New England* (Boston, MA: Northeastern University Press, 1992).

27. "Overseers of the Poor," pp. 124, 129.

28. Cray, *Paupers and Poor Relief*, pp. 191–92; Cray, "White Welfare and Black Strategies," 281–83; Smith, *"The Lower Sort"* pp. 174–75.

29. "Overseers of the Poor," pp. 362, 416. While only 29 of 119 cases of native-born whites appearing before the overseers were related to illness, more than half (18 of 30) of cases involving African-Americans concerned either sickness or injury to either the deponent or the deponent's spouse. Two thirds of immigrants (12 of 18) appeared for reasons of illness and debility. The cases of at least eight African-Americans in the poor record were brought to the overseers by individuals other than the African-Americans themselves.

30. "Overseers of the Poor," pp. 132, 182.

31. "Overseers of the Poor," pp. 17, 218, 221.

32. "Overseers of the Poor," p. 256.

33. "Overseers of the Poor," p. 273.

34. "Overseers of the Poor," pp. 192, 202, 292–93.

35. "Overseers of the Poor," pp. 3, 43, 130, 271–72, 351, 364, 388.

This article originally appeared in the *Hudson Valley Regional Review*, Volume 14.2.

From Merchant to Manufacturer: The Economics of Localism in Newburgh, New York, 1845–1900

Mark Carnes

Our Men of Property, 1846–1892

> Our trade has left us and it will continue to do so. Last fall a great many of the farmers from the towns of Montgomery and Crawford, and Minisink, sent their produce and butter to market by the Erie Rail Road from Goshen, and next May when that railroad is finished to Middletown, we must expect to lose all the trade of those towns.— How shall we make up the loss? Why do not some of our men of property take measures to have manufacturing establishments erected on our wharves?
>
> —*The Newburgh Journal*, February 18, 1843

On an early Monday morning in August, 1845, a great bell roused the residents of the northeastern section of Newburgh. Those who lived on the steep banks of the Hudson peered towards the waterfront, and although the sun had not cleared the mountains to the east, it was possible to discern a steady stream of people—mostly nervous young women—crossing a footbridge to the sixth-story entrance of the new cotton factory. The scene was strangely evocative of the previous day when hundreds of people responded to the summons of church bells throughout Newburgh. But the call of God was noticeably less strident than that of the factory, for the factory bell continued throughout the day and into the "still hours of the night." Despite the complaints of the townspeople, the clamor persisted during the days and weeks to come, relenting only on the Sabbath. The factory then—and only then—acceded to the less temporal demands of the church.[1]

The factory bell eventually fell silent, its deep sonorities replaced by the shrill sound of the steam whistle. In the cotton factories of New England, established some fifteen to twenty-five years earlier, the great bell was a reflection of the avowedly religious aspirations of the factory founders as well as a useful means of mass comunication.[2] But in Newburgh there was no technological explanation for the factory bell; unlike the water-powered cotton factories of New England, the Newburgh Steam Mills—as proclaimed by its corporate name—employed a new source of power: the steam whistle was available from the outset.

Why were the Newburgh Steam Mills equipped with an innovative and unproven power source? Indeed, why was there a cotton factory in Newburgh at all?

It is impossible to give straightforward answers to these questions; the local newspapers and histories scarcely touched on the subject. But this much is known: Homer Ramsdell, Thomas Powell, Benjamin Carpenter, David Crawford, Christopher Reeve and several other freighters invested a total of $100,000 to establish the Newburgh Steam Mills in the spring of 1844.[3] In so doing Newburgh's main forwarding merchants shed their mercantile vestments and donned those of the industrialist. They had learned the ritual from others, most notably the merchant princes of New England—Francis Lowell, Nathan Appleton and Amos Lawrence—who had abandoned trans-Atlantic trade and had built scores of cotton textile factories throughout New England during the 1820s and 1830s. Confronted with a similar economic crisis, Newburgh's freighters carefully repeated each detail of the ceremony: they patterned their corporate charter after the New England companies, they differentiated each floor of the factory by production function, and they copied the architecture of the earlier factories, including even the cupola and bell. Insofar as Newburgh's freighters imitated the great merchants of New England, it is useful to review the rise of the cotton textile industry in that region to understand the motives of Newburgh's freighters.

The merchants of the major port cities of New England initially decried the development of domestic manufacturers, arguing that local factories destroyed more jobs in foreign trade than were created in manufacturing.[4] The antipathy of the merchants towards manufacturing was founded in a belief that the activities were inherently competitive; a self-sufficient economy, they reasoned, had little need for trade. The most prosperous merchants also believed that manufacturing inevitably culminated in the emergence of grimy mill towns populated by a dispirited working class. Furthermore, the well-publicized failure in the early 1800s of a large cotton factory in Beverly, Massachusetts convinced most New England merchants that their opposition to domestic manufacturing was well-founded.[5]

However, the War of 1812 and the subsequent decline of the Atlantic maritime trade altered both the opinions and profit margins of the New England merchants. Men who had reinvested surplus capital in mercantile pursuits began to look for more lucrative investments; their search led them to upland New England, where swift-flowing rivers could provide the power for textile machinery. Throughout New England, merchants began to redirect capital into cotton textile manufacturing. In places such as Lowell, Lawrence, and Chicopee, Massachusetts—where there was no pre-existing town to speak of—they built workers' housing, schools, and churches and extended rail lines to establish an uninterrupted flow of raw materials and finished cloth. Yet these impressive efforts at city-building on the part of the prominent merchants of Boston were but the most visible examples of a general mercantile transition to cotton manufacturing in New England during the 19th century.[6]

While the decline of oceanic trade in the early 1820s provided the incentive for New England's merchants to build cotton textile factories, the impact of the Erie Railroad in the early 1840s caused a similar economic transformation of Newburgh. And much as the merchants of New England initially opposed the development of local manufactures, the forwarding merchants' main concern from the outset was to block the Erie Railroad and to maintain the existing commercial network. But the completion of the railroad to Goshen in 1841, which provided Orange County farmers with easy access to New York City markets, signaled the end of Newburgh's mercantile heyday. The freighters decided to recast Newburgh's economic base, and the cotton factory was the first step in this process. The cotton textile industry had initiated the industrial revolution in Great Britain in the late 18th century and New England in the early 19th century; Newburgh's forwarding merchants hoped it would do the same for their town in the 1840s.

The construction of a massive cotton factory by Newburgh's forwarding merchants was, above all else, an act of faith. It stemmed from the conviction that the world of the future was to be shaped by coal, iron and machines, a conviction, moreover, that the great merchants of New England had discovered the way to that world. Newburgh's freighters-turned-manufacturers, like any novitiates, scrupulously patterned their efforts after their mentors—Lowell, Appleton, and Lawrence.

But there was one significant difference: the machinery in the Newburgh cotton factory was powered by steam engines. Although a handful of cotton factories made use of steam engines before 1844, water-powered mills remained a characteristic feature of New England textile manufacturing until well after the Civil War.[7] Since Newburgh's forwarding merchants had imitated the merchant-manufacturers of New England on so many other matters, why did they choose an innovative and unproven power source?

If their main objective was to profit directly from cotton manufacturing, they could have invested in established New England firms, or built a more conventional water-powered factory in nearby Walden.[8] Yet they located the cotton factory in Newburgh, and this was made possible by the availability of the still-experimental steam engine. The cotton factory was sited on the riverfront not for access to water power (the Hudson was slow-moving) but to make use of the freighters' idled steamboats to carry raw cotton and finished goods to and from the factory's docks. Should the cotton factory fail to return a dividend, increased freighting revenues might compensate for any losses in manufacturing, much as the old turnpikes had contributed to the wealth of the merchants without ever turning a consistent profit themselves. Newburgh's freighters believed, moreover, that the factory would repopulate the village, quicken the pace of business, and most important, increase the value of their lands.

The directors of the Newburgh Stearn Mills had little difficulty finding the men and women to take the low-paying jobs as loom and spinning machine operators. Although the crisis precipitated by the Erie Railroad forced hundreds of Newburgh artisans and craftsmen to seek opportunities elsewhere, nearly as many unskilled Irish laborers were enticed to Newburgh by the lower cost of living (especially the cheap rents) caused by the local depression of 1841 to 1845. And if the forwarding merchants had misgivings over the social impact of the cotton factory, the severity of the local economic crisis overcame them.

The cotton factory succeeded in sparking Newburgh's industrial development. Whereas the largest previous manufacturing firm employed at most twenty-five workers, the cotton factory listed over three hundred employees, most of them women.[9] The cotton factory also gave rise to what was known as the "cotton complex," a clustering of cotton mills with nearby iron foundries. The first large local foundry specialized in producing steam engines, looms and other machinery designed for cotton mills[10]; presumably the Newburgh Steam Mill was its major source of demand. Newburgh's forwarding merchants played an important role in developing these subsidiary industries. Benjamin Carpenter and his brother built the town's first major iron foundry while Homer Ramsdell established the Washington Iron Works.

However, the rise of Newburgh's metal and machinery industries pointed up the town's inadequate transportation. If Newburgh was to become an industrial city, it needed access to the coal fields of western Pennsylvania and the iron ore of areas farther west. The freighters became convinced that Newburgh's nascent industries required rail connections, and they renewed efforts to attain that objective.

Ironically, the Erie Railroad gave the freighters their chance. Although the railroad was unfinished in 1840, the Erie had exhausted the initial State loan; despite intense criticism it applied for yet another. Thomas Powell and Homer Ramsdell, heading a delegation of local forwarding merchants, worked with state representatives to block relief legislation for the Erie Railroad. Ramsdell eventually proposed a compromise which the Erie accepted in 1845: the Erie would build and operate a special railway spur from Goshen to Newburgh and a Newburgher would serve as a director of the corporation. In return, Newburgh's freighters were to renounce the charter of the dormant Hudson and Delaware Railway, to support the legislative aims of the Erie, and to raise $140,000 for the construction of the spur. With Newburgh's support, the relief legislation passed. By 1849 the forwarding merchants had raised the necessary funds (see Table 1) and the spur was completed within two years. Newburgh at last had access to the coal and iron of the Midwest.[11]

With the support and guidance of the forwarding merchants, Newburgh's industrial development proceeded rapidly. From 1844 to 1879 Newburgh's value added by manufacturing (adjusted for price fluctuations) increased ten-fold (see Table 2). Newburgh's transition from a commercial village to an industrial city was further reflected in a change in the nature of its manufactures. In 1835 eighty-five percent of Newburgh's value added by manufacturing derived from the town's commercial functions: local breweries, gristmills, tanneries and sawmills processed the grain, animal skins and timber of nearby farmers; in all cases the manufacturing process resulted in a substantial weight loss, thereby reducing freight charges considerably. Yet within ten years of the establishment of the cotton factory, sixty-one percent of Newburgh's value added by manufacture came from the industries associated with the cotton complex—cotton textiles and metal machinery. By 1880 commerce-related manufactures accounted for less than fifteen percent of Newburgh's manufacturing output (see Table 3).

Accompanying the shift in Newburgh's economic base were changes in its physical structure. Prior to the mid-century industrial transformation, the built-up area was concentrated along a half-mile section of the riverfront (refer to Map 1 on page 54; the heart of the old village is screened). Surrounding this commercial and residential district were the estates of the forwarding merchants. After the completion of the Newburgh railroad spur, Newburgh's industrialists were no longer obliged to site their factories along the riverfront, and the proliferation of factories to the south and west of the old village reflected this change in transportation. Homer Ramsdell, anticipating the direction of Newburgh's industrial development, purchased large sections of land abutting the Erie spur; by the time of the Civil War, he had erected several factories and leased them to promising entrepreneurs.

Although it is not known for certain that the forwarding merchants initiated Newburgh's industrialization to drive up real estate prices, that was an important consequence of their actions. The old residential section of Newburgh failed to accommodate the rapidly expanding industrial population, and new streets and housing tracts were built to the south and west (refer to Map 1; the dotted lines indicate street extensions between 1835 and 1879). The census schedules of 1870 listed Isaac Van Duzer's son as owning $65,000 in real estate while Benjamin and Isaac Carpenter (the latter describing himself as a "speculator in real estate") owned $210,000. Unequalled, however, were the landholdings of Homer Ramsdell which reportedly totaled $714,500. The lands of Henry Robinson, purchased for approximately $250 per acre in 1835, were subdivided by developers and sold by the lot for what amounted to $4,000–5,000 per acre in 1887.

Rising land values are often an indication of increasing population, but as Newburgh industrialized there was a change in the nature as well as the size of the town's labor force. As a commercial center, Newburgh's work force largely consisted of the craftsmen who tended to the needs of the visiting farmers. With the depression that followed the construction of the Erie Railroad, however, these artisans were the first to seek opportunities elsewhere. It is impossible to calculate precisely the extent of this demographic dislocation since the census schedules prior to 1850 failed to list detailed occupational information about the town's residents. Information from 1850 to 1870 confirms the expected decline in the importance of craftsmen in Newburgh's economy (see Table 4).

The occupational statistics also indicate the importance of construction in Newburgh's mid-century economy. Industrial growth created a demand for new factories, houses, tenements, sewers, water lines and other types of construction, and by 1870 nearly twice as many men were employed in construction as in

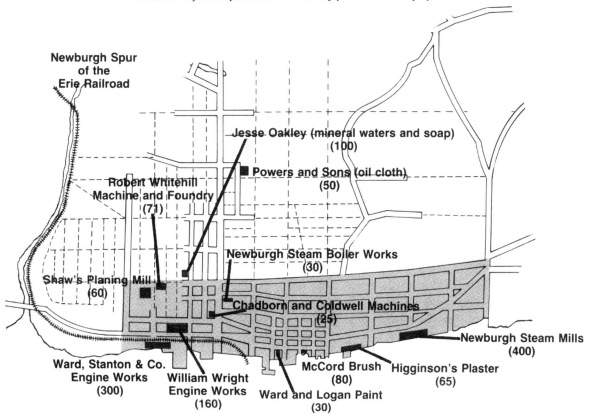

MAP 1:
Spatial Distribution of Factories in Newburgh, 1879
(Dotted lines represent streets built from 1835–1879)
Include only those factories with twenty-five or more employees.

Newburgh Spur of the Erie Railroad

Jesse Oakley (mineral waters and soap) (100)

Powers and Sons (oil cloth) (50)

Robert Whitehill Machine and Foundry (71)

Newburgh Steam Boiler Works (30)

Shaw's Planing Mill (60)

Chadborn and Coldwell Machines (25)

Newburgh Steam Mills (400)

Ward, Stanton & Co. Engine Works (300)

William Wright Engine Works (160)

Ward and Logan Paint (30)

McCord Brush (80)

Higginson's Plaster (65)

Source: *Census Schedules of Manufactures, 1880*

factory production. For these construction workers and general laborers a healthy Newburgh was, by definition, ever growing; if industries failed to grow, or if new industries did not move to town, the demand fix residential and industrial construction would dry up. Due to the magnitude of the construction sector, the town was confronted with paradox: Newburgh could maintain its population only through growth.

It seems unlikely that many Newburghers initially shared the forwarding merchants' sense of localism, which had derived from marital ties and real estate investments. But by mid-century this largely private attachment to Newburgh had evolved into a pervasive and strident boosterism. The people of Newburgh seemed to be aware of the subtle balance of the town's economic mechanism, for a failure.

Newburgh's industrial transformation thus marked a change in emphasis from external to internal growth. When Newburgh functioned as a commercial center, its forwarding merchants exploited the economic potential of the hinterland; their concern was not with the growth of Newburgh *per se,* but with the expansion of the outlying agricultural region. But to protect their commercial and real estate holdings, the freighters chose to exploit the internal aspects of Newburgh's economy. Once set in motion, their economic system was apparently self-sustaining: industrial growth brought new factory workers who required housing which in turn led to a further expansion of the construction and service sectors of Newburgh's economy to grow would generate a retrogressive cycle: an exodus of construction workers, less consumer demand, reductions in the service sector, still less construction and so on. Since over thirty-five percent of Newburgh's

TABLE 1
Mercantile contributions to the Newburgh spur of the Erie

Firm	Amount
Thomas Powell & Co."	$45,000
Benjamin Carpenter & Co.	10,000
Crawford, Mailler & Co.	25,000
John P. DeWint	25,000
N. Reeve	1,000
	$106,000

Not listed above is a $29,000 contribution of the Beveridge Brewing Company which often acted in consort with the freighters.

[a]In all, Thomas Powell and his son-in-law, Homer Ramsdell, made land purchases and cash advances to the Erie that totaled $202,219.

Source: Ruttenber, *History of Orange County*, pp. 120–121.

TABLE 2
Value added by manufacture for Newburgh, 1839–1899, adjusted to 1879 prices

Year	Value added by manufacture (current prices)	Value-added price deflators[a] (1879= 100)	Value added by manufacture in 1879 prices
1839[b]	87,550	126	54,246
1844	106,750	107	99,766
1849	470,109	92	5 10,988
1854	54 1,600	98	552,653
1859	701,480	95	738,400
1869	1,162,485	151	769,858
1879	1,035,480	100	1,035,480
1889[c]	2,403,000	90	2,670,000
1899[c]	2,764,500	81	3,455,623

[a]Rascal on Robert E. Gallman, "Commodity Output, 1839–1899," in the National Bureau of Economic Research, *Trends in the American Economy in the 19th Century, Vol. 24*, (Princeton University Press. 1960), p. 56. Deflators were rounded to the nearest whole number.

[b]The 1839–1840 Census Schedules for Newburgh are missing. The 1839 Value-added figures were interpolated from 1835 and 1845 data.

[c]The Manuscript Schedules for Manufacturing for 1889 were destroyed by fire. The data for Newburgh for 1889 and 1899 were derived from published schedules of manufacturing and are not necessarily comparable to the earlier figures.

Source: Refer to Appendix B.

TABLE 3
Distribution of Newburgh's value added by manufacture by industry, 1835–1880 (by percent)

Type of Industry	1835	1845	1850	1855	1860	1870	1870
Iron foundries and metal machinery	—	14	7	30	21	29	46
Textiles	14	24					
Clothing	—	—	—	—	1	10	14
Gristmills and brewing	72	36	20	8	18	13	1
Sawmills, wooden items	4	—	9	14	12[b]	13	4
Leather Products	9	22	9	16[a]	8 [a]	3	9 [a]
Mineral processing	—	—	11	—	1	—	—
Chemicals	—	—	—	—	—	2	8
Miscellaneous	1	4	13	19	10	9	2

[a]Includes soap manufacturing, which was largely dependent on animal fat and accordingly was grouped with leather products. By 1880, the figure represents solely soap manufacturing.

[b]Includes some other construction materials.

Sources: The Federal Census Schedules for Manufacturing for 1850–1880 and the, Manuscript Schedules for the New York State Census for 1835, 3845, and 1855. The 1840 Federal Schedule is no longer available while the 1865 and 1875 State Censuses were incomplete.

TABLE 4
Occupational distribution of male workers in Newburgh, 1850–1870

Occupational group by sector	1850 total	% male labor force	1870 total	% male labor force	Percentage change 1850–1870
Manufacturing					
Factory work	199	11.2	831	18.2	+7.0
Artisans	289	16.3	416	9.1	-7.2
(sub-total)	(27.5)	(27.3)	(-0.2)		
Construction					
Skilled	140	7.9	575	12.6	+4.7
Laborers	557	31.3	1.056	23.2	-8.1
(sub-total)	(39.2)	(35.8)	(-3.4)		
Transportation	100	5.6	243	5.3	-0.3
Services	493	27.7	1,439	31.6	+3.9

Source: Original manuscript Census Schedules of Population for Newburgh for 1850 and 1870.

families owned their homes, the economic decline of the city would spell financial ruin for the town's middle classes. The promotion of Newburgh became not a stratagem for a few, but the fundamental concern of the entire community.

As the commitment to Newburgh—to localism—was becoming widespread, the forwarding merchants began to relinquish their pre-eminent position in the community. A grateful population accorded them honors testifying to the success of their plan of development; main streets were named after Powell, Carpenter, Robinson, Walsh and Smith (Ramsdell no doubt disdained the comparison implicit in such an honor).

But the task of sustaining Newburgh's growth was left to a new generation of entrepreneurs, mostly industrialists. These new men—immigrant machinists with a gift for invention, or self-made entrepreneurs with lots of energy and optimism—were eager to superintend Newburgh's continued growth. Robert Whitehill, born in Glasgow, worked in a Newburgh foundry. As an apprentice he invented a machine for sizing and dressing cotton yarn, and by 1890 was president and chief owner of several large machinery factories. Patrick Delany, a refugee from the Irish potato famine, could tell a similar story: He worked in a boiler works, devised several patents and established his own factory. Horatio Beckman began as a machinist in Newburyport and invented a machine that "revolutionized the entire comb trade"; he became long-standing superintendent of the Newburgh Steam Mills and a major stockholder in the local electric company. A final example of this new generation is William Wright, who purportedly invented the nation's first rotary engine at the age of twenty-seven; armed with a handful of patents and an impressive reputation, Wright gained Ramsdell's support and opened the town's largest machine factory.[12]

The visible success of these self-made men made them natural heirs to the forwarding merchants' legacy of town promotion. Although these inventor-entrepreneurs were newcomers, the town accepted them almost immediately. Whitehill was elected alderman and chosen as president of the Board of Trade; Delany, too, was elected alderman; Beckman served as water commissioner and alderman; Wright became the most prominent member of the Board of Trade. Newburgh's "society" also opened ranks to admit these ostensible parvenus: Wright, Whitehill and Beckman were charter members of Newburgh's prestigious private club.[13]

While the forwarding merchants' concerted efforts to "boost" Newburgh were strongly influenced by their substantial investments in local real estate, the localism of the subsequent generation of manufacturers can best be understood as the result of social rather than economic factors. They sought status and promised economic growth in return. An indication of the manufacturers' good faith was the formation of the Board of Trade in 1882 which symbolized the shift from the collective entrepreneurship of the old freighters to a more formal collective entrepreneurship of manufacturers.[14]

By 1891 it was clear that the forwarding merchants had succeeded. Townspeople celebrated the rise of their industrial city by subscribing to a new history of the city. John Nutt, the town biographer, emphasized in 1891 the parallel of Newburgh's industrial growth with its period of turnpike expansion under the leadership of the early freighters; in his words, "the tidal wave of prosperity that swept over the village a hundred years ago has returned." United in purpose and infused with a sense of localism, the people of Newburgh acclaimed the achievements of Whitehill, Wright, Delany, Heckman, and others, and anticipated "a new era" of expanded growth. Nutt concluded, "All the indications are that the growth is healthy. There is every reason to expect the continuance of the 'good times.'" The situation and advantages of the place are now such that it is not likely to lose its share of good things going.[15]

A Slow Appearance, 1893–1900

A stranger from Middletown: "Isn't Newburgh rather slow? it seems to be falling behind."

Newburgher: "No; the conditions have changed. The city has lost its old time commercial buzz, and is engaged in manufacturing. Hence, we do not see so many people on the streets as we did. Manufacturing towns always have a slow appearance during the day."

—*Newburgh Sunday Telegram*, September 23, 1900

It seemed that only an astute outsider, making periodic visits, could have perceived the dimensions of change that occurred in Newburgh during the closing decades of the 19th century. The built portion of the city had surmounted the crest of hills to the west and began to spill onto the estates of the old forwarding merchants. The Newburgh and Cochecton Turnpike, once the chief artery of hinterland trade, was renamed "Broadway" and began to compete with the older commercial streets along the riverfront. Streetcars, initially drawn by horses, connected the growing residential areas with the factories near the river. Those who walked to work found the going somewhat easier as storm drains and stone pavements graced a number of the more-travelled streets that were formerly inundated by mudslides each spring.

But as the stranger from Middletown observed, even these main thoroughfares were remarkably quiet during the day. Was Newburgh "falling behind"? Had it succumb in some mysterious way to external competitive pressures? Or were the protestations of the Newburgher substantially correct? The Newburgher didn't explain exactly why manufacturing towns had a slow appearance, but perhaps he was referring to the large percentage of women in the labor force. Or perhaps the daily round of shopping that had absorbed the attentions of housewives was increasingly being postponed until later in the day as more women went to work in the new garment factories. Or perhaps the Newburgher was thinking of the absence of artisans—displaced by factories and retail stores—who had combined production and retail functions while tending to the needs of the back-country farmers. But if Newburgh appeared to be falling behind in 1900 there was an alternative explanation:

For several decades Newburghers had been uneasy over the fate of the Newburgh Steam Mills, which in 1845 had initiated the city's transformation from a mercantile to a manufacturing city. By 1850 the forwarding merchants who had built the cotton factory sold it to Garner and Company of New York City. This firm was mostly owned by Thomas J. Garner, an English millionaire who exported and marketed inexpensive American cotton textiles. To ensure that he could fulfill contracts with European textile merchants, Garner acquired upstate New York cotton textile factories. He soon owned majority stock in the Harmony Mills (Cohoes), the Rocky Glen Company (Dutchess County), the Franklin Dale Company (Clinton County), the Haverstraw Print Works, the Ingham Mills Print Works, and the Newburgh Steam Mills. When Garner died in 1867 he had gained full ownership of the Newburgh factory. His son, though, was fond of yachts and fancy homes, and he neglected the business. By the early 1870s the directors of the Newburgh Steam Mills, appointed by Garner, were loaning Garner and Company large sums of money with that firm's paper as collateral. The younger Garner died in 1876 and left Garner and Company to his nine-year-old daughter. The will provided that four executors would manage the estate until 1892, when his daughter would attain the age of twenty-five. Two of the executors were dead when the will was read. One of the others, William Thorn, lived in Newburgh and had supervised Garner's interests there. As executor, Thorn appeared to take pains to protect and expand the Newburgh Steam Mills. Perhaps Thorn's efforts were too zealous, for Garner's widow sued Thorn for dissipating the family's fortune. Eventually the suit was withdrawn, but when the daughter turned twenty-five—in 1892—she closed the Newburgh Steam Mills.

The following year would be worse. The Panic of 1893, and the depression that followed, were disastrous for Newburgh. In July the Whitehill company declared bankruptcy, followed by the Wright Engine Works four months later.[16] In April, 1894 the Delany boiler shop reported that only ten of its employees remained on a payroll that had approached one hundred.[17] During the following years a number of other manufacturing firms failed, the most embarrassing being the pride of the Board of Trade: the Kilmer Wire Works.[18]

Newburgh's industries had been buffeted by other depressions, especially those following the financial panics of 1857 and 1873, but in general they had lasted only briefly and were regarded simply as resting points along the march of industrial progress. But the metal and machinery industries of Newburgh were in a weak position even before the Panic of 1893.[19] The local firms were neither large enough to make use of scale economies nor located sufficiently near raw materials to achieve savings in transportation.

Although Newburgh's industrial development was initiated by the cotton factory, the metal and machinery industries soon accounted for the greater part of the city's industrial output. More important, the metal and machinery firms were "male-employing" as contrasted to the cotton factory and the newer garment factories that relied on cheap female labor.[20] The machinists, boilermakers and molders earned two to three times more than the semi-skilled laborers or construction workers.[21] Thus, the insolvency of Whitehill's, Wright's, Kilmer's and other companies precipitated a severe economic crisis.

Within five months of Wright's closing, between five and eight hundred people left Newburgh, "the vacant houses and apartments being silent witness to the truth of this statement.[22] One newspaper reported that nearly six hundred skilled workers were unemployed[23] while the "best mechanics—the molders and machinists—had left town in search of work in the Midwest.[24] Despite the exodus of skilled workers, newspaper estimates of the number of unemployed ranged from 1,400 to 4,000, the latter amounting to nearly fifty percent of the entire work force.[25]

What had begun as an industrial crisis quickly spread to other branches of Newburgh's economy; residential and industrial construction came to a standstill, throwing still others out of work.[26] As increasing numbers of wage earners found their jobs eliminated or their wages recluses, the city's retail trade deteriorated. Pressed to extend credit to their unemployed customers, the proprietors of the nearly two hundred grocery and liquor stores found it difficult to maintain their businesses; a large number of retail stores, both small and large, failed.[27] Espousing a Darwinian solution, the *Sunday Telegram* claimed that the city would be better served if ten percent of the stores went out of business or moved elsewhere.[28]

Relocation, however, was an option that most Newburghers found untenable. Many had invested their lives and their money in establishing their shops. Others owned homes that could now be sold only at a great loss. Still others thought the prospect of breaking family and neighborhood ties unbearable. Most Newburghers believed, furthermore, that the situation could improve, and they thought it the duty of the town's leaders to set that process in motion. After all, had not the experience of the previous decades proven that change comes from within? A city grows not because of its inherent locational advantages, but because its leaders possess the vision and enterprise to exploit whatever potential does exist. Indeed, the crisis brought about by the Erie Railroad in the 1840s motivated the Ramsdells, Powells, Carpenters, and

Crawfords to build an industrial city. The current crisis, they reasoned, must have been the fault of the new leaders—the Wrights, Whitehills, Beckmans, and Delanys—for, as one paper complained, "the old aggressive spirit of development seems to have died with Homer Ramsdell." [29]

Money as well as leadership was needed to bring about economic recovery. During the two years following his declaration of bankruptcy, William Wright appealed to local sources to raise the $10,000 necessary to satisfy the Engine Works' main creditor, a "rapacious" New York City bank. Wright noted that if he were able to commence operations he would rehire two hundred "resident mechanics" and thereby inject $10,000 in wages into Newburgh's prostrated economy each month. But owing to what Wright termed "the indifference of the moneyed class of the city," his efforts failed. As the date for the public sale of the Engine Works was set—July 18, 1895—Wright bitterly complained that if Homer Ramsdell were still alive he never would have had to "beg" for the money to put his firm back in order. [30]

Whitehill encountered similar problems and was forced to put his factory up for sale at public auction two days prior to the sale of the Wright Engine Works. A syndicate of outside creditors had become dissatisfied with the actions of a locally appointed receiver and had begun to pressure the local judge to dispose of the firm's remaining assets more equitably. [31] A number of prominent Newburghers reasoned that once the firm was sold there would be "no doubt of its prompt transfer to local interests and immediate resumption. [32]

The auction took place in the office of the factory with scores of "capitalists, machinists and workmen" milling around outside awaiting word of the disposition of the old enterprise and the plans for the new. What developed inside was a heated struggle between "local capital" and "New York money," the former being represented by Whitehill and his friends, the latter by the major New York City creditors. A third faction, headed by Colonel William Dickey (a major real estate speculator in the Heights section of the city) began to bid with the others, but soon dropped out, overawed by the "display of New York money." The New York faction, "exhibiting the dash and nerve that is characteristic of their city" and led by a member of the Whitney family, gained ownership of Whitehill's factory. They departed the city close-mouthed about their plans. [33]

As the New Yorkers descended towards the railroad terminal, Whitehill, Dickey, and the other local capitalists, as well as the machinists and laborers, no doubt wondered whether the people of Newburgh still possessed the resources and leadership necessary to control their city's destiny. The sale of Wright's two days hence loomed ominously in their minds, and the belated and clumsy efforts of the Board of Trade to found a joint-stock company to preserve the local factory seemed especially disheartening. [34] As was the case with Whitehill, Wright had amassed a number of short-term commercial notes which could not be repaid as orders slackened with the onset of the industrial depression. Wright's decision to pay his workers and "other local creditors" just before declaring bankruptcy exacerbated the wrath of the firm's creditors. [35] On the day of the sale, the same gathering of Newburghers that had watched the departure of the Whitney group no doubt flinched as a company of well-dressed people emerged from the New York train and climbed the hill towards the courthouse. Once again Colonel Dickey, with representatives of the Newburgh Real Estate Company, commenced the bidding after proclaiming his intention to start the shop, rehire the workers, and place Wright hack in charge. But the Newburghers were outbid by the New York creditors. Wright's, too, became the property of absentee owners. Observing that "the idea that Newburgh people may be called into the concern seemingly exists more in hope than in material substance," the *Sunday Telegram* complained that "local capital lost its opportunity. [36]

Within four months of the sale of the Whitehill and Wright factories, local capital sustained yet another "severe blow." The Kilmer Wire Works, which had been brought to Newburgh by the Board of Trade through a local subscription of $100,000 in capital stock, declared Bankruptcy in October.[37] The failure was precipitated by the major supplier of the Kilmer Works, namely the Troy Iron and Steel Company which no longer agreed to let its $106,000 account go unpaid. The Kilmer stockholders, mostly Newburghers, found their stock certificates worthless as the total debts of the firm rose to over $800,000.[38] Proclaiming it "the most disastrous failure ever known in Newburgh," the public-spirited capitalists who had invested in the enterprise singled out the Board of Trade for "soaking them."[39] A major supporter of the venture was both vice-president of the Board of Trade and a large investor in local real estate; a partner of the firm that marketed the stock locally was found to be related by marriage to the Kilmer family, all of which increased Newburghers' apprehensions. The *Sunday Telegram* observed that "the next man or organization that can float any stock around this town will have to be a freak.[40]

Since it no longer appeared likely that local capital was either willing or able to direct Newburgh's industrial recovery, Newburgh's leaders looked expectantly to see what the absentee owners intended to do with the Newburgh factories. One leader predicted that with the sponsorship of wealthy New York syndicates, Newburgh's iron and machinery firms would conduct operations of "gigantic" proportions.[41] Gradually, however, these optimistic projections faded. The absentee owners of Wright's retained only skeletal crews while the owners of the other two firms sold their patents, machinery and inventories to non-local producers.[42] Confronted with local judges who were more sensitive to the economic needs of Newburgh than the bankruptcy statutes, the creditors of Wright's and Whitehill's had purchased the bankrupt firms simply to supervise the disposition of their assets.

Optimism abounded over rumors that the Troy Iron and Steel Company, closely tied to Standard Oil, would take over Kilmer's.[43] The ambitions of Newburgh's industrialists and realtors appeared to be more than realized when the nation's largest wire trust—the Washburn and Moen Company—acquired the Kilmer Wire Works in 1899.[44] The optimism subsided when the Trust immediately released all of the firm's salesmen and some of its machinists. The Wire Trust made its intentions explicit within several months: the Newburgh factory was to be dismantled. Soon afterwards the machinery was removed and shipped to other parts of the country while the unusable remainder of the firm's assets were "junked." The Newburgh wire mill had been purchased solely to prevent others from using the facilities. An astonished *Telegram* concluded, "And so ends the desert mirage held out in the distant visions of hundreds of skilled mechanics and cottages filled by the families of contented workingmen."[45]

In 1900 the *Telegram* observed "It has taken Newburgh exactly seven years to strike to the bottom."[46] The nation as a whole was well on the way to recovering from the depression of 1893 to 1897, but in Newburgh the situation had scarcely improved. The census for that year confirmed that there had been no appreciable increase in the city's population for the first time since the crisis brought about by the Erie Railroad in the 1840s. The iron and machinery business had "gone to pot" and recovery seemed unlikely since the wave of late 19th century industrial consolidations had strengthened the position of the Pennsylvania and mid-Western competitors.[47] The building trades, formerly the largest sector of Newburgh's employment, were completely inactive. Ten years earlier nearly two hundred homes were built annually; but only three houses were constructed in 1899, and none through the first half of 1900.[48] Rents declined sharply and one realtor lamented, "There is no real estate market to quote, and hasn't been for a number of years.[49] The city's more enterprising unemployed took to planting potatoes in the vacant lots of the city, and some fifty families were sustained by these rustic experiments in urban economics.[50]

Those who had waited patiently for the city's economic recovery began to give up hope. The city's leaders—Wright, Whitehill, Delany, Kilrner, Beckman, Dickey and others—had been unable to save their own firms, much less rebuild the economic foundations of the entire city. Wright died penniless in a Brooklyn tenement. Whitehill, too, died shortly after his firm's failure, and his brother was left to fight unsuccessfully for local control of the engine works. Ramsdell had divided the largest portion of his estate among his grandchildren thereby minimizing the extent to which his wealth could be immediately wielded for local enterprise after his death in 1895. Beckman was fired shortly after his gas and electric company had been absorbed by General Electric. And if local industrialists had proven incapable of orchestrating Newburgh's economic revival, it now seemed doubtful that the various absentee owners would take on Newburgh as their charge.

These were the undercurrents, then, that the aforementioned Newburgher disingenuously omitted from his discussion with the traveler from Middletown in the autumn of 1900. Newburgh had indeed undergone a transition from a commercial town to a manufacturing city—that part of the tale was correct—but the "slowness" attributed to the city was largely a consequence of the fact that the industrial foundations of the city were collapsing. In boosting his city the Newburgher was perpetuating the tradition of localism established by the forwarding merchants nearly a century earlier. As the city's factories were passing into the hands of disinterested absentee owners and distant corporations, and as the local leaders were becoming powerless to direct the city's recovery, it was imagined that the spirit of localism would somehow breathe life into the city's prostrate industries.

But even as the Newburgher was explaining (or dissembling) the ramifications of Newburgh's transition to a manufacturing city, another metamorphosis was taking place. If the well-travelled Newburgher had visited the workers' district in the southern portion of the city, particularly the section bordering the Negro neighborhood, he would have noticed the Italians, eastern Europeans and Russian Jews who were moving into the houses and tenements that had been all but abandoned during the depression of the 1890s. The most significant legacy of the Panic of 1893—low rents and inexpensive housing—eventually furnished the basis for the city's industrial rejuvenation by attracting immigrant labor. Newburgh's garment factories and sweatshops, requiring little capital but ample supplies of cheap labor, flourished. Several clothing companies moved to Newburgh, often occupying the vacated premises of the iron and engine works.[51]

Once again Newburgh was to receive its share of progress. But just as some Newburghers were made uneasy by the clanging of the factory bell and the arrival of Irish immigrants in the summer of 1845, some Newburghers despaired of the alien newcomers at the turn of the century, imputing to them the rise in crime and corruption, the increasingly ramshackle tenements and overcrowded lots, and the growing sense of pessimism over the fate of the city as a homogeneous community. Some went so far as to reject the long-standing economic definition of progress, arguing that the garment factories should be closed. "These pauper labor concerns," they claimed, "are a detriment to any town."[52]

Industrial Newburgh began as a gamble—a desperate attempt by a close-knit group of merchants to protect their real estate investments. Conceived as an economic instrument and sustained by a pervasive commitment to local economic growth, Newburgh was unprepared at the beginning of the 20th century to question the consequences of industrialization. During the decades that followed, Newburgh's garment industries prospered and subsequently faded; after World War II another massive demographic change transformed the city. Yet over the years the willingness to regard the city as an economic contrivance remained unshaken.

The Book of Progress

Newburgh will have a population of 60,000 in 1950, and say 125,000 in the year 2000. . . . Cut this prediction and paste it in your hat. The logic of increase and development is irresistible. Nothing will arrest it in the natural order of things. It is written in the book of progress.

—Newburgh Sunday Telegram, April 14, 1895

Animating the urban-industrial revolution of the 19th century America was a faith in progress—a conviction that the nation's economic and social institutions were evolving to some higher form. Fired in the crucible of competition, the factories, railroads, banks, and even the individual entrepreneurs and their cities were the products of a vaguely understood Darwinian alchemy: the "fittest" survived and prospered, while those that were in some way deficient did not. Although this notion of competitive, evolutionary progress was applied broadly to many endeavors during the 19th century, it often achieved its most explicit expression in reference to the destiny of particular cities. Local newspaper editors, politicians and promoters persistently conjured the spectra of a ghost town—or at least the prospect of "falling behind"—to enlist public support for various developmental schemes. Americans, moreover, showed a remarkable willingness to part with their public and private funds to ensure the prospects of their town.

Why parochial attachment should be so strong in 19th century urban America is not self-evident, for American cities were made "in a few years out of nothing," as Seth Low put it.[53] While European parochialism was nurtured by deep-rooted traditions and ageless family ties, American cities were the setting of endless demographic upheavals.[54] And if European parochialism was tempered by tradition, American localism took on a strident character: the huckster and booster were almost indistinguishable.

The fusion of these ideas—a faith in economic progress and a self-conscious sense of localism—decisively influenced Newburgh's development during the 19th century. The emphasis on local economic growth, emanating from the marital practices and real estate investments of the freighters, shaped the mercantile village of the early 1800s and necessitated its industrial transformation at mid-century. Originally a device of the mercantile elite, localism became acceptable by all classes. Laborers and building tradesmen, comprising the largest segment of the labor force, recognized the need for unlimited growth to maintain their economic position. Middle class families, whose status was confirmed by home ownership, sought population growth to protect their major investment. Similarly, the late 19th century industrial parvenus, financed by the old forwarding merchants and elevated to positions of community leadership, gladly accepted the responsibility for ensuring the town's growth. Closely identified with economic self-interest, localism thus became the unifying concept of 19th century Newburgh.

It was an idea, however, which became increasingly outmoded as the century progressed. Geographic specialization eroded the economic foundations of many small industrial cities such as Newburgh which lacked any particular competitive advantage. The extension of railroad track and the reduction in railroad freight rates during the last third of the 19th century favored the "efficiently producing centers over inefficient and nonproducing cities."[55] In accordance with Adam Smith's well-worn dictum, the widening of the national industrial market encouraged geographical specialization, much as the high transportation costs earlier in the century protected industrialists in one area from more efficient competitors elsewhere. The efforts of Newburgh's forwarding merchants to create an industrial city in the mid-1800s succeeded partially because the industrial market was fragmented by high transportation costs. By the 1890s, however, Newburgh's engine factories were buying iron castings from Ohio at a cost below that of local foundries.[56]

TABLE 5
Value-added by manufacture per worker, the United States and Newburgh
(in 1879 prices)

Year	U.S.	Newburgh
1839	$399	?
1849	542	684
1859	605	613
1869	529	505
(a)		
1896	521	505
1879	617	577
1889	900	772

(a)Robert Gallman emphasizes that because of qualitative changes in manufactured goods, it is senseless to compare value-added statistics over too great a time span; the data from 1839–1869 are comparable, as are the data from 1869–1899. One should not make comparisons between these two groupings.

Sources: U.S. data based on Robert E. Gallman, *op.cit.*; Newburgh material based on Table 3 (page 113) and Appendix B.

The evolution of a national investment market during the last third of the 19th century[57] further weakened Newburgh's industries. Lance Davis has noted that in the early 1800s capital moved from one area to another "only when the savers themselves moved with their capital."[58] Newburgh's forwarding merchants mastered this locally-oriented economic system. Through the practice of mercantile intermarriage, they consolidated local investment capital and channeled it into local turnpikes, hotels, real estate and finally into local industries. As non-local investments became accessible to Newburgh's capitalists during the 1870s and 1880s, however, the elaborate system of local capital mobilization deteriorated. Forced to compete in the nation's emerging investment markets, Newburgh's industries began to suffer from a shortage of capital during the 1870s and 1880s, as suggested by a comparison of the value-added output per manufacturing worker for Newburgh and for the rest of the nation (see Table 5). During the period from 1849 through 1869, when Newburgh's mercantile community was transferring capital into manufacturing, the output per worker in Newburgh was considerably above the national average. But by the 1870s and 1880s the trend was reversed—an indication that relatively less capital was flowing into Newburgh's industries. This failing became all too evident following the Panic of 1893.

The pattern of Newburgh's population growth relative to the rest of the Northeast paralleled the flow of capital into manufacturing (see Figure 1). Newburgh's rate of growth when it functioned as a mercantile center had little in common with the average growth rate of cities in the Northeast; after the completion of the Erie Railroad, Newburgh's loss of population from 1840 to 1845 (refer to Appendix A; Figure 1 does not include data from the New York State Census) was especially unusual. But as the forwarding merchants redirected their capital into manufacturing during the late 1840s, the 1850s and the 1860s, Newburgh's growth

FIGURE 1

The rates of growth for Newburgh, New York and the median rate for cities
of over 10,000 population as of 1950 in the Northeast.

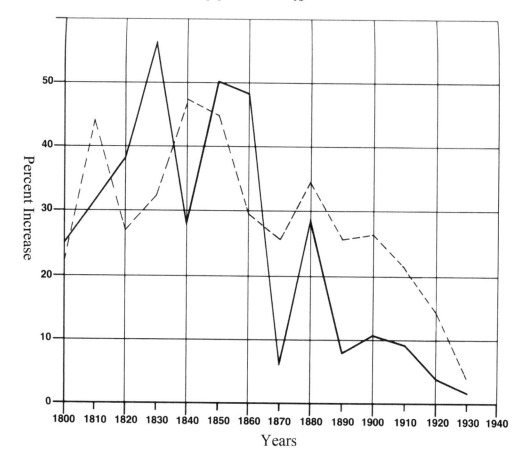

Sources: Carl Madden, "Some Spatial Aspects of Urban Growth in the United States," *Economic Development and Cultural Change*, Vo.4, 1956. p. 376. Refer also to Appendix A.

rate exceeded that of the region as a whole. By the 1870s, however, a new pattern was established—one that would last to the present: Newburgh grew at a rate consistently lower than that of most other cities in the Northeast.

Geographic specialization and the evolution of a national investment market were major elements in the economic rationalization of the nation during the last two decades of the 19th century. Yet economic progress, defined as increasing specialization, output and efficiency, eventually devastated the economic system established by the forwarding merchants.

"The economic significance of cities," Shigeto Tsuru has written, "lies in the external economies they provide." By "external economies" Tsuru means those benefits "which cannot be directly attributed to the action of the private individual firm," such as a nearness to markets and complementary producers, and the availability of a large and specialized labor force.[59] As a small industrial city, however, Newburgh provided few external economies; it lacked a competitive advantage in proximity to raw materials or markets; its labor force was small and relatively unspecialized. That it became an industrial city at all is remarkable. But

Newburgh's forwarding merchants were not content to watch as outside economic forces overwhelmed their town in the 1840s. Their success in the creation of an industrial city stemmed in part from their ability to muster local resources—capital, entrepreneurship, and leadership—to compensate for a lack of external economies.

From the outset, however, the freighters' foremost concern was the growth of their city rather than the profitability of their industries; both were clearly related, but the *intent* of the forwarding merchants must be considered the crucial causal factor: They chose to industrialize because they believed it the best way to further Newburgh's urbanization—and their real estate investments. Their motives and methods were founded in an as yet ill-defined localism. That they succeeded in creating a prosperous industrial city demonstrated the strength of a well-coordinated nexus of local economic forces in the mid-1800s; that they ultimately failed indicated the extent to which a rationalized economy had pervaded the nation by the close of the century. The forces of a broad economic market now dictated the city's future.[60]

Notes

Our Men of Property, 1846–1892

1. *Newburgh Telegram*, August 21, 1845.

2. See Winslow Homer, New England Factory Life-"Bell Time" *Harper's Weekly*, Julv 25, 1868, p. 492. A copy is reproduced in Edward Kirkland, *Industry Comes of Age* (New York: Quadrangle, 1967). P. 336pp.

3. *Newburgh Telegram*, May 30, 1844. The owner of a riverfront brewery (which functioned as its own forwarding agent) also became closely tied to the management of the cotton factory.

4. *Report of the Committee of Merchants of Boston*, p. 7, 1820, cited in Caroline F. Ware, *Early New England Cotton Manufacture*, and (New York: Russell. 1966). pp. 79–80.

5. Ware, *Ibid* pp., 20–21

6. " See, for example, Thomas R. Smith, *The Cotton Textile Industry of Fall River, Massachusetts* (New York: 1944). for a study of the establishment of cotton textile factories by a local group of merchants in Fall River.

7. Victor S. Clark, *History of Manufacturers in the United States*, Vol. I (New York: Peter Smith, 1929). p. 411; also Ware, *Early Cotton Man.* p. 152.

8. According to the State Census Schedules of Manufacturing for Orange County for 1845, Newburgh had a total value added by manufacture of $106,750, or a per capita figure of $17.39; Walden, on the other hand, with hut 2,300 inhabitants, produced nearly $60,000 in value-added, for a per capita figure of $24.58. At the time of the survey, the Newburgh cotton factory had not yet commenced production.

9. Employment data on Newburgh's manufacturing firms is based on the original schedules of the *U.S. Census of Manufactures*. With the exception of the 1855 census, the New York State manufacturing censuses were astoundingly incomplete.

10. *The Highland Courier*, June 13, 1845.

11. .Ruttenber, *History of Orange County*, pp. 118–122. As a representative of Newburgh's interests, Homer Ramsdell was named a director of the Erie Railroad and eventually became President of the company for a period. Throughout his association with the Erie, Ramsdell sought to promote Erie Railroad connections with New England. The idea was that Newburgh would become the point of connection, and steamboats from Newburgh—his steamboats—would ferry the trains across the river. The scheme worked for a time.

12. John Nutt. *Newburgh: Her Institutions, Industries, and Leading Citizens*, (Newburgh: J.Ritchie and Sons. 1891) pp. 236–239. 247, 264–265, 243–245.

13. *The Powelton Club, 1893*, (Newburgh: Newburgh Journal Printing House, 1893). The initial publication of Newburgh's most prestigious voluntary association.

14. Nutt, *Newburgh*, pp. 189–191. The Board of Trade as composed of 29 manufacturers, 19 retail merchants, 6 wholesale merchants, 6 real estate agents, 3 professionals, 2 transportation moguls, and a number of city officials and building contractors in 1891.

15. Nutt. *Ibid.*, frontispiece; also pp. 27, 65

16. *Newburgh Sunday Telegram* (hereafter cited as *Telegram*) July 23, 1893, November 12. 1893, and January 7. 1894.

17. *Telegram*, April 1, 1894.

18. *Telegram*, December 8, 1895.

19. *Telegram* April 2, 1899.

20. Refer to Appendix C, The Newburgh newspapers were careful to distinguish between "male-employing" and "female-employing" concerns, the former were regarded favorably, the latter critically.

21. See, for example, David Cole, *Immigrant City* (Cambridge: Harvard Univ. Press, 1937), pp. 121–122.

22. *Telegram*, June 24, 1894.

23. *Telegram*, April 1, 1894

24. *Telegram*, May 20, 1894, July 7, 1895, August 4, 1895

25. *Telegram*, December 24, 1893

26. *Telegram*, December 23, 1894

27. *Telegram*, December 23, 1894.

28. *Telegram*, December 23, 1894, April 1, 1894

29. *Telegram*, March 24, 1895

30. *Telegram*, March 31, 1895.

31. *Telegram*, November 19, 1893.

32. *Telegram*, July 7, 1895.

33. *Telegram*, July 21, 1895.

34. *Telegram*, March 31, 1895.

35. *Telegram*, January 7, 1894.

36. *Telegram*, July 21, 1895.

37. *Telegram*, October 27, 1895.

38. *Telegram*, December 8. 1895.

39. *Telegram*, December 15, 1895.

40. *Telegram*, December 15, 1895; also December 8, 1895.

41. *Telegram*, July 28, 1895.

42. *Telegram*, May 8, 1909.

43. *Telegram*, March 8, 1896.

44. V. S. Clark, *History of Manufacturers*, Vol. III, pp. 122–125.

45. *Telegram*, April 30, 1899, April 3, 1899, February 5, 1899.

46. *Telegram*, May 6, 1900, August 12, 1900.

47. *Telegram*, April 2, 1899.

48. *Telegram*, May 6, 1900.

49. *Telegram*, June 3, 1900, July 15, 1900.

50. *Telegram*, May 20, 1900.

51. *Telegram*, April 9, 1899.

52. *Telegram*, November 13, 1909.

The Book of Progress

53. Low's statement cited in Richard Hofstadter, *The Age of Reform*, (New York: Vintage. 1955). p. 176.

54. Stephen Thernstrom, *The Other Bostonians: Poverty and Progress in the American Metropolis* (Cambridge, Mass.: Harvard University Press, 1973). p. 224. Thernstrom has noted that, "The migratory impulse seems to have been surprisingly strong and uniform over a period of almost 170 years." (p. 224).

55. Alan R. Pred, *Geographical Review*, Vol. 55, (1965), p. 174.

56. *Newburgh Sunday Telegram*, March 31, 1895.

57. Lance E. Davis, "The Investment Market, 1870–1914: The Evolution of a National Market," *Journal of Economic History*, vol. 25 (1965), pp. 360–365.

58. Lance E. Davis, "Capital Immobilities and Finance Capitalism: A Study of Economic Evolntion in the United States, 1820–1920." *Exploration in Entrepreneurial History, vol.1 (1963), pp. 100–101*

59. Shigeto Tsuru, "The Economic Significance of Cities," in Oscar Handlin and John Burchard., *The Historian and the City* (Cambridge, Mass.: M.I.T. Press, 1963) p. 45.

60. The causal significance of local groups of merchant-entrepreneurs has not escaped the notice of urban economic historians. Thomas Smith studied the rise of the cotton textile industry in Fall River, Massachusetts, and noted that many of the investors in the initial cotton factory were merchants who sought to increase the value of waterfront property (pp. 26–33). The central element in the town's industrial development was the "presence of an aggressive, closely knit group of local entrepreneurs." (p. 53). Later in the hook, Smith concludes that several of the cotton mills "were built largely for speculative purposes, to increase real estate values." (p. 78). Constance Green, in a study of the industrialization of Holyoke, Massachusetts, noted that even though Boston merchant investors established the town's first cotton factory, the town's most important industry—paper manufacturing—developed from local sources: "At least half of the capital invested in the paper mills belonged to Holyoke people and most of the rest came from Springfield, a situation in marked contrast to what obtained in the textile industry." (p. 91). Hut why the resurgence of local industrial enterprise? Green wasn't sure: "Whatever the explanation—a kind of entrepreneurial provincialism, a belief that investment in Holyoke was sounder than in most places, the fruit of civic pride and ambition, or mere chance-noteworthy is the extent to which Holvoke's business enterprises were locally financed with an increasing network of intertwining interests." (pp. 175–176). The same dynamic was found in Chicopee, Massachusetts. The cotton factory was established by absentee industrialists, but the arms factories found their "capital requirements met by the combined efforts of local merchants and important salaried employees of the mills." (p. 89). Thomas R. Smith, *The Cotton Textile Industry of Fall River, Massachusetts (New York: King's Crown Press, 1944)*, Constance M. Green, Holyoke, *Massachusetts: A Case History of the Industrial Revolution in America* (New Haven: Yale University Pr., 1939), and Vera Shlakman, *Economic History of a Factory Town: A Study of Chicopee, Massachusetts* (Northampton, Mass.: Smith College. 1935). The dynamic of urban-industrial growth outlined in this essay seems to have parallels elsewhere.

This article originally appeared in the *Hudson Valley Regional Review*, Volume 3.1.

APPENDIX A

The Population of Newburgh from 1790 through 1900

Studies of the growth of cities are complicated by changes in municipal boundaries, usually result of annexation. The problem in reconstructing the population growth of the area contained in the city limits of Newburgh as constituted in its charter of 1865 is somewhere different. The village of Newburgh was created as an administrative subdivision of the Town of Newburgh in the early 1800s, although local residents distinguished between the relatively dense settlement in the village and the outlying town even ill the 1700s.

Although some censuses separated the population figures for the town and the village of Newburgh, it has not been possible to locate a complete population series during the 19th century for both the Village and the Town of Newburgh. Individual canvasses for the village are available for 1782, 1790, 1814, 1817, 1822, 1835, 1845, 1850, 1855, 1865, 1870, 1875, 1880, 1890, 1892, and 1900 [in 1865, the boundaries of the Village of Newburgh became roughly the boundaries of the new City of Newburgh.] The sources for this data include Ruttenber, *History of Orange County*, p. 286, the *Newburgh Gazette*, August 27, 1845, the *Newburgh Telegram*, October 31, 1850, and the New York State Census for 1865 and the *Newburgh Telegram*, December 16, 1900.

On the other hand, a continuous series of population data was available for the combined Town and City Village of Newburgh from 1790 to 1900. It was therefore possible to create a reasonably accurate population estimate for the missing years of the Village of Newburgh by using proportionate interpolations. The table which follows is based on these figures.

Mark Carnes

Population of the Village of Newburgh (1782–1860) and the City of Newburgh (1865–1900)

Year	Population	Rate of Increase	
		(ten year period)	(five year period)
1790	1,487	—	1—
1800	1,696*	14	—
1810	2,105*	24	—
1815	2,370		13
1820	2,754	3 1	16
1825	3,499*		27
1830	3,807*	3 8	9
1835	5,118		34
1840	5,951*	56	16
1845	5,784		-3
1850	7,623	28	32
1855	9,599		26
1860	11,426*	50	19
1865	13,905		22
1870	17,014	49	22
1875	17,322		2
1880	18,049	6	4
1890	23,087	28	
1892	24,5361		
1900	14,943	8	

*Denotes interpolation.

APPENDIX B

Preparation of Value-Added Tables

The tables on Newburgh's value-added by manufacture are based on the original federal census schedules of manufacture for the years 1850, 1860, 1870 and 1880. The federal published schedule is used for 1890 and 1900; the state census manuscript schedules for 1875, 1845 and 1855.

The firms included in the tabulations all had at least four employees; those with fewer were omitted. The definition of what constitutes "manufacturing" has repeatedly changed; Robert E. Gallrnan, *op.cit.* established the guidelines for such a study of value-added and they have been followed in the preparation of Newburgh's value-added by manufacture tables.

In general, those activities now regarded as "services" such as hiking, printing and publishing have been omitted, as have various aspects of construction (carpenter sub-contractors, painters, and so on). Small retail operations that included an assembling function, such as tobacconists, were also excluded. Public utilities, including the gas companies, were excluded. These exclusions are consistent with Gallman.

See also the table that follows concerning the distribution of manufacturing employment in Newburgh by industry, prepared from the same tabulations:

The distribution of manufacturing employment in Newburgh by industry, 1850–1880.

Type of Industry	1850	1855	1860	1870	1880
Iron foundries and metal machinery	8	21	17	30	35
Textiles	46	47	31	32	26
Clothing	—	—	5	5	6
Gristmills and brewing	8	8	5	4	1
Sawmills, wooden items	3	13	18[b]	12	9
Leather Products	7	12[a]	10[a]	3	12[a]
Mineral processing	24	—	1	—	—
Chemicals	—	—	—	3	5
Miscellaneous	4	—	13	11	6

[a] Includes soap manufacturing. By 1880 within this category leather processing had been entirely replaced by soap manufacturing.

[b] Includes other construction materials.

[c] Includes the manufacture of lime, which was used as a fertilizer. Also included are several brick factories which may not have been located within the geographical area of the village/city.

Sources: Federal Census Schedules for manufacturing for Newburgh 1850–1880. New York State Census for 1855 (includes listing of industries).

APPENDIX C

Sectorial Distribution of Newburgh's Labor Force, 1850–1870

The data on the next page were derived from the original federal census schedules which list the occupation of each resident of Newburgh. The occupations for women were not regularly listed in the 1850 Census, so the data below is only for men.

The occupations changed considerably during the twenty-year period, so that several of the larger shifts may have simply reflected changes in occupational nomenclature. The grouping of most occupations was fairly obvious, but there were some problems, particularly regarding certain artisanal occupations.

Finally, the data on the next page are further segregated by city ward and ethnic group and are available from the author on request.

Occupations	1850	% total force	1870	% total force	Change in % 1850/1870
Manufacturing					
Engine work related: boilermakers, machinists, molders engineers, etc.	61	3.4	352	7.7	+4.3
Other factory work brush, soap, plaster factories	49	2.8	335	7.3	+4.5
Cotton Factory: spinners, weavers	74	4.2	88	1.9	-2.3
Manufacturers: owners or superintendents	15	.08	56	1.2	+0.4
Artisans: chandlers, blacksmiths, tailors furniture makers, coopers, shoemakers	289	16.3	416	9.1	-7.2
Construction					
Skilled workers: masons, painters, stone masons, carpenters, planers, roofers, etc.	140	7.9	575	12.6	+4.7
Laborers: (no additional designation)	557	31.3	1056	23.2	-8.1
Transportation					
Carters, teamsters, boatmen, etc.	100	5.6	243	5.3	-0.3
Services					
Waiters, gardeners, other personal, services	60	3.4	158	3.5	+0.1
Clerks, salesmen	102	5.7	409	9.0	+3.3
Butchers, bakers	36	2.0	114	2.5	+0.5
Shopkeepers	120	6.7	273	6.0	-0.7
Merchants (wholesale)	37	2.1	87	2.0	-0.2
Bookkeepers, agents	7	0.4	89	2.0	+1.6
Professionals: lawyers, physicians	27	1.5	8.4	1.8	+0.3
Government workers	9	0.4	34	0.7	+0.3
Teachers, clergy	18	1.0	40	0.9	-0.1
Farmers	38	2.1	48	1.1	-1.0
Miscellaneous	40	2.2	103	2.3	+0.1

The Hudson River Railroad and the Development of Irvington, New York, 1849–1860

Rohit T. Aggarwala

Introduction

Close by Sunnyside is one of those marvelous villages with which America abounds: it has sprung up like a mushroom, and bears the name Irvington, in compliment to the late master of Sunnyside. A dozen years ago, not a solitary house was there. . . . Piermont, directly opposite, was then the sole terminus of the great New York and Erie Railway and here seemed to be an eligible place for a village, as the Hudson River Railway was then almost completed. Mr. Dearman had one surveyed upon his lands; streets were marked out, village lots were measured and defined; sales at enormous prices, which enriched the owner, were made, and now upon that farm, in pleasant cottages, surrounded by neat gardens, several hundred inhabitants are dwelling . . . Morning and evening, when the trains depart for and arrive from New York, many handsome vehicles can be seen there. This all seems like the work of magic. Over this beautiful slope where few years ago the voyager upon the Hudson saw only woodlands and cultivated fields, is now a populous town. The owners are chiefly business in [sic] of New York, whose counting rooms and parlours are within less than an hour of each other.

—Benson J. Lossing, *The Hudson*, 1866[1]

Irvington, New York, was created by the coming of the Hudson River Railroad. Nearby towns such as Tarrytown, Yonkers, and Ossining had all existed in colonial times, but what was Justus Dearman's single farm in 1849—the year the railroad began—was, in 1860, a village with 600 inhabitants, recognized as one of the premier suburbs of the day. [2]

There were two Irvingtons. The first, the one well known later in the century for its architecture, surrounded the town, used its post office and railroad station, and was comprised of luxurious estates like Sunnyside owned by gentleman farmers who aspired, like many in England did at the same time, to the life of the country nobleman. The second Irvington, less well known but perhaps more important, is in the village laid out by Mr. Dearman's surveyors onto lots, owned by small merchants and craftsmen, some of whom commuted to New York, but some of whom were locals. These were the runners of the millions who fled the cities in the 20th century: middle-class families seeking a home with a healthier, safer lifestyle in the country.

The story of Irvington illustrates how a transportation innovation altered the pattern of city growth, and how rural regions not only were turned into extensions of a metropolitan region, but fully supported and participated in that transformation themselves. The story includes fortunes made overnight, successful and failed land speculation, technological advances, industrialization, the growth of the home as a refuge from the cold world of business. It involves old-family farmers, wealthy merchants, small-time entrepreneurs, craftsmen, and immigrants.

This paper will attempt to tell that story for the first ten years of the town's existence, until 1860. It will examine how Irvington was formed, who moved there, who profited from it; further, it will attempt to understand why they moved there and what life was like for these early suburbanites. It will describe the changes that antebellum suburbanization brought to Westchester.

Antebellum suburbanization has been dealt with, notably in Kenneth T. Jackson's *Crabgrass Frontier* and John R. Stilgoe's *Borderland: Origin of the American Suburb, 1939*, but usually as a prelude to the boom in suburbanization that came after the war. The change from rural to urban ways of life is demonstrated in *The Urban Threshold*, a study of Kingston, New York, on the west bank of the Hudson, by Stuart M. Blumin. But Kingston is a city which grew for internal reasons, and his study applies to Irvington only in limited ways. There is very little work done on Irvington itself, and little of that focuses on the crucial years of 1849–1860: *Woolfert's Roost*, a 1971 illustrated history with no listed author passes quickly from revolutionary times to the post-Civil War era, giving only a few paragraphs to the subdivision of the farms, and is very concerned with prominent local families. An unpublished typescript, "History of Irvington," at the Westchester Historical Society focuses mainly on pre-1850 history. The Irvington Historical Society published for a time a magazine, *The Roost*, from which I have used two articles, but again, it mainly misses this period and is involved with local stories rather than history.

The Coming of the Railroad

On September 29, 1849, an inaugural special opened the Hudson River Railroad from 30th Street on the west side of Manhattan to Peekskill, 47 miles up the river, and the lower Hudson Valley was changed forever.[3] The Hudson River was one of America's great highways of commerce, connecting New York, the nation's largest city and greatest port, and Albany, a major city in the 19th century. The river towns along its length had never been isolated—mail from and to New York (22 miles) frequently took only a day.[4] Still, the river valley's connection with New York depended on a river only navigable eight months out of the year, or on tedious, long carriage journeys. The railroad brought all of Westchester within a ninety-minute journey of Manhattan, on a route unaffected by weather.

The line had been envisioned for some time, but steamboat interests and the objections of the New York & Harlem Railroad and its investors had delayed it. The Harlem was chartered in 1838 to connect lower Manhattan with the Harlem River, and had by 1844 reached White Plains, 20 miles north of the city. It was planning to continue its inland route to Albany.[5]

The inland route worried some in the established cities on the river—notably Poughkeepsie, where Matthew Vassar, the wealthy brewer and merchant, had organized a preliminary survey for a riverbank railroad as early as 1842.[6] In 1846 the Hudson River Railroad Company was organized, and by March of 1847 it had raised the $3 million capital that the state legislature had required for it to be granted a charter. The first section opened two years later, and the line was complete to Greenbush [East Albany] in October 1851. The following year, the Harlem line reached the state capital.[7]

Before the railroad, Westchester County was primarily agricultural. A few river towns, like Tarrytown, had been around in colonial days, and local industry concentrated in those places. The bulk of the population of Westchester was in the northern half of the county, where there were large farms that provided New York City with much of its food.

There had been suburban estates in Westchester before the railroads—Washington Irving's Sunnyside, Colonel James Hamilton's Nevis, former New York mayor, William Paulding's Paulding Manor—but only for the very wealthy who could afford the second home or hotel expenses that sporadic commuting by boat or carriage required. With the railroad, middle-class New Yorkers could commute to the city every day. The lower part of the county began to grow in population and in importance. The railroad access led many farmers to begin dairying, and the Harlem River Railroad made $40,000 a year shipping fresh milk into Manhattan every morning.[8] One farmer in Carmel, 35 miles north of New York on the Harlem, switched to dairy cows from beef cattle and sheep when the railroad came, and in 1850 grossed $3,600 from the sale in New York of milk and cream from his fifty cows.[9]

The Hudson River Railroad also expected commuters to be among its passengers. Upon the railroad's opening, it published a tariff for discounted daily commutation fares. A one-way ticket from Tarrytown to New York was 35 cents; a commuter paid 22 cents each way if he bought them in quarterly installments of 120 tickets.[10] These fares allowed the middle class to commute—one hundred dollars a year was a good amount of money, but not a fortune.

The railroad was not entirely egalitarian. It began with one standard of service, but soon adopted the European system of first- and second-class cars; it must have had a diverse ridership.[11] More importantly, fares were based on mileage; while the commuter paid 22 cents, the fare to Manhattanville (now in the Bronx) was only 10 cents.[12] This was unlike omnibus lines, which charged per ride rather than by distance. These distance-based fares kept working-class New Yorkers from moving farther out than what is now the Bronx, preserving Westchester for the prosperous middle class.

Mount Vernon, New York, on what is now the Westchester-Bronx border, provides an example of how suburbanization was sorted by class according to distance from the city and, therefore, by commutation fares. In 1850, a group of New York tradesmen, employees, "and other persons of small means" organized themselves into the New York Industrial Home Association #1, which proposed to secure homes for its members and escape "the exorbitant rentals then exacted by landlords in the city."[13] By the spring of 1851, the group had selected a site at the intersection of the New York and New Haven Railroad with the New York & Harlem, in Westchester but close to Manhattan. One year later, three hundred houses were under construction; by 1860, Mount Vernon had 1161 residents, compared to 600.[14]

Even Mount Vernon would not be an enduring working-class community. A poor economy in the 1850s forced homeowners individually to sell to outsiders wealthier than themselves. In 1860, Mount Vernon looked like the rest of Westchester; the workers had returned to the city, leaving suburban commuting for the professionals and business-men.[15]

There was also an established market for the upscale country home. Alexander Jackson Downing had popularized the suburban cottage and villa in his magazine, *The Horticulturalist*, and other writings. The New York Evening Post frequently carried advertisements for auctions of suburban land in its front-page "Public Sales" column, and classified advertisements offering Westchester, Rockland, New Jersey, and Long Island farms and lots were common. All stressed the availability of railroad commuting to New York. A classified ad on April 19, 1850 offered two farms in Westchester and one in Rockland County, listing for each the closest rail line and station. It concluded: "All the above named farms possess many advantages for gentlemen wishing to reside in the country, and doing business in the city."[16] It said "reside in country," not summer or vacation there.

The Beginning of Irvington

On March 29, 1849, a farmer in Westchester County, New York, sold a quarter-acre of riverfront land to the Hudson River Railroad.[17] The line had been buying land since 1847, and would open as far as Peekskill in September. Dearman's neighbor, Calista Crosby, had sold three-quarters of an acre to the railroad in 1847 and only got $250; because he had waited to sell, the old farmer got $700 for his plot one-third that size.[18]

Dearman had owned his land since 1817, when he bought 140 acres of a neighbor's farm, and he had bought an additional 14 acres a few years later.[19] His farm lay directly across the river from the Piermont, New York terminal of the newly constructed New York & Erie Railroad. With the arrival of the Hudson River Railroad, it would be a logical place for a village.

Dearman saw this far in advance of the railroad's actual arrival. Only one month after the railroad opened, he sold his 154 acres to a New York broker, Gustavus A. Sacchi, for the astounding sum of $26,500.[20] Sacchi had already bought some land from Dearman's neighbor, Calista Crosby.[21] The property was surveyed and divided into lots measuring valued altogether at $39,000. They varied in price: the lots closest to the river were twice as expensive as those farther up the hill towards the Albany Post Road.[22]

On March 26, the following advertisement appeared in the "Public Sales" column on the front page of the New York *Evening Post:*

> **Building Sites on The Hudson River**
>
> —Situate [sic] between the Albany Post Road and the River, at to be sold at auction on the 25th of April, at the Merchant's Exchange, by COLE & CHILTON, Auctioneers. . . . A part of the property fronting the water will be sold in village lots, and in plots on the upland to suit purchasers. The premises are now being laid out, planted and improved. . . .
>
> Seventy-five per cent of the purchase money may remain on bond and mortgage. For further particulars application may be made at the station house on the premises to Mr. GEO. W. DEARMAN, at 5 Broad Street, to G.A. SACCHI or at the Auctioneer's office, 9 Wall st, where maps of the premises can be seen.
>
> N.B. Persons wishing to build for the summer, can purchase at *private sale*, on very liberal terms, on immediate application as above.[23, 24]

Advertisements were also placed in the New York *Courier, Tribune,* and in the magazine Home Journal.[25]

It is significant that Dearman's son, George W. Dearman, is listed as a contact person; it means that the farmer and his family participated fully in the sale; he was not swindled by a group of New York speculators. Dearman saw a great opportunity, and took it; the old farmer was not sentimental about his farm being subdivided when there was money to be made.

Sacchi probably assumed that large numbers of middle-class New Yorkers would move to the lower Hudson Valley as quickly as workingmen moved to Mount Vernon, but very few of the lots sold at the first auction. He was not alone in this assumption. On April 30, only four days after the auction, the Sing Sing, New York *Hudson River Chronicle* reported erroneously: "there are some three or four hundred buildings contracted for and in progress" at Dearman's. It may have misinterpreted the auction map, which showed 266 lots for sale; it may have been reporting the plans rather than the reality. The article went on to stress its faith in the area's suburban future:

The proximity of the County of Westchester to New York, and the decided advantages which it possesses as a place of residence for the business community of the city, over other neighboring counties, renders it peculiarly beneficial in all points of view, as a resort at all seasons of the year, for all classes and descriptions of businessmen.[26]

The paper's editors must have seen in the map what they had wanted to see. Westchester residents seem to have been even more eager for suburbanization than the New Yorkers were.

The same day as the Chronicle article, the New York Evening Post carried another Cole & Chilton advertisement:

Tuesday, June 11

At 12 o'clock at the Merchant's Exchange

Cottage sites at on the Hudson River Railroad—

The balance remaining unsold of those beautiful plots of ground at the above place, will be sold on the above day, if not previously sold at private sale. Persons wishing to purchase at private sale can do so by applying to the auctioneers, No 9 Wall street. Persons wishing to build immediately, 90 per cent of the purchase money may remain on bond and mortgage for a term of years. Several choice parcels are yet unsold.[27]

This ad ran for the entire month of May and into June, with the heading "Private Sale." Meanwhile, Cole and Chilton ceased holding their auctions at the Merchant's Exchange, and when the June 11 auction was finally advertised again, it was to take place in Dearman's itself. The firm advertised 100 plots yet unsold—after one auction and six weeks of private sales advertised daily—and a special train to take New Yorkers to the auction. The agents had finally realized that there was a market for the land outside of New York; in addition to the special train, they had arranged for the ferry to offer free rides from Piermont, "for the convenience of the citizens of Rockland and Orange counties."[28] Though Cole & Chilton did not, other New York auctions (and auctions on the premises by New York firms) were being advertised in the *Hudson River Chronicle*.[29]

Whether all the lots sold on that date is unclear. However, Sacchi either lost interest in the land or had overextended his capital. He mortgaged the land back to Dearman and, before long, had trouble making his payments to the farmer.

A Manhattan druggist, Franklin C. Field, had noticed Dearman's early. On October 27, 1849, two days after Sacchi bought his land from Dearmans, he sold some of it to Field. Field's drugstore was at 34 Beekman Street, and it must have done a good business, because he not only lived at the posh Metropolitan Hotel on Broadway but also had money to invest in land speculation.[30]

On June 4, 1850, before the second auction even took place, Field began to acquire the land out from under mortgage by paying for it lot by lot.[31] He may have lacked the thousands to pay for it all at once; or he may have had the wisdom to realize, as Sacchi did not, that the land would take time to sell. Field deposited the auctioneer's map with the county government as the official map of the village of "Dearman," and in the 12 separate transactions, he acquired most of the 266 lots. The area was known variously as Dearnman, Dearman's, Dearman's Station, and Dearman's Landing; in 1854, the residents ended the confusion by renaming the settlement Irvington, in honor of their august neighbor at Sunnyside.[32]

Sacchi seems to have lost almost all the property in Irvington to Field, and probably made little money for his effort. But the one setback at Dearman's did not stop Sacchi's land speculation; between 1849 and 1895 he sold over 600 parcels of land in Westchester.[33] Similarly, although Cole & Chilton may not have been entirely successful with the sale of Dearman, they kept up their interest in Westchester: an advertisement on June 11—the very day of the second Dearman's auction—promised an auction of lots at Sing Sing, only a few miles further upriver.[34] With time, Field did very well on Dearman's; by 1858, the druggist had become a full-time broker, with an office at 50 Exchange Place in New York.[35] Dearman also did well for himself: he died in 1855 with an estate of over $17,000. Like many farmers who made money, his newfound wealth seems not to have altered his lifestyle, as it did Field's: his estate inventory shows a silver tea set and six gold spoons to be his only extravagances.[36]

The Suburban Aesthetic

The auction map of Dearman's shows the streets Dearman and Sacchi laid out.[37] First Street, marked "70 feet wide," runs east from the railroad station up the sloping farm to Broadway. Also called the Albany Post Road, Broadway was the main north-south road of the area and ran into its namesake in Manhattan. The other east-west street in Dearman's, unnamed on the map, connects Broadway to the dock and ferry landing, with a bridge over the railroad. There were eight north-south cross-streets, approximately 50 feet wide, lettered from the river up the hill as A Street, B Street, and so on to H Street one block west of Broadway.[38] This design resembles the grid map of New York; it has nothing to do with the landscape or the countryside.

At the top of the map are two sketches of cottages and ground floor plans, based on Downing's designs and published in his book, *Cottage Residences*. The larger, "A Cottage in the English or Rural Gothic Style," was to cost $4,500 to build. Downing envisioned it on a plot of 200' x 1600', with elaborate landscaping. Downing included a bedroom on the main floor, an unusual composition (most houses had all bedrooms on the second floor); he mentions that "there are many families mainly composed of invalids, or persons advanced in years, [who require] little or no necessity for ascending or descending stairs." It was intended for the comfortable among the middle-class—the largest rooms are the library and the parlor. There were to be one or two servants, but the lady of the house would be fully in charge of the household.[39] A family in this house would have entertained guests frequently.

The second design, slightly smaller, is "A Small Cottage or Gate Lodge," which would only cost $830 to build. Downing supplies this second design as appropriate for the gardener or farmer of a larger manor in the same style. "It would otherwise," he writes, "make a neat and picturesque dwelling, if properly located, for a small, respectable family who wish to lead a quiet and simple life."[40]

The two houses show at what part of the market Dearman, Sacchi, and Field were aiming. The auction map was advertising, and these imagined houses would more effectively entice prospective buyers than a sketch of the farmland that Dearman's was at the time of the auction. The use of Downing's designs shows that the suburb's promoters always knew that the scenery, distance from New York—and higher potential profits—made their targets the professional and business classes.

The respectability and neatness of the village was a high priority. Quiet and property concerned the first suburbanites; an early deed for land in Dearman's from Field contains the stipulation that "no dwelling house shall at any time be erected . . . of less than $500 and [prohibited any] trade or business [that] may prove a nuisance to the neighborhood or injurious to the value of the adjoining premises."[41] Health was also stressed: the Cole & Chilton advertisements all claim that Dearman's has a "position perfectly healthy." Cholera

Rohit T. Aggarwala

had returned to America in 1849, and many city residents—especially in New York, the hardest-hit—saw country life as a way to avoid the diseases of the city.[42] The things that made people escape the city—noise, smells, crowds, disease, business, perhaps the lower classes—would be prevented from the very beginning.

Downing's success with his home designs—and the motive to put drawings of houses, rather than of Hudson Valley scenery, on the map—came from the increasing American love of the home. The Reverend William G. Eliot, Jr., told an audience of women in 1853 that

> the foundation of our free institutions is in our love, as a people, for our homes. The strength of our country is found, not in the declaration that all men are free and equal, but in the quiet influence of the fireside, the bonds which unites together in the family circle. The comer-stone of our republic is the hearth-stone.[43]

He expressed a popular sentiment that was at that moment finding buyers in Dearman's. That he eschews the importance of the equality of man is significant in an ideology that excluded the poor from its vision and was fully to be achieved only by the rich.

The New Suburbanites

Elisha S. Chapin, who sold shoes in New York, was one of Field's early customers in New York, purchasing two plots in 1853.[44] He had a townhouse on Barrow Street in Manhattan and, by 1856 a store at 46 Dey Street, in the center of town.[45] Chapin's business was growing; Dey Street in the 1840s had been a tenement neighborhood, and only in early 1850s converted completely to dry goods shops. He must have had the money to move both store and home at the same time.[46] With his wife and two-year-old son, he brought a family of servants to his new home in Dearman's. In 1860 he claimed real estate of $10,000 and personal property of $2,500. He maintained his townhouse on Barrow Street in New York until at least 1856, but gave it up by 1860; perhaps it took him a few years to depend entirely on daily commuting.[47]

Another New York buyer was John Woodhead, who bought land in 1855. An Englishman married to an American, he was 65 years old and had three children, aged 9 to 15. In the New York City directory of that year, he listed a home on Fourth Avenue in New York and an importing business on Warren Street; he also had a home in London, and probably made several trans-Atlantic crossings for business each year.[48] In 1860, his 19 year-old son, Albert, joined him in business.[49] While he maintained his New York townhouse and probably stayed there when working late, Irvington was his permanent residence, and his family was there year-round. Wealthier than Chapin, Woodhead had a personal estate of $8,000 in 1860, and employed a coachman and two female servants.[50]

Just south of the Dearman property, one of Irvington's wealthiest new residents was collecting property and building a mansion. In 1853, Theodore McNamee, a New York silk merchant, assembled four pieces of land into a gentleman's farm with a broad view of the Hudson.[51] He built a large Italianate villa, four stories tall, complete with a greenhouse.[52] The estate was a working farm, and McNamee was listed in the 1860 Westchester County Directory under "Farmers."[53, 54]

McNamee was only 38 in 1853; his wife was 42, and they had several children. His domestic staff included 3 female Irish servants, a coachman from New York, and a gardener from France. In 1860, he possessed real estate worth $100,000 and had personal assets of $20,000—making him among the very rich for that era.[55] He had moved to Irvington from a townhouse at 134 10th Street, at the corner of Brevoort Place, several blocks from his silk business at 112 Broadway.[56] But McNamee commuted every day; by 1855 he had sold the townhouse and listed Irvington as his only address.[57]

Of these early commuters, several generalizations can be made: all came to Westchester with families; all were established in their businesses or professions. For all, as for most of their contemporaries in mid-19th century America, movement was a part of life: Chapin moved home and store in 1853, McNamee's business moved from 112 to 320 Broadway in 1857,[58] Woodhead had transatlantic connections, Field changed both occupation and place of business.

In moving out of town, they all sought a pastoral ideal which only McNamee could truly attain—with his vast grounds, farm, and river vista. For the others, Irvington was a compromise that allowed them only small lots—probably not much bigger than their New York townhouses—in exchange for the quiet of suburban life, a picturesque setting on the Hudson, and such amenities as a vegetable garden and the ability to design their own homes. Despite the drawbacks, they came, testifying to the power of the suburban ideal in the 1850s.

Local Irvingtonians

In providing the free ferry rides to the second auction, the land speculators recognized what would become a major part of their business: local craftsmen and small businessmen who saw a lucrative market in the new settlement. One of Field's first sales was to John J. Banta, a young carpenter, who bought lot 22, a mid-block parcel one block away from the river, for $240 in October 1850.[59] Such a low price was still too much for the craftsman to afford outright; two months later he mortgaged the land to Colonel James A. Hamilton, grandson of Alexander Hamilton and a rich local lawyer.[60]

Another local who arrived in 1850 was Benson Ferris, Jr., the son of one of the area's most prominent men; his father had owned Sunnyside before Washington Irving. The younger Ferris went to the Tarrytown Institute, a private school for young men, and later taught there. He opened the first store in Dearman's, which he kept until he returned to Tarrytown in 1856 to open a hardware store. He was an active citizen, serving on the Greenburgh Board of Education and, in 1855, organizing the Westchester County Republican Party.[61]

Peter Warman had always lived in Dearman's, as a laborer doing odd jobs for various neighbors, including Washington Irving. He and his family—his mother, wife, and four children—probably lived as informal tenants on Dearman's farm because there is no recorded lease for him or his family until 1854.[62] In that year, his mother, Lavinia, leased a plot from Isaac Lent, who may have just bought the land from Field or Dearman and wanted a formal agreement.[63] Warman profited directly from the railroad's approach—in 1851 he became the railroad's station agent at the new Dearman station.[64]

In 1853, Field sold land to Benson F. Jewell, a tanner, cousin to Benson Ferris, Jr.[65] Jewell came from an established local family—his grandfather, John Jewell, had been imprisoned in Tarrytown by the British during the Revolution, and after the war bought 340 acres nearby.[66] John Jewell, Jr., Benson's father, was born in 1785 and had just died in 1851, worth $20,000. His will forgave $1,000 that Benson had borrowed just before his father's death; Benson had several siblings, and it seems that this was all he got from the estate.[67] Jewell prospered as the town grew around him; by 1860, he called himself a "gentleman." Some of his wealth may have come from his brothers or the estate of his father; Benson's wife, Julia, was Justus Dearman's granddaughter, but Dearman left her only $25 upon his death in 1855.[68] Later, Jewell opened a county store in the town with a partner.[69]

Rohit T. Aggarwala

Stephen Crosby, another tanner, bought a lot in 1850, and moved in with his mother, his wife and child, two Irish servants, and two black laborers. [70] His mother was Calista Crosby, the neighbor who had sold her land to the railroad too early to make much profit. She had bought two plots from Gustavus Sacchi in 1849, and Stephen, perhaps on his mother's advice, acquired three plots in Dearman's. [71] The profits of tanning and land speculation combined to give Crosby, too, the ability to call himself a gentleman in 1860. Although he had lost his laborers and one of his servants by then, he had the assets to claim the title: $6,000 in real estate and $10,000 in personal assets.

Another early Dearman's family was that of Justus' son, George Dearman, who lived at the top of the village, on Broadway, and ran a grocery store there. He and his wife, Euphemia, who came from the prominent Odell family, had four children. When George died in 1855, his widow sold the business to J.J. Banta, the carpenter, who became the major grocer of the town. Banta mortgaged the store to the estate. [72]

Caleb Wildey, Jr., was a blacksmith in Dearman's, and also lived near Broadway. His father had been one of the early settlers of nearby Tarrytown, and in 1845 had a street named after him. [73] But Caleb, Sr., died the next year, when Caleb, Jr.—the oldest son—was 14, and without enough children to work the farm, the family must have fallen on hard times. [74] They listed no real estate in the 1850 census; the farm was probably sold to support the family, but Caleb's mother may have saved enough from the sale to allow her son to purchase the land to set up his shop.

These residents demonstrate the way the local population was changed by and profited from the move to the suburbs. Some, like Dearman and Crosby, saw it coming and made a profit from land sales. Others, like Wildey and Banta, found new customers who bought goods the local farmers either made themselves or did without. Several, including Ferris, only stayed for the very first years of the village, when their knowledge of the area may have given them a business edge over competitors; for Ferris, simply being the first was probably all the edge he needed.

Suburban Immigrants

As Banta, Jewell, and Crosby left their trades, Irish immigrants moved in to take their places in the new community. Michael Bray arrived from Ireland in 1853 with his wife, bought a plot near Broadway and opened a blacksmith shop. Shortly thereafter, he and his wife had a son and a daughter. His business grew, and by 1860 Bray had $5,000 in property and $500 in cash, and had two other Irish blacksmiths and an Irish wheelwright working and living in his shop. [75] Unlike some immigrants, Bray intended to stay: he filed a declaration of intention to naturalize in 1853 and was granted citizenship in 1855. [76]

Abbottsford was a second Irvington that sprang up on the other side of Broadway, on the former Harmse farm. It was divided and sold at about the same time, and some of it also by Franklin Field, but its lots, less scenic than Dearman's, were mainly sold to immigrant servants of the local mansions. One example was Christopher Fitzsimmons, a coachman on Colonel Hamilton's Nevis estate. In 1863, he sold his house and lot in Abbottsford to another Irishman, John Huston, who put $5.00 down on the $2,500 price, and got a job on the Hudson River Railroad. [77]

A Complete Town

By 1855, Dearman's was a complete, functional village, like many emerging suburbs along the railroads in Westchester. Tarrytown and Yonkers showed the same trends, but those two towns had existed before the railroad; Dearman started out as a suburb, and so the suburban trends could be seen there most purely.

It had a coal and lumber business at the pier by the railroad station, a post office, and a grocery store. Five years later, it had acquired a confectioner, a carriage maker, a butcher, two shoemakers, a house painter, and a hotel—all catering to a middle-class, commuting population.[78] Greenburgh Public School #2 had been on Broadway well before Dearman contemplated subdividing his farm.[79] However, the local population of children was increasing: in 1851, there were 150 children aged 4–21 in School District #2, and in 1853 there were 171.[80] (District #2 included areas outside of Dearman's; but a good part of that increase might be ascribed to it.) Most of the Hudson River Railroad's trains stopped at Irvington.

Although some of the local residents who moved to Dearman's or speculated in its land may have prospered from the new suburb's emergence, the town's effect on its residents was not mainly one having to do with prosperity or social mobility. It is in the change in life-style that the suburb itself is important. The increase in population and urbanization across the country meant that new customers could be found in growing towns like Tarrytown, nearby. Ferris' good timing in being the first storekeeper in Dearman's gave him a small edge, but he soon gave it up to return to Tarrytown and open a store there. Craftsmen like Banta and Crosby went into business in many established towns, and laborers like Warman found jobs related to the transportation and industrial revolutions all over America; it did not take a new town to accomplish these social movements.

Rather, Irvington is significant in that it affected the life-style of all who lived there. There was direct and constant connection with New York City—but the Hudson Valley had always had a good connection to it, and the coming of the railroad changed the valley in that way much less than it did Binghamton or New Jersey. The significant factor of the suburb is that, in a rapidly urbanizing society, many people strove to return to smaller towns—not only New Yorkers, but people from Westchester and other outlying areas as well. Tarrytown had a population of 1,000 in 1842, but it had grown greatly by 1860.[81] It is likely that, in 1860, life in Irvington, with 600 neighbors, more closely resembled life in the earlier Tarrytown than Tarrytown itself did in 1860.

Another significant fact is that Irvington was not a community of New Yorkers in a pastoral setting; if anything, it was a few families of commuters set in a Westchester village. The level of interaction between New Yorker and local was great; while the commuters themselves went to the city during the day, their families stayed in Irvington. Mrs. Chapin and Mrs. Woodhead probably did some of their own shopping, and would have known the various storekeepers such as Dearman and Banta. Their children, at least during their elementary school years, would have attended either the local common schools or the Tarrytown Academy, where they would have joined the local elites such as the Ferrises. The commuters, interestingly, seem not to have had any political involvement; Westchester leaders such as Ferris, Jr., Colonel Hamilton, and T.W. Crisfield held the local offices.

The houses in Dearman's were substantial; neat and attractive if not always elegant. Many houses as well as mansions were designed by major architects of the day, such as Alexander Jackson Davis and George Woodward, and several aspired to architectural interest.[82]

None of the houses could have been very small, due to the restrictive clause in the deeds, and all would have been solid and big enough for a large family; family life was a major part of the suburban ideal. Up the hill at Broadway and in Abbottsford, where the Irish lived, there were pigs and chickens in the street; Downing saw the immigrant population as a cause of village ugliness, writing "wherever they [the Irish] settle, they cling to their ancient fraternity of porkers, and think it no free country where pigs can't have their liberty."[83] Most of the houses had gardens, though none had the space to grow anything as elaborate as Downing envisioned.

Downing himself objected to nearly everything about Dearman's, and would have objected to the use of his designs for its promotion. He intended his cottages for spacious grounds, not small lots. He wrote in *The Horticulturalist* of his anger at the land speculator (like Sacchi and Field) who "covers the ground with narrow cells, and advertises to sell or rent them as charming rural residences." He specifically condemned Dearman's, charging that its developers wasted a beautiful setting by building "mere rows of houses upon streets crossing each other at right angles and bordered with shade trees."[84]

Dearman's straight streets represented the best city planning of the Enlightenment: straight streets, right angles, numbers instead of names to make address-finding easy. But Downing and others in the artistic world looked to a new ideal, the Romantic, which sought closeness with nature and personality rather than efficiency. Downing preferred curving roads following the terrain, large plots for gardens and woods around each house, isolated settings with grand vistas.[85] Dearman was born in 1765; a practical farmer from a rational age, he would have seen nothing romantic in nature.[86] To him, straight streets would have meant progress; it also meant cheaper surveying, more lots fronting on a street, more profit. Romanticizing the wild was something only wealthy city-dwellers would do.

A Changed County

Westchester County in the 1850s was a contrast between areas of "prosperity" and those of "slovenliness," and the difference between the two was mainly the distance from one of Westchester's three railroads, as John R. Stilgoe notes in *Borderland: Origins of the American Suburb.*[87] Nathaniel P. Willis, a writer who lived on the west side of the Hudson at Cornwall, near Newburgh, remarked upon a ride he took up the Harlem River Railroad:

> Miles upon miles of unmitigated prosperity weary the eye. Lawns and park-gates, groves and verandas, ornamental woods and neat walls, trim edges and well-placed shrubberies, fine houses and large stables, neat gravel walks and nobody on them—are notes upon one chord and they certainly seemed to me to make a dull tune of Westchester. . . . Westchester wants a dash of wretchedness to make it quite the thing.[88]

Suburbanization also disrupted the farming that had previously been Westchester's main occupation. Solon Robinson, editor of *The American Agriculturalist* looked at the county's farms in November 1850, and marveled at the Harlem line not for its passengers but for its annual freight bill for raw milk.[89] "Tillable land has increased in value," he wrote, but the problems of new neighbors overwhelmed the farmers. Orchards were abandoned because too much fruit was stolen, and coal smoke from the local brickyards had already ruined many trees; domestic dogs attacked sheep. Feeling helpless, many farmers neglected the upkeep of their properties: "Everything has an ancient . . . behind-the-age appearance," Robinson wrote.[90]

According to Robinson, one indication of the farmers' inability to adapt quickly to their new neighbors was the fact that the houses of commuters were usually supplied mainly from the city; even the gentlemen farmers were not self-sufficient. Local farmers continued to supply the city with milk, and failed to turn to the market gardening and supply the commuters' families with the fresh meat and vegetables they wanted. Robinson concluded that "Close as this county is to the city, the majority of the inhabitants have not yet caught the infecting spirit of improvement."[91] The result was that even more aspiring suburbanites bought the farms, improved them, and carried on agriculture as a hobby or sideline.

Robinson failed to see what was really going on around him. The few farmers left in central Westchester were holdouts, continuing dairy farming in an increasingly expensive area when competitors from farther-out areas, accessible by rail and ferry but more inconvenient for the commuter, such as Orange County on the Erie Railroad, Putnam and Dutchess Counties on the Harlem, and Long Island, had lower expenses because they did not have suburban neighbors raising the property values that Robinson himself noted were increasing. Dairy farming was probably not a bad living, but when contrasted to the "prosperity" New Yorkers brought with them, even well-run farms were apt to look slovenly.[92] Robinson may even have been comparing old farms run as sidelines: McNamee's farm did not need to show a profit each year; it only had to please its rich owner. The native farmers—the ones who, unlike Dearman, Crosby, and Ferris, had not seen that suburbia was the future of Westchester—could hardly keep up with their rich neighbors' cosmetics even if they could get by economically.

The population growth of the lower part of the county was dramatic. Between 1845 and 1855, Westchester's population expanded from 47,394 to 80,678; of this 33,284-person increase, 22,461 were in the towns newly served by railroads. Greenburgh, the town in which Irvington and Tarrytown sit, alone grew by 6,230.[93] The time and cost of commuting kept this growth south of Tarrytown and White Plains: "Merchants and professional men, obliged to go to New York every day, hardly find it easy or profitable to live higher up the river than Tarrytown, and accordingly we shall find that the large towns north of that village owe their growth rather to internal than external causes."[94]

Still, it is easy to ascribe this growth entirely to the railroads. The figures quoted above also show a ten-year increase of 10,000 persons in towns not served by railroads; Westchester was growing itself. The local buyers of small plot—the Bantas and Ferrises and Jewells—were the sons of local farmers who could not continue farming in the area because there was not enough land. This may explain why Westchester's residents, like the editors of the *Hudson River Chronicle*, were so eager for the business of New York to move upriver; it would give their sons something to do. The locals who became the storekeepers in the new suburbs probably had brothers who went west to continue farming.

Conclusions

The experience of Dearman's illustrates the changes that took place in Westchester—and in many suburbs of major railroads—allowed daily commuting beginning in the 1840s. Everyone—local farmers, city speculators, country newspaper editors—expected suburban growth to follow the railroad. The local people—farmers, merchants, and laborers—welcomed it, participated in it, and many prospered from it. The slovenly farmers Solon Robinson reported on were the few who had not seen it coming and did not have the enterprise to adapt to the new situation. In fact, suburbanization followed less quickly than expected, in a steady stream rather than in a rush, to the detriment of those, like Sacchi, who expected quick sales. It also involved many who had not worked in New York, but found jobs or enterprise in a newly commercial society based not on farming but on salaries and wages drawn in New York by the commuters.

What is remarkable about Irvington is the extent to which the local population participated in the remaking of their county. Irvington is not a story about big-city developers taking away land from content farmers. It was Justus Dearman who sold his land and provided the mortgage for his first broker; his son was an agent in the sale, and most likely paid close attention to the sale's progress, if only because he might never collect on his mortgage if things went badly. The first sales of land were not only to speculators from New York, but also to speculators from the neighboring towns, and Dearman's first residents were not commuters but locals who came to establish the basic businesses every small town in the 1850s required. In the few local histories, Irvington has often been portrayed as a community of housekeepers and servants, but it was not so homogeneous. Woodhead and Chapin from New York were wealthier than most of the local families, but not all; Peter Warman who as a hired hand for Washington Irving would have held his hat before the writer, could, as a station agent, sell tickets and provide assistance to passengers without subservience. Theodore McNamee was probably wealthy and aloof on his estate, but he was an exception, high above the shopkeepers and farmers but also beyond the social reach of the smaller city merchants like Woodhead and Chapin.

Irvington was bound for a change after the Civil War. During the Gilded Age of the 1870s and 80's, some of the most extravagant villas of New York financiers were built there, and many of the first residents' homes were bought and enlarged into mansions. But in its first decade of existence, Irvington was not a suburb as much as a suburban town, where a few commuters provided the seed money around which a Westchester community grew.

Notes

1. Benson J. Lossing, *The Hudson From the Wilderness to the Sea* (New York: Virtue & Yorston, 1866), 353.

2. J.H. French, *1860 Gazetteer of New York State* (Syracuse: R.P. Smith, 1860; repr., Interlaken, N.Y.: Heart of the Lakes, 1980), 699.

3. Advertisement, *New York Evening Post*, September 28, 1849, 3.

4. Lucille Hutchinson and Theodore Hutchinson, *The Centennial of North Tarrytown* (Cambridge, M.D.: Western Publishing Company, 1874).

5. Kenneth T. Jackson, *Crabgrass Frontier* (New York: Oxford University Press, 1985), 35.

6. Louise Hasbrouk Zimm, et al., *Southeastern New York* (New York: Lewis Historical Publishing Company, 1946), 361.

7. John Brown and W. Colchester Yron, *Historical, Descriptive, & Illustrated Atlas of the Cities, Towns, and Villages on the Lines of the Hudson River and New York Central Railroads* (New York: Francis B. Hart and Company, 1862).

8. John R. Stilgoe, *Borderland: Origins of the American Suburb, 1820–1939* (New Haven: Yale University Press, 1988), 69.

9. Paul W. Gates, *The Farmer's Age: Agriculture, 1815–1860, vol. 3 of The Economic History of the United States*, Henry David, et al., eds. (New York: Holt, Rinehart, & Winston, 1960), 240.

10. Edward Hungerford, *Men and Iron: The History of New York Central* (New York: Thomas Crowell Co., 1938), 150; Philip Green, *The Railroad in Croton in History of Jane Northshield*, ed. (Croton-on-Hudson, N.Y.: Croton-on-Hudson Historical Society, 1976), 84.

11. Alan Keller, *Life Along the Hudson* (Tarrytown, N.Y.: Sleepy Hollow Restorations, 1976), 160.

12. Hungerford, *Men and Iron*, 151.

13. Frederic Shonnard and W.W. Spooner, *History of Westchester County* (New York: New York History Co., 1900), 579.

14. Shonnard and Spooner, *History of Westchester*, 580; J.H. French, *1860 Gazetteer of New York State* (Syracuse: R.P. Smith, 1860; Interlaken, N.Y.: *Heart of the Lakes*, 1980), 699–700.

15. Jackson, *Crabgrass Frontier*, 85.

16. Advertisement, *New York Evening Post*, May 10, 1850, 1; advertisement, *New York Evening Post*, May 11, 1850, 1; advertisement, *New York Evening Post*, April 19, 1850, 4.

17. Deed, Justus Dearman to Hudson River Railroad Company, March 29, 1849, Westchester County Records Center (WCRC), N.Y., Liber 133, 155.

18. Deed, Calista Crosby to Hudson River Railroad Company, August 19, 1847, WCRC, Liber 121, 58.

19. *Profile: Village of Tarrytown* (White Plains, N.Y.: Westchester County Association, 1974).

20. Deed, Justus Dearman to Gustavus A. Sacchi, October 25,1849, WCRC, 139,109.

21. Index of Deeds by Grantee, WCRC, s.v. G.A. Sacchi, see Deed, Calista Crosby to G.A. Sacchi, October 18, 1849, WCRC, Liber 141, 72.

22. Deed, Justus Dearman to Franklin C. Field, September 9,1850, WCRC, Liber 153, 27.

23. Advertisement, *New York Evening Post*, March 26, 1850, 1.

24. See Appendix 1.

25. Advertisement, *New York Evening Post*, April 8, 1850, 1.

26. "Growth of the County of Westchester!" (Sing Sing, N.Y.), *Hudson River Chronicle* April 30, 1850, 2.

27. Advertisement, *New York Evening Post*, April 30, 1850, 1.

28. Advertisement, *New York Evening Post*, May 1, 1850, 1; advertisement, New York Evening Post, June 5, 1850, 1.

29. Various advertisements, (Sing Sing, N.Y.) *Hudson River Chronicle*, various issues, May-July 1850.

30. H. Wilson, *Trow's New York Directory, 1855–6* (New York: Trow City Directory Co.,1855).

31. Deed, Justus Dearman to Franklin C. Field, September 9, 1850, WCRC, Liber 153, 27; Deed, to Franklin C. Field, November 12, 1850, WCRC, Liber 156, 26; Index to Deeds by Grantor, WCRC, s.v. Justus Dearman.

32. In this paper the town will be called either distinguish it from the fanner himself—or depending on the frame of reference.

33. Index to Deeds by Grantor, WCRC, s.v. G. Sacchi.

34. Advertisement, *New York Evening Post*, June 11, 1850, 1.

35. H. Wilson, *Trow's New York City Directory 1858–1859* (New York: John F. Trow, 1858).

36. Estate Inventory of Justus Dearman, File 1855–33, WCRC.

37. Auction map in Westchester County Record Center.

38. "Map of the Village Lots and Cottage Sites at Westchester Co., adjacent to the Hudson Station & Piermont Ferry Depot to be sold at auction by Cole & Chilton on Thursday 25th April at 12 o'clock, at the Merchant's Exchange, N.Y." WCRC.

39. Andrew Jackson Downing, *Victorian Cottage Residences* (1842; repr. New York: Dover, 1981), 40.

40. Downing, *Victorian Cottage Residences*, 138.

41. Deed, Franklin C. Field to J.J. Banta, October 28, 1850, WCRC, Liber 153, 233.

42. Charles E. Rosenberg, *The Cholera Years: The United States in 1832, 1849, and 1866* (Chicago and London: *University of Chicago Press*, 109.

43. Jackson, *Frontier*, 48.

44. Index to Deeds by Grantee, WCRC, s.v. Elisha Chapin.

45. *Trow's 1856–57.*

46. John A. Kouwenhoven, *The Columbia Historical Portrait of New York* (Garden City, N.Y.: Doubleday & Co., 1953), 247.

47. *Trow's 1856–57*; H. Wilson, *Trow's New York City Directory, 1860–61* (New York: John F. Trow, 1860).

48. *Trow's 1855–56.*

49. *Trow's 1860.*

50. Manuscript schedules of the United States Census of 1860.

51. Index to Deeds by Grantee, s.v. Theodore

52. *Villas on the Hudson* (New York, 1860; repr. New York: DaCapo Press, 1927).

53. Thomas Hutchinson, *Westchester County Directory for 1860–61* (New York: Thomas Hutchinson, 1860).

54. See Appendix 2.

55. 1860 U.S. Census manuscript schedules; Stuart M. Blumin, *The Urban Frontier* (Chicago: University of Chicago Press, 1976), 5

56. Doggett's *New York City Directory, 1850–1* (New York: John Doggett, Jr., 1850), 328.

57. *Trow's 1855–56*

58. *Trow's 1856–57*; *Trow's 1858–59.*

59. Deed, Field to Banta, October 28, 1850.

60. Index to mortgages by mortgagor, WCRC.

61. J. Thomas Scharf, *History of Westchester* County, *New York* (Philadelphia: n. p. 1886) 2:260.

62. McLaughlin, "Census Transcription."

63. Index to Deeds by Grantee, WCRC, s.v. Lavinia Warman.

64. Kate R. McLaughlin, "1850 Census Transcription of Greenburgh," 1962 typescript, WCRC; will of John Jewell, 1851, Westchester County Surrogate Court proceedings, WCRC, Liber 33–1851, 265.

65. McLaughlin, "1850 U.S. Census transcription."

66. Scharf, *History of Westchester,* 2: 189

67. Grenville C. Mackenzie, *Families of the Colonial Town of Philipsburg* (Tarrytown, N.Y.: Sleepy Hollow Restorations, 1976). Jewell chapter, vol. 1.; estate inventory of John Jewell, Estate Inventories File 78–1851, WCRC; will of John Jewell, Liber 33–1851, 265.

68. 1860 U.S. Census manuscripts; will of Justus Dearman, 1855, Westchester County Surrogate court proceedings, WCRC, Liber 37–1855, 251.

69. J.H. Lant, *Westchester* County *Directory* (Albany: Weed, Parsons, Co., 1864).

70. McLaughlin,"1850 Census Transcription."

71. Westchester County Index to deeds by grantor, WCRC; Westchester County Index to deeds by grantee, WCRC.

72. Westchester County Index to mortgages by mortgagor, WCRC.

73. Jeff Canning and Wally Buxton, *History of the Tarrytowns* (Harrison, N.Y.: Harbor Hill Books, 1975), 48.

74. McLaughlin, "1850 Census Transcription,"60.

75. 1860 U.S. Census Manuscript schedules.

76. Michael Bray, *Declaration of Intent to Naturalize,* March 23, 1853, WCRC.

77. Robert Insdorf, "Abbottsford Properties Can Be Traced Back to Harmse Farm," *The Roost,* vol. 1(Irvington, N.Y.), 1 (March, 1977); Adele Wamock, "The Huston Family, Residents of Abbottsford Since 1863," *The Roost,* vol. 2 (June 1978).

78. See Appendix 2.

79. *Woolfert's Roost* N.Y.: Washington Irvington Press, 1971).

80. "1851 Towns of Westchester—Statements of the Number of Children Between 4 and WCRC; "Report of the Superintendent of Common WCRC.

81. *Gazetteer of the State of NewYork* (Albany J. Disturnell, 1842), 391.

82. John Zukowsky and Robbe Pierce Stimson, *Hudson River Villas* (New York: Rizzoli, 1985).

83. Andrew Jackson Downing, "Country Cottages," *The Horticulturalist* vol. 4, (June 1850) 539.

84. Jackson, *Crabgrass Frontier,* 65.

85. Jackson, *Crabgrass Frontier,* 65.

86. Mackenzie, *Families.*

87. Stilgoe, *Borderland,* 68.

88. Quoted in Stilgoe, *Borderland,* 68.

89. Stilgoe, *Borderlands,* 69.

90. Quoted in Stilgoe, *Borderland,* 69–70.

91. Stilgoe, *Borderland,* 70.

92. Gates, *The Farmer's Age,* 238–240, 248.

93. Shonnard and Spooner, *History of Westchester,* 577–8.

94. James Miller, *Miller's New Guide to the Hudson River* (New James Miller, 1866).

This article originally appeared in the *Hudson Valley Regional Review,* Volume 10.2.

Appendix 1

First Advertisement for the auction of land at Dearman's.

New York *Evening Post,* March 26,1850, page 1, "Public Sales" column.

Building Sites on the Hudson River

-Situate between the Albany Post Road and the River, at Dearman to be sold at auction on the 25th of April, at the Merchant's Exchange, by COLE & CHILTON, Auctioneers. The distance from the city by the Hudson River Trains, is three-quarters of an hour. The fare is the same as to Dobb's Ferry and may be commuted quarterly or by the year. A part of the property fronting the water will be sold in village lots, and in plots on the upland to suit purchasers. The premises are now being laid out, planted and improved. The views are commanding and beautiful, and the position perfectly healthy. The Ferry with Piermont affords constant communication between this point and the opposite shore, and connects the Hudson River and Erie Railroads. The neighborhood is excellent, including in the immediate vicinity the country seats of Messrs. Washington Irving, Ambrose C. Kingsland, Gen. Paulding, Mrs. Colford Jones Messrs. Henry Sheldon, James A. Hamilton, and George Schuyler, besides the residences of many gentlemen belonging to Westchester county.

Seventy-five per cent of the purchase money may remain on bond and mortgage. For further particulars application may be made at the station house on the premises to Mr. GEO. W. Dearman at 5 Broad Street, to G.A. Sacchi; or at the Auctioneer's office, 9 Wall st, where maps of the premises can be seen. All the trains of the Hudson River Railroad stop at Dearman and Gentlemen who would view the premises, may take the cars at Chambers street, at 7, 8 ½ A.M., 3, 4 ½ and 6 P.M., and leave Dearman, returning at 7 25, 9 24 A.M. and 129 529, and 10 12P.M.

N.B. Persons wishing to build for the summer, can purchase at *private sale,* on very liberal terms, on immediate application as above.

Running Advertisement for the first auction.
New York *Evening* Post, April 8, 1850, page 1, "Public Sales" column.
Also ran April 9, 10, 11, 12, 13, 15, 16, 17, 18, 19, and 20.

Bruce A. Chilton, Auctioneer
BY COLE & CHILTON
[Several other auctions of New York City property listed]

THURSDAY, 25th
At 12 o'clock at the Merchants' Exchange
Building Sites on the Hudson River, at Dearman, between Dobb's Ferry and Tarrytown. For full particulars, see advertisement in Courier, Tribune, Evening Post, and Home Journal, or enquire of the auctioneers, where maps are now ready and can be had.

Main Advertisement for the first auction.
New York Evening Post, April 22, 1850, page 1, "Public Sales" column.
Also ran April 23 and 24.

Bruce A. Chilton, Auctioneer
BY COLE & CHILTON
[Two auctions for Manhattan properties precede Dearman auction]

THURSDAY, 25th
At 12 o'clock, at the Merchants' Exchange
Cottage sites for Summer Residences on the east bank of the Hudson River, at Dearman, between Dobb's Ferry and Tarrytown.

The premises are situated between the Albany Post Road and the river at Dearman, in the town of Greenburgh, each lot being 50 feet by 100 feet. The distance from the city by the Hudson River trains is three quarters of an hour. The fare is the same as to Dobb's Ferry, and may be commuted quarterly or by the year. A part of the property fronting the water will be sold as village lots, and in plots on the uplands to suit the purchasers. The premises are already laid out, planted, and improved. The views are commanding and beautiful, and the position perfectly healthy. The Ferry with Piermont affords constant communication between this point and the opposite shore, and connects the Hudson River and Erie Railroads. A wide avenue leads from the post road to the river, gently sloped, well graded, and lined with a double row of trees. The neighborhood is most excellent, including in the immediate vicinity the country seats of Messrs. Washington Irving, Ambrose C. Kingsland, Gen. Paulding, Mrs. Colford Jones, Messrs. Henry Sheldon, James A. Hamilton, and George Schuyler, besides the residences of many gentlemen belonging to Westchester county. The homestead of the former proprietor, Mr. Dearman will be sold with the out buildings.

Only ten percent of the purchase money will be required on the day of sale, and if purchasers build immediately, the whole of the balance may remain on bond and mortgage. In the case of purchasers not building, seventy-five per cent may so remain.

For further information, application may be made at the Station House on the premises, to G W Dearman, at No. 5 Broad st to G.A. Sacchi or at the auctioneer's office No. 9 Wall st, where maps of the premises can be had.

All the trains out of the Hudson River Railroad stop at Dearman, leaving Chambers street at 7 o'clock and 8 22 o'clock A.M., and at 3, 4 ½ and 6 o'clock P.M. and leave Dearman returning at 7 o'clock 25 minutes and 9 o'clock 24 minutes A.M. and 1 o'clock 29 minutes, 5 o'clock 29 minutes, and 10 o'clock 12 minutes P.M.

A number of plots have been sold at private sale, which will be pointed out by the auctioneer. The Hudson River Railroad Company are now laying a double track between this point and the city, and are also making improvements at Dearman Station which, as the point of union of the great Northern and Western routes, possesses peculiar and important advantages over the adjoining villages. A branch Railroad is in contemplation from Dearman to Port Chester or William's Bridge, to connect the Erie and New Haven routes.

Running advertisement for the second auction.
New York *Evening Post*, April 30, 1850, page 1, "Public Sales" column.
In Cole & Chilton's regular box. Ran throughout May with heading "PRIVATE SALE," without date, time, or place of auction.

TUESDAY, June 11
At 12 o'clock at the Merchant's Exchange
Cottage sites at Dearman, on the Hudson River The balance remaining unsold of those beautiful plots of ground at the above place, will be sold on the above day, if not previously sold at private sale. Persons wishing to purchase at private sale can do so by applying to the auctioneers, No 9 Wall street. Persons wishing to build immediately, 90 per cent of the purchase money may remain on bond and mortgage for a term of years. Several choice parcels are yet unsold.

Main Advertisement for the second auction.

New York *Evening Post*, June 5, 1850, page 1, "Public Sales" column. Also ran on June 7 and 8.

TUESDAY, June 11

At 3 o'clock, on the premises.

Cottage sites and village lots at Dearman, on the Hudson River—The balance of the lots remaining unsold at Dearman, opposite Piermont, comprising about 100 in number.

The Dearman premises front upon the Hudson River and Railroad, and extend thence easterly on a fertile slope to the Albany turnpike, with a gradual ascent of 130 feet. From all parts there is a beautiful and extended view up and down the river. The lots near the railroad, 50 feet by 100, are well adapted for business purposes, and the plots on the upland for private residences are unrivalled in their commanding and healthy position, fine scenery and excellent neighborhood. A wide avenue, well graded and lined with a double row of trees leads from the postroad to the river.

In the immediate vicinity are the country seats of Messrs. Washington Irving, Ambrose C. Kingsland, Moses H. Grinnell, Gen. Paulding, Mrs. Colford Jones, Messrs. Henry Sheldon, James A. Hamilton, and George Schuyler, besides the residences of many gentlemen belonging to Westchester county. The distance from the city by the Hudson River trains is three quarters of an hour, and all the property is within five minutes walk of the station.—The fare is the same as to Dobb's Ferry, and may be commuted quarterly, or by the year, at rates varying from 18 to 23 cents, according to the number of tickets taken.

Numerous plots have already been disposed of at private sale, in addition to those sold at the first auction.

The ferry with Piermont, under the management of the Piermont and Dearman Ferry Company, which was incorporated at the recent session of the Legislature, with a capital of $80,000 C. Seymour, State Engineer, President) affords constant communication between this point and the opposite shore, and connects the Hudson River and Erie Railroads; and the Hudson River Company are making large improvements at Dearman to meet their consequent increase in business. A branch railroad is in contemplation from Dearman to Port Chester or William's Bridge, to connect the Erie and New Haven routes; and application is being made for a post office at this station.

These combined advantages give to the property at Dearman, as the point of union between the great Erie and Hudson routes, and the probable point of connection between the Erie Road and those of New England, an actual perspective value in incalculable magnitude.

Only 10 per cent of the purchase money will be required in cash from purchasers who intend to build immediately. The whole of the balance being allowed to remain on bond and mortgage. In case of purchasers not building, sixty per cent may so remain.

For further particulars, application may be made at the Station House on the premises, at No. 5 Broad street, to G A Sacci, or at the auctioneer's office, No. 9 Wall st., where maps of the premises can be had, showing the unsold plots.

The Hudson River trains for Dearman leave Chambers street daily at 7, 8.15 A.M. and 3, 4 45 and 8.30 P.M. and leave Dearman returning at 7 25, 9 42 A.M. and 1.39, 550 and 10 18 P.M.

Rohit T. Aggarwala

Arrangements have been made with the Hudson River Railroad company for a special train on the day of the sale, to leave Chambers street, New York, at 115 P.M. and return after the sale is over, and for the convenience of citizens of Rockland and Orange counties, the Piermont and Dearman Ferry Company have directed the ferry boat to run without charge on the day of the sale.

Appendix 2

List of Businesses in in 1860.

Source: Thomas Hutchinson, *Westchester County Directory for 1860–1* (New York: Thomas Hutchinson, 1860).

Blacksmiths

Michael Bray

Caleb Wildey, Broadway near First Avenue

Boot & Shoemakers

Alexander Hectos, Broadway & First Avenue

John Thomas, First Avenue near C Street

Butchers

James Lent, First Avenue near Broadway

Carpenters & Builders

M.B. Demarest

Charles Lawrence

Clergymen

C.H. Mc Hugh, Presbyterian

W.A. Mc Vicar, Presbyterian-Episcopalian

S.H. Orcutt

Coach & Carriage Makers

Gustavus Schillinkey

Coal Dealers

Storms & Lockwood, Railroad near dock

Confectioners

Henry Twitchings, First Avenue & B Street

Dry Goods

Banks & Evans, First Avenue & Railroad

John J. Banta, Broadway & First Avenue

Grocers

Daniel Cashman, First Avenue near C Street

Banks & Evans, First Avenue near Railroad

John J. Banta, Broadway & First Avenue

Arthur Kilpatrick, First Avenue near C Street

Hotels
Irvington House (Henry S. Downes, proprietor)

Lagerbier Saloons
Lewis Hoffer, First Avenue near Railroad

Lumber Dealers
Storms & Lockwood, Railroad near dock

Painters, House & Sign
George Mayo, First Avenue & B Street

Harness & Saddle Manufacturers
John C. Clark, Railroad near First Avenue

Tin & Sheet Iron Workers
Stephen T. Wright, Railroad near First Avenue

Farmers
Jabez L. Ellis
Theodore McNamee
Nathaniel O. Tompkins

Postmaster
T.W. Crisfield

Public School #2—F. B. Abbott, Principal

Appendix 3

Advertisment for Farms

New York *Evening Post*, April 19, 1850, page 4, classified section.

> FOR SALE—A desirable Farm of 80 acres together with the crops and stock, in Mamaroneck, Westchester county, near the New Haven and New York Railroad Deport, [sic] Price for Farm, crops, and stock $7,000.

> Also, a Farm of 20 acres, in the town of Yonkers, near the Tuckaho Depot of the New York and Harlem Railroad. Price $2,200.

> Also, a farm of 80 acres in county, eight miles from Piermont, and one mile from Clark's Comer Depot of the New York and Erie Railroad. Price $6,000. All the above named farms possess many advantages for gentlemen wishing to reside in the country, and doing business in the city. They are well improved with abundance of various kinds of grafted fruit, &c. &c. Apply to W. M. P. MOSS, No. 1 Nassau, cor. of Wall st.

Irish Immigrant Workers in Antebellum New York: The Experience of Domestic Servants at Van Buren's Lindenwald

Patricia West

Domestic service presented a problem to nineteenth-century Anglo-Americans. Political ideology celebrated republican equality and independence; "servitude" and "slavery" were metaphors for the worst political perils. Domestic ideology glorified the home as an insular "haven in a heartless world," safe from the discord of public life.[1] Yet these ideals clashed with the wish for household servants, which introduced large numbers of Irish Catholic immigrants into northern homes, blurring the supposedly separate public and private "spheres" and causing that bane of nineteenth-century "true womanhood," the "servant problem." Domestic service has been a problem for historians, too, because the preponderance of documentary evidence about servants was written by the very Anglo-American employers for whom domestics symbolized the dissonance between cherished ideals and the real world of the nineteenth century.

Ralph Waldo Emerson speculated on the relationship between antebellum class-based political strife and the "servant problem" in 1840:

> The case of the menaced & insulted monarch is not quite aloof from our own experience . . . For see this wide society in which we talk of [the interests of] laboring men [and yet] we allow ourselves to be served by them. We pay them money & then turn our backs on them . . . [T]his tree always bears one fruit. In every household the peace of the pair is poisoned by the malice, slyness, indolence, & alienation of domestics. In every knot of laborers or boys the rich man . . . does not feel himself among friends but . . . enemies [,] and at the polls he finds them arrayed in a mass in distinct opposition to him. Yet all these are but signs of an opposition of interest more deep which give[s] a certain insecurity & terror to all his enjoyments[,] for he feels himself an insulted & hated noble.[2]

Emerson testified to the essential unease wealthy and middle-class antebellum northerners; felt with the introduction of the human embodiment of the European-identified class system into American democracy and into American homes.

Emerson's reference to the political independence of what he perceived as a hostile laboring class also registers an important change in the male workplace. The old order of commercial capitalism had been based on a less exploitative, even paternalistic, relationship between employer and employee in which employers were responsible for the moral and physical well-being of their employees, as well as for their apprenticeship in a trade. This gave way to new relationships characteristic of the industrial order, in which the responsibility of the employer for the welfare of the employee was diminished if not eliminated. To meet the needs of an increasingly competitive market, employers in the new manufactories asserted the freedom to fire employees at will and imposed a rigid "work discipline" on their workers. During the decade heralded by Emerson's observations, this change coincided with the massive influx of Irish immigrants, many of whom could vote as a result of the recent realization of white manhood suffrage. Soon the old Jeffersonian vision of a nation of independent rural republicans became more elusive than ever as America's own "dark satanic mills" drew hundreds of thousands of poor immigrants whose arrival transformed the north.[3]

Secondly, household service was a problem in domestic ideology because it was the reified Victorian home that was supposed to protect each middle-class family from the ravages of the turbulent public realm. Yet, as Fay Dudden explains, domestic service introduced into the "private sphere" the ethnic and class conflict that had rocked the political world. According to Emerson, it was this tension that inhibited the private "enjoyments" of the middle class. The transition from the traditional employment of "help," the familiar neighbor girls of essentially the same cultural background as their employers, to the hiring of Irish Catholic "domestics" was the equivalent of the change in the public male workplace. Women employers and employees now keenly experienced the divergence of interests outlined by Emerson. Dudden points out that "the home" of Victorian prescriptive literature was in reality highly permeable to the infusion of such values as "time discipline" from the public world of men.[4]

Nevertheless, as both the trades of men and the textile production of women (in which "help" was so often employed) gradually left the home to be taken over by factories, "the home" took on greater symbolic power as the culture's moral center, locus of women's special responsibility to offset the turmoil of the morally corrosive, highly competitive male world of business and politics. Middle-class women, now ensconced in "woman's sphere," were less engaged in productive labor and more engaged in the symbolic labor of elaborate calling and dining rituals, which are so deeply associated with Victorian life. Dudden suggests that the paid labor of poor women freed middle-class employers from the drudgery of housework to pursue education and participation in reform. Hence the meaning of Dudden's double-edged title *Serving Women*.

However, domestic service also made the middle-class "cult of domesticity" possible, for while "ladies" cultivated personal delicacy in ever more genteel domestic settings, immigrant and black women were assigned the back-breaking labor of maintaining stylish parlors and wardrobes, the props upon which the intricate iconography of the Victorian home was constructed.[5] Dudden argues that the change from "help" to "domestic" was rooted in such an "elaboration of employers' needs."[6] But the shift away from "help" and to "domestic" laborers introduced a rough-and-tumble marketplace style of conflict into the home, sullying the wished-for placidity of the "woman's sphere." Domestic service disrupted the ideal of "the home" even as servant labor made the lavish Victorian lifestyle possible.

Of course, because men could vote and women could not, the modernization of the male workplace translated into the unmuffled political excitement of the Jacksonian era. It was this climate of political experimentation that nurtured the rise of the brilliant and opportunistic Martin Van Buren (1782–1862), dubbed by detractors and boosters alike the "Little Magician," or the "Red Fox of Kinderhook." Historians have linked the decline in republican values in the workplace to the political ferment that spawned the second American party system, that is, to the rise of the Whigs in opposition to the Democrats, the latter the vehicle of Van Buren's ascent to power and the former the agent of his downfall.[7] The contours of the Jacksonian period have been the subject of a legion of books and articles and the source of rich debate. In summary, the era was characterized by increasing urbanization, growth in business and banking, westward expansion, technological advances (in particular in paper production and printing), and the "transportation revolution." Mass immigration and the expansion of the electorate provided the immediate catalyst for the development of the second two-party system, the amplification of egalitarian political rhetoric, and the dubious invention of the mass-media political campaign.[8] Van Buren's rise from obscurity to lead the New York political machine and to initiate the establishment of a two-party system, which he hoped would reorder politics and transcend the looming north-south split, was a classic example of the possibilities and limitations of the Jacksonian moment.[9] As Emerson noted, the problem of domestic service, of the so-called "stranger in the gates," resonated with conflicts that matched the mercurial nature of antebellum politics. Thus Martin Van Buren's political career was inextricably linked to the social changes well symbolized by his Irish domestic servants.

The mass immigration of the Irish, beginning in the 1820s and 1830s and reaching colossal proportions by the 1840s, was both a major source of political innovation and at the root of the domestic transformation described by Dudden. To put mass Irish immigration in local perspective, from 1830 to 1845 the Irish population of Albany rose from 8 percent to 40 percent.[10] In general, the Irish came to America because of limited economic opportunity in Ireland. By the years of the famine from 1845 to 1849, they were pushed from their homeland by sheer, unmitigated poverty. Hasia Diner has outlined the sequence of events leading to the Famine: the potato, brought to Europe as part of the "Columbian exchange," made it possible to produce enough food to feed a family on ever smaller parcels of land; parents then began to divide their land between a number of offspring, which encouraged early marriage and population growth; when a fungus invaded the virtual monoculture of potatoes, massive starvation ensued. Diner argues that the famine induced a return to less risky, traditional patterns of agriculture and land inheritance. Subsequently, parents granted the inheritance of land, and therefore the ability to marry, to eldest sons only. This meant that younger sons had to venture to the cities for jobs, and that women had less of an opportunity to marry, encouraging them to emigrate as well. So while famine itself activated immediate emigration, it also supported long-term changes, reinforcing emigration as an economic strategy.[11]

The tendency toward delayed marriage or non-marriage was one of the reasons that Irish women, by contrast with Italian and Eastern European women, became domestic servants. The Irish were the only immigrant group in which women migrants outnumbered men. Unlike the culture of middle-class American women, Irish culture fostered female self-assertion and social independence. On the other hand, the social world of Irish men and women was based on firmly bounded "separate spheres." Therefore it was not a problem for single Irish women to migrate, delay marriage, and accept the relative isolation of jobs as live-in house servants. And though it was hard work with long hours, domestic service was alluring because it paid relatively well. Not only did Irish women need their wages to survive, they also frequently assisted relatives left behind in Ireland. One study indicates that Irish workers from New York City alone sent over twenty million dollars to their families back home in the decade following the famine.[12]

Meanwhile, in the world of American politics, Martin Van Buren's career had waxed and waned. Having steadily advanced from New York politics to the Senate, the vice-presidency, and, finally, the presidency in 1837, Van Buren was resoundingly defeated in his bid for a second term in 1840. His suppression of controversial issues (like the annexation of Texas) in hopes of maintaining the Union, and his Jeffersonian minimalism in response to both the Panic of 1837 and the boisterous campaign tactics of the Whigs, lost him reelection.[13] As his stormy political career ended, Van Buren came to terms with retirement to his Kinderhook estate, wearily vowing:

I will mature my plan for that life of quiet contentment for which I have so long looked in vain and the opportunity to enjoy that which has been so suddenly, and I cannot think but fortunately, thrust upon me.[14]

Some years before, then-President Van Buren had purchased a plain but commodious Federal-style brick house in Kinderhook, New York, that he renamed Lindenwald. Urged on by his fashion-conscious son, Smith Thompson Van Buren, the ex-president hired sought-after architect Richard Upjohn to renovate the house in 1849. An amazing metamorphosis resulted: the formerly stolid house now sported a rather imposing Italianate tower, copious Gothic Revival details, and a puzzle of a floor plan featuring numerous additional rooms and halls. This was the Lindenwald the house servants of this study knew, a Federal house in eclectic Victorian garb. It was the perfect analogy to the aging Van Buren, the Jeffersonian cum Jacksonian whose political career had risen and fallen in accordance with the vast cultural changes that swept the first half of America's nineteenth century.

At Lindenwald, Van Buren entered a new phase of life as a retired statesman and gentleman farmer. The home of the gregarious Van Buren, a widower with four sons, was regularly filled with visiting family and friends. However, documents describing his formal parlors and lavish dinners also imply the other side of the coin of Victorian life: that of the domestic servant. Recognition of the lives of house servants has the potential to historicize the romantic image of antebellum culture and politics to which house museums have so often subscribed.

The problem with which all students of nineteenth-century domestic service must grapple is the relative documentary obscurity of the house servant. First, almost all the written sources about domestic service were left by employers, because house servants lacked the leisure and, frequently, the literacy to write letters and diaries. Material culture resources are similarly biased. It was, after all, the material world of their employers that the servants were assigned to maintain and preserve. The work dresses and tools of the domestic rarely survived their periods of usefulness, while the Victoriana that stocks house museums was carefully tended and later collected by curators. Furthermore, detailed personal sources are limited generally because domestic service was the painful relationship to which Emerson bore witness, an episode in the history of the home that was often shoved under the carpet, so to speak, both contemporaneously by domestics and employers themselves, and subsequently by museums. In addition, as Dudden points out:

> The selectivity of memory has worked against domestic service not only because it was painful but also because it was part of female experience and its pains were considered private, disconnected, and undignified.[15]

Historians and curators must seek innovative methods to clear the smoke screen of domestic ideology, including class and ethnic prejudice, from the history of nineteenth-century households, in order to uncover the lives of domestics, as workers, as immigrants, and as women.

Bridget Clary, Margaret Kelly, and Hannah O'Connor—this sampling of names reminds us that the Lindenwald domestics were real human beings. Insight into their lives at Lindenwald (in the 1850–62 period to which the house is restored) was gleaned by combining secondary sources on domestic service with primary sources on nineteenth-century housework, and applying them to the material culture and documentary sources at Lindenwald. Census records reveal a core household staff of four young Irish women at any given time, each census indicating a complete turnover.[16] This rate of turnover could be explained by a number of factors, including seasonal house closings and dismissals. And it was far from unusual for servants to quit jobs at which they were unhappy, having no contracts or other commitments to their employers and good prospects for other jobs.[17] Considering Lindenwald's rural location, servants may have experienced particularly keenly the isolation from the kitchen-stoop conviviality of urban neighborhoods, not to mention the lack of nearby Catholic services.[18]

The specific occupations of the female servants were not listed in census records but may be deduced by cross-referencing Van Buren's correspondence with an estimation of the work necessary to run a house like Lindenwald. Based on what historian Daniel Sutherland calls "the domestic hierarchy," the cook was probably the eldest worker or the worker whose residence in America was the longest (both qualities denoting more experience and skill). In earlier correspondence Van Buren referred to a waitress and a chambermaid in addition to the cook.[19] This leaves only one position undetermined, perhaps a parlormaid or a laundress. If the fourth position was a parlormaid, then one of the other servants had the considerable additional responsibility of the laundry.

A domestic's hours of work were long and somewhat irregular, depending upon the wishes of the employer. The lack of leisure had a generally negative impact on the health of servants.[20] Most servants worked from sunrise to sunset, at least ten hours a day, with a full day averaging eleven to twelve hours. In this period a full day off for servants was rare; generally servants had one evening or half-day off per week. Servants were always "on call," because houses like Lindenwald had extensive bell systems reaching even into servants' bedrooms. Domestics were ignored as some organized workers achieved legislation for shortened work hours, a measure Van Buren had supported.[21]

The physically demanding nature of nineteenth-century housework called for adequate nutrition. Whether a servant received it varied from household to household. Servants generally ate leftovers from the family meal, which might or might not be enough.[22] At Lindenwald, adjacent to the basement kitchen, there remains what has been identified as a servants' dining room, rather generously decorated with flowered wallpaper. More commonly servants ate, worked, and snatched leisure moments in the busy kitchen.

When a servant's day was finally through, she retired to her quarters. Typically, servants' rooms were either in the attic or the basement, and they were furnished with family cast-offs—a bed, perhaps a chair and a washstand, probably no carpets, curtains, or architectural decoration. These contrasts reinforced the social distance between employer and servant. Servants' rooms lacked the privacy enjoyed by employers; not only were they vulnerable to the intrusions of the call bell, they were often shared with other servants.[23] At Lindenwald, there are three adjoining servants' rooms on the attic floor. The mid-century alterations included dormers, which converted the low-ceilinged garret to livable rooms. The whitewashed plaster walls and pine floors are in dramatic contrast to family areas. Rows of pegs on the walls suggest the absence of chests of drawers and a meager wardrobe. Even with twentieth-century heating, the rooms are hot in summer and cold in winter. There are no fireplaces in these rooms, no furnace ducts, and no evidence of stoves.

Given the close living conditions, it is not surprising that conflict was endemic to domestic service. Van Buren rendered his perspective on one such clash at Lindenwald:

> The two women I made swear eternal friendship got jealous of each other, the cook could no longer keep down the Devil that I saw in the corner of her eye when she first arrived . . . and I have sort of a Riot downstairs. Finding that soft words were of no effect I assumed toward them an aspect more sour and ferocious than you can imagine, suspended the cook and a very devout Irish chambermaid, who with all her piety is a devil of a bully . . . The female waiter has escaped unhurt . . . [24]

Referring to such an intra-household conflict as a "Riot" was a potent metaphor with significant political connotations, as antebellum New York had been plagued by Catholic/Protestant riots.[25] America's social stratification was manifested within affluent nineteenth-century American homes by the layout of rooms, halls, and decorative effects. House design expressed the fundamental American uneasiness with the concept of domestic service through concerted attempts to minimize direct contact between the family and servants. Halls separating work areas from "family" areas, servants' quarters tucked away in awkward places, back stairs and servants' entrances—all comprised an effort to make servants and housework virtually invisible to the family.[26]

Lindenwald's architecture incorporates this nineteenth-century predilection. A basement door on the west side of the house probably served as the servants' entrance. The tower stairs, sharply circular, steep, and narrow, served as the back stairs and the only access to the servants' quarters, connecting them directly to the basement work areas. Popular nineteenth-century architectural oracle Andrew Jackson Downing claimed servants' stairs added "greatly to the comfort and privacy of even small villas." He was referring, of course, to the comfort and privacy of employers. In nineteenth-century architecture, the segregation of the family from housework took precedence over efficiency, thanks to that ubiquitous "Victorian labor-saving device," a large staff of servants.[27]

Lindenwald was also typical in the distancing of the kitchen and the servants' quarters from rooms inhabited by employers, a practice analogous, in fact, to tendencies in urban neighborhoods. Nineteenth-century architecture emphasized the importance of assuring adequate space between dining rooms and kitchens, designed, in the language of architects, to "protect" the family from experiencing the sounds and smells of cooking. It was argued that servants' rooms ought to be "entirely separate" from "main" areas, and that servants should have access to these "main" areas only through "passages."[28] Lindenwald, fashionable home that it was, incorporates all of these standards to some extent. Thus, as Daniel Sutherland puts it, servants were "in the household but not of it."[29] They constituted a separate society within a society, inhabiting especially awkward and uncomfortable spaces while tending to the comfort of others, forced to recognize the glaring contrasts between two distinct lifestyles under one roof.

Some servants, however, rarely required access to "main" areas of the house. Cooks and scullions spent most of their time in the kitchen, which in the northeastern United States was frequently in the basement. Lindenwald's cooks labored countless hours in the basement kitchen, with its plastered stone walls and tiny windows. A sink and hand pump were located in the southwest corner of the room. On the north wall, a Gothic-style coal-burning Moses Pond Union cookstove, manufactured about 1850 in Boston, still stands near a brick bake oven.[30] Very little evidence exists to indicate precisely how the kitchen was furnished. If typical, it would have been a hot, crowded room, sooty and dirty by our standards, with cupboards, work tables, and perhaps a chair or two.[31]

The nineteenth-century kitchen required an enormous amount of care, and at Lindenwald this was probably the work of the cook, perhaps aided by the waitress. Commercial cleaning products were virtually unknown at this time, the task accomplished instead by sand, salt, camphor, lye, vinegar, and various home-made mixtures of these. Advice manuals suggested two thorough cleanings per week, and daily sweeping and wiping. Sinks were scalded with lye, work surfaces rubbed with old cotton, windows rinsed, floors mopped, and tools cleaned.[32]

We know very little of actual daily menus at Lindenwald, though records of formal dinners, records of the garden at Lindenwald, and archaeological analysis of food storage areas indicate a diet including mutton, potatoes, and root vegetables in winter, and fresh fish and vegetables in summer. Lindenwald had a wine cellar, a pantry, a larder, and a root cellar.[33] By combining period recipes with knowledge of household technology, some understanding of the labor of Lindenwald's cooks can be gained. The rare descriptions of Van Buren formal dinners lend further insight:

> The Dish before him contained a fine ham; then comes two side dishes of potatoes and peas; then an enormous one of fricasee: then potatoes and peas with a sprinkling of butter, cucumber, and then in front of John another supply of fricasee. Four bottles of champagne completed the carte for the first course. The second was pies, custard, jelly, of excellent make, and the third of fine-flavored seegars![34]

At Lindenwald, family dining occurred in one of two places. Informal family dining was held in the "breakfast room" adjoining a stairway leading to the basement. Formal dinners were staged in the ornate center hall, featuring a table that could be extended to seat more than twenty people. A banquet of this magnitude would have presented considerable trouble to the servants, particularly the waitress, who would have been called upon to carry laden and precious trays from the basement kitchen, up a narrow set of stairs, and further on a circuitous route through rooms and halls.

The actual serving and eating of food was a complex, mannered ritual in the nineteenth century. The availability of servants contributed to an increasingly elaborate and coded etiquette, the mastery of which created an ever larger rift between the deportment of employers and servants.[35] Emerson discovered this in 1841, when he invited his servants to regularly join the family at dinner. They surprised him by refusing; the cook explained that she was "never fit to come to table."[36]

When all of the dishes had been carried into the kitchen for washing, the parlormaid's work began. The parlormaid cleaned and ordered the main floor rooms: hallways, libraries, drawing rooms, and parlors. The work of the nineteenth-century parlormaid was similar to that of the cook in that technical innovations had not resulted in a reduction in the amount of work, because these improvements were accompanied by a concurrent rise in standards of cleanliness and display.[37] Household tasks multiplied as machine-made upholstery and ornate furnishings filled prosperous homes. Lindenwald's Brussels carpets, mohair upholstery, and carved furniture bespeak a life of unremitting dusting and sweeping for the parlormaid, as well as the changes in the industrial economy that made these goods available in remarkable abundance.

Upstairs, chambers were typically aired and dusted daily after the family went to breakfast. Chamberpots were emptied and cleaned. Advice books suggested that the servant be instructed to quietly smuggle the chamberpots downstairs, as the family had "sensitive feelings" to be considered. Next, fireplaces were cleaned and washbasins emptied. Beds were made; soap, towels, and candles were resupplied. A servant's last duty in the bedchambers was to supply them with warm water and fresh drinking water.[38]

Of all household tasks, none elicited more complaints than laundry, a chore redoubled by complicated and delicate Victorian clothing. If a household could afford to hire only one servant, it was someone to help with this hated chore. Lindenwald's 1850 addition contains what Upjohn called the "wash room." A lead-lined sink with a hand pump stood in the southwest corner of the room. Although there were advances in technology in this period (pumps, hand-cranked ringers, sinks with drains), washing machines had not come into general use.[39] Water was heated on the stove, and wash was done in tubs using a stick and a washboard. Nineteenth-century laundry equipment extant at Lindenwald includes two large wooden drying racks, wash-boilers, and an iron. An order for household tools for Lindenwald included sadirons and stands. Since no evidence of a stove exists in this room, wash was probably done on the stove in the adjacent kitchen.

The Lindenwald servants, after a long day of labor, had little time or opportunity for recreation. Though it was a lovely estate, young Irish women most certainly would have missed the communities of friends and family in urban areas. We know the Lindenwald servant did not stay for long, perhaps leaving for local mills and factories or, more likely, seeking supportive communities in nearby Albany or New York. When she left Lindenwald, under whatever circumstances and for whatever destination, traces of her hard life remained—a cookstove, a washtub, a row of pegs in a garret room.

The prevailing popular image of a precious and charming Victorian past is built upon repression of the harsh lives of laboring women. In this sense we have based our collective memory on the nineteenth-century rhetorical constructs of egalitarian politics and the "cult of domesticity" rather than on historical reality, merely reflecting rather than interpreting the ideological dilemma of affluent Victorians. The case of the Lindenwald domestics reveals the impossibility of sifting politics from "the home," the private from the public, men's history from women's history. Uncritical readings of biased material culture and documentary evidence has led to serious underestimations of the historical significance of the lives of domestics. We need to uncover these stories and demystify the ideology of "the home," our inheritance from the nineteenth century and beyond. If it could still be said that the lives of domestic servants were somehow insignificant to nineteenth-century cultural and political history, perhaps we should reflect upon the words of English house servant Hannah Cullwick: "i felt a bit hurt to be told i was too dirty, when my dirt was all got while making things clean for *them*."[40]

Acknowledgments

This article was originally presented as a paper for a symposium, "Those Who Served: Domestic Servitude in Rural New York, 1776–1930," held at Bard College on November 16, 1991, and sponsored by the Hudson Valley Studies Program at Bard College and the Friends of Clermont, with funding from the New York State Council on the Humanities. The author wishes to thank fellow panelists Sally Bottiggi Naramore, Faye E. Dudden, A. J. Williams-Myers, and Gretchen Sorin, as well as Michael Henderson and John Miller of Martin Van Buren National Historic Site, who read and commented on earlier drafts.

Notes

1. The roots of this dimension of nineteenth-century American political ideology are described by Bernard Bailyn, *The Ideological Origins of the American Revolution* (Cambridge: Harvard University Press, 1967), and Gordon Wood, *The Creation of the American Republic* (Chapel Hill, N.C.: University of North Carolina Press, 1969), among others. The phrase "haven in a heartless world" is from Christopher Lasch, *Haven in a Heartless World: The Family Besieged* (New York: Basic Books, 1977).

2. Ralph Waldo Emerson, *The Journals and Miscellaneous Notebooks of Ralph Waldo Emerson, vol. 7.*, ed. A. W. Plumstead and Harrison Hayford (Cambridge, Mass.: Belknap Press, 1969), 343.

3. E. P. Thompson, "Time, Work-Discipline, and Industrial Capitalism," *Past and Present (December 1967)*: 56–97; Herbert Gutman, *Work, Culture, and Society in Industrializing America* (New York: Vintage Books, 1977); Paul Johnson, *A Shopkeeper's Millennium: Society and Revivals in Rochester, New York, 1815–1837* (New York: Hill and Wang, 1978); Sean Wilentz, *Chants Democratic: New York City and the Rise of the American Working Class, 1788–1850* (New York: Oxford University Press, 1984).

4. Faye E. Dudden, *Serving Women: Household Service in Nineteenth-Century America* (Middletown, Conn.: Wesleyan University Press, 1983). In making this case, Dudden implicitly challenged the tendency of historians of nineteenth-century women to construct arguments based on the rhetoric of "separate spheres." Nancy Cott, for example, used Thompson's concept of "time discipline" to argue that industrialization caused male work life to differ markedly from that of women, creating separate, gendered cultures because women's work continued along traditional lines. Dudden's predecessors in the field of domestic service had by and large concurred, arguing that the "servant problem" was caused by an anachronistic "master-servant" relationship ill-suited to the modernizing world. Nancy Cott, *The Bonds of Womanhood: "Woman's Sphere" in New England,*

1780–1830 (New Haven: Yale University Press, 1977); Daniel E. Sutherland, *Americans and Their Servants: Domestic Service in the United States from 1800 to 1920* (Baton Rouge: Louisiana State University Press, 1981).

5. Historians have argued that the ideology of middle-class feminine domesticity arose in part as a means by which middle-class women could distinguish themselves from the new class of working women. See Linda Kerber's discussion of the historiography of nineteenth-century domesticity in "Separate Spheres, Female Worlds, Woman's Place: The Rhetoric of Women's History," *Journal of American History* 75 (June 1988): 9–39.

6. Ducklen, *Serving Women*, 107.

7. See Johnson, *A Shopkeeper's Millennium*, passim.

8. Lee Benson, *The Concept of Jacksonian Democracy: New York as a Test Case* (Princeton: Princeton University Press, 1961); Glyndon Van Deusen, *The Jacksonian Era* (New York: Harper and Row, 1963), 1–25 and passim; Edward Pessen, *Jacksonian America: Society, Personality, and Politics* (Hornewood, Ill.: Dorsey Press, 1978), 33–34, 55, passim; Daniel Walker Howe, *The Political Culture of the American Whigs* (Chicago: University of Chicago Press, 1979); William Nisbet Chambers, "The Election of 1840," in *History of American Presidential Elections, vol. 1*, ed. Arthur Schlesinger, Jr. (New York: McGraw-Hill, 1971), 651, 647–49.

9. See James C. Curtis, *The Fox at Bay: Martin Van Buren and the Presidency* (Lexington: University Press of Kentucky, 1957); Robert Remini, Martin Van Buren and the Making of the Democratic Party (New York: Columbia University Press, 1968); Richard P. McCormick, "Van Buren and the Uses of Politics," in *Six Presidents from the Empire State*, ed. Harry J. Sievers (Tarrytown, N.Y.: Sleepy Hollow Restorations, 1974), 30–32. For an exhaustive study of Van Buren's life and career, see John Niven, *Martin Van Buren: The Romantic Age of American Politics* (New York: Oxford University Press, 1983).

10. Pessen, 35; William Rowley, "The Irish Aristocracy of Albany, 1798–1878," *New York History* 52 (July 1971): 275–304.

11. Hasia R. Diner, *Erin Daughters in America: Irish Immigrant Women in the Nineteenth Century* (Baltimore: Johns Hopkins University Press, 1983), 1–29.

12. Diner, *Erin's Daughters*, 20–42, 90; Dudden, *Serving Women*, 65–66, 219–22; Sutherland, *Americans and Their Servants*, 103–14; Carol Groneman, "Working-Class Immigrant Women in Mid-Nineteenth Century New York: The Irish Woman's Experience," *Journal of Urban History* 3 (1978): 260.

13. Curtis, *The Fox at Bay*, 63, 191–94; Robert Gray Gunderson, *The Log Cabin Campaign* (Lexington: University Press of Kentucky, 1957); Remini, *Martin Van Buren*, 125; Chambers, "The Election of 1840," 647; McCormick, "Van Buren and the Uses of Politics," 30–32; James C. Curtis, "In the Shadow of Old Hickory: The Political Travail of Martin Van Buren," *Journal of the Early Republic I* (Fall 1981): 249–67.

14. Martin Van Buren to James Wadsworth, 8 June 1844, National Park Service, Martin Van Buren National Historic Site, Kinderhook, N.Y.

15. Dudden, *Serving Women*, 2.

16. The following are names and ages of domestics from the 1850, 1855, and 1860 *censuses, respectively:* Sarah O'Connor, 46, Hannah O'Connor, 24, Catherine Jordan, 20, Catherine Link, 25; Sarah Hail, 42, Mary McEntire, 40, Margaret Kelly, 22, Ellen McDonough, 26; Bridget Clary, 35, May O'Brien, 26, Ann Gray, 35, Margaret Neeling, 26. Van Buren had other servants aside from the standard household staff of four, principally when his sons' families *were in* residence, including an occasional governess and some native-born women whose occupations were unspecified. Columbia County, N.Y., Census Records, 1850, 1855, 1860. Columbia County Courthouse, Hudson, N.Y.

17. Dudden, *Serving Women*, 49–55; Sutherland, *Americans and Their Servants*, 130–32.

18. Dudden found a dramatic contrast in the number of servants in rural versus urban areas of New York. For example, in 1855, for every four families in the cities of New York and Buffalo there was one servant, but *there were* only two servants in an entire population of twenty thousand in rural Warren County. Dudden, *Serving Women*, 73. In the 1850–62 period, there were only two Catholic churches in Kinderhook's Columbia County, *where* Lindenwald is located, both of which *were probably* too far for even the most devout servant to travel in her very limited "free time." St. Mary's in Hudson, about *fifteen miles* away on the post road, was established in 1847, and St. Patrick's in Chatham, organized in 1855, was about eight miles away. Franklin Ellis, *History of Columbia County* (1878; reprint, Chatham, N.Y.: Sachem Press, 1974), 118, 295.

19. Sutherland, *Americans and Their Servants*, 88. Martin Van Buren to James K. Paulding, 4 January 1845, original at Morristown National Historical Park, Morristown, NJ., microfilm copy at Martin Van Buren National Historic Site, Kinderhook, N.Y.

20. Dudden, *Serving Women*, 194–96; Sutherland, *Americans and Their Servants*, 99–102.

21. Sutherland, *Americans and Their Servants*, 97–99. When president, Van Buren issued an executive order limiting workdays on *federal projects* to ten hours (without a reduction in pay). Arthur M. Schlesinger, *The Age of Jackson* (Boston: Little,

Brown and Company, 1953), 265.

22. Dudden, *Serving Women*, 195–96; Sutherland, *Americans and Their Servants*, 113–14.

23. Sutherland, *Americans and Their Servants*, 114–17.

24. Martin Van Buren to James K. Paulding, 4 January 1845, original at Morristown National Historical Park, Morristown, NJ., microfilm copy at Martin Van Buren National Historic Site, Kinderhook, N.Y.

25. *See* Wilentz, *Chants Democratic*, 267.

26. Sutherland, *Americans and Their Servants*, 30–34.

27. A. J. Downing, *The Architecture of Country Houses* (1850; reprint, New York: Dover, 1969), 272; John Gloag, *Victorian Comfort: A Social History of Design, 1830–1900* (Newton Abbot, England: David and Charles, 1973), 30.

28. Downing, *The Architecture of Country Houses*, 287, 331, 334, 360. See also Calvert Vaux, *Villas and Cottages* (1864; reprint, New York: Dover, 1970), 162, 344.

29. Sutherland, *Americans and Their Servants*, 34.

30. By mid-century, cookstoves were produced nationwide. They were a technological improvement but they nonetheless demanded a great deal of care and tending. In an experiment at Boston's School of Housekeeping in the late nineteenth century, time spent on stove care was quantified. In a six-day period, it took twenty minutes to sift ashes, twenty-four minutes to lay fires, one hour and forty-eight minutes to tend fires, thirty minutes to empty ashes, fifteen minutes to carry coal, and two hours and nine minutes to black the stove. Two hundred and ninety-two pounds of coal, twenty-seven pounds of ashes, and fourteen pounds of kindling were hauled. Susan Strasser, *Never Done: The History of American Housework* (New York: Pantheon, 1982), 36–41; Siegfried Gideon, *Mechanization Takes Command* (1948; reprint, New York: W. W. Norton, 1969), 527–29; Linda Campbell Franklin, *From Hearth to Cookstove* (Florence, Ala.: House of Collectibles, 1975), 145; Dudden, *Serving Women*, 131.

31. Sutherland, *Americans and Their Servants*, 114–15; Frances Parkes, *Domestic Duties* (New York: J. J. Harper, 1828), 128; "The Miseries of Mistresses," *Harper's New Monthly Magazine* (October 1856): 717–18.

32. Strasser, *Never Done*, 89; Parkes, *Domestic Duties*, 128; Catharine Beecher and Harriet Beecher Stowe, *The American Woman's Home* (New York: J. B. Ford, 1869), 371–76.

33. Kathleen Fiero, *Lindenwald Historic Structures Report: Archeological Data Section* (National Park Service, 1983), 68, 171.

34. Smith Thompson Van Buren to Angelica Singleton Van Buren, 30 July 1837, Presidential Papers Microfilm: Van Buren Papers (Washington, D.C.: Library of Congress, 1958).

35. See Kathryn Grover, ed., *Dining in America, 1850–1900* (Amherst: University of Massachusetts Press, 1987).

36. Ralph Waldo Emerson, *The Letters of Ralph Waldo Emerson*, vol. 2, ed. Ralph L. Rush (New York: Columbia University Press, 1939), 389.

37. Ruth Schwartz Cowan, *More Work for Mother: The Ironies of Household Technology from the Open Hearth to the Microwave* (New York: Basic Books, 1983).

38. Strasser, *Never Done*, 88; Sutherland, *Americans and Their Servants*, 92; Parkes, *Domestic Duties*, 137; Pamela Horn, *The Rise and Fall of the Victorian Servant* (New York: St. Martin's Press, 1975), 65.

39. Ducklen, *Serving Women*, 142; Giedion, *Mechanization Takes Command*, 565–66.

40. Hannah Cullwick in *Victorian Women: A Documentary Account of Women's Lives in Nineteenth-Century England, France, and the United States*, ed. Erna Olafson Hellerstein, Leslie Parker Hume, and Karen M. Offen (Stanford, Ca.: Stanford University Press, 1981), 351.

This article originally appeared in the *Hudson Valley Regional Review*, Volume 3.1.

Business Women in the "Land of Opportunity": First- and Second-Generation Immigrant Proprietresses in Albany, New York, 1880

Susan Ingalls Lewis

The United States has long been extolled as the "land of opportunity" for businessmen of the nineteenth-century; indeed, one could argue that by the late 1800's, the celebrated model of self-made, immigrant tycoon Andrew Carnegie had become central to American national identity. But what of the immigrant businesswoman? How did she fare in the "new world" of big business, horizontal and vertical integration, the development of mass markets, and the managerial revolution? What part did she play, if any, in the remarkable economic growth of this period in American history?

In order to address these questions, this paper explores the business careers of first and second generation immigrant proprietresses in Albany, New York. Although it never rivaled the port city of New York in size or prominence, during the mid-nineteenth-century Albany was not only the capital of New York State but a thriving center of commerce and industry, quadrupling in population from approximately 24,000 individuals in 1830 to 98,000 in 1880. Because of its pivotal location at the juncture of the Hudson River and the Erie Canal, Albany served as an important conduit for goods shipped from New York City to the Great Lakes region of the American mid-west, and vice versa. During this same period, immigrants from Europe—especially Ireland and Germany—also transformed the ethnic and religious character of a city previously dominated by a native-born, Protestant elite of Dutch and English ancestry.[1]

My investigation of female entrepreneurs in mid-nineteenth-century Albany originally focused on the most prominent and successful of the hundreds of women in the local business community, particularly those whose endeavors had been recorded in the credit ledgers of the R.G. Dun & Co. Mercantile Agency.[2] Continuing research has revealed, however, that exceptional businesswomen constituted only the tip of the iceberg in terms of women's economic activity in the marketplace. Currently, my project faces the challenge of exploring the rest of that iceberg—the part of the story that lies hidden in the murky depths below the surface of narrative records such as credit reports and civic histories, is a history that must be uncovered through painstaking research in city directories and census records.

Social and cultural historians have long been aware of the problem of "privileging" the experiences of upper and middle-class people over those of the working classes and poor, who—as we know—represented the majority, if not the most powerful segment of, the population. Women's historians have also encountered difficulties in creating models that include working class women, immigrant women, and women of color in their understanding of gender history. In terms of business history, big business tends to be "privileged" as a topic worthy of scholarly attention, while very small businesses are seen as relatively unimportant, or at best peripheral to the grand narratives that dominate the field. Similarly, local historians who study business history tend to concentrate on prominent individuals and large firms, neglecting what might be described as the "underbelly" of the regional business community. Local, female-run businesses that operated on a minute, virtually microscopic, scale are usually relegated to a hidden area, an area of activity that we know existed, but almost no one seems to believe sufficiently worthwhile to investigate.

In light of common assumptions about separate spheres in mid-nineteenth-century America, the sheer number of businesswomen in Albany who are documented in city directories, in federal and state census records, or in the R.G. Dun & Co. Collection of credit ledgers is astonishing. Information gleaned from city directories, for instance, reveals over 400 women in the city of Albany operating businesses in their own names in the single year 1880, while the federal census of 1880 adds approximately 100 additional names of women running small enterprises to the list, and research in the R.G. Dun & Co. Collection has identified dozens more female entrepreneurs who were active at the same time. Indeed, ongoing research has uncovered more than 1,250 women "in business" in the city of Albany who were active in the decade between 1875 and 1885 alone.[3]

As might have been predicted based on the findings of previous scholars, most of Albany's businesswomen were engaged in the female enclaves of dressmaking and millinery (402 and 60, respectively), or in operating boarding houses (139), but these trades represented slightly less than half (48%) of the entire group.[4] The remaining business categories under which Albany's female shop-keepers, service providers, artisans, and manufacturers were listed in city directories, the federal census, or the R.G. Dun & Co. Collection's credit records between 1875 and 1885 included, in descending order: groceries and provision stores (195 female proprietors), saloons and restaurants (145), fancy and dry goods stores (117), confectionery and candy shops (55), variety and toy stores (49), commercial laundries and women who "took in" washing and ironing (27). hair "work", hair jewelry, and hair dressing concerns (15), bakeries (13), hotels and inns (11), and cigar & tobacco shops (10). Trades in which fewer than ten women were listed as proprietors included (again, in descending order): houses of prostitution, newsstands, book stores, clothing stores, junk shops, boot and shoe shops, shirt and collar manufacturers, shops supplying "furnishing goods" (such as underwear) for ladies or gentlemen, manufacturers of wax flowers, corset and hoop skirt manufacturers, undertaking establishments, fruit stores, jewelry stores, drug stores, dealers in fish and oysters, umbrella sellers, dyers, plumbers, cooperages, and breweries. Rare enterprises and trades, each represented by only a single businesswoman during this ten-year period, included a blacksmith, a piano manufacturer, a furniture store, a meat market, a glove manufacturer, a root beer manufacturer, a florist, a seller of tinware, a crockery dealer, a gold-leaf beater, an embroidery stamper, a dealer in cloths, woolens, and cassimeres, a passenger agent, a stationer, a dealer in fishing tackle, a coal dealer, a pawn broker, and the proprietor of a milk depot.[5]

In previous papers, I have spoken of exceptional entrepreneurial women such as Julia Ridgway, an ambitious innovator and for more than thirty years the proprietress of the largest plumbing establishment in Albany.[6] In order to sample "the rest of the iceberg"—that is, the business experiences and patterns of women who were not exceptionally notable or successful, according to the yardsticks applied by the business community during this period itself—I will be using as examples female proprietors located in the 1880 federal manuscript census. I have deliberately selected the type of women whose enterprises have not been discovered (and probably were not recorded) in the R. G. Dun & Co. Collection of credit reports, or whose entries comprised only a few cryptic lines. To summarize key findings regarding this sub-group of small businesswomen, one can conclude that: 1) almost all operated their ventures "at home"—in their places of residence, rented or owned; 2) the majority were first or second generation immigrants from Ireland or Germany (reflecting the ethnic composition of their urban neighborhoods), and 3) most of their tiny businesses provided a means of self-employment for widows or the mothers (married or widowed) of young children.

In lieu of the complete statistical, demographic analysis of businesswomen in Albany which composes part of my larger study, I have prepared a micro-mini review of women identified thus far as female grocers and saloon-keepers in the 1880 federal census. Of the 105 businesswomen in this group, 56% were widows, while 38% were married—only five individuals were single, and one was divorced. Their ages ranged from nineteen to seventy-nine, with an average age of forty-two. In terms of nativity, 78% (eighty-two individuals) were foreign-born: of these first generation immigrants, the overwhelming majority—95%—were from Ireland (68%) or Germany (27%), while the rest were single individuals from Canada, England, Scotland, and Luxembourg. Of the 22% of female grocers and saloon keepers born in New York, the majority were also of Irish descent—thus making first and second generation Irish immigrants 64% of the total number of businesswomen in this population. In contrast, only 6% of proprietresses in the entire group were the native-born daughters of native-born parents.

Of the married women who constituted approximately one-third of the group, most of their spouses worked in manual or artisanal occupations (including several laborers, carpenters, and moulders, plus two painters, a printer, a cabinet maker, a paper hanger, a stone and brick mason, a stonecutter, a wheelwright, a blacksmith, a stove mounter, and a machinist). A smaller percentage of their husbands (approximately 30%) were identified as having commercial careers in the same or similar occupations as their wives (as saloon keepers, grocers, butchers, bakers, or peddlers); other businessmen included a merchant of kindling wood, a contractor, and a builder.

The vast majority of the married and widowed female grocers and saloon keepers (86%) lived with their children. The ages of such children ranged widely—both within the sample group and within individual families. Surprisingly, more than one-third of these businesswomen were caring for children aged five and under, while another 30% lived with grown children over the age of twenty. Children in their late teens and above, especially sons, were almost always employed. The employments of these sons—echoing those of the surviving husbands—included a variety of blue-collar occupations and skilled trades, including laborers, carpenters, stove mounters, and moulders, plus single individuals working as a printer, a jeweler, a watchmaker, an apprentice plumber, a mason, a boatman, a segarmaker, a shoe maker, a nickleplater, a cutter, a brewer, a bartender, a baker, a teamster, a fireman, a worker in a brick yard, and a boy in a tobacco factory. A few sons had moved into white collar work as store clerks (it is difficult to determine whether in their mother's businesses or elsewhere), one was a telegraph operator, and another worked in a telephone office; only one was listed as a merchant (alongside his father). Daughters were much less likely to report occupations (once again, it is difficult to know whether or to what extent they may have been assisting in the family business, or perhaps shouldering domestic responsibilities); jobs listed for daughters included positions as dressmakers, store clerks, servants, laundresses, and workers in shoe factories. The youngest age of a working child for any businesswoman in this sample group was thirteen years, though most children of that age were still in school: the oldest child still in school was seventeen.

One fascinating detail gleaned from census records is that 13% of the female grocers in this sample were actually illiterate—that is, they could not read, or write, or both. This was particularly true of Irish women, 21% of whom were reported as illiterate. One wonders about the impact this disability had on carrying on their businesses. The presence of children in most households may have alleviated this problem, or perhaps these micro-entrepreneurs were able to function based on memory and the ability to count money.

Moving from the aggregate to the individual, let us consider a fairly typical example of one of Albany's immigrant female microentrepreneurs—this case, a saloon-keeper. Mary Devlin was the forty year old Irish-born wife of fifty-one year old paver and contractor John Devlin. Mary, described as "keeping house and saloon" in the 1880 census, was also the mother of eight children ranging in age from two to fifteen. Her description in the "occupation" category of the census report failed to note, however, that the Devlin household also included a boarder. Nor did Mary Devlin's name appear under "saloons" in the business listings of the city directory, nor has she been located in the R.G. Dun credit ledgers.

In order to analyze and interpret data concerning petty entrepreneurs such as Mary Devlin, one must somehow fit information about the stories of their businesses and lives into a meaningful theoretical framework. Yet, as I have argued elsewhere, the framework common to most historians of American business in the nineteenth century—the onward and upward narrative of business expansion and consolidation—has little to offer the historian of female proprietors. As grocers and saloon-keepers, boarding house operators and confectioners, as the owners of fancy goods and variety stores, these "penny capitalists" operated concerns that have been characterized as small and short-lived, in an area that has usually been conceptualized as on the very edge of the thriving nineteenth-century marketplace.

In several ways, this paper represents an ongoing dialogue between my own research and thinking and issues recently raised by other historians of business-women, most notably Wendy Gamber, whose research on milliners and dress-makers in Boston at times parallels, at times complements, and sometimes challenges—and is challenged by—my own work.[7] Gamber's excellent historiographic overview—"A Gendered Enterprise: Placing Nineteenth-Century Businesswomen in History" delivered at the Hagley Conference on "Conceptualizing Gender in American Business History" in November of 1996—has served to sharpen and reinforce many of my own ideas.[8] One might say, however, that she has been approaching these conceptual problems globally, while I am approaching them locally. That is, she has been analyzing the whole range of American business history to determine how women fit into the picture, while my work has been much more focused on using a specific population of nineteenth-century businesswomen as laboratory cases against which to test current theoretical questions. Thus, I would like to consider here not only what I have learned about immigrant women involved in modest business ventures in Albany, but also how we might approach the analysis and interpretation of data concerning such businesswomen, and ultimately what the attempt to create such an analysis demonstrates about the limitations of standard business history terms, categories, and concepts when dealing with Albany's "petty" capitalists. After discussing these limitations, the challenges they present, and some possible solutions to the problems I have raised. I hope to create a dialogue between the local—that is, my findings and suggestions—and the global—the grand narrative of business and economic history.

Interpretive challenges

As I have argued previously, the analysis and interpretation of data concerning small businesses owned and operated by women presents a series of challenges when using the standard models and categories provided by business history.[9] In order to generate a useful statistical analysis, for instance, one must be able to identify such basic information as whether an individual should be considered the actual proprietor of a concern, her particular line of business, and the dates when she entered and left the commercial arena.

Susan Ingalls Lewis

Yet for many—if not most—of Albany's female microentrepreneurs, proprietorship may be hidden by the presence of male relatives, evidence on trades may be ambiguous or even contradictory, and the length of business activity may prove extremely difficult to determine with accuracy.

Let us consider specific cases that illustrate the questions outlined above. First, what constitutes a business? As Wendy Gamber has pointed out, if we consider business enterprise as identical with "the firm," then few women in nineteenth-century America—including Albany—would qualify as being in business. But if we consider business to encompass all forms of proprietorship and self-employment, then many more women would qualify. I would like to propose that for mid-nineteenth-century Albany, all cash-generating ventures exclusive of wage-work should qualify as business ventures. That is, female peddlers should be included along with the owners of large dry goods stores, and women who "took in" washing in addition to the proprietors of commercial laundries. Still, gray areas remain. What of sixty-six year old Catharine Hannah, a basket-maker born in Baden, or Mary McEwen, a second-generation Irish daughter who "made" children's clothing, or the numerous Irish and African-American women designated as "taking in" washing and ironing? In such cases it may prove impossible to decide whether the individual was self-employed or not.

Once a historian of businesswomen has decided what he or she will categorize as a business, the vital question becomes—who was the proprietor? Often, women were hidden under a male presence; both in family businesses and in female-run businesses listed under male names. Evidence of such situations abounds in the entries of the R.G. Dun & Co. credit examiners—as in notations such as this one appearing under the name of the fancy goods "dealer" Peter Hecker in 1874: "He works at RR Depot wife attends to the business & is help'd by daughters who are smart girls."[10] But, as noted previously, entries for smaller concerns such as those I am discussing today tend to be nonexistent or quite limited. Thus, credit records cannot be depended upon to provide information on proprietorship for the "owner & operators" of Albany's most modest business ventures.

However, I believe that it is possible to use census entries to extrapolate information about female involvement in commercial concerns. For instance, the 1880 census describes Irish immigrant Cornelius Droogan as keeping a grocery store at 15 Morton Street—his family's place of residence—while his Irish-born wife Marie's occupation was given as "keeping house." Yet Cornelius was a sixty-five year old sufferer from rheumatism, according to the census, while his wife was only forty-four, with no recorded physical ailments. Thus, in addition to caring for five children ranging in age from five to twelve, Marie Droogan almost certainly took part in the grocery business—along with Cornelius's daughter Katie, twenty-four, who was described simply as "at home." Shall we count Marie Droogan and Katie as businesswomen—or not? In this particular case, a credit report of 1882 indicates: "the business is managed by his wife in his name," but how can we know at what point Marie assumed this responsibility, and to what extent she was involved in the business all along?[11]

In another case, the manuscript census for Albany lists John O'Connell, Jr. as a "Hotel Keeper"; his twenty-nine year old wife, Bridget, (a second generation Irish immigrant) was identified merely as "keeping house." Yet her household included twenty-eight individuals besides herself and her husband, twenty-four male boarders and four live-in female servants. Are we to conclude that her husband "ran" the hotel while Bridget remained in the "domestic sphere" of their private suite? Or is it far more realistic—and accurate—to assume that Bridget O'Connell was involved in the daily operation of the hotel officially recorded under her husband's name?

An even stronger case can be made for identifying married women as the proprietor managers of boarding houses and hotels when their husbands were carrying on a separate trade or business. Thus, although Irish-born Bridget James received a notation of "keeping house" next to her name in the census records, the fact that her husband James was running a retail liquor store suggests that Bridget played a vital role in taking care of the seven boarders listed as part of their household. Similarly, I would argue that Ann King, an Irish immigrant, should be considered at least the joint proprietor of what was officially her husband's boarding house, since her husband Patrick worked as a produce dealer. Thus, in the case of boarding houses listed under male names, I believe it is important to translate the term "keeps house" in commercial as well as domestic terms for their wives (or other female relatives living under the same roof, such; sisters, daughters, or mothers.) And, if so, doesn't this mean that one needs to examine all city directory entries for hotels, inns, and boarding houses listed in male names, and check the census records for the presence of female relatives—wives, mothers, daughters, sisters—who played an essential part in this type of family business?

An unanticipated question that arose when doing research on Albany's immigrant businesswomen was how to identify, and differentiate between, their trades. Although we may believe that we understand the difference between a grocery store and a saloon, for instance, in the mid-nineteenth-century the divisions between these common business enterprises appear to have been ambiguous. In fact, women identified as grocers in one source were often described as saloon-keepers or retail liquor dealers in another, and vice versa, while several businesswomen named in the census were given the double designation of "keeping a grocery and bar room." (Indeed, Virginia Penny, the noted nineteenth-century advocate of employment for women, observed with concern that most small groceries in New York City sold liquor.)[12] The necessary solution here requires research into a variety of sources—including fiction and reform literature—to elucidate truly the nature of those trades in which nineteenth-century women were engaged.

How to determine the length of time in which a woman was engaged in her business can also be difficult. How should one record the commercial activity of, say, a female grocer who was married to a husband/official business proprietor for fifteen years, was left the entire business at his death, and then, as a widow, ran the same concern for seven more years in her own name? Is the correct length of her business career seven, or twenty-two years? Perhaps we should stop conceptualizing widows as "stepping into" their husband's shoes and rather imagine them as "stepping up" into the light of the historical record. Indeed, I believe that it is time to stop perpetuating the myth that family businesses, located within the household, were "individual" concerns with sole proprietors.

In the case of those home-based trades where we know that widows regularly carried on businesses after their husbands' deaths—such as bakeries, groceries, saloons, fancy goods and dry goods stores, for instance—it would be most accurate not only to include the years before the husband's death as "years in business" for widows, but to count the wives of men engaged in such home-based ventures as businesspeople too.

Lest I seem to have been grappling here, in my obsession with accurate counting, with minor issues, consider how the adjustments I have suggested would change the profile of the female business community as presently understood. The needle trades—dressmaking and millinery—have often been seen as those with most female participation. Yet could this be simply because these were the fields in which women would be far more likely to be running businesses in their own names, and thus be recorded as proprietresses in city directories and census records? If one goes back and adds to a list of female proprietors the wives of men who were recorded as operating small shops in their own homes, specifically in those trades that were often carried on by women after their husbands died, would the predominance of the female-dominated needle

Susan Ingalls Lewis

trades hold up? Would we still believe that married women were only rarely involved in business enterprises? As Wendy Gamber has pointed out, a precise accounting of the number of nineteenth-century female entrepreneurs in the United States is not possible. Nevertheless, I believe that a far more precise or at least comprehensive accounting ought to be conceived of and attempted in community studies like mine. Surely there is a real need to generate some approximate numbers to counter the stubborn, continuing myth that women were not present in the nineteenth-century marketplace.

New interpretive paradigms

Once one admits that the type of microentrepreneur I have been describing—whether female, male, immigrant, or native-born—cannot be comfortably assimilated into the mainstream of American nineteenth-century business and economic history as it is currently constituted, the need for a different interpretive framework is evident. In seeking an interpretive lens through which to understand how private enterprise functioned in the economic lives of Albany's first and second generation immigration business-women and their families, I have concluded that the patterns associated with Albany's nineteenth-century immigrant businesswomen suggest a variation of the family wage economy described by Joan Scott and Louise Tilly in their groundbreaking study *Women, Work and Family*.[13] What I would like to propose is a large area of commercial activity that seems to have less relationship to the expanding mass markets of the nineteenth century, to industrialization, and to the risk-taking aspects of entrepreneurial capitalism, and more to do with the constantly varying attempts of women—and men—single, married, widowed, with and without children—to negotiate the capitalist economy, and especially to maximize efforts to provide the money—the cash—that was so necessary to survive in this type of environment. That is, I would like to argue for the existence of what one might call a mixed family economy, where family businesses supplemented and supported family wage work, and vice versa.

Consider the case of Maria Pendergast, born in Ireland, the forty-seven year-old wife of a carpenter and builder—a man who was at once both an artisan and an entrepreneur. According to the occupational entry in her census listing, Maria was involved in both running a saloon and keeping a boarding house, while the Pendergast household included four adult children—three of whom were employed at trades—two daughters as dressmakers and one son as a carpenter. One daughter remained "at home"—one presumes to assist her mother in saloon-keeping and caring for nine male boarders. Such a mixed family economy defies strict dichotomies between "bourgeois" and "working class" individuals, and situates small, home-based businesses as one among several cash-producing options for the immigrant family.

Putting small business at the center

It is clear that the study of businesswomen is currently poised on the brink of making an important contribution to the field of women's history. But can it make an equally important contribution to the study of business history? Or, as Joan Scott asked in her commentary at the 1996 Hagley Conference on "Conceptualizing Gender in American Business History," so what? What difference can the inclusion of women make to the business history field? When considering how to "fit" women into business history, it will clearly not be enough simply to locate their activities at the edges of traditional narratives, nor just to "insert" a few outstanding female examples into their rightful places. Instead I would like to propose turning our conception of nineteenth-century business history inside out.

Suppose, instead of thinking of these small businesses as located on the fringes of the real marketplace, we consider the ways in which female owned and operated businesses provided an everyday, essential conduit for goods and services, and especially cash, throughout the economy of the working class community. Were such small and almost informal business enterprises really located "at the margins" of the capitalist market economy, or should we re-conceptualize micro-business as being at the center of monetary exchange the poor and working classes in the urban centers of the nineteenth-century? Where, in other words, did most of Albany's laboring class spend its money? In what ways did this network of small shops provide the economic underpinning for Albany's wholesale houses and larger markets? Should we really be looking at the "progressive" development of huge department stores, or did these represent merely the most dramatic and visible shopping opportunities in a community where most goods were still sold by neighbors to neighbors within the neighborhood? [14]

The story of female penny capitalists and the mixed business wage economy in which they operated also challenges our discrete and oppositional definitions of nineteenth-century class structure based on a dichotomy between capital and labor, and the division of historical schools into categories such as "labor," "business," and "gender" history. The very fact that female micro-entrepreneurs fall into the cracks between women's, business, and labor history can be interpreted as a sign that the fragmentation of history into discrete sub-disciplines has outlived its usefulness in explaining historical phenomena. Should history, including business history, continue to be conceptualized on a linear perspective, as a narrative of progress and change? Or is it time to delve more deeply into the continuous and simultaneous aspects of business and economic history—the manner in which small business and the economy have remained similar over centuries, and the ways in which different "stages" or levels of development existed simultaneously, especially in the nineteenth-century?

I would like to argue that across the entire "Western World" of the later nineteenth-century, women were involved in the same types of endeavors discovered by researchers of earlier eras. As Pat Hudson and W. R. Lee have observed, European women of the medieval, early modern, and modern period have continued to be involved in "irregular, low-status employments which do not readily enter the historical record."[15] According to these scholars:

Spinning, sewing, millinery, silkworking, laundering, nursing, and petty retailing, as well as dairywork, much food and drink preparation and low-status fieldwork seem to have been predominantly in female hands over many centuries even though the structure of the economy and market environment had changed dramatically. [16]

What Hudson and Lee have described very well here is the linkage between low-status employments and what they call "petty retailing," as well as the association of female business (and labor) with the preparation of food and clothing. By adding shelter, in the guise of hotels, inns, and boarding houses, to this list, one would have a fairly comprehensive representation of the trades in which the vast majority of Albany's businesswomen were involved in 1880.

Conclusion

Thus, this essay does suggest at least some definite conclusions regarding immigrant businesswomen in the land of opportunity. Based on my preliminary research, it appears that most women involved in business ventures in mid-nineteenth-century Albany were not responding to any exceptional opportunity provided by the United States with its huge internal mass market, nor did these women take advantage of the dramatic business expansion and consolidations of this period in American history. On the contrary, their modest, home-based businesses often represented a continuity with the "old country—as when Irish women operated saloons and grog shows.[17] My strongest conclusion is that as historians begin to study the entire scope of women's business activity, we will discover more continuity than change in the occupations of most businesswomen over time and across geographic location, and that small business has provided an "irregular, low-status employment" for a significant proportion of working women from medieval times to the present.

Finally, I would like to propose that we look forward in time as well as backward, and consider similarities between patterns I have uncovered—self-employment, dual-income families, working mothers, women's representation in trades related to the domestic concerns of food, clothing, and shelter, the location of businesses at home, micro-entrepreneurships and the place of female workers in today's post-industrial economy. At the risk of being "presentist" isn't it more up-to-date to include small business and self-employment as well as big business when considering the economic engines of capitalism? Though historians have described history as the story of "change over time," shouldn't history also include an understanding of continuity over time? I believe that this type of re-focusing not only opens up the whole story of women's participation in the capitalist, cash economy from the middle ages to the present, but would also serve to enrich the linear narrative of business history, adding complexity to a story that has been conceptualized on "bigger-is-better" assumptions about modernization and progress that appear somewhat outdated in the service and information-based economy of the post-modern world.

Notes

1. The economic, social, and ethnic context of mid-nineteenth-century Albany is considered in detail by Brian Greenberg in *Worker and Community, Response to Industrialization in a Nineteenth-Century American City, Albany, New York, 1850–1884* (Albany: State University of New York Press, 1985); however, Greenberg assumes that both workers and the local business community were exclusively male.

2. See Susan Ingalls Lewis, "Female Entrepreneurs in Albany, 1840–1885," *Business and Economic History*, 21 (1992), pp. 65–73. The R.G. Dun & Co. Collection is housed in the Baker Library of the Harvard University Graduate School of Business Administration; entries for the city of Albany fill eight large volumes

3. I am defining women as "in business" who 1) were listed under their own names in the business sections of city directories, 2) were identified as having business occupations in the individual listings in city directories, 3) were identified as having business occupations in the manuscript census of 1880, and/or 4) were identified as running businesses in their own names or in the names of male relatives in the credit reports of R.G. Dun & Co. I am defining as a "business" any commercial, artisanal, service, or manufacturing venture which provided self-employment (versus wage work) and generated cash (versus unpaid domestic labor.)

4. Both Mary P. Ryan and Suzanne Lebsock concluded that millinery and dressmaking businesses provided the best opportunities for female entrepreneurial success in Utica, New York and Business Women in the "Land of Opportunity" Petersburg, Virginia, respectively, in the period before the Civil War. Mary P. Ryan, *Cradle of the Middle Class: The Family Oneida County, New York, 1790–1865* (Cambridge: Cambridge University Press, 1981) p. 205; Suzanne Lebsock, *The Free Women of Petersburg: Status and Culture Southern Town, 1784–1860* (New York: W. W. Norton &Company, 1985) p. 180.

5. The total here adds up to more than 1250, because some women were engaged in more than one trade, either simultaneously or serially over their business careers; these numbers are based on current figures from my central database linking information from all three of my primary sources. However, this research is still in progress and I expect to identify several hundred additional businesswomen for the decade 1875–1885.

6. Susan Ingalls Lewis, "Who Were the Female Entrepreneurs in Mid-Nineteenth-Century America?", paper delivered at the Exeter Conference on Women, Trade, and Business from Medieval Times to the Present, in July 1996.

7. Recently, the first scholarly work of the last 20 years to concentrate on businesswomen has been Wendy Gamber's detailed study of the female-dominated, genteel trades of dressmaking and millinery. Wendy Gamber. *The Female Economy: The Millinery and Dressmaking Trades, 1860–1930* (Urbana: University of Illinois Press, 1997).

8. Wendy Gamber, "A Gendered Enterprise: Placing Nineteenth-Century Businesswomen in History," paper presented at the

Hagley Museum and Library Conference on Conceptualizing Genderin American Business History; November 1996.

9. Susan Ingalls Lewis, "Beyond Horatia Alger: Breaking through Gendered Assumptions about Business 'Success' in Mid-Nineteenth century America," *Business and Economic History,* Volume twenty-four, no. I, Fall 1995, pp. 97–105. 6

10. *New York Vol. II,* p. 224, R.G. Dun & Co. Collection, Baker Library, Harvard University Graduate School of Business Administration.

11. *New York Vol. 13,* p. 5, R.G. Dun & Co. Collection, Baker Library, Harvard University Graduate School of Business Administration.

12. Virginia Penny. *How Women Can Make Money* (Springfield, MA: D. E. Fisk & Co., 1870; reprint edition New York: Amo Press & *The New York Times,* 1971), pp. 121–22.

13. Louise A. Tilly and Joan W. Scott. *Women, Work, and Family* (New York: Routledge, 1989)

14. I am indebted here to the sophisticated conceptualization developed by Elizabeth Ewan in her paper "Hucksters in the High Street: petty retailers in late medieval Scotland," delivered at the Exeter Conference on Women, Trade, and Business, from Medieval Times to the Present in July 1996.

15. Pat Hudson and W. R. Lee. "Women's Work and the Family Economy in Historical Perspective," in Pat Hudson and W. R. Lee, eds. *Women's Work and the Family Economy in Historical Perspective* (Manchester: 1990), p. 2.

16. Hudson and Lee, p. 5.

17. As described in Roy Rosenzweig. *Eight Hours for What We Will: Workers of Leisure in an Industry in City, 1870–1920* (New York: Cambridge University Press, 1983) pp. 42–45.

This article originally appeared in the *Hudson Valley Regional Review,* Volume 14.2.

Painters, Poets, and Writers

The "Prophetic Eye of Taste": Samuel F. B. Morse at Locust Grove

Robert M. Toole

> *. . . the landscape gardener, it is he alone who with the "prophetic eye of taste," sees prospectively. . . . and selects with a poet's feeling . . .*
>
> —Samuel F. B. Morse, Lecture One, April 1826.

Introduction and Historical Background

Locust Grove is located on the Hudson River at Poughkeepsie, Dutchess County, seventy miles north of New York City. A farm estate since the Colonial period, Locust Grove became the home of Samuel F. B. Morse in 1847. Samuel F. B. Morse (1791–1872)[1] had been an influential American artist, but in 1847 he was the principal inventor of a new technology—the telegraph—that would revolutionize communication in the pre-Civil War years. With the financial returns from his patents beginning to materialize, Morse, at age fifty-five, was for the first time in his life in a position to own a substantial residential property such as Locust Grove.

Morse purchased a seventy-six acre parcel that remained intact until his death in 1872. It was not until 1920 that the boundaries of Locust Grove changed significantly. Today, the Young-Morse Historic Site occupies a 135-acre museum property that preserves nearly all of Morse's historic holdings as well as buffer land along the river (fig 1).

During the residency of Samuel F. B. Morse, Locust Grove was a remarkably varied ornamental landscape (fig. 7). The site's natural form was decisive in determining the historic development and its layout. The primary feature is the bluff (or escarpment) which parallels the river. The bluff rises about 100 feet on a precipitous slope and is a prominent physical feature.

Above the bluff is a nearly level plateau. Here the house stands close to the bluff, surrounded by a parkland of lawn and trees. From the lawn terrace, west of the house, a spectacular panoramic view opens across the Hudson River Valley. The raised plateau, with its fertile soil, was the center of residential and horticultural activities, while the half-mile-wide river front, below the bluff, was developed as an extensive, picturesque landscape garden that melded agricultural and ornamental themes.

Offsetting a sense of separation between the house grounds and the river front is a long ravine that cuts through the bluff and extends into the upper plateau along the north property line. This ravine formation was utilized early in the site's history as an access ramp, called the grade road, leading from the river to the plateau (fig. 7).

While the house grounds are nearly flat, the area below the bluff is highly varied. Here, topography generally falls toward the river, but the land is also shaped by a stream that crosses the site diagonally and

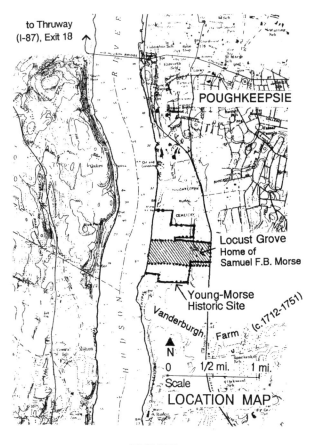

FIGURE 1

Location Map, R.M. Toole, 1994
Today's 135-acre historic site includes nearly all of the 76-acre parcel (cross-hatched on the map) owned by Samuel F.B. Morse in the mid nineteenth century. Located south of Poughkeepsie, Locust Grove looks out over the "Long Reach" of the Hudson River. The site retains its historic prospect, with the western shore generally undeveloped. Adjacent open space, the Poughkeepsie Rural Cemetery and a conservation zone help to insulate the historic landscape from modern strip development on Route 9.

forms a substantial ravine. A smaller brook, that includes a pretty waterfall, joins the larger stream near the center of the property. In addition, the river front land is punctuated by numerous ridge lines and small hills that give accent and third-dimension to the topography. Ground conditions in the river front vary from nearly level wetlands to cliff-like slopes. Open fields, used for grazing and hay production, defined an intricate spatial pattern, today obscured under uniform second growth woods. For Morse, open space, combined with topographic dips and hollows, formed micro-locations that were the basis for the highly evocative landscape design composition. Open to views from the house and lawn above the bluff, the river front was a landscape prized by a designer practicing the nineteenth century art of landscape gardening. As Samuel F. B. Morse put it in 1847: "Its 'capabilities,' as the landscape gardeners would say, are unequalled."[2]

For Samuel F. B. Morse, Locust Grove was a single entity, an estate landscape with a visual character and sense-of-place achieved through the practice of art. Samuel F. B. Morse's development of Locust Grove is representative of regional landscape design themes of great significance to American history. The landscape design heritage of the Hudson River Valley had its full flowering in the Romantic period (roughly 1800 to the Civil War), a "Golden Age" when prosperity and cultural ambitions encouraged excellence in a variety of artistic endeavors. These achievements included the writings of Washington Irving and the Knickerbockers, poetry of William Cullen Bryant and Walt Whitman, the picturesque architecture of Alexander Jackson Davis and Andrew Jackson Downing, the painting of Thomas Cole and the other members of the Hudson River School, and the landscape gardening that ennobled estate properties throughout the Valley. In this period, landscape gardening was practiced as a fine art and Locust Grove was one of the finest examples that remains extant today.[3]

Samuel F. B. Morse brought special credentials to his landscape gardening at Locust Grove. Much of Morse's historical significance rests on his invention of the telegraph, but we also celebrate his role as an important early American artist. Morse practiced his art from the time he was a student at Yale University in 1810. He abandoned artistic endeavors in the late 1830s in pursuit of the telegraph. As an artist Morse involved himself in the promotion of the arts in America, and this interest included study and appreciation of landscape gardening. In order to understand the designed landscape at Locust Grove, it is necessary to place the work within the background of landscape design as known to Morse, and to identify his artistic predilections and motivations. While Samuel F. B. Morse lived at Locust Grove as the renowned inventor of the telegraph, his role as a shaper of the designed landscape and architecture at Locust Grove may be seen as a continuation of his artistic background. Morse's Locust Grove was a work of art and one of Morse's finest artistic achievements.

Samuel F. B. Morse was immersed in his painterly vocation for nearly thirty years. As a teenager, he traveled to England to study with fellow American Washington Allston and he remained as an artist until age forty-six, when in 1837 he was rejected for the important commission to paint a historical subject for the Capitol rotunda in Washington, D.C. After that disappointing incident, which occurred five years after Morse's first conception of the telegraph, the artist turned his full attention to his invention and gave up painting altogether. After this, Morse's artistic sensibilities were most notably channeled into the landscape and architectural transformation of Locust Grove.

Morse's years as an artist, the decades from 1810 to the 1830s, coincided with the formative era of the American republic. Morse's skills were considerable, his education privileged, and this prepared him for a position as a leading artist of his generation. Still, this was a frustrating period for the arts in America. The eastern states (all was wilderness and raw frontier further west), were in Morse's youth and young adulthood a provincial, artistically conservative society where patrons were few and inspired artists fewer. Morse struggled as an artist because of the limitations of the period and also, perhaps, because of his lofty ambitions. Morse yearned to achieve more than the excellent portrait paintings for which he is best remembered today.[4] Like others of his generation, Morse wanted to paint historical subjects, then considered the highest branch of painting. Landscape painting was to achieve preeminence as America's first distinctive contribution to the arts—the hallmark of the Hudson River School—but for Morse it was a secondary interest. While his career crossed into the beginnings of the Hudson River School, Morse's artistic approach was focused on the legacy of older artists such as Benjamin West, John Singleton Copley and Gilbert Stuart, all of whom he admired.

During Morse's years as an artist there is only occasional evidence that he had active experience with landscape gardening or architectural design.[5] Given Morse's activities there would have been little opportunity for direct involvement, yet the artist's travels and experience introduced him to landscape and garden art, especially the pivotal English background. When he visited England for the first time in 1810 Morse was exposed to the long tradition of English landscape gardening. Still no record survives of whatever impressions he had on the topic. His studies seldom took him out of London, where as a young art student he lived on a tight budget.

Morse worked as a portrait painter after his return to America. He travelled throughout New England and for a time found a loyal following in Charleston, South Carolina. Morse had broad artistic interests. He painted an occasional landscape and used landscape backdrops to good effect in a number of his portraits (fig. 2).[6] This is notable because in this period the treatment of landscapes on canvas had direct reference to the manipulation of real landscapes in the practice of landscape gardening. In 1825, Morse moved to the emerging metropolis of New York City. A year later he was influential in the founding of the National Academy of Design, serving as its first president.[7]

Also in 1826, seeing "an opportunity of doing something for the Arts in this country, the object at which I aim,"[8] Morse produced a written discussion on landscape gardening as part of a comprehensive discourse on the arts, the "Lectures on the Affinity of Painting with the Other Fine Arts." Morse prepared four separate lectures, delivered for the first time in April 1826 for the New York Athenaeum. While not published in his lifetime, Morse's "Lectures" have been recently edited and interpreted and have been called "the authoritative version of Morse's artistic thoughts."[9]

Morse's lectures discussed all the arts, but his treatment of landscape gardening was exceptional as one of the earliest and most interesting to survive from this formative American period. In turn, Morse's lectures are important to a consideration of Locust Grove because they outline his understandings of landscape design principles twenty years before he undertook the Locust Grove improvements.

That Morse included landscape gardening in his lectures on the fine arts was not unusual. The English landscape garden had been described as a fine art by many eighteenth and nineteenth century commentators.[10] Morse's inclusion of landscape gardening confirmed the high regard the practice then enjoyed. Still, in 1826 very few in America had developed theories of landscape or garden design.[11] For advice on landscape gardening, Americans consulted the works of English theorists and were inspired by English practice. In fact, throughout the early decades of the nineteenth century, and even earlier, sophisticated Americans generally clung to the older Anglo-Dutch garden traditions that were held over from the Colonial period.[12] In 1826, Americans had only limited experience with landscape gardening, which Morse called "little known or practiced in our country."[13] While there were few opportunities for practice, there were even fewer skilled gardeners and nurseryman available along the eastern seaboard to offer guidance.[14]

In this context, Morse's lectures on the fine arts offered a unique analytic discourse on the position of landscape gardening in relation to the other fine arts written by an American stressing the crucial theoretical foundation on which the study of any art form is predicated. Morse's lectures also provided examples illustrating the practical application of landscape garden theory. In this way, Morse prefigured the writers on landscape gardening who would come later. Andrew Jackson Downing's famed book, *Treatise on the Theory and Practice of Landscape Gardening Adapted to North America* (1840) comes to mind in this regard. Yet it must be remembered that Downing, today considered America's most prominent mid-nineteenth-century landscape gardener/landscape architect, was a ten year old boy when Samuel F. B. Morse first delivered his systematic, learned discourse to the sophisticated and fashion conscious elite of New York City.

Morse began his lectures by describing five "perfect fine arts—painting, sculpture, poetry, music and landscape gardening." These he considered "perfect" because they did not obtain their effects from a mixture of other arts. Morse described landscape gardening as the art of

> arranging the objects of Nature in such a manner as to form a consistent landscape . . . the art of hiding defects by interposing beauties; . . . of contriving at every point some consistent beauty so that the imagination in every part of the theatre of his performance [the site] may revel in a continual dream of delight. His main object is to select from Nature all that is agreeable, and to reject or change every thing that is disagreeable.

The objective of landscape gardening, as with all the fine arts, was to "please the imagination." One who practiced landscape gardening must:

> possess the mind of the Landscape Painter, but he paints with the objects themselves[;] . . . it is not the laborer who levels a hill, or fills a hollow, or plants a grove that is the landscape gardener, it is he alone who with the "prophetic eye of taste," sees prospectively the full grown forest in the young plantation, and selects with a poet's feeling passages which he knows will affect agreeably the imagination.

FIGURE 2

Engraving, after original drawing by Samuel F. B. Morse entitled "Blithewood," frontispiece from Alexander Jackson Davis, Rural Residences, *1837*

A. J. Davis's book was America's first pattern-book for picturesque architecture. Morse's art work shows the epitome of Davis's theme that the landscape and house were to be a unified composition and attests to Morse's sensitivity to the fine art of landscape gardening.

It should not be thought that Samuel F. B. Morse, in *1826*, had attained the skills of an experienced landscape gardener. In fact, as noted above, he had no opportunity to attain such direct experience. But his lectures confirm that he did consider the topic in detail. Morse was directly influenced by Thomas Whately (d. *1772*) who he cited often in the lectures. Whately had written an influential book, *Observations on Modern Gardening*, published in *1770* from writings compiled by about *1765*. This book, and a few others from this period, served as standard texts on the topic of English landscape gardening as it had evolved to a mature practice in the period from the *1720s* to the *1770s*. While initially an up-to-date commentary, by *1826* Whately's preferences were often out-of-fashion in England, where he was thought of as an authority on earlier practices. Still, Morse called, Whately—who had been dead for more than fifty years—"an accomplished writer as well as gardener." While it is not documented, Morse probably became familiar with Whately's work from the time of his initial stay in England in *1810*.

From a historical perspective, Whately's influence on Morse shows the persistence of the long-evolving English landscape gardening tradition. English practice was established in the age of Lancelot "Capability" Brown and Humphry Repton, and continued to evolve to the start of the nineteenth century with the so-called "picturesque improvers," who championed a fully natural look.[15] The evolution of English landscape gardening, from the early decades of the eighteenth century to the late eighteenth century, was then interrupted and altered in the nineteenth century by individuals like J. C. Loudon. Loudon's numerous books and periodicals on landscape and garden design were widely consulted during the period of Morse's residency at Locust Grove, but by then Morse's approach to landscape design was well-established.[16]

For Samuel F. B. Morse, and many of his contemporaries, landscape gardening began with the earlier tradition and its practices. Morse agreed with Whately that landscape gardening was "entitled to a place of considerable rank among the liberal arts."[17] Morse's inclusion of landscape gardening in his treatment of the fine arts attests to his general sympathy with Whately's argument on this point. It is noted that Thomas Whately showed a preference for what he termed the "expressive" over the "emblematic," i.e. associative in garden design. This distinction largely sums up the shift from the early landscape gardens to those favored in the second half of the eighteenth century, when "picturesque" effects and natural appearances dominated taste in landscape design. Whately's writings favored an all-natural approach, revealing what Whately called a landscape's "original character," which landscape gardening exposed in an "expressive approach." Borrowing heavily from Whately for his lectures, Morse, in his lectures, described the "materials and methods" employed in the practice of landscape gardening. There was "ground, wood [trees and shrubs], water, rocks and [the exterior appearance of] buildings." Morse clearly emphasized the supremacy of the picturesque (natural appearing) over artificial effects in landscape design, largely defined the distinction of an American approach.[18] A strong indication of this was in Morse's treatment of the unity of Nature and God, tied together as an entity from which man gained truth. This spiritual link was widely shared by Americans of Morse's generation.

"Nature is full of objects that naturally affect the imagination," wrote Morse in the 'Lectures'. As an "art," landscape gardening was "not arbitrary nor dependent on mere authority, but . . . [has its] origin deeply rooted in the principles of nature." Morse preferred landscape forms closely reflecting natural scenery, a point mirrored in his evaluation of the allied art of landscape painting. Morse wrote, for example, that "in painting too there are many scenes which require only the mechanical imitation of the Painter to give them their poetic effect on the imagination." In the realistic work of the Hudson River School, wilderness and pastoral American scenes were captured by near "mechanical imitation," applied to reinforce a sense of oneness with nature, where meaning sprang from truthful delineation. [19]

Again citing Thomas Whately, Morse quoted his description of Dovedale, a picturesque beauty spot in Derbyshire, England. Here, as in other destinations where the English of this period sought the picturesque, outdoor aesthetics was considered best experienced not in the garden so much as in a dramatic wilderness. But why not in the garden? This was the preference of the "picturesque improvers," but in England there were few natural situations deemed worthy, and few individuals willing to undertake garden making truly imitative of nature. It was in America, a few decades later, that the picturesque approach found an appropriate setting and modicum of popular sentiment that allowed "Picturesque" garden making, as distinct from a more "Graceful" or "Beautiful" design, to flourish.[20] By following closely Morse's articulate ideas from the lecture series, the evolution of landscape gardening, as it had been employed in England and appreciated in America, can be traced.

Finally, and most significantly for our consideration of Locust Grove, Morse concluded his treatment of landscape gardening in his lecture series by illustrating what he called its "transforming powers." In this part of his lecture Morse showed his audience two sketches, one a "before" scene and the other of the same scene "after" improvements had been made. While the sketches have not survived, the narrative provides a clear description that allows their conjectural reconstruction.[21] The technique of "before and after" sketches had been used by landscape gardeners since the eighteenth century. Humphry Repton's 'Red Books' made this practice famous before 1800. The fact that Morse utilized this technique took advantage of his artistic skills and rounded out his discourse as a persuasive and complete treatment.

The "before" sketch used by Morse in his lecture showed a neoclassical-style house with "three monotonous rows of windows; . . . [a] bare roof without eaves or balustrade; . . . four equi-distant chimneys and [an] abortive pediment, altogether appearing as if the Genius of Desolation had been the Architect." Here,

Morse was describing a generic Federal style house, a common site in 1826 America. Morse described the hypothetical residential landscape "before" improvements with scorn equal to his architectural critique. He pointed out its straight approach walk that bisected the front lawn, and the finicky "patchwork" fencing. He thought ill of a rigidly aligned, badly pruned row of Lombardy poplars and two "unconnected woodsheds," scattered in the view. A barren meadow, "without tree or shrub" stretched toward a river that was "disclosed [i.e., open] to view in its whole passage," leaving an exposed and boring prospect.

Morse's "after" sketch illustrated alterations that could be exhibited by the skilled landscape gardener. These changes included alterations to the house exterior, that gave the structure a more interesting, though still classical appearance.[22] Morse illustrated a sweeping circular drive, replacing the offensive straight walk, "enclosing the area and making one beautiful lawn." The hodgepodge fencing was replaced with a neat green hedge. Toward the river, the exposed meadow was "enclosed as a lawn by trees and shrubs" and views were enlivened with new plantings that provided "mystery." In this way the former desolate house site was "made to appear not only tolerable but even fascinating."

It is clear that Morse's discourse on landscape gardening was not the voice of a lone artist, but his ideas on landscape gardening had been well-prepared, confirming his understandings of the art form at a critical moment when his words could be received by a receptive audience. With the Romantic period, even as Morse gave up painting to concentrate on his invention, the practice of landscape gardening gained a heightened aesthetic purpose. The Hudson River Valley, long considered the paragon of scenic beauty in America was by 1847 a center of landscape gardening in America.[23] Locust Grove was Morse's opportunity to practice the art form he had considered so carefully. The landscape gardening at Locust Grove including architectural remodelling and the redesign of a seventy-six acre property, is rightly called one of Morse's most important artistic works, given the place of landscape gardening in the arts of this historic period.

Site History

You have no idea how lovely [Locust Grove] is. Not a day passes that I do not feel it . . . I have peace and love, and happiness at home.

—Samuel F. B. Morse, letter to his brother Sidney, 18 Dec.1848

The site of Locust Grove was originally a small portion of a wilderness land patent given to Col. Peter Schuyler of Albany in 1688. Before 1700, a good portion of this patent had been purchased by a prominent New York City businessman, Dirck Vanderburgh (also spelled Van Der Byrgh or Vander Burg).[24] Dirck Vanderburgh died in 1709 but his only son, Henry, developed a large farm on part of the property from about 1712 and raised a family of ten children there before he died in 1750. This farm, containing more than 700 acres, extended north and south of today's Locust Grove on both sides of the public road (now, Route 9) (fig 1).

After his death, Henry Vanderburgh's farm was subdivided by his heirs, with about half purchased by a neighbor, Henry Livingston (1714–1799). Henry Livingston was a third generation member of the prominent Livingston family. He was born in Kingston, the son of Gilbert Livingston.[25] Henry moved to the Poughkeepsie area in the 1730s. He lived in a riverside house just north of the Vanderburgh farm. As his neighbor's land came on the market, beginning in 1751, Henry began to acquire individual parcels.

The land Henry Livingston acquired was located on the Hudson River, on the west side of the public road, called then the King's Highway. His first purchase included part of the river front of what is today Locust Grove. In 1751, this was woodland, located in the northwest corner of the old Vanderburgh farm. The parcel was described as being "about eighty yards to the westward of the valley [i.e., a ravine] coming from the Old Dwelling House. . . ."[26] The deed and plan information from this period are somewhat inconclusive, but the description of an "Old Dwelling House" suggests that the site of Locust Grove may have been a farm residence before Livingston's purchase. The construction date of the original farmhouse at Locust Grove is uncertain. In the mid nineteenth century, a family historian described the farmhouse as "160 years old"[27] placing the construction at about 1700. While this is not confirmed by other documentation (the house was demolished in the late nineteenth century), old notations suggest a farmhouse of great age. As early as 1800 it was called an "antique domicile,"[28] and in 1821 was described as "the famous old mansion of stone."[29] Given the circumstantial evidence, it seems probable that a house existed on the site of Locust Grove before Henry Livingston acquired the site, perhaps built by one of the Vanderburgh heirs or even by Henry Vanderburgh or his father, as far back as 1700. As such, Locust Grove may trace its heritage as a residential property through nearly 300 years of history.

Eventually, Henry Livingston, Sr., acquired some 358 acres of the former Vanderburgh farm and in 1771 he and his wife Susanne sold their Vanderburgh property to their son Henry Livingston, Jr., (1748–1828).[30] Henry Livingston, Jr., was a man of considerable local distinction. He has been described as "a soldier [in the Revolutionary War], poet, illustrator and musician."[31] He was also a local judge, a skilled surveyor and of course a farmer. As a poet, he is credited, by some, as the author of the traditional American rhythm, "The Night Before Christmas."[32]

Shortly after Henry Livingston, Jr., received the farm he married and settled on the property, which he called Locust Grove for the dense stand of black locust trees that were planted between the farmstead and the highway.[33] In 1799, Henry prepared a map of the Poughkeepsie area which included a depiction of his land. This is the earliest plan record of the site. A cluster of three buildings is shown at the end of a short straight road coming into the property from the public road. Henry's house was set on the north side of the entrance road. While the site is preserved, all above ground evidence has disappeared and the exact location of the structure is presently unknown. A somewhat later map of the property, dated to about 1806 (fig 3), again prepared by the surveyor, Henry Livingston, Jr., shows in more detail the farmhouse clustered in a group of five buildings, possibly including a barn, a stable/carriage house, sheds, an outhouse, and other outbuildings. A well was located nearby.[34] Arable land and orchards were arranged to the south along the upper plateau. The sizable kitchen garden was probably laid out south of the farmhouse. This early farmstead layout was typical for the period. The house did not have a river view and this was also typical of an era that valued the practicality of the home setting close to the farm operation over aesthetic concerns.

Henry Livingston, Jr.'s, house was at the top of the ravine and here was developed the grade road providing access down to the river front. This road led to a river landing—called in one deed "Wood Landing"— an essential access in an era when the river was the primary transportation link. It seems that the river front was being cleared of timber throughout Henry Livingston, Jr.'s, residency. A saw mill complex is shown on the 1799 map, and identified as a "sawmill dam" on the 1806 map. This was located close to the river along the site's major stream. The saw mill was also illustrated in 1792.[35]

Twenty years later the need for a sawmill seems to have ended and at Henry Livingston, Jr.'s, death in 1828, a sales notice described:

> 250 acres of excellent land. . . . The farm is in a high state of cultivation, well watered & well fenced, beau-
> tifully situated on a fertile plain bordered on the east by the Highland Turnpike Road & on the west by
> the Hudson River, it possesses advantages of profits & elegance equal to any in the County.

Robert M. Toole

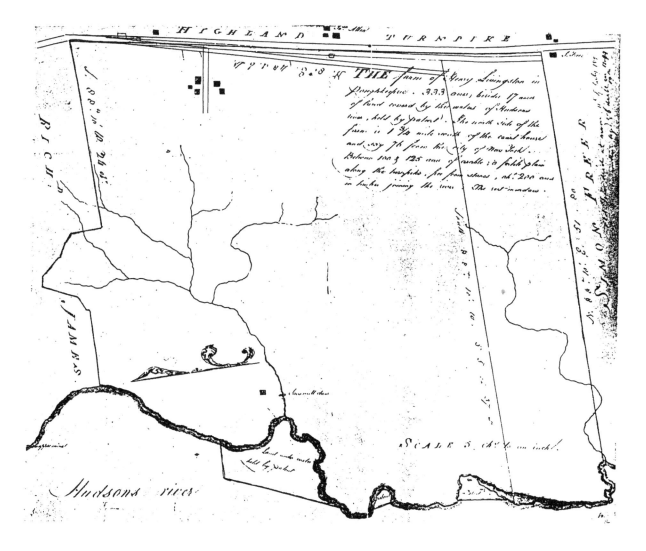

FIGURE 3

Map entitled "The farm of Henry Livingston in Poughkeepsie, . . . " by Henry Livingston, Jr., no date, c. 1806
This early plan shows a clustered farmstead of five buildings grouped along an approach drive close to the "Highland Turnpike." The
site's major stream is shown emptying into the river near a "Saw-mill" with a related building (house?) nearby. Livingston's Locust
Grove extended both north and south beyond the boundaries of Samuel F. B. Morse's later property. The inscription (upper right)
reads: "333 acres besides 17 acres of land covered by the waters of Hudson's river, held by patent. The north side of the farm is 1-3/4
miles south of the court house and say 76 miles from the City of New York. Between 100 and 125 acres of arable [land]; a fertile plain
along the turnpike, free from stones, etc. 200 acres in timber joining the river. The rest meadow."

In 1830, the old farm and its "250 acres of excellent land" were purchased by John B. Montgomery (1785–1861), an Irish immigrant who had lived for many years in New York City. Montgomery was apparently not a farmer.[36] Little is known of his background, but Montgomery's development of Locust Grove seems to have been considerable. He built a new house overlooking the river. This structure is now the central section of the present house. The design was an austere example of the Federal style, a type long established and a bit old-fashioned in 1830. The house design employed two nearly identical facades, the east elevation, with its broad stairway leading to the carriage drive and a similar grand stairway facing the river on the west.[37] In addition to his new house, Montgomery can be presumed to have relocated the old farmstead from the area that was now his entrance park. The venerable Livingston farmhouse was retained but the farm-related buildings and yards around the house were of necessity removed. At this point farm operations seem to have been developed below the bluff where these utilitarian operations could be isolated out of view. This would have allowed Montgomery to clean up the old Livingston farmstead, which was now part of the new approach driveway and park. The new driveway looped from the old straight entrance to form a circle. The driveway was planted with sugar maples arranged informally on both sides of the new drive.

Beginning with John Montgomery's seventeen year residency, the new house, the park, the lawn terrace, and the critical area of the property lying between the new house and the river, received design consideration as an ornamental landscape but the details or extent of the improvements are not known. Montgomery's purchase represents the start of landscape changes that altered the original emphasis on the property's agricultural use. This shift would be culminated by Samuel F. B. Morse but to a considerable extent Montgomery's earlier changes must be recognized as significant. Further research and archaeology are needed to document the extent and nature of Montgomery's landscape design contributions and the landscape development during this period, before the property was sold to Samuel F. B. Morse in 1847.

In October 1846, Samuel F. B. Morse, a widower living in rented quarters in New York City, expressed his immediate interest in securing a home. Speaking of his twenty-three year old son, Charles, Morse wrote: "Charles has little to do . . . He is desirous of a farm and I have made up my mind to indulge him . . . I shall go up the river in a day or two and look in the vicinity of Po'keepsie. . . ."[38]

After this autumn 1846 trip, Morse let the matter rest through the winter, but by spring his finances were becoming more secure and in June 1847 he was again "farm" hunting, writing his brother that he expected "next week to go into the interior of the State with Charles . . . to look for a farm for my boys."[39] The second son was twenty-two year old Finley, who was mentally handicapped from a youthful illness.

Morse visited the Poughkeepsie area in late June or July when several properties were examined. In July, Morse wrote his brother again, enclosing what he called "a diagram of a place" he "fancied." But then, at the end of the month, he announced to his brother Sidney that he had been "informed of a place for sale, South of this village two miles, on the bank of the river. . . . I have this day concluded a bargain for it. There are about one hundred acres. I pay for it $17,500."[40] In this letter we have Morse's first description of the property which he called "far superior." Morse's words were laced with references to landscape gardening:

> I am afraid to tell you of its beauties and advantages. It is just such a place as in England could not be purchased for double the number of pounds sterling. Its "capabilities" as the landscape gardeners would say, are unequalled.[41] There is every variety of surface, plain [i.e., the plateau], hill, dale, glen, running stream, and fine forests, and every variety of distant prospect. . . . I will not enlarge [on the description]: I am congratulated by all in having made an excellent purchase, and I find a most delightful neighborhood within a few miles around. . . . The new railroad will run at the foot of the grounds (probably) on the river and bring New York within 2 hours of us. There is every facility for residence-good markets, churches, schools. Take it all in all I think it just the place for us all. If you should fancy a spot on it for building, I can accommodate you, and Richard wants twenty acres reserved for him.[42]

The last two sentences broaden Morse's intentions by expressing a hope that his brothers Sidney and Richard would also have houses on the property, attesting to Morse's wish to have his family beside him after many years of separation. The brothers never took up the offer, but Locust Grove quickly become a family

Robert M. Toole

gathering place, with frequent visits by the brothers and also Morse's daughter Susan, who had married in 1842 and lived in Puerto Rico.

The deed recording the sale of Locust Grove was dated August 10, 1847. The 100 acre parcel was the northern part of the Livingston/Montgomery farm. Included was the house and grounds, the park and the immediate farm areas above the bluff, including orchards, meadows and the kitchen garden. In the river front was the farm complex, including a farmhouse, barn, sheds, and yards. At this date, the river front was generally open, though the boundaries and steep slopes were even then wooded, constituting the "fine forest" Morse praised to his brother.

Morse and his sons quickly moved to Locust Grove. In September 1847, Morse revealed his intentions for the property. Referring to it as a "delightful retreat" and "the farm," he said it "gains in my affections at every days residence. . . . [The house and] the grounds can be gradually improved as means and inclination dictates."[43] By October, the immediate family members had come to inspect the place and Morse had decided to call the property 'Locust Grove'. He wrote Sidney: "Locust Grove it seems was the original name given to this place by judge [Henry] Livingston [Jr.], and without knowing this fact I had given the same name to it, so that there is a natural appropriateness to the designation of my home."[44]

From the evidence it is clear that Morse undertook landscape garden development from the first. In the autumn of 1847 he asked his brother for help, if he "should chance upon any practical works on Landscape Gardening, with numerous designs, you may get it for me. I have Whately and Loudon already."[45] As an early example of his landscape gardening Morse built a pond in 1848. This was located in the river front close to the south property line. It was, Morse said, developed with great care, with his daily involvement, "selecting and marking carefully those trees which were to be removed and charging them not to cut a single twig that I had not selected and marked. The shade of the trees was calculated and essential for my purpose."[46] These and similar projects seem to have continued at an ongoing, steady pace for the first five or six years of his residency at Locust Grove.

By November 1847, with Morse away on one of numerous business trips, events indicate that Morse's son Charles had been placed in charge of the property as had been planned from the first. Charles wrote his father in the tone of a manager directing farm operations: "Everything here is going well, the two Patricks, Fin [Finley] and myself are engaged in getting out the rocks that impede the plough in the lower lot bordering on Mr. James' bluff [i.e., the north side of the property] and I think the time and labor profitably employed."[47]

But Charles did not last. In the spring of 1848, Morse hired "Mr. Teller," as the property's farmer, indicating a change in the role of Charles Morse. Later that summer, after Charles married, Morse shed light on the shifting situation. He still considered having Charles live at the property, saying that "I think of fitting him up a house near me; perhaps the old Livingston house, now my farm house," but to live there not as a farmer but in a "regular business [technical drawing]." Morse elaborated that "farming is pleasant to talk and think about but it requires a different sort of mind from Charles' to make farming profitable."[48] Soon after this Charles and his new wife would leave Locust Grove behind.

The abortive attempt to settle Charles on a farm, which had motivated the early decision to "indulge him" by purchasing Locust Grove, together with the campaign to have his brothers Sidney and Richard develop separate homes at Locust Grove, all came to an end after Morse married his second cousin, Sarah Griswold (1822–1902), on August 10, 1848. Although Morse was fifty-seven, his wife was twenty-six and a new family would grow to occupy Locust Grove. In July 1849, a son, Arthur, was born followed by Cornelia in 1851, William in 1853 and Edward, born in 1857 when Morse was sixty-six years old (fig. 4).

FIGURE 4

Photograph, c. 1858
Seated in the driveway on the south side of the porte cochere of the remodeled house at Locust Grove are Samuel F. B. Morse at the
center, flanked by his second wife, Sarah (left), and two of their young children, Cornelia (b. 1853). On the right is Morse's daughter
from his first marriage, Susan and far right, Sarah's mother. Susan's husband, Edward Lind, stands behind his wife, with Samuel's
son by his first marriage, Finley (b. 1825) standing to the left. Note the boxwood hedge (right), spruce tree (left) and trellis with vines
(behind).

The role farming would play at Locust Grove was now clarified. In the spring of 1850 Morse extended
his original boundary to the south by purchasing additional acreage from John Montgomery. This was the
first of two land transactions that reconfigured Locust Grove into the seventy-six acre parcel Morse knew as
home for his remaining twenty years, and that would continue to constitute Locust Grove until 1920. The
south expansion seems to have been directly related to the ornamental landscape gardening then under-
way. The land included orchard and meadow acreage above the bluff, but more importantly it widened the
wooded south side of Morse's river front adding extra forested acreage that included the outlet of the site's
major stream. This woodland enclosed Morse's river front helping to define a separate place. No open farmland was added below the bluff. Morse confirmed the inevitability of the farm's reduced importance when
he sold about one-third of the property (more than forty-three acres) in March 1850. This was a distinct
parcel of open farmland on the north side of his holdings. Here a new residential property, called 'Edgehill',
was to be constructed.

It is important to remember that the Locust Grove farm had been much reduced from its acreage during the Livingston and Montgomery periods and profitable farming under these circumstances was difficult.
Morse naturally resisted this, annoyingly writing a friend on March 5, 1850: "I have indeed a farm out of

Robert M. Toole

which a farmer might obtain his living, but to me it is a source of expense." In reality, Morse had at this date resigned himself to creditable but subsidized farming. In Morse's period, Locust Grove was not a farm enterprise but a full range of farming operations continued even as the landscape became a broad palette for landscape gardening.

By 1850 Morse turned his focus to the landscape's principal feature, the Montgomery house, which he had said derisively had "no pretensions to taste."[49] Before he undertook remodeling, in the spring of 1851, Morse contacted a long-time acquaintance, the notable architect Alexander Jackson Davis (1803–1892), then at the height of his career as America's foremost practitioner of picturesque architecture.[50] It seems that even before this date Morse had begun to sketch his ideas for the house alterations, beginning with drawings of the existing situation and then applying, eventually with Davis's help, a variety of development options for the old-fashioned Federal style house.[51]

The exterior was remodeled in the Italian style, transforming it to what one drawing identified as a "Tuscan Villa." A substantial porte cochere was added on the east, while the west was dominated by a tower ("campanile"), and on the south by a veranda ("piazza"). Davis visited Morse in Poughkeepsie for the first time in April 1851, spending three days there. He sketched a small map of the property,[52] but despite this landscape drawing there is no evidence that Davis had direct or professional responsibility for any site-related projects. Still, there were landscape design improvements occurring at this time and certainly Davis can be presumed to have discussed all matters of the property's development on his numerous site visits. Davis's indirect influence on the landscape work may be inferred.

Davis's building plans were prepared in May 1851. An early presentation drawing of the house is inscribed: "here given as originally designed in concert with S. F. B. M," attesting to the involved role of Morse. After Morse's review, the plans were quickly amended and completed. By June, a building contractor had been hired and construction started in early August. Davis visited in August and again in October. Progress continued over the winter and Davis visited for a last time in May, calling the work "nearly completed."[53] At the end of the summer Davis wrote a follow-up letter, enclosing a bill for the design work ($192.50), and "curious to hear how you find your new house, and what you are doing to make the grounds beautiful."[54] Morse immediately responded, paying the bill and updating Davis on the landscape work he had asked about. Morse's correspondence has not survived, but Davis's reply confirms that carefully considered landscape gardening was underway:

> Of course your landscape gardening is going on according to Whately, Repton, Loudon & Downing, and is immediately to exhibit the most finished illustration of Natural Beauty—the art modestly retiring with the background![55]

Then, focusing on several landscape garden issues, Davis continued:

> Allow me to suggest that you terrace the north side of the house, and so trellis and plant as to balance or symmetrise with the south veranda. Also, that the plantations so approach the house that portions [of the house] only may be seen from any one point, peeping from forth the verdure, and so playing upon the imagination that an idea of great extent of accommodation and an infinite variety of picturesque beauty be presented to the exercised mind.

From this point, with the land transactions concluded and the house remodeled and landscape gardening having been undertaken, life at Locust Grove seems to have settled into something of a routine. There are frankly long gaps in the documentation on matters concerning the property. Clearly work continued, but few manifest changes seem to have occurred after 1852. The practice of landscape gardening was no doubt pursued as a subtle refinement of the situation at hand with improvements made over time. So, for example, Morse constructed a rustic style summer house, seen on a later photograph and noted in later diary accounts.[56] The summer house was located along the bluff edge overlooking a ravine south of the house. From the summer house, a path and flight of rough, timber (log?) steps were installed leading down the face of the bluff through the ravine to the river front. Around the house, paths extended along the terrace edge and rustic seats and features were set out on the lawn. There were urns, and a fountain was installed east of the house centered on the porte cochere.

In 1855, his financial claim to the telegraph assured (by ruling of the U.S. Supreme Court), Morse purchased a house in New York City to serve as a winter residence. After 1855, the family spent winters in the city while spring through autumn was enjoyed at Locust Grove. There were gaps in this routine. Early in June 1856, Morse took his family to Europe, returning to New York in the autumn. Then, in April 1857 he again visited Europe on telegraph business, again returning in the autumn. The next summer he returned to Europe for a third time with the family, in this case delaying his return home until the spring of 1859. At this point, Morse had been absent for three summers, with winters spent in New York.

By 1859, the property's gardener was Thomas Devoy who was to remain at Locust Grove for the remainder of Morse's occupancy. Devoy appears to have had the skills and importantly the temperament (Morse called him "faithful"), for success. His involvement after 1859 seems to have enabled Morse to achieve horticultural projects that gave him great pleasure throughout the rest of his life. For example, after 1860 there is increasing talk of grape culture, with Morse saying that Devoy was "very successful in the culture of grapes."[57] In 1864, Morse talked of a grape he was sending Devoy as "a valuable addition to our varieties,"[58] and in 1871, he mentioned his "cold and hot house graperies, a larger quantity than ever before, of exotic varieties."[59] Devoy seems to have allowed Morse to practice horticulture and Morse apparently delighted in his managerial role and in exhibiting the results of their joint efforts. In 1859 the farmer was Thomas Luckey, at least the third individual to hold the precarious position of farmer since Morse purchased the property just eleven years earlier. Mr. Luckey would in turn be let go after 1864, at which point Thomas Devoy seems to have been given the joint position of farmer and gardener.

At some point, probably after Morse returned from the extended stay in Europe in 1859, a greenhouse was erected. This is first mentioned in a letter from the winter of 1864. The greenhouse was attached to the east side of a stable building with its horticultural exhibits oriented toward the south. An earlier engraving of this area suggests that an older building may have been removed to allow its construction.

While not conclusively documented, Morse may also have built a separate greenhouse, called a "grapery," specifically designed for grape production, south of the house near his orchard and kitchen garden. The "garden" mentioned in Morse's correspondences was located southeast of the immediate house grounds and seems to have been a continuation of the earlier Livingston's kitchen garden.

In June 1866 Morse and the family went again to Europe and remained there for two years returning in June 1868. In their absence Locust Grove was rented. On return, Morse wrote lovingly of being home, now at age seventy-seven, an old man: "The farm looks splendid," he wrote, "Never did the Grove look more charming. Its general features the same, but the growth of trees and shrubbery greatly increased."[60] Thus began Morse's last years at Locust Grove. Despite the inevitable need to manage the rampant vegetation, it is not likely that extensive landscape alterations were made after 1868. None are recorded. Morse spent his last summer at Locust Grove in 1871 and died in New York City on April 2, 1872 just short of his eighty-first birthday.

After Morse's death, Locust Grove was retained as the family home. Still, there was little stability in the property's ongoing use. Finley was almost forty-seven, but in need of care, he eventually moved to other relatives. Morse's wife, Sarah, age fifty, remained on the property for a time but her children were approaching adulthood. Arthur was twenty-three and he left the area before dying tragically in New Orleans in 1876. Cornelia, in her twenties, married and moved to Germany. Her mother later followed her and did not return to Locust Grove.

Samuel Morse's sons are most closely associated with Locust Grove after their father's death. William was nineteen in 1872. He married a year later and continued to summer on the property. In the 1880s, after the death of his first wife, William remarried, undertook house remodeling and planned to make Locust Grove a year-round home. Then after a year the plans changed and he moved away. Morse's youngest son, Edward Lind Morse, was 15 at the time of his father's death. He remained with his mother for several years but eventually he returned to Locust Grove and was instrumental in the property's sale in 1900.

The development of the landscape and gardens during the unsettled if continued Morse family ownership is not well documented. Only fragmentary information survives from this period.[61] At some point in the 1880s, the old Livingston farmhouse was torn down and a new gardener's cottage built.[62] The first tenant of the new cottage was said to be Thomas Devoy who had then been on the property for about twenty-five years. In this period, Devoy was apparently employed managing a substantial commercial greenhouse operation. It seems that William Morse, perhaps even before his father's death, decided to raise flowers (reportedly roses). His brother Edward joined with William in this endeavor.[63] Four, one hundred-foot-long commercial greenhouses were constructed. These were laid out in a north-south orientation, along a line of garden beds, sheds and perhaps an earlier greenhouse (grapery?), that had been constructed about 200 feet south of the house. A row of hemlock trees was planted as a screen.

Photographs taken during the late nineteenth century, twenty years after Morse's death, show that planting around the house had been simplified. For example, no vines or foundation shrubs are shown and the boxwood hedge that flanked the porte cochere during Morse's time had been removed. The site's more refined garden elements—flower beds cut into lawns and seasonal maintenance—declined after Morse's involvement ended but this reduced care did not change the landscape layout. Trees and shrubs slowly matured and in some areas went wild but the landscape garden arrangement known to Samuel F. B. Morse remained generally uncompromised (fig. 6).

In November 1900, William H. Young (d.1909), a successful lawyer who lived in Poughkeepsie, purchased Locust Grove from the Morse trustees.[64] The Young family included William's wife, Martha ("Dolly") (d.1946), and their children, Annette (d.1975) and Innis (d.1953). Before its purchase, the Youngs had rented Locust Grove as a summer residence and they eventually lived there for eighty years, the site's last and longest period of family occupancy. The Youngs have gained a reputation for respect and appreciation for Samuel F. B. Morse and his legacy,[65] and over their tenure the family does seem to have generally preserved the landscape features and effects as they found them. No wholesale design alterations were imposed.

Still, changes were made. A wing was added to the house immediately after its purchase. Within a few years, new outbuildings were built while old structures were remodeled. An old dwelling below the bluff was demolished. By 1902, Morse's greenhouse had been removed from the east side of the stable/carriage house, and the service related functions concentrated there were set behind a screen planting of evergreen trees.

Young planned a new, more ornamental stable building, but the plans were not executed and the old building was instead rehabilitated.

Elsewhere, the Youngs took several steps to screen the property's edges, this to enhance privacy and set the landscape off from the increasing development and traffic along the Post Road. Early in 1901, an extensive tree and shrub planting was installed, intended "for [a] screen look."[66] Elsewhere, in April 1902, 200 white pine were installed along the north boundary line and hemlocks were added on the south, perhaps in 1903 when "120 hemlock spruce," are recorded to have arrived at Locust Grove.[67] While William Young screened the east, north and south boundaries from views, the river vista was "widened somewhat"[68] and maintained throughout William Young's residency. This situation is well illustrated in photographs from this period (fig. 5).

The Youngs were avid gardeners. Even in the years when they rented the property, a large "main garden"[69] was maintained. This was located west of the gardener's cottage in the same location as Morse's more utilitarian kitchen garden. The Youngs maintained a large flower garden in this area throughout their residency. Elsewhere

LOCUST GROVE.

FIGURE 5

Locust Grove.
Engraving, from Benson J. Lossing, "The Hudson-from the Wilderness to the Sea," New York: Arts Journal, 1860–1861
This evocative image shows the Locust Grove landscape during the residency of Samuel F.B. Morse. The view looks west from the public road, today Route 9. The height of the Italianate house tower has been exaggerated for artistic emphasis. Note, in the middle distance, an old structure from the earlier Livingston farm and the characteristic limbs of black locust trees along the entrance drive. Benson Lossing said of Locust Grove:

> *"The mansion is so embowered that it is almost invisible to the traveller on the highway. But immediately around it are gardens, conservatories, and a pleasant lawn, basking in the sunshine, and through vistas between magnificent trees, glimpses may be caught of the Hudson, the northern and southern ranges of mountains, and villages that dot the western shore of the river. For a man of taste and genius his home is one of the most charming retreats to be found on the banks of the Hudson from the wilderness to the sea."*

in the house grounds, the Youngs maintained floral displays in urns and incidental beds that no doubt changed somewhat over time. Morse's long-abandoned lawn beds west of the house were not reestablished. A new flower bed layout was installed on the level lawn south of the veranda, in a location where Morse might have had some garden feature earlier. Young's layout, which came to be called the "French Garden,"[70] was a geometric arrangement of triangular beds around a center rectangle, cut into the lawn and intended for bedding out. These and other incidental changes in the house environs reflect the period taste for refinement and classical formality, themes sympathetic to the earlier Morse approach.

In the river front, a continuing taste for the picturesque aesthetic also helped preserve Morse's landscape garden and the panoramic views. Open space in the river front was kept cleared and in *1901* William Young built a large, natural appearing pond by damming the site's major stream. New roads and stone walls were also built.

Robert M. Toole

After William Young died in *1909* the pace of landscape and garden changes moderated considerably. The property was preserved more or less unaltered over the next 65 years. One change in maintenance was profound. In the *1920s* mowing and grazing were discontinued and the remaining open areas of the river front grew into woods, obliterating Morse's nineteenth-century landscape garden.

After Mrs. Young died in *1946*, Annette Young continued her full time residency at Locust Grove, with Innis Young also spending time on the property before his death in *1953*. In the *1960s*, as Annette Young reached her eightieth birthday, she became committed to the preservation of the property. Her motivations seem to have focused on the importance of Locust Grove's association with Samuel F. B. Morse and concern for the Young family possessions in the house, which she had cared for over the years.[71] Annette Young also expressed concern for the wildlife that inhabited the property, foreseeing a sanctuary in the river front. In *1963* the property was declared a National Historic Landmark, due to the association with Samuel F. B. Morse.[72] Annette envisaged the future site as the "Samuel F. B. Morse Museum,"[73] and her will states that the property "be maintained in perpetuity as a historical site for the enjoyment, visitation and enlightenment of the public."[74] After Annette Young's death in *1975* Locust Grove opened as a museum property governed by a Board of Trustees who are dedicated to the site's preservation, restoration and presentation to the public, as stipulated in Annette Young's will.

Landscape Design Description

> [Locust Grove] is the handsomest place on the river.
>
> —Samuel F. B. Morse, *9 July 1848*

Figure 7 shows the plan of Locust Grove as it is thought to have been at the end of Samuel F. B. Morse's lifetime.

The house was a feature above the bluff. The elegant "Italianate" structure was appropriate to its owner—Samuel F. B. Morse—and to its setting on a nearly level site.[75] An embellished and somewhat geometric treatment of the ground surrounding the house imparted refinement over a rustic or picturesque effect. This was referred to as a "Graceful" or "Beautiful" landscape design, an approach epitomized in the grandeur of the flat parkland, lawn terracing, and the elaborate display of flowers and urns in the house grounds at Locust Grove.[76]

Each side of the house was distinctive. In elevation the architecture was nearly symmetrical and Morse developed the immediate landscape to reinforce a balanced effect. For example, on the east, twin larch trees were planted on either side of the porte cochere and a fountain was sited on the lawn directly on the east-west center line of the house. The loop driveway passed through the port-cochere and each side was edged with matching sections of clipped boxwood hedge.

Symmetry continued on the south. Here, Morse's study opened onto the vine embowered veranda, focusing domestic life to this sunny orientation, joining house to landscape in a finely crafted ensemble. From the raised veranda, a broad flight of steps was aligned on the north-south center line of the house. The steps led down to an earthen terrace, raised above the surrounding lawn by a geometric turf bank. The terrace overlooked floral displays cut into the lawn on the south. A turn east or west on the terrace led to separate side steps that descended to the ground. Matching urns flanked the terrace and paired sugar maples on the lawn framed the scene. Although loosely formed, the symmetry here is complete and the layout while modest in scale and components is elegant and classical in effect.

On the west, the Italianate tower provided an architectural focus equal to its expansive setting (fig. 8). The tower dominated the level lawn terrace which served as a natural platform for the house and a belvedere overlooking the panoramic view to the west. The abrupt drop along the bluff face resulted in a nearly architectural look, a natural evocation of the artificial terraces typically seen at Italian villa sites. With the encouragement of his architect, A. J. Davis, Morse further developed the terrace theme when he raised the ground around the house by about three feet using a geometrically formed turf bank that traced the house on the south and west sides. This terracing provided the substantial platform on which the house stands with heightened monumentality.

Two photographs from late in Morse's residency and several engravings illustrate the scene. The photographs, from about 1870, shows numerous curvilinear flower beds cut into the lawn. In one view (fig. 8), a circular bed is shown centered on the tower, flanked by at least eight other beds on the north and south. These beds were planted seasonally, using bulbs, annuals and tender exotics that were over-wintered in the nearby greenhouse. This type of lawn bed was very typical of taste in the post-Civil War period.

East of the house, was the entrance driveway and park, with agricultural activities located to the southeast and south. The old straight driveway remained the main entry into Locust Grove. Along the driveway, the grade road turned off to the right (north) before turning west toward the river. A map drafted in about 1851[77] also shows the grade road making direct connection with the public road and so providing Locust Grove with a separate service entrance. Dominated by the sugar maples, the park east of the house also displayed a variety of other specimen trees, including spruce and oaks. Closer to the public road, the straight driveway was lined with rows of black locust trees, a typical Colonial period planting that remained from Locust Grove's early history.

This area had undergone an active development and remnants of earlier uses were incorporated into Morse's arrangement. Most conspicuous in the park was the siting along the driveway of the old Livingston house. The old house was apparently somewhat dilapidated at the time of Morse's purchase, but it was retained as valuable accommodation, and as a fond reminder of the property's past.

Around the old farmhouse the original ensemble of buildings and fenced yards had been tidied-up. The presence of the stable/carriage house (service) complex northwest of the house, and the presence of a separate barn/farm complex below the bluff, attests to a concern for separating divergent uses and enhanced amenity in the house grounds.

A later resident, Innis Young, identified grounds to the southeast of the house as the site of the "former gardens." In a correspondence to his gardener of 1858, Morse spoke of his "garden," and went on to clearly describe it as a kitchen garden, identifying such crops as "corn, squashes, beets and early potatoes. . . . melons. . . . asparagus." In another letter Morse also mentioned "onions, cabbage. . . . turnips, parsnips, carrots, salsify, celery. . . . [and] lettuce." Morse's garden seems to have evolved from the property's earlier use. The area would have been the immediate grounds south of the old Livingston farmstead, a likely location for Livingston's earlier kitchen garden. By Morse's period, the northern portion of this early garden, together with the farmstead development lying on the south side of the driveway, had been removed so as not to intrude on the new loop drive and park fronting the 1830 house. The garden beds lying further south were apparently retained and as need arose were expanded further south. These gardens served as the kitchen garden during the Montgomery and Morse periods, and thereafter increasingly as an ornamental flower garden in the Young residency after 1895.

As in the case of Morse's kitchen gardens, the orchard at Locust Grove seems to have been established before Morse's ownership. The orchard occupied the level ground west of the kitchen garden and extended close to the loop drive on the north. A few old fruit trees can be seen close to the driveway in photographs from about 1900, and so it may be concluded that Morse allowed the orchard trees to remain close to the house. In this way the orchard melded with the park. Even more evocative was Morse's vineyard ("grapery"), which was possibly located west of the orchard, just back from the bluff face south of the house. Morse may have had a special greenhouse for grape cultivation in this area, and his vineyard would have likely extended to the south.

The presence of Morse's summer house along the bluff close to the orchard and vineyard attests to the mix of ornament and agriculture that was a goal of landscape gardening in this period. The summer house is shown indistinctly in one photograph from about 1900. A notation on the back of the photograph describes it as a rustic style structure. Its overall dimensions and design detail are unknown. In addition to this shelter, rustic seats were sited along the path overlooking the bluff. These paths seem to have been cleanly edged and carefully maintained. Away from the house, paths were no doubt less refined. One path, fitted with timber steps, descended the bluff from the site of the summer house. This path entered the river front on the south side of the property, complementing the access from the grade road on the north side. This paired access to the river front was an important design condition. Path alignments were crucial components in the overall landscape composition because they created a visual sequence for those moving through the landscape.

The bluff face was cleared from the small ravine south of the house, almost to the grade road on the north. At the edges, vegetation was retained to screen the farm complex below the bluff, but even then the horizon to the northwest was included in the panoramic view. Across the nearly 500-foot wide cleared bluff face, only occasional specimen trees, including several cedars, were retained for foreground scale and interest (fig. 6). As the land dropped away, the woodland understory thickened. Periodically, selected clearing operations were undertaken to return the desired look. The bluff face was an organic composition in constant need of management.

Below the bluff, screened by vegetation, a farm house, barn and perhaps other farm related outbuildings were constructed before Morse's purchase. The matter of the farm complex on what was called the "lower flat" focuses attention on the important question of Morse's agricultural use of the river front. Locust Grove was a real farm, not solely a suburban residential property. Farming operations were considered essential to the perception of a country seat during Morse's period. Even as late as 1868, Morse called Locust Grove "the farm."

In our interpretation, Locust Grove was an "ornamental farm"[78] because farming was not the only role of the landscape and farming operations were melded imperceptibly with aesthetics. In 1851, a few years after his purchase and with his son Charles settled elsewhere, Samuel F. B. Morse showed a depleted interest in farming by significantly reducing the site's agricultural acreage, selling about half the open land while he encouraged woodland to return in other areas. Morse had presumably concluded that the acreage sold was expendable given his intentions for the property. In this way, Morse's actions show a preference for landscape gardening over farming. Locust Grove was a gentlemen's farm, a modest agricultural operation subsidized by a man of wealth and taste. As such, Morse's farm was intended for aesthetics and rural authenticity, but not profit. These modifications had a profound influence on landscapes throughout the Hudson River Valley in this period.

At Locust Grove, these themes were best illustrated in the river front, below the bluff. The grade road descended to the area where it became the lane, continuing for about 800 feet beyond the lower farm complex, ending at an open field on the river. The lane was clearly defined, partially bounded by a field stone wall and partially by fence lines, with old sugar maples and other trees placed along it forming an established edge that Morse used in setting the north boundary of his property. The lane provided access to several fields. A "bar-way" (gate) is noted in one deed at a point on the lane just west of where the dominant stream passed under the lane. This gate gave access to the south on a dirt track that followed along the west side of the stream. It would seem that this route led originally to the old mill site. Near the river, another spur from the lane led south along the east side of the stream. This alignment may have continued along one of several routes and led eventually to the early river landing. These early roads were by Morse's period downgraded as the mill and landing no longer functioned.

The original arrangement of fields in the river front was established during the Livingston and Montgomery periods. This layout was altered decisively by the close of the Morse residency. The most important element Morse worked with was the pattern of woodland vegetation that defined the open spaces. An analysis of the river front reveals that except for isolated pockets and individual field trees, most of the area below the bluff was open ground by the close of the Livingston period in 1828. It was in the Montgomery and especially the Morse period that this cleared landscape was selectively returned to woods. By the close of the Morse residency only about one-third of the river front acres remained open—being pastures, meadows, or wooded areas partially cleared of trees.[79] Morse preserved a wide swath of wooded ground along his south boundary (fig. 7). He understood that the open land defined by his woodland belts established spatial interest and revealed the land's variety as a three dimensional composition. In deciding on this spatial definition of wooded vs. open ground, Morse effectively created a landscape garden in the river front.

Farm fields were an integral part of Morse's landscape garden and the stone walls and fence lines that edged the fields were important landscape design elements. It seems that at least three north-south wall lines, each running perpendicular to the lane, existed before Morse's residency (fig. 7). These walls defined the farm fields. A map, drawn in about 1851[80] shows four such demarcation lines, at least three of which were wall lines (the other appears to be a fence). A 1850 deed described these as "cross walls."[81]

The positioning of site walls, as modified by Morse, represents important landscape design decisions both for themselves and also for the resulting arrangement of open fields and wooded ground. The two walls closest to the river were constructed across low areas so that they are not seen in the panoramic view from the house and the upper terrace. Unlike the others, the wall closest to the house was located on the east facing side of a low, north-south ridge line. This wall was clearly visible from the upper lawn terrace. At some point after 1851 Morse had this wall dismantled and erected a new wall, not shown on the 1851 plan, several hundred feet further to the west where it was tucked on the west side of the low ridge where it was hidden from the house.

Originally, the north-south cross walls extended from the lane, on the north, to an east-west wall line several hundred feet to the south. This south line was an old demarcation established in the eighteenth century. As a survey line, this straight wall had no relationship to the land's character. It dipped arbitrarily into a steep ravine and crisscrossed the stream that paralleled the south boundary of Morse's original purchase. Understandably feeling cramped by this awkward edge, Morse added a 300 foot wide strip of woods in 1851.

FIGURE 6

Photograph, 1902

This view records the river front landscape garden thirty years after Morse's death. It is the earliest known illustration of the area and shows Morse's designed landscape generally unchanged except for the added tree growth. A close comparison between this image and the existing conditions verify the historic composition.

With this wooded buffer, Morse then physically altered the old wall line to an arrangement more sensitive to the land's configuration. These alterations to older wall lines are instances where Morse's landscape gardening resulted in aesthetic improvements to an earlier utilitarian farm layout.

Farm fields were maintained within the wall and fence lines. Immediately below the bluff was the "lower flat." About six acres of open ground. The woodland edge that defined this grazing field curved around rocky ground in the northwest corner of the area. A wooded knoll was maintained in the center of the field. On the south, Morse located a fence line along the stream that formed a natural field edge on this side. From above, the design provided a heightened sense of third-dimension and depth of field, a testimony to Morse's subtlety as a landscape gardener (fig. 6).

The most clear cut of the agricultural fields in the river front was a meadow maintained on a large rounded hill, later called the "Great Green Hill," that occupied the field between two cross walls just east of the river. This six-acre field rises to an elevation of about 100 feet and was a commanding open space in the panoramic view from the house.

Just east of the "Great Green Hill" was a complex area of about six acres, bisected by the site's major stream. This area included steep, rocky portions where woodland conditions seem to have been in place even before Morse's purchase. Generally unsuited to mowing or crop cultivation, this area was otherwise marginal pasture. Under Morse this former grazing area served the visual concerns of landscape gardening. Grazing and mowing were severely restricted. One small field was left, but Morse also built a pond in the area close to the waterfall that served as a natural feature. A composition of woodland and selected open space was maintained elsewhere.

Also by Morse's period, grazing was apparently reduced in certain areas of the immediate river edge. This was a sizable area of twelve or thirteen acres and included a headland sixty feet above the river. Except along the immediate river edge, and in the rocky headland, this area seems to have been open before Morse's ownership. Afterward, a wider wooded edge was maintained with trees cleared only in a low gap that was a central feature of the scene from the house. Native vegetation was grown along the immediate river edge and on the headland to screen the railroad from view.

The visual unity of the landscape garden design Morse created in the river front is a hallmark of the property in this period. Working at a large scale, most importantly from the generally fixed vantage point of the upper lawn terrace and house, Morse formed the landscape into a vast park-like scene, freely borrowing the neighbor's fields, the Hudson River and the pastoral backdrop on the western shore, to extend and

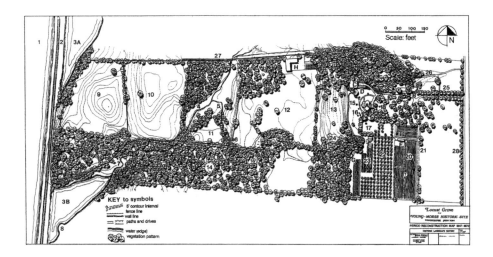

FIGURE 7

Period Reconstruction Plan, Locust Grove Landscape Components, 1872, R.M. Toole, 1994
This plan shows Locust Grove as it is thought to have appeared during Samuel F.B. Morse's lifetime. The plan is based on nineteenth-century written, cartographic and illustrative descriptions of the property, research concerning all phases of the property's development, and modern survey information. The existing site remains intact and has experienced few alterations since the historic period. Key to numbers and letter identifications are as follows:

> *1, Hudson River; 2, Railroad; 3A, Sunfish Cove; 3B, Stream Outlet; 4, Dominant Stream; 5, Secondary Stream; 6, Pond and Waterfall; 7, Site of Old Mill; 8, River Landing (abandoned); 9, River-Edge Pasture (5.5 acres); 10, "Great Green Hill" (6 acres);11, Center Section (6 acres); 12, "Lower Flat" (6 acres); 13, Bluff Face (6 acres); 14, Woodland Buffer (24 acres); 15, Lawn Terrace; 16, Flower Beds on lawn; 17, South Façade (w/steps and terrace); 18, East Façade (w/larch trees, boxwood hedge and fountain); 19, Parkland; 20, Kitchen Garden; 21, Old Road (early public road?); 22, Orchard; 23, Vineyard (?); 24, Path (down bluff); 25, Approach Avenue (w/black locust trees); 26, Grade Road; 27, The Lane; 28, Public Road (Albany Post Road). Buildings: A, Main House (1830, remodeled, 1851); B, Livingston House and Farmstead site (colonial); C, Coach House/Stable; D, Greenhouse; E, Grapery; F, Garden Shed (Tool House); G, Summer House; H, Barn (and Farmhouse?).*

complete the panorama, called in 1914 a "Picture," where "the whole scene is a unit for the boundaries are distinctly marked."[82]

While many of the elements of this composition were in place in 1847, Morse enhanced the scene to his taste, and then maintained it to constitute a designed entity. The design principle and quality of the work may be evaluated in light of Morse's achievements as an accomplished and learned artist. Discussing painting in 1826, Morse said:

> A picture then is not merely a copy of any work of Nature, it is constructed on the principles of nature. While its parts are copies of natural objects, the whole work is an artificial arrangement of them similar to the construction of a poem or a piece of music.[83]

Or a landscape garden, for indeed these thoughts have direct application to landscape gardening as Morse understood it at Locust Grove. Certainly these scenes were "picturesque" as that term was applied in common usage—"like a picture." In addition, Morse's appreciation of the river front evolved from its natural situation, a testimony to the Picturesque design mode he exhibited there.[84] The river front was a complex scheme, melding natural elements (native woodland and swamps, exposed rock and undulating land forms) in a mix of pastoral parkland and agricultural acreage. While the land's physical character largely determined the landscape design, the composition of open and wooded areas produced a visually interesting, unified

FIGURE 8

Photograph, c. 1870
This important photograph shows the lawn terrace at the end of Morse's lifetime. Samuel F.B. Morse is seated (with white beard) on the right with family members and friends clustered nearby. Note the flower beds on the lawn and the greenhouse on the left.

arrangement. As Morse described it in his lecture series, "these are the means in the possession of Landscape Gardening by which it aims to please the imagination."

Morse called the property "as beautiful a landscape prospect as the noble Hudson affords,"[85] and he presented Locust Grove to a visitor with a simple claim: "I can not promise you anything here of interest but beautiful natural scenery."[86] These sentiments attest to Morse's reliance on the natural attributes of his landscape which he subtly manipulated for maximum effect to convey the essence of Hudson River Valley scenery.

Samuel F. B. Morse's landscape gardening at Locust Grove, especially as exhibited in the river front, represents a distinctive phase of landscape design in the pre-Civil War period. This period was influenced by Romanticism and its deeply felt appreciation for nature. Samuel F. B. Morse's river front was intended to conjure up heightened notions of local scenery and promote romantic sentiment in empathy with the native environment. As such, landscape garden design at Locust Grove was integral to Morse's times and to the artist himself, remaining his, and one of his generation's most notable design achievements. The site's present state of preservation underscores its significance.[87]

Endnotes

1. There are a wide range of background studies concerning Samuel F. B. Morse and his career as artist and inventor. A selected list would include: Carleton Mabee, *The American Leonardo; A Life of Samuel F. B. Morse*, New York, 1943; Samuel I. Prime, *Life of Samuel F. B. Morse*, New York, 1875; Oliver Larkin, *Samuel F. B. Morse and American Democratic Art*, Boston, 1954; Paul Staiti, *Samuel F. B. Morse and the Search for the Grand Style*, Ann Arbor, 1979; William Kloss, *Samuel F. B. Morse*, New York, N.Y., 1988.

2. Letter: Samuel F. B. Morse (hereafter cited SFBM) to Sidney Morse, 7/30/1847. Letters are cited from Edward Lind Morse, ed., *Samuel F. B. Morse: His Letters and Journals*, 2 Vols., Boston, MA, 1914, copy, Young-Morse Historic Site (hereafter cited as YMHS). Morse's use of the term "capabilities" had direct reference to the long history of landscape gardening. See below, note 15.

3. In addition to Locust Grove notable examples of landscape gardening that remain in the Hudson River Valley, listed from south to north, include: Sunnyside (Washington Irving's home, 1835–1859), and Lyndhurst (initiated as "Knoll" in the period 1836–1864), both in Tarrytown, N.Y.; Springside (Matthew Vassar's home and A. J. Downing's only known and extant landscape garden design, laid out in 1850–52, located 1/2 mile north of Locust Grove); Hyde Park (today's Vanderbilt Mansion National Historic Site, initiated in period 1763–1835); The Point (Hoyt House, 1852), at Staatsburg, N.Y.; Montgomery Place (operated by Historic Hudson Valley) at Annandale-on-Hudson; Clermont State Historic Site and several dozen other old estate properties in the Hudson River National Historic Landmark and finally, Olana State Historic Site (Frederic Church's home), south of Hudson, N.Y. As a group, these historic landscapes are considered to have national and even international significance.

4. William Kloss, *Samuel F. B. Morse*, New York, N.Y.: Harry N. Abrams, Inc. 1988. Kloss called Morse the "finest portrait painter of his generation" (p. 11), and also evaluated his significance in broader terms, saying he "ranked high among Americans of the revolutionary and federal era whose lives were distinguished by the breath of their interest and knowledge and their success in varied endeavors" (p. 9). Also, Paul J. Staiti, "Ideology and Politics in Samuel F.B. Morse's Agenda for a National Art," *Samuel F. B. Morse*, New York, N.Y.: National Academy of Design, 1982, pp. 7–53. Staiti says "He [Morse] was a major participant in and shaper of nineteenth century American culture" (pp. 45–46).

5. Morse had given some attention to architecture. He studied the Italian villa on his trip to Italy in 1830 and afterward showed interest in the topic, sketching a variety of building types.

6. Morse scholar William Kloss described Morse's landscape work as "utterly naturalistic in light and color and in the observation of foliage and architecture."

7. The National Academy of Design, which still exists, was founded in reaction to the established American Academy which was widely regarded as conservative and unresponsive to the needs of working artists.

8. Letter: SFBM to Lucretia Morse, 8/1823.

9. Nicolai Cikovsky, Jr., "Editor's Introduction," Samuel F. B. Morse, *Lectures on the Affinity of Painting with the Other Fine Arts*, Columbia, Missouri: University of Missouri Press, 1983, p. 17. Cikovsky's book reproduces Morse's four lectures verbatim.

10. Lucia H. Albers, "The Perception of Gardening as Art," *Garden History*, Vol. 19, No. 2, Autumn 1991, P. 170. William Shenstone (1714–1763), who is credited with coining the term "landscape gardener," put it this way in his essay: "Unconnected Thoughts on Gardening" (1764): "I have used the word landscape gardener; because in pursuance to our present taste in gardening, every good painter of landscapes appears to me the most proper designer."

11. Brenda Bullion, "Early American farming and gardening literature: 'Adapted to the climates and seasons of the United States'," *The Journal of Garden History*, Vol. 12, No. 1, January-March, 1992, pp. 29–51.

12. See: R.P. Maccubbon and P. Martin, eds., *British and American Gardens in the Eighteenth Century*, Williamsburg, VA.: The Colonial Williamsburg Foundation, 1984. Also, Barbara Wells Sarudy, "Eighteenth Century Garden's of the Chesapeake," *Journal of Garden History*, Vol. 9, No. 3, July-Sept., 1989.

13. Cikovsky, *Lectures*, pp. 50–51. All Morse quotations used in this discussion of the "Lectures" are taken from the Cikovsky volume. The significance of English landscape gardening has been widely concluded. Kenneth Clark, in his popular work, *Civilization* (1969), called it "the most pervasive influence that England has ever had on the look of things." Morse's 1826 critique that landscape gardening was "little known or practiced" was edited within a decade to read: "Landscape Gardening . . . recently both studied and practiced in our country," showing the progress in American landscape gardening that occurred in the 1820s and 1830s. See: Cikovsky, pp. 50–51 and 116, note 1–32.

14. Therese O'Malley, "Landscape Gardening in the Early National Period," *Views and Visions*, Washington, D.C.: The Corcoran Galley of Art, 1986, pp. 133–159.

15. Lancelot "Capability" Brown (d. 1783) was famous in his own lifetime as England's greatest landscape gardener. He did not produce a body of written principles so that in nineteenth-century America his work was less well understood in its specifics than simply as a legend. Brown called himself a "place-maker" indicating the importance of engendering a "sense of place" to a work of landscape gardening. It was this concern that created the great English estate grounds, such as Castle Howard, Blenheim, Stowe and Stourhead. Brown was called "Capability" for his habit of telling clients that their properties had "capabilities" (i.e., potential) for ornamental landscape improvements, Humphry Repton (d. 1818) was the most important of a group of "landscape gardeners" who carried on where Brown left off, extending the tradition of English landscape gardening into the nineteenth century. Unlike Brown, Repton produced a body of written work that clearly articulated the principles of landscape gardening as practiced from the Brown era. Repton was also an early eclectic practitioner, working with the

design tastes of the Regency period while admitting appreciation for the often wild and natural-appearing landscapes championed by the "picturesque improvers," notably Uvedale Price (d. 1829) and Richard Payne Knight (d. 1824). For more on the English background of landscape gardening, see: J.D. Hunt and Peter Willis, eds., *The Genius of the Place, The English Landscape Garden, 1620–1820*, Cambridge MA: M.I.T. Press, 1990; and David Jacques, *Georgian Gardens, The Reign of Nature*, Portland, Oregon: Timber Press, 1983.

16. John Claudius Loudon (d. 1843) was the preeminent English landscape gardener during Morse's adulthood. Loudon's ideas became popular in the late 1820s and as such had a limited influence on Morse's (or American) attitudes on landscape gardening before the 1840s. Loudon ushered in the garden tastes referred to generally as 'Victorian,' amounting to a highly eclectic range of design components, effects and options that marked a departure from the more single-minded English landscape garden tradition and picturesque sensibilities of the past. "Victorian" themes descended on American landscape and garden design only fitfully before the Civil War, but with a vengeance thereafter. See: Melanie Louise Simo, *Loudon and the Landscape*, New Haven, Conn.: Yale University Press, 1988.

17. Thomas Whately, *Observations on Modem Gardening* (1770). Whately went on: "[Landscape Gardening] is as superior to landscape painting, as a reality is to a representation: it is an exertion of fancy, a subject for taste; and being released not from the restraints of regularity, and enlarged beyond the purposes of domestic convenience, the most beautiful, the most simple, the most noble scenes of nature, are all within its province."

18. For a lucid description of the implications of landscape gardening in America, see: George B. Tatum, "Nature's Gardener," *Prophet With Honor: The Career of Andrew Jackson Downing*, Washington, D.C., t989, pp. 43–80.

19. The Hudson River School painters all used this "mechanical imitation" in common and the trait has been the subject of much commentary. See, for example: Barbara Novak, *Nature and Culture, American Landscape and Painting, 1825–1875*, New York: Oxford University Press, 1980. "[For the Hudson River School] Nature is not so much seen through pictures (i.e. the picturesque), but rather pictures instruct on how to see nature for itself' (p. 234).

20. Andrew Jackson Downing, *Treatise on the Theory and Practice of Landscape Gardening Adapted to North America*, New York, N.Y.: Wiley and Putnam, 2nd ed., 1844, "Section II-Beauties and Principles of the Art," pp. 47–65. Downing contrasted the "Picturesque" with the "Graceful" or "Beautiful" as separate design modes of what he called the 'Modem, Irregular or Natural Style," by which he referred to the long tradition of Brown and Repton (often referred to today as the English landscape garden). See below, notes 76 and 84.

21. See: *Young-Morse Historic Site, Locust Grove Historic Landscape Report*, 1992, Figure 11.

22. The picturesque, Italianate transformation used later at Locust Grove would have been unthinkable in 1826 when classical architecture remained unchallenged in America.

23. A. J. Downing, *Landscape Gardening*, 1st ed., New York: Wiley and Putnam, 1841. In the 1st edition, Downing reported on the status of landscape gardening in America, describing a half-dozen properties, all but one of which were located in the Hudson River Valley. In the much expanded 2nd edition, 1844, five properties in the Boston and Philadelphia areas were discussed first. Then Downing says that "There is no part of the Union where the taste in Landscape Gardening is so far advanced, as on the middle portion of the Hudson," and follows this with discussion of more than a dozen examples in the valley. This reportage occurred about three years before Morse purchased Locust Grove. See also: U. P. Hedrick, *A History of Horticulture in America* to 1860, Oxford: Oxford University Press, 1950, pp. 186–211, and J. E. Spingarn, "Henry Winthrop Sargent and the Early History of Landscape Gardening in Dutchess County, New York," Dutchess County Historical Society *Yearbook*, and Albert Fein, "Landscape Architecture and the Hudson River Valley: The Juncture of Nature and Technology," *Charmed Places*, New York, N.Y.: Harry N. Abrams, Inc., 1988, pp. 19–41. Fein concluded: "Landscape gardening [was] one of the major private art forms of the [Romantic] period."

24. Background information on the Vanderburgh family by H. A. Thomas, from genealogical data compiled from Richard Schermerhorn, Jr. and family records of Ida Thomas, "Lucas Dircksen Vanderburgh of New Amsterdam and his son Dirck, Progenitors of the Vanderburgh Family of Dutchess County, N.Y.," not published, Oct., 1951 (source: The Holland Society of New York).

25. Gilbert Livingston (1690–1746) was the last son of Robert Livingston (1654–1728), founder of the important Hudson River Valley Livingston family. Gilbert married Cornelia Beekman (daughter of Henry Beekman) in 1711 and lived at Kingston, N.Y. Henry was one of Gilbert's nine sons, several of whom established homes in Dutchess County.

26. As quoted in: William J. Powers, Jr., "Disposition of Henry Vanderburgh Estate, Poughkeepsie, N.Y.," Nov. 1991. Early land transactions are summarized from deed information recorded at the Dutchess County Court House (hereafter cited as DCCH). Also, see: Clifford Buck, "Abstract of Land Acquisition," c. 1978, YMHS.

27. Cornelia Livingston Goodrich, "Sketches of a few Gentleman of Ye old Colonial Days," unpublished essay, c- 1914, p. 8, YMHS.

28. Henry Livingston, Jr.,'s daughter, quoted by Dr. William S. Thomas, "Henry Livingston," Dutchess County Historical Society *Yearbook*, 1919, p. 37.

29. Ibid.

30. Ibid., pp. 32–46. According to Dr. Thomas, Henry was called "Junior" only until his father died in 1799. He was also referred to as 'Major Livingston' for his military rank, and later as "Judge Livingston," by Samuel F.B. Morse, and others.

31. Cornelia Goodrich, essay (c- 1914).

32. W. Stephen Thomas, "Does 'The Night Before Christmas' Belong to Dutchess County?" not published, 1977, copy, YMHS.

33. According to Dr. Thomas (*Yearbook*, 1919), Henry Livingston, Jr., married Sarah Welles in c. 1774. After Sarah's death in 1783, Henry married Jane Paterson. Together, twelve children were raised on the property in Livingston's residency there.

34. Ibid., quoting Henry Livingston, Jr.,'s daughter: "Near the house was a well, forty feet deep, from which the water bucket was drawn by a wheel and chain."

35. *New York Magazine or Literary Repository*, August, 1792. The published engraving was accompanied by a caption that declared "the natural beauties of the cascade on which this saw, mill stands, are not equalled perhaps by any in America."

36. Helen Wilkinson Reynolds, "The Story of Locust Grove," Dutchess County Historical Society *Yearbook*, 1932, p. 23.

37. Young-Morse Historic Site, *Historic Structure Report for Locust Grove, Estate of Annette I. Young*, prepared by Building Conservation Technology, Inc., Spring, 1978.

38. Letter: SFBM to Sidney Morse, 10/29/46.

39. Ibid., 6/15/47.

40. Ibid., 7/30/47.

41. Ibid. This is a direct reference to the English landscape garden tradition, and specifically to Lancelot Brown, England's great 18th century landscape gardener, whose nickname was, 'Capability" (see above, note #15).

42. Letter: SFBM to Sidney Morse, 7/30/47.

43. Ibid., 9/12/47.

44. Ibid., 10/12/47.

45. Ibid.

46. Letter: SFBM to M. Sherell, 4/4/49. The letter makes clear that this work took place in the previous season.

47. Letter: Charles Morse to SFBM, 11/23/47.

48. Ibid., 7/9/48.

49. Letter: SFBM to Sidney Morse, 9/12/47.

50. Morse knew Davis from his early years in New York City in the 1820s. For back, ground on A. J. Davis, see: Jane B. Davies, "Davis and Downing: Collaborators in the Picturesque," *Prophet with Honor: The Career of Andrew Jackson Downing*, Washington D.C., 1989, pp. 81–123.

51. See: *Historic Structure Report* (1978). The primary space concerns were for additional bedrooms, storage and a study/office.

52. The map is entitled (in Davis's handwriting), "Morsestan [:] Plot of Ground," c. 1851, YMHS.

53. A. J. Davis Daybook, 5/14/52, copy YMHS.

54. Letter: A. J. Davis to SFBM, 9/l/52.

55. Ibid., 9/5/52. The references to "[Thomas] Whately, [Humphry] Repton, Dohn Claudius] Loudon & [Andrew Jackson] Downing," seems to be in response to Morse's use of the names, though this is not certain.

56. Diary entry: Innis Young, 11/5/1920, YMHS. The summer house was described on the back of the one photograph that survives as the "lovely old SFBM rustic summer house." The exact date of its construction is unknown.

57. Letter: SFBM to William Brightly, 10/13/62.

58. Letter: SFBM to Thomas Devoy, no date.

59. Letter: SFBM to a cousin, 8/12/71.

60. Ibid.

61. See: Leila Livingston Morse, "Samuel F.B. Morse," Dutchess County Historical Society *Yearbook*, 1932, p. 29.

62. The exact date is not recorded but Dr. W. Stephen Thomas, in "Henry Livingston," *Yearbook*, 1919 says "[The house] has since been razed. There are persons living today [who] would remember [it]." In c. 1914, Cornelia L. Goodrich said "old residents of Poughkeepsie will doubtless remember [the Livingston house]." These quotations suggest that the old house was

removed after Morse's death in 1872, perhaps in the early to mid-1880s. It is said that the gardener's cottage contains materials salvaged from the farmhouse demolition, though this has not been substantiated. The gardener's cottage was built after 1882.

63. *Poughkeepsie Journal*, quoting Annette Young, 1/31/1965, copy YMHS.

64. The sale was made through an intermediary. While the sale seems to have been finalized late in 1900, the deed was dated April 19, 1901, just after the property was purchased by Clifford P. Hunt, whose deed is dated May 27, 1901, DCHS.

65. *Poughkeepsie Journal*, quoting Annette Young, 1/31/1965, copy YMHS. Also, H.W. Reynolds, "The Story of Locust Grove," *Yearbook*, 1932, p. 25. "[The Youngs] have looked upon [Locust Grove] as a trust from the past." Also, Charles Hasbrouck, relating conversations with Annette Young, notes, YMHS.

66. Diary entry: Hasbrouck Innis, 5/17/1901, YMHS.

67. Ibid.: Innis Young, 1903, YMHS.

68. Ibid.: Hasbrouck Innis, 1/19/1902, YMHS.

69. Ibid., also called the "north Garden," and simply, using capital letters, "The Garden."

70. Innis Young, untitled essay (Harvard University), 1914, p. 19. There is no reference to the name "French Garden" in the diary accounts. Innis described the garden as "of geometrical shaped flowers (sic) beds fitted with a turf background," YMHS.

71. Newspaper accounts, copies YMHS. The household possessions were focused on the family's long ancestral roots in the Hudson River Valley. Annette's mother was a relative of the Hasbrouck family whose roots in the valley are traced to seventeenth-century New Paltz. Today, Kenneth E. Hasbrouck, Sr. serves as President of the Young-Morse Historic Site.

72. See nomination document: U.S. Department of the Interior, "National Survey of Historic Sites and Buildings," "Locust Grove," 5/20/1963, copy YMHS.

73. *Poughkeepsie Journal*, quoting Annette Young, 1/31/1965.

74. Last Will and Testament, Annette I. Young, dated: September 20, 1974.

75. A. J. Downing, in *Landscape Gardening*, 1st ed., 1841, recognized that the "Italian style" was called "the most beautiful mode for domestic purposes" (p. 311). It "recalls images of the land of painters and the fine arts" (pp. 315–316) suited to the "cultivated mind. . . . a man of wealth and taste" (P. 317). "He who has a passionate love of pictures, and especially fine landscapes, will perhaps, very naturally prefer the modern Italian style for a country residence" (p. 341). Downing also offered a "general principle... that classic architecture [including the Italian Style] should always be selected when the neighboring ground, or the surrounding scenery is simply beautiful or elegant" (p. 338).

76. See above, notes 20 and 75. Referring to the 'Beautiful' design mode, Downing said: "And finally, considering the house itself as a feature in the scene, it should, properly, belong to one of the classical modes—the Italian, Tuscan, or Venetian forms are preferable" (P. 56), and that "residences of a country of level plains, usually allow only, the beauty of simple, and graceful forms." (p. 59). Downing's description and analysis is included here for illustrative purposes only.

77. The "Morsestan Map," c. 1851.

78. Albert Fein, "Landscape Architecture and the Hudson River Valley: The Juncture of Nature and Technology," *Charmed Places*, 1988, p. 24. The term "ferme ornee was coined in England before the mid eighteenth century, first used by Stephen Switzer *Ichnographic Rustica* (1742). A. J. Downing, in his second book, *Cottage Residences* (1842), called the ferme ornee, "a term generally applied to a farm, the whole or the greater part of which is rendered in some degree ornamental by intersecting it with drives, and private lanes and walks, bordered by trees and shrubs, and by the neater arrangement and culture of the fields."

79. Innis Young, untitled essay, (Harvard University), 1914. Young said that most of the wooded areas are "formed by a vigorous seedling growth [from field abandonment] which must have started some hundred years or more ago." In 1849, Morse commented on the age of his woodland acres, saying: "Who can raise those trees again short of twenty years," Letter: SFBM to M. Sherell, 4/4/1849. These quotations suggest that selective reforestation began at about the time of Montgomery's purchase, in 1830. Historic photographs and on-site evidence indicates that the general woodland tree growth that replaced the formerly open fields in the river front is approximately 165 years old. It seems that Montgomery's residency (1830) would encompass all but a few individual trees or tree remnants existing in the area today. In all, about 54 acres were included in the river front. Of this total, it seems that perhaps 40–45 acres (about 80%) was open land at the time of Mongomery's purchase in 1830. By the close of Morse's ownership, approximately 25 of these acres had been selectively returned to woodland, so that at the close of Morse's period only about 35% of the total was open space.

80. The "Morsestan Map," c. 1851.

81. Deed: Book 92, p. 303, dated April 1, 1850 (John B. Montgomery and Isabelle, his wife to SFBM), DCCH.

82. Innis Young, untitled essay (Harvard University), 1914.

83. SFBM, lecture four, 1826, as quoted in Cikovsky.

84. See above notes 20 and 76. The design approaches (modes) indicative of Downing's "Picturesque" and "Graceful" or "Beautiful" were, by 1850, well established, referenced to the themes Downing and others defined as prevalent in the Hudson River Valley in this period. Samuel F. B. Morse may be presumed to have had an informed sense for the design implications of the themes implicit in Downing's "Picturesque" and "Beautiful," but there is no documentation to suggest that he consciously made the distinction between the "Picturesque" and "Beautiful" or used the terms himself A. J. Downing was not directly linked to landscape development at Locust Grove.

85. Letter: SFBM to Charles F. von Fleischmaan, 3/6/52.

86. Letter: SFBM to John P. Brown, 4/4/51.

87. See: Young-Morse Historic Site, *Locust Grove Historic Landscape Report*, prepared by The Office of R.M. Toole, Landscape Architect, 1992, funded by a grant from The J. M. Kaplin Fund. This article is based on the comprehensive report. The author would like to thank the Board of Trustees, Young-Morse Historic Site, Kenneth E. Hasbrouck, Sr., President, and Timothy J. Countryman, for cooperation in the preparation of this report.

This article originally appeared in the *Hudson Valley Regional Review*, Volume 12.1.

The Commerce of Art in the Nineteenth-Century Hudson Valley

Richard C. Wiles

The names of Asher Durand, J.F. Kensett, Thomas Cole, and Albert Bierstadt, among others, today conjure up in our minds visions of luminous paintings with golden-hued views of Hudson Valley scenes or renderings of man versus nature parables. Such familiarity is the result of a century of exhibits and book and catalog reproductions of the work of such artists of the Hudson River School.

But what was their impact on their contemporary world of the nineteenth century? Did the ordinary resident of the Hudson Valley or the mountain region have any knowledge of such art? Did he or she have access to Cole's work in Katterskill Clove or Frederick Church's renderings of the Hudson from his beloved Olana? Did the paintings of the lower Hudson, its lighthouses, and density of its boat traffic gain their attention?

In fact, many opportunities existed for nineteenth century travellers and admirers of the American "picturesque" to view these paintings, not as originals but in reproduced forms, as illustrations in the numerous publications of the day.

Was the popularization of these regional subjects merely artists' expanding the reach of their original works in another form? Were the images, on the other hand, merely "hypes" of a commercial nature, sold as advertising by railroads, steamboat lines, hotels, and resorts to attract the traveller of the day to visit the American scene? Or was the appearance of such engravings, lithographs, and prints simply a part of the romantic movement in the representation of nature? An amalgam of such reasons is difficult to construct, but it is quite clear that all three had some role to play.

Throughout the nineteenth century, a bewildering array of artists, print makers, literary figures and publicists attempted to carve out a niche for a "picturesque" that was truly American. This was not simply a derivative from representations of English and Continental European scenery, place, and romantic imagery. As Dennis has recently shown, from 1790 onwards, travel articles available to U.S. audiences began to stress U.S. topics. The views of nature of Hawthorne and Cooper were part of this search for the picturesque in nature that was widely accepted in American by the 1840's.[1] As aesthetic in objective as this search may have been, there was also a nativist element in its course. In his popular offering, the monumental volume gift book *Picturesque America* (1872), William Cullen Bryant defended the isolation of American nature and its scenery. Bryant, in his Preface, wrote of the Old World nature having become overcivilized:

> It will be admitted that our country abounds with scenery new to the artist's pencil, of a varied character,
> whether beautiful or grand, or formed of those sharper but no less striking combinations of outline which
> belong to neither of these classes. In the Old World every spot remarkable in these respects has been vis-
> ited by the artist; studied and sketched again and again; observed in sunshine and in the shade of clouds,

and regarded from every point of view that may give variety to the delineation. . . . Art sighs to carry her conquests into new realms.[2]

This search for American aesthetic values was answered in this volume work of U.S. "places" via steel engravings of artists' work. Photography, according to Bryant, even at this date, would not do: "Photographs, however accurate, lack the spirit and personal quality which the accomplished painter or draftsman infuses into his work."[3] Thomas Cole had expressed the same sentiments thirty years earlier: " . . . the art of painting is a creative, as well as imitative art, and is in no danger in being superceded by any mechanical contrivance."[4]

Bryant's work, popular as it was, had a long ancestry which attempted earlier to do—perhaps not so self-consciously—what *Picturesque America* did for the nature-loving American and traveller of the late nineteenth century. Representation, by original work or engraving, print, or lithograph from the art of others, drew the attention of audiences and travellers, actual or in imagination, to the wonders of America. The Hudson Valley was an important phase, especially by mid-century, in such a process. The appeal extended beyond the American viewer and reader. John Howatt cites the *London Times'* statement in reference to Cropsey's "Autumn on the Hudson" (1860): "American artists are rapidly making the untravelled portion of the English public familiar with the scenery of the great western continent."[5]

Thus the celebration of American scenery was a process that went on throughout the entire nineteenth century. In its popular art forms, this pride weathered the decline of interest in landscape painting, especially by the Hudson River artists in the later decades of the century. The raw materials for such a campaign had been produced either as original paintings, drawings, or in other genres of representation. Reproduction could continually take place and did so via popular magazines, view books, travel guides, commercial pamphlet advertisements, etc. The lure for traveller and tourist as well as vicarious armchair viewer was ever in demand.

Popular response was to the representation of scenes that were accessible by public and private transportation—not pilgrimages to the sites of artists' activity, but to spectacular and picturesque land forms, cataracts, and the frequently nearby tourist accommodations of the mountain house type. While the Hudson Valley figured prominently in supplying this need, it did not, as we shall see, have a corner on the market. Even its own artists such as Cole and his successors sought out equally challenging scenic spots in the White Mountains of New Hampshire and the Adirondack area of New York State. The extent of the artist's trampings is shown in the variety present in their sketchbooks. For example, Sanford R. Gifford's pencil sketches in one of his notebooks show the geographical diversity of his travels and renderings: drawings from the Beaverkill and Neversink Valleys of Orange and Sullivan Counties to views of the more rugged scenes in the Adirondacks.[6]

Popularization of these artistic interpretations by the Hudson River artists began early in the nineteenth century, though the pace accelerated dramatically from the Civil War years. In the Hudson Valley, the Catskill Mountain House probably deserves first place in terms of frequency of representation in engraving and lithograph, due in large part to its spectacular setting and long list of celebrity visitors from home and abroad, but also stemming from its early date of service to a vacationing populace. As early as 1828, *Rural Repository*, published in Hudson, New York, presented an engraving of the Mountain House sitting on its promontory in the Pine Orchard of Greene County. This view was a harbinger of things to come for the remainder of the century.

View of the Hudson River, Looking Towards Newberg, in Frank Leslie's Illustrated Newspaper, New York, Dec. 8, 1886. *This engraving, extolling the "exquisite beauty," "mighty hills," and "noble bay at Newberg," spread majestically across half a page.*

While the discussion of scenery by the aesthetic theorists of the day and the seeking of prime subjects for reproduction transcend our area of concern, it is no accident that so much work, and early in the process, had its location in the Hudson Valley and its mountains. In many ways it was a perfect laboratory in which the burgeoning aesthetic views could be worked out. In one of the most successful and meaningful publications of the time, *The Home Book of The Picturesque: or, American Scenery, Art, and Literature,* published in 1852, a series of essays by prominent writers interprets for the layman the philosophy of scenery. Here the reader is introduced to some of the theories that Cole, Church, Durand, Kensett, and others worked out in their painting or wrote of in their explanations of landscape art. Interspersed between engravings, many of the Hudson Valley, these essays ran the gamut from the inevitable comparison of the Hudson to the Rhine River by James Fenimore Cooper (who rates the Hudson higher on a scenic scale), to discussions of that famous dichotomy of the period, the distinction between the "picturesque" and the "sublime." Cooper's daughter, Susan Fenimore Cooper, like many of the Hudson River School, concludes that for scenery to be either picturesque or sublime, man and nature are needed in conjunction. In representing such scenes, one needs the hand of man visible, in fields and clearings, and not only the untapped forest. Yet, at the same time, men must not do too much: she goes on to complain that the last Dutch house in New York is gone and laments: "We are the reverse of conservators in this Country."[7]

It was the river and the mountains that were heralded in these works, but it also was more than that. It was the mood, the mystery, and the scale of scenes in the Catskills, the Highlands and throughout the valley as a whole that the visual presentation of such word pictures would exploit. The man versus nature theme so familiar to the viewers of Hudson River School painters is present in these writings in an admixture of mystery, grandeur, and the power of nature. John Burroughs in 1886 states precisely a theme common to the description of our landscape in an essay explaining his personal response to the Hudson on whose banks he had lived for years at West Park:

> A small river or stream flowing by one's door has many attractions over a large body of water like the Hudson. One can make a companion of it; he can walk with it and sit with it, or lounge on its banks, and feel that it is all his own. It becomes something private and special to him. You cannot have the same kind of attachment and sympathy with a great river; it does not flow through your affections like a lesser stream. The Hudson is a long arm of the sea, and it has something of the sea's austerity and grandeur. I think one might spend a lifetime upon its banks without feeling any sense of ownership in it, or becoming at all intimate with it: it keeps one at arm's length. [8]

Burroughs clearly sees the conjunction of river and landscape as a dualism which is really the subject of the depictions of the Hudson Valley: "But there is one thing a large river does for one that is beyond the scope of the companionable streams—it idealizes the landscape, it multiplies and heightens the beauty of the day and of the season." [9]

Such ideas were the foundations for travel books, scenery, and view books as well as more literary assessments of the valley. It was not simply a "sense of place" or the mere touting of the Catskill Mountain House or Cozzen's Hotel at West Point that was the message. It was a deeper and more all-encompassing atmosphere that writers, artists, and the travellers alike created from the geography and topography of the valley. Surrounded with such an atmosphere, the specific visual reproduction and the vivid word portraits of scenes move to a synthesis that became the Hudson Valley and into which the railroad, steamboat, and resort literature could intrude with their more mundane fare of rates, recreation possibilities, and timetables. An image had been created; the exploitation of it was a more commercial, though important matter: the appeal to the public via the popular press that would hold out the prospect of "on site" investigation of both the atmosphere and its concrete embodiment in the burgeoning resort industry of the region.

In the nineteenth and twentieth centuries attempts were made to isolate a meaning or series of meanings for the Hudson Valley region and to interpret them from an aesthetic point of view. But such attempts lacked a framework within which to view the area and often ended up in overromanticized results with the "creation" of an aesthetic, even changing place names to fit the ideal of what a land feature should be.

In recent years there have been novel attempts to cover this old ground in new ways, stressing denotation as well as the earlier connotation of the landscape. These newer works are not from the usual sources; they are by geographers and geologists who treat the Hudson Valley not as a static series of topographical features but as a unique blend of land and water forms that have elicited a bewildering array of responses from those who lived there or from those who sought to interpret them via paint, engraving, sketch, or words.

Raymond J. O'Brien's 1981 work *American Sublime* analyzes part of this region—the Hudson Highlands and Palisades—in such a manner, showing the growth of a sense of place and how economic and commercial development, which threatened to destroy it, allowed residents and others to step back and take a closer look. O'Brien approaches his topic in an interesting manner, arguing that geological aspects are joined by

View of the Rondout, *a Currier and Ives print from a drawing by Fanny Palmer. The goal of this famous New York printmaking firm was to market large quantities of typical American scenes at very reasonable prices.*

historical associations and the sublime appearance of the sites to bring about the regional identification. If one ponders why the Hudson Valley has been unique, it is perhaps useful to consider Paul Shepard's concept, developed in 1961 in the journal *Landscape*. Shepard isolates the Hudson Valley, among other U.S. landscapes, as a perfect example of what he calls the "Cross Valley Syndrome," a geological formation in which a water gap or river crosses ridges or mountains over years and creates "topographical passages," resulting in historic and economic landmarks and spectacularly "wild" scenery. As Shepard explains: "From a distance the cross valley has an emotional impact, since, unlike most mountain valley landscapes, it may be observed looming above a horizontal foreground."[10] Both Shepard and O'Brien see the nineteenth-century literary and artistic activity in the Hudson Valley as a "revolution in American sensibility to the habitat" and therefore as an unlimited series of experiences that could be brought to the public's awareness for a variety of commercial purposes.[11]

But a habitat is not simply topography. Changes were happening in the valley and the mountains during the nineteenth century. Away from the river, nascent industrialization was taking hold in the pre-Civil War decades with the demands of the major force in U.S. economic history, making a widespread impact on topography—denuding the slopes of millions of virgin hemlocks and polluting the streams so beloved by the artists of the region. A bit later, the quarrying of bluestone in the mountains and the exploitation of the Highlands and Palisades for stone also had their impacts. The river banks themselves were intruded upon and their "wildness" was tamed by the appearance of brick works in Putnam, Ulster, Dutchess, and Greene counties. Cement factories, their raw materials exhumed from the bowels of the river hills, also appeared and continue to exist in the twentieth century. Hudson Valley industries were not easy on the environment. The post-Civil War rise of textile factories, breweries, and relatively large scale iron foundries on both sides of the river further added to the changes from economic developments. The overall effect was a formidable contrast to earlier years.

What was the response to this? First, what changes in economic and social relationships occurred over these years in terms of in and out migration? What ethnic groups entered and left? Did they have a sense of what was happening to their place? One usually looks for visual records of such dramatic occurrences beyond the data of demographic change. Yet the records and responses are not only to be sought in artists' renditions. Valley residents in their journals and other accounts saw what was happening around them and viewed the developments as carrying mixed blessings, with the possibility of a loss of the sense of place they had known.

Secondly, what was the aesthetic dimension and what forms did it take? Did the artist have the sensibility of the ordinary resident and document these commercial and industrial intrusions or did the painter "paint out"? Did the landscape architect design with imagined surroundings in mind? In short, the industrial transformation of the valley, pre- and post-Civil War, should be investigated in the light of aesthetic output and interpretation of valley scenes.

Yet industrialization in the sense of the exploitation of natural resources and the growth of manufactures is not the only impact. Transportation changes in the forms of steamboat and railroad affected the river proper on its banks as well as in the fastnesses of the mountains. The rails to the mountain top opened the cloves to smoking engines as well as to visitors seeking respite from the city and artists seeking remote and unspoiled scenery. The resort period of the region, both a cause and effect of the railroads in the Catskills, also is of importance. Was it a retreat to the "wilderness" with one artistic result being a re-creation of scenery that, if one looked closely or in a different direction, had been severely disfigured? Some saw this clearly. John B. Jervis, engineer for the construction of the Hudson River Railroad on the east bank of the Hudson, responded to the hue and cry of mid-nineteenth century "environmentalists" and their objections to the railroad in this manner:

> To a very great extent the construction of the Road will improve the appearance of the shore; rough points will be smoothed off, the irregular indentations of the bays be hidden and a regularity and symmetry imparted to the outline of the shore; thus by a combination of the works of nature and of art adding to the interest, grandeur and beauty of the whole. [12]

The art of the region, in many ways, responded to the situation much as did Jervis and simply ignored the "improvements" of the railroad.

The purveying of this vision of the Hudson Valley region to the general public—both for aesthetic and commercial pay-off—involved a fascinating and complex marketing effort by artists, engravers, and publishers via the popular journals and books of the day. While this was an effort that lasted virtually throughout the entire nineteenth century, the golden age for this type of literature and artistic reproduction was heavily concentrated from the 1820s through the 1850s. The growth of steamboat and rail travel during the period created a new access, especially to the valley, for the readers of travel books, periodicals, and annuals of the time. Armchair travellers were now joined more frequently by excursionists.[13]

Popular representation of American scenery took on an almost overwhelming variety of formats and genres. Whether lithograph or engraving, the prodigious number of reproductions of Hudson Valley scenes,

Richard C. Wiles

in many cases, defies a definite provenance for the "original" of the scene. Some of the hand-tinted lithographs and engravings were original works, some copied from photographs; others were renderings of the famous products of painters of Hudson River settings. The publications in which these images appeared were also prodigious in number. One must, however, isolate some of the more prominent reproductions of such art to gain a flavor of the extensiveness of the practice as well as the personalities involved in their presentation.

One of the most obvious of the success stories in this literature was the production of *Picturesque America,* mentioned above. Announced in 1870 as a publication of Appleton and Co., New York, it was first published in monthly parts in 1872 through 1874, finally appearing in two gigantic volumes. The November 19, 1870, issue of *Journal* printed a call for subscription to the new publication. Care was taken to make the work "one of the most valuable pictorial series ever issued of American localities." The engravings produced "will be what is technically known as 'fine book-work,' and not of the ordinary inferior newspaper execution."[4] With William Cullen Bryant as editor, the two volumes contained remarkable scenes of the U.S. with several representations of the Hudson Valley region, especially the Kaaterskill Falls and mountain house areas. Though *American Picturesque* was probably the best known of this type of work and one of the most handsome volumes to be produced, other earlier successful attempts had also popularized the landscape of the region.

The work of William Henry Bartlett ranks foremost among the popular presentations of this type of art in the Hudson Valley. As artist, observer, and traveller through the U.S. and Canada, Bartlett provided the new material for many of the engravings in the mid-nineteenth century. As his biographer, Alexander M. Ross, points out, our knowledge of Bartlett as a watercolorist is limited: he is known for hundreds of black-and-white illustrations of his paintings and sketches, the latter sketched on site and sent to engravers to reproduce. His best known products are the companion books *American Scenery* and *Canadian Scenery,* which appeared, like *Picturesque America,* first in separate issues, each containing a few engravings and selling for very little. By March 1839, twenty of a total of thirty parts were offered to the public. Sketches for these widely circulated engravings, which retain their popularity today, were done by Bartlett during his three visits to America in 1838, and 1841. The idea of a book devoted to American scenery was the suggestion of N. Parker Willis, a well-known literary figure of the time in the Hudson Valley. Bartlett's work contained 120 steel engravings, a quarter of which were devoted to Hudson River subjects. These engravings were later copied profusely in the view books of the 1850s.

Unlike many of his contemporaries who wished to filter out undesirable elements from the landscape, Bartlett sketched his scenes warts and all in many cases. City buildings and streets in New York City, Albany, and Utica were a favorite subject. He also had a fascination for transportation in his work. His "vista" work on Hudson Valley sites includes Fort Putnam, Hyde Park, Newburgh, and Peekskill Landing.[15] He had the appropriate connections to coordinate his supply of potential engravings to both England and the U.S., for he was an employee of George Virtue's press in London, which produced the engravings. Virtue also owned the *Art-Journal* in the U.S. and sold books featuring engravings here and abroad. The circularity of this process of production is shown by the fact that much later landscape painting was based on engravings or aquatints like those of Bartlett. As William Diebold has written recently, "Bartlett's views did much to shape the way people came to see the Hudson. They were copied in magazines in the United States and several other countries, with and without credit. Currier and Ives used them with no acknowledgement, ..."[16] Examples of prints "after" W. H. Bartlett are colored engravings produced in the 1830s of the Palisades and views from West Point and Hyde Park. One of the most famous is E. Benjamin's engraving of Bartlett's drawing of the "Catterskill Fall (From Below)."

The voyage from painting or sketch to engraving and back to painting was, thus, a common part of the production of popular representation of the American landscape and Hudson Valley subjects in particular. Many of the names most revered as members of the Hudson River School enter this chain of production-reproduction at more than one spot. In fact, the connections between many of these artists began first in their work at engraving and only later in the world of landscape painting.

John F. Kensett, for example, in the late 1820s went to New York City to work in the shop of Peter Maverick, the best known engraver in the U.S. This Maverick connection was to lead to a remarkable inter-relationship of Kensett and other Hudson River School artists. In the shop, Kensett met John William Casilaer who also arrived to study with Maverick. Asher Durand learned the art of engraving also with Peter Maverick and went on to become a partner in the business. After Maverick's death in 1831, Kensett, Casilaer, and another familiar name in the school, Thomas Rossiter, studied with Asher Durand as engraving students.[17] In fact, in 1832, Kensett applied for a permanent position with Durand but was refused, so moved to Albany to work with an engraving firm. During his formative years in England and Europe, Kensett exploited his engraving talents and supported his travels and study by sending engravings back to his U.S. employers.

Though Kensett turned away from the engraving process after his stay in Europe, engravings of his work and of his associates continued to flood the American travel guide and journal markets. Kensett's famous painting "The White Mountains—From North Conway" was purchased by the American Art-Union which had it engraved for its 13,000 subscribers. [18] The engraver of this major work was James Smillie, a name that was to become famous for Hudson Valley subjects. Smillie produced fine steel engravings of landscapes of well-known artists, notably Thomas Cole. One of Smillie's most prominent engravings was his famous view of the Catskill Mountain House, which was taken from a drawing of the mountain house by George Harvey.

Perhaps the most interesting popular offering involving reproductions of major artists was the 1852 appearance of the above mentioned *Home Book of the Picturesque*. Containing essays on the picturesque by Bryant, Irving, and Cooper, the aging giants of the American literary scene, it presents thirteen steel engravings based on the work of what Motley F. Deakins calls, in his 1967 reprint of the book: ". . .the honor roll of our first great school of painters."[19] The popularity of this offering was impressive. Later the same year another edition appeared under the title *Home Artists* while sixteen years later, in 1868, Putnam, the original publisher, refashioned the work and issued it under yet a third title, *A Landscape Book*.

Dedicated to A. B. Durand by the publisher, the original edition's engravings include a rendition of Kensett's "Catskill Scenes" by H. Beckwith, a second engraving of Durand's "Catskill in the Clove," and an S. V. Hart engraving of R. W. Weir's painting "The Church of the Holy Innocents, West Pt" along with non-Hudson Valley scenes by T. A. Richards, F. E. Church, Durand, and Thomas Cole.

Such major works and popular gift books were joined, however, by a whole panoply of popular journals, profusely illustrated throughout the nineteenth century with engravings of the fantastic and the tragic as well as with beckoning glimpses of watering holes, mountain retreats, and peaceful vistas to be sought out and enjoyed on the spot. *Frank Leslie's Illustrated Newspaper, Appleton's Journal, and Harper's Weekly*, to name a few, presented continual spreads of engravings of events and sites in half page, full page, and even fold-out doubled-paged versions. *Frank Leslie's Illustrated Newspaper* for December 8, 1860, contained a fine reproduction of a "Scene on the Hudson River, Looking towards Newberg," accompanied by a commentary on the view from Cold Spring, noting: "At all seasons of the year this view is charming, but in the leafy summer time it is inexpressibly lovely."[20] *Harper's Weekly* for January 16, 1869, presented an engraving after a photograph by the Slee Brothers depicting the Hudson Valley nineteenth-century craze "Winter sports-

Ice Boats on the Hudson."[21] Iceboating, the pastime of the well-to-do whose estates lined the banks of the Hudson, added to the picturesqueness of the views. Though the books and periodicals cited here are only a small sample of the outpouring of such popular offerings of Hudson Valley vistas and places of beauty and sojourn, they do present an accurate flavor of the character of this type of art.

Yet another variant was to arrive on the scene and catch the imagination of the American public: the work of the firm Currier and Ives. Already a successful printmaker, Nathaniel Currier was joined by James Ives in 1852, the same year as the first appearance of the *Home Book of the Picturesque*. Thus began the association that would present hand-colored lithographs until the firm's dissolution in 1907. The goal was unabashedly to give the public prints "that were easy to understand and appreciate, pictures that were typically American, and pictures not only with subjects that were to widen the knowledge and experience of the average man but at prices that were within the range of his pocketbook."[22] No struggle with the sublime or picturesque here. The firm's interest was admirably realized, for their attributed output of over 7,000 prints was distributed at the wholesale price of 6¢ each, while the retail price ranged from 15 to 25¢ per print. Large folio-sized lithographs were higher, with unit prices ranging from $1.50 to $3.00.

The "production line" for such a vast output was similar in form to the process of popular engravings discussed, except that in the case of Currier and Ives, the artists were, in most instances, hired by the firm. In addition, a large number of their prints, like the engravings in the popular magazines, were copies of well-known paintings and line engravings which were available for lithographic reproduction, since copyright protection was virtually non-existent. Many of the prints were done communally by more than one artist so that they often are difficult to attribute.[23]

The firm had international distribution outlets for its products, even maintaining a London office. In New York City, pushcart peddlars handled their prints and sold them on the streets. One of the most productive of the Currier and Ives artists, Fanny Palmer, dealt mainly with rural and suburban scenes in her work, as in her "View on the Rondout." Palmer and others produced works reflecting not only the firm's location in New York City but also the fact that New York, the Hudson, and the Erie Canal were the important links for travel west and the route taken by most New York City immigrants. Several of the lithographs portray these regions: "Upper and Lower New York Bay," "The Entrance to the Highlands," and Washington Irving's "Sunnyside" on the Hudson and the "Mill Dam at Sleepy Hollow."

John Kowat in his well-known work on the Hudson River School, documents the denouement of the popularity of landscape painting in the Barbizon-Rome style and its replacement with a variety of French influences. In his work on Kensett, the theme is taken up with the statement that Kensett's death at the relatively young age of fifty-six in 1872 allowed him to escape the "anxiety of seeing his art hidden away from public view and almost forgotten in basements and attics across the nation," a fate experienced by Church and Bierstadt in the 1870s and '80s.[24]

The popularization of art and the scenes portrayed held on a little longer. In 1872, the year of Kensett's death, *Picturesque America*, the finest example of the popular presentation, appeared. Prints, engravings and lithographs would hold the public's and potential travellers' imaginations for another two decades before photography and the growth of affluence and mobility would thrust such literature and reproduction aside. It had served in some measure a dual function over the century: the creation of accessibility to the art and style of the time, and the linkage of such art with public appreciation of the picturesque as well as with its commercial application.

Notes

1. Dennis Berthold, "Charles Brockden Brown, Edgar Huntly and the Origin of the American Picturesque," *William and Mary Quarterly* XLI (January 1984), 62–84.

2. William Cullen Bryant (ed.) *Picturesque America* 2 Vols. (N.Y.: D. and Co., 1872), p. iii.

3. Ibid., p. iv.

4. As quoted in John Wilmerding, *A History of American Marine* Little, Brown and Co., 1968), 66.

5. John K. Howat, *The River and its Painters* (N.Y.: The Viking Press, 1972), 46.

6. Sanford Sketchbooks in Exhibit "Familiar Vistas: Columbia County Artists and their Environment" at the Columbia County Historical Society, Kinderhook, N.Y. July 25 to November 20, 1987. Loan from Private Collection.

7. *The Home Book of the Picturesque(1852)*, Facsimile Reproduction and Introduction by Motley E. Deakin (Gainesville, Florida: Scholars' Facsimiles and Reprints, 1967), 89.

8. John Burroughs, *Signs and Seasons*, 3rd ed. (Boston: Houghton Mifflin and Co., 1887), 203.

9. Ibid., 203.

10. Paul Jr., "The Cross Valley Syndrome," *Landscape* 5.

11. Ibid., 5.

12. Alvin F. Harlow, *The Road of the Century* (N.Y.: Creative Age Press, 143.

13. Alexander M. Ross, *William Henry Bartlett: Artist, Author, and Traveller* (Toronto: University of Toronto Press, 1973), Preface.

14. *Appleton's Journal*, IV, #86 (November 19, 1870), 620.

15. Ross, *Bartlett*, 27, 38, 45–46.

16. William Diebold "Old Prints of County," *South of the Mountains* 30 (July-September 1986), 7.

17. Clara Endicott Sears, *Highlights Among the Hudson River Artists* (Boston: 1947), 110.

18. John Paul Driscoll and John K. Howatt, *John Frederick Kensett, An American Master* (N.Y.: W. W. Norton and Co., 1985), 67.

19. *Home Book of the Picturesque*, Introduction.

20. Frank Leslie's *Illustrated Newspaper* XI (December 8, 1860), 36.

21. *Harper's Weekly* XIII (January 16, 1869), 33.

22. Harry T. Peters, *Currier and Ives* (Garden City, N.Y.: Doubleday, and Co., Inc., 1942), 3.

23. Ibid., 19.

24. Driscoll and Howatt, *Kensett*, 47–48.

This article originally appeared in the *Hudson Valley Regional Review*, Volume 5.1.

The Moral Geography of Cooper's *Miles Wallingford* Novels

Donald Ringe

Because he is so well known for his five Leatherstocking tales, James Fenimore Cooper is most often associated with such New York settings as Otsego Lake, the scene of *The Pioneers* (1823) and *The Deerslayer* (1841), or other parts of the upstate wilderness, the setting for *The Last of the Mohicans* (1826) and *The Pathfinder* (1840). But these are not the only parts of New York that Cooper uses in his novels. Equally important is the lower Hudson Valley between Albany and New York City, an area he used in both *The Spy* (1821) and in parts of *Satanstoe* (1845), but which plays an especially significant role in his double novel of 1844, *Afloat and Ashore* and *Miles Wallingford*. The ashore part of his book is set for the most part on Clawbonny, a farm in Ulster County. It is the home of five generations of Miles Wallingfords, the first of whom "had purchased it of the Dutch colonist who had originally cleared it from the woods."[1] This is the point from which the latest Miles, the narrator of the novel, embarks on his four sea voyages and to which he returns at last when his many adventures are over.

Though the action of the novel takes place between 1797 and 1804, the narration occurs some forty years later as the sixty-year-old Miles Wallingford recounts the adventures of his youth. This method of narration gives Cooper a number of advantages. It creates so great a distance between the events and the telling as to allow the narrator, now an aging man, to order and interpret his experience from the point of view of more than a generation later. He sees his youth in a way that would not have been apparent to him while he was living it, at times commenting on his youthful follies; and he can perceive a pattern of meaning in the events of his early life that only the perspective of forty years can give. To achieve these aims, however, Cooper had to keep before the reader a sense of the lapse of time, and Miles repeatedly observes that most things have changed, that the Hudson Valley, New York City, and the world at large were quite different places when he was a young man.

Travel on the Hudson in those days, Miles tells us, was by sloop, a type of sailing vessel that sometimes had to wait for the tide to change and occasionally went aground in low water so that days might pass on a trip between Ulster County and Manhattan or on one to Albany. On one occasion, a character even finds it quicker to go ashore on the east bank of the river and travel to New York by land. Unlike the steamboats which, at the time of the narration, hurry passengers along with a great deal of noise and bustle, the sloops, often commanded by a phlegmatic Dutch master, made leisurely trips through the beautiful Hudson Valley. Their pace allowed time for the passengers to enjoy pleasant meals with their friends or to gather on deck "to look at the beauties of the hour," as the characters do at one point in the novel, when, "about a mile above Hudson," they look "toward the south" at what, Miles comments, "is, perhaps, the finest reach of this very beautiful stream" (MW, p. 11). Miles knows, of course, that steamboats are more efficient vessels, but he cannot help regretting the loss of the pleasant life that their advent has rendered impossible.

Miles also recalls what New York was like in his youth and the change that has since taken place there. When the novel opens, he describes the city as beginning "a short distance above Duane street" with "a mile and a half of open fields" between the town and "Greenwich, as the little hamlet around the State prison was called" (AA, p. 38). He observes that Wall Street in 1799, when he returns from his first voyage, was still the site of private dwellings, and he mentions the main attractions of the city: "a circus kept by a man of 'the name of Richetts—the theater in John Street, a very modest Thespian edifice—and a lion, I mean literally the beast, that was kept in a cage quite out of town, that his roaring might not disturb people." The site, Miles observes, was somewhere in the vicinity of what was to become Franklin Square (AA, p. 117). As the novel closes, moreover, he reveals the rapid growth of the city in the removal of his townhouse up the island to escape the advance of commerce: from Wall Street to Chambers Street in 1805, to Bleecker Street in 1825, and finally to Union Place in 1839 (MW, p. 438).

Cooper maintains a firm sense of the past throughout the novel, keeping before the reader details that recall the period of the action. He even introduces real people who were prominent at the time. In the very first chapter, Miles informs us that when he was a boy, Governor George Clinton, himself "an Ulster County man" and later Vice President of the United States, was an occasional visitor to Clawbonny (AA, p. 3). At other points in the novel, Miles associates with or hears about important New Yorkers, among them the merchants John Murray, Archibald Gracie, and William Bayard,[2] who are consulted by the Reverend Mr. Hardinge, Miles's guardian, when he seeks advice on buying a ship for the young man. On his return from his second voyage in 1802, Miles learns that Dr. Benjamin Moore has recently been elected Episcopal Bishop of New York,[3] and the passengers Miles rescued in the Pacific, the British Major Merton and his daughter, are taken in hand by the British Consul General, Colonel Thomas Barclay, a native New Yorker who had fled to, Nova Scotia after the Revolution but returned in his official capacity in 1799.[4] Miles even receives dispatches from James Madison, Secretary of State, for delivery in Hamburg, the destination of his final voyage in 1803.

Among the professional men introduced is Miles's lawyer, Richard Harison, who draws up wills for both Miles and his cousin John and who represents Miles when he returns from his last voyage ostensibly a ruined man. Harison had been a Federalist delegate to the Constitutional Convention at Poughkeepsie in 1788 and served as the first United States Attorney for the Federal District of New York from 1789 to 1801.[5] Also included are a number of medical men. When his sister Grace becomes seriously ill, Miles sends Neb, his black slave, across the river to summon Dr. Samuel Bard, who lived at Hyde Park; and in a letter to Moses Marble, his first mate, he includes a list of New York physicians, among them David Hosack, Wright Post, Richard Bayley, and William Moore, directing him to go down the names until he finds a doctor who will come to Clawbonny. Miles even thinks of sending to Philadelphia for Benjamin Rush,[6] but is "deterred from making the attempt by the distance and the pressing nature of the emergency" (AA, p. 489). Bard is not home when Neb delivers the message, but Marble brings the second man on his list, Wright Post, a "tall, slender, middle-aged man, with a bright dark eye" (AA, p. 510), who prescribes for the ailing Grace.

In social matters, too, Cooper remains faithful to the historical past. Slavery was still legal in New York at the time of the action, though the process of gradual emancipation had just begun with a law passed in 1799. By 1804, the state, Miles writes, "was on the point of liberating [the] slaves, leaving a few of the younger to serve for a term of years, that should requite their owners for the care of their infancies and their

Donald Ringe

educations" (MW, p. 420). Though Miles, even as an old man, defends the institution as he knew it in his youth, he is not opposed to emancipation. He offers Neb his freedom while they are both young men, and although Neb refuses to accept it, once he marries Chloe, Lucy Hardinge's serving girl, Miles gives the couple their freedom papers "at once [relieving] their posterity from the servitude of eight-and-twenty, and five-and-twenty years, according to sex, that might otherwise have hung over all their elder children, until the law, by a general sweep, manumitted everybody." Neb and his wife remain at Clawbonny, but their children gradually move away "as ambition or curiosity [carry] them into the world" (MW, pp. 434–435).

Although Miles is a slaveholder and the owner of a substantial property, he does not stand very high in turn-of-the-century New York society. Those who lived on the west bank of the Hudson did not move in the social circle of those who lived on the east, and the position of the Wallingfords "midway between the gentry and yeomanry of the State" is at best equivocal (AA, p. 523). As a result, Miles's position in New York City is not among the elite, and his occupation, once he becomes the captain of a merchant vessel, further confirms his social inferiority. Though Miles is willing to accept such distinctions, he is very much annoyed that Major Merton and his daughter soon move in the best circles of New York—higher even than they could aspire to at home—merely because they are English. "In that day," he writes, "the man who had served against the country, provided he was a 'British officer,' was a better man than he who had served in our own ranks" (AA, p. 346). Miles resents the undue influence that the British exert on New York society only twenty years after the close of a Revolution that was fought to establish American independence.

In his treatment of the national and international scene, Cooper is equally careful to maintain a sense of the past. During the course of the action, the quasi-war with France occurs (1798–1801), and hostilities between France and England break out in 1803. Miles is affected by both conflicts. While he is returning to America in the course of his first voyage, the ship he is on, the Tigris, has a brush with a French privateer from the island of Guadaloupe, and shortly thereafter, she meets the Ganges, under the command of Captain Richard Dale. This was the first American warship—actually a converted Indiaman—to go to sea for the protection of American commerce, then suffering much from the depredations of French privateers.[7] Miles is much impressed with Dale and feels an impulse to join the fledgling navy. Had he done so then, he says, or later in New York when he saw ships fitting for war and young men appearing in uniform, his career would certainly have been different, and he might have become, by the time he is writing, "one of the oldest officers in the service" (AA, p. 95). He decides, however, to remain on merchant vessels.

The quasi-war has, nonetheless, important consequences for him. On his second voyage, as third mate of the Crisis, a letter of marque, the ship encounters a French privateer, La Damede Nantes, and captures her after a brief struggle. The Americans also recapture a prize the French ship had taken, and as Miles, who is placed in charge of it, beats his way up the English Channel, he barely escapes assault by a French lugger. The most extended conflict occurs, however, months later in the Pacific, when Moses Marble, now in command of the Crisis, anchors at what seems to be a desert island. The ship is captured by a Frenchman, Monsieur Le Compte, who with his men had been shipwrecked there. But when Le Compte sails away with his prize, he leaves behind a schooner, believing that he will be far away before the craft can be readied for sea. The Americans fit out the schooner in short order, pursue Le Compte to the coast of South America, and after a fierce assault, retake the Crisis on the very last day, they soon learn, that such a recapture could be considered legal. Peace had been made and the quasi-war with France was over.

The war between England and France causes Miles even more trouble. He learns of it first when, on his third voyage, as captain of the Dawn, he is stopped by a British frigate in the Straits of Gibraltar, but at the time—May 1803—he is not molested. Later that year, however, he puts to sea again in the *Dawn*, bound for Hamburg with a cargo of sugar, coffee, and cochineal, and his troubles multiply. As he is leaving New York, he sights the *Leander*, a British man-of-war that had been with Nelson at the Battle of the Nile in 1798. The British ship gives chase, and fearing that he will be boarded and sent to Halifax or Bermuda where his cargo might be confiscated, Miles evades the British cruiser and escapes into the Atlantic. But before he can reach Europe, he is detained by the *Speedy*, a British frigate. When the British captain learns that part of what Miles is carrying was grown on St. Domingo, a French island, he places an English crew on board and orders the *Dawn* into Plymouth, where a British judge will decide on the disposition of both ship and cargo.

Even if they should not be seized, Miles knows that a delay of several months could ruin him. He decides, therefore, to retake his ship and manages to set adrift the British crew. While making his escape, however, he falls in with a French corsair, whose captain claims him as a prize because he has been in the hands of the English. Though Miles again escapes, he is now so short-handed that the *Dawn* is wrecked by a violent gale and both cargo and ship are lost. Picked up by a British frigate that eventually falls in with the *Speedy*, Miles suffers still more injustice. He is arrested and carried to England because it is claimed that he must have murdered the prize crew that had taken control of the *Dawn*. Though innocent of the charge—he saw the men picked up by a British ship bound for the West Indies—Miles has no reason to trust British justice, and he escapes for a third time to make his way home in September 1804. In his own person, Miles has thus suffered the wrongs heaped upon neutral Americans by both belligerents during the Napoleonic wars.

That Miles recalls the past in such detail makes credible his observations on how the world has changed in the intervening forty years. Much of what he valued has been lost, especially the old New York feeling that had derived from a population long settled on the land. Strangers have overrun the state, a "throng from Ireland and Germany . . . now crowd the streets" of the city (AA, p. 347), and advocates of change and progress foster the building of "railroads and canals" (MW, p. 424). Miles knows that things must change. The party, he writes, "which sets up conservatism as its standard" is as dangerous to the state as "that which sets up progress: the one is for preserving things of which it would be better to be rid, while the other crushes all that is necessary and useful in its headlong course." Miles is opposed to both. "No sane man can doubt that, in the progress of events, much is produced that ought to be retained, and much generated that it would be wiser to reject" (MW, p. 436). How then is one to distinguish between them? Miles does not say directly, but through his experience both afloat and ashore, Cooper makes clear where permanent values lie.

Miles acquires his experience in three sharply contrasted areas: the open sea, the farm at Clawbonny, and the city of New York.[8] Each exists as an actuality presented in realistic terms, but each takes on as well a symbolic meaning, much like that described by W. H. Auden in *The Enchafed Flood*. In the romantic iconography of the sea, Auden explains, there are three primary elements, the sea itself, the city, and the romantic island, each of which may best be understood in relation to the others. The city represents the restrictions of the human community from which the voyager may escape into the freedom, openness, and potentiality of the sea, the place of both possibility and primitive power. The island is the romantic refuge where the voyager may pause in his quest.[9] In Cooper's version of this spatial metaphor—one that he shares with Hawthorne, Melville, and others—[10]city, sea, and island play crucial roles. The farm at Clawbonny is for Miles an island of security in a changing world, the city of New York is a place of social distinctions where he can never be entirely comfortable, and the sea is the questing ground where he can develop qualities of manhood and independence that he could never acquire ashore.

Though Miles's experience at sea is crucial to his life, he does not initiate it himself. It is Rupert Hardinge, his guardian's son and a boyhood friend who first suggests that they run away and who sails with him in the *John*, a merchant vessel bound for China. They make their decision purely in the spirit of adventure, but life afloat quickly reveals a fundamental difference between the two. Miles takes to the sea at once, grows and develops rapidly during the voyage, and arrives at New York at its end an accomplished seaman. Rupert does none of these things. He never returns to sea, therefore, deciding instead to study law in New York. Miles embarks alone on his second voyage, shipping as third mate in the *Crisis* on a journey that eventually takes him around the world and consumes some three years. During this time, Miles matures as a seaman, advancing quickly up the ladder of promotion as vacancies occur. Before the voyage is over, Miles has become captain of the ship. The sea has been his proving ground, the open space of freedom and opportunity where he develops his potential as a seaman and as a man.

Yet the sea has also a sinister side that presents the voyager with manifold dangers. Terrible storms buffet the vessels in which Miles sails, and one particularly violent tempest, combined with a powerful current, drives the *Crisis* wildly through the Straits of Magellan while the men, unable to determine their position or alter their course, can do little more than ride out the storm. Miles enters a dangerous world when he goes to sea, a world made worse by the depredations of greedy men. Pirates lie in wait among the eastern islands, their proas poised to attack any ship that enters the Straits of Sunda, and Indians on the northwest coast of America wait in ambush for those who come to trade. If the opportunity presents itself, they fall upon the unsuspecting ship, seize the cargo, and murder the crew. Yet even if the voyager escapes the assaults of such native marauders, he may still be attacked by Europeans—the Frenchmen, for example, who, as we have seen, preyed on American vessels during the quasi-war. Nature and man combine to make the sea a very dangerous place for those who venture upon it.

Not all who sail the sea can meet the challenge. Three of the captains under whom Miles serves prove to be inadequate to the task. Captain Robbins, a well-meaning but dull man who has developed a theory of ocean currents, loses the *John* on the coast of Madagascar when, following his theory, he places the ship in so dangerous a position within a reef that it cannot be extricated. Captain Williams, another well-meaning man, develops a false sense of security on the northwest coast of America and fails to take the necessary precautions to protect his ship from the Indians who capture it and kill him. And Moses Marble, first mate of the *Crisis*, who assumes command after Williams is killed, sails to a Pearl Island where, again through a failure to take precautions, the ship is captured by the Frenchmen who have been shipwrecked there. Though all three men are experienced seamen, none prove worthy of the rank they have attained. Marble, much to his credit, recognizes his limitations and decides to remain a subordinate officer. Because he perceives that Miles has already developed those qualities of mind and character that fit him for command, he agrees to serve under him.

Miles achieves success afloat, but it has its price. He has had to turn away from the stable values of his life ashore. From the first pages of the novel, the farm at Clawbonny is established as an island of peace and security, ample to satisfy any reasonable needs of its owner. It consists "of three hundred and seventy-two acres of first-rate land, either arable or of rich river bottom in meadows, and of more than a hundred of rocky mountain side, that was very tolerably covered with wood." The farmhouse, begun in 1707 and added to by subsequent owners, "had an air of substantial comfort without, an appearance that its interior in no manner contradicted." Though the ceilings might be low and the rooms not large, it was "warm in winter, cool in summer, and tidy, neat, and respectable all the year round." The "barns, granaries, sties, and other buildings of the farm, were of solid stone, like the dwelling, and all in capital condition," while all around were "orchards, meadows, and ploughed fields" (AA, pp. 2–3). On such a place Miles could have remained as "a comfortable and free housekeeper, . . . living in abundance, nay, in superfluity, so far as all the ordinary wants were concerned" (AA, p. 20).[11]

Yet Clawbonny is much more than a place of material comfort. It has other important aspects that make it emotionally satisfying. A tradition of simple living has been carried on for nearly a century, a legacy that includes the local Episcopal Church that dates from the days of Queen Anne. Here the Reverend Mr. Hardinge, who succeeded his father as spiritual guide to the little community, maintains an established order that contributes to the peace and security of the farm. Miles does not, however, value these qualities sufficiently. Though he knows that his father, who had also been a sailor, gave up the sea when he took possession of his paternal acres, the young man, who, because of the early death of his parents, has already gained his inheritance, is willing to do the opposite: leave his patrimony to pursue a life at sea. It is only when he and Rupert actually depart and are sailing down the Hudson on their way to New York and adventure, that Miles feels regret for what he is leaving behind: "all that belonged to the farm, began to have a double value in my eyes, and to serve as so many cords attached to my heartstrings" (AA, p. 35).

Miles is soon engrossed in his new occupation, but thoughts of Clawbonny recur at moments of danger. After the *John* is lost, he begins "to think of Clawbonny, and its security, and quiet nights, and well-spread board, and comfortable beds, in a way [he] had never thought of [them] before" (AA, p. 78), and just as the *Tigris* is about to engage the French privateer, his thoughts return to the farm and the people he left there. But the contrast between life afloat, with its violence and danger, and life ashore, with its peace and security, comes to him most sharply when he finally gets home. "Clawbonny never looked more beautiful than when I first cast eyes on it that afternoon." House and orchards and meadows, fields of corn and ruminating cattle standing beneath the trees—all "seemed to speak of abundance and considerate treatment. Everything denoted peace, plenty, and happiness. Yet this place, with all its blessings and security, had I willfully deserted to encounter pirates in the Straits of Sunda, shipwreck on the shores of Madagascar, jeopardy in an open boat off the Isle of France, and a miraculous preservation from a horrible death on my own coast!" (AA, pp. 105–106).

Despite this recognition, Miles soon goes to sea again on a voyage that will take him away for three years. He doesn't really know why he embarks. The tearful farewells of his sister Grace and Lucy Hardinge elicit the comment: "Man must be a stern being by nature, to be able to tear himself from such friends, in order to encounter enemies, hardships, dangers and toil, and all without any visible motive. Such was my case, however, for I wanted not for a competency, or for most of those advantages which might tempt one to abandon the voyage. Of such a measure, the possibility never crossed my mind" (AA, p. 127). Part of his reason for going is the romantic attraction of the ship's purpose, to sail around the world, but part involves his belief that voyaging is what he is fated to do. This journey is, of course, the one that makes him a man, but when he returns, it is not just Clawbonny which confronts him with an alternative way of life. New York City becomes a third locus of value, and one that is as crucial to his ultimate welfare as his experience at sea or his position as owner of Clawbonny.

It is not so much the social distinctions of New York society that affect Miles. He knows his place precisely and does not envy those above him. What does disturb him, however, is the acceptance by that society of Rupert and Lucy Hardinge, his childhood friends, and the consequences to himself. Both have been taken up and introduced to the New York social world by Mrs. Bradfort, a wealthy and socially prominent cousin of their father. Rupert is a weak, self-indulgent, mercenary young man who soon climbs into the society of New York Anglophiles. He loses interest in Miles's sister Grace, whom he had once promised to marry, and abandons her for Emily Merton, the British major's daughter. Yet after Grace's death, Rupert accepts her bequest of $20,000, which Miles feels bound in honor to pass on to him. Miles knows Rupert well, has seen his failure to grow and mature at sea, is aware of the shabby way he treated Grace, and knows he has lived on money both he and Grace have given him. Yet Rupert moves freely in social circles to which Miles, though clearly the better man, can never be admitted.

Even more serious is the effect on Miles of Lucy's rise in society. Although he loves her deeply, he has never revealed his affection to her. Both were still too young when he made his first two voyages to be aware of their feelings, and now that he is able to offer her his love, she has moved into a social set to which he cannot aspire. Though Miles as owner of Clawbonny would have been a suitable match for Lucy before Mrs. Bradfort took her up, her new position in New York society and his as a ship captain have, in the eyes of the world, moved them so far apart socially that a marriage would not now be even considered. When Mrs. Bradfort dies, moreover, and makes Lucy her heir, the girl acquires a wealth much greater than his own, a fact which, in Miles's view, separates her even more from him. Miles learns too that Lucy is being courted by Andrew Drewett, who moves in the same circles as she, and that everyone, including Lucy's father, believes that they are engaged. Small wonder then that Miles becomes embittered at the change which New York has made in his relations with the girl.

What Miles does not recognize in his frustration is that Rupert and Lucy react in totally different ways to their change of fortune. Rupert revels in his new social position and either patronizes or snubs his old friend when he meets them. Lucy does not. Indeed, she gives no indication that her change in status as at all affected her warm, frank, and honest nature. Miles, in his folly, acts in such a way as, inadvertently, to make her believe that he loves Emily Merton, with whom he had spent much time on his ship, and he tells her that he does not intend to marry. Miles is, of course, a very confused young man. He has left the peace and security of Clawbonny to sail the open sea, and while he was away, the girl he has come to love seems to have moved beyond his reach. With the social world of New York closed to him, and Clawbonny having few attractions now that Grace is dead and Lucy apparently lost, Miles decides to go once again to sea. On this final voyage, the greed of both French and British captains and the violence of a tempest all but destroy him.

Though the voyage seems at first to have been an unmitigated disaster, it provides the experience Miles must have if he is ever to learn where permanent values may be found. He is already well aware that the social life of the city does not embody them. He has seen, in Andrew Drewett's mother, that a commonplace, unthinking woman may lay claim to social distinction, and, in the career of Rupert Hardinge, that a shallow nature is no bar to social acceptance. He has seen more. On a visit to London during his second voyage, he discovered the iniquity to be found at the lower levels of the social order, where well-known rogues operate openly knowing full well that the law can do little to deter them. Miles even meets a man who escorts him around London with an ulterior motive. Miles has brought a captured ship into port, and the Englishman offers "his services in smuggling anything ashore that the *Amanda* might happen to contain, and which I," Miles writes, "as the prize-master, might feel a desire to appropriate to my own particular purposes" (AA, p. 160). Miles is repulsed by the social world at its highest and lowest levels.

In his frustration Miles misuses both island and sea. He embarks on his fourth voyage with a purpose quite different from those that motivated the first three. Miles had achieved his maturity by the end of the second voyage, and although he embarked on the third as owner as well as master of the *Dawn*, he merely sailed from port to port as cargoes offered. When he embarks for Hamburg, however, in 1803, he has filled his ship with goods he has bought himself to sell at his own advantage for the high profits he has heard they will command in Europe. Miles does not need the money. He already has the wealth required to satisfy any reasonable want, yet to pay for his cargo, he borrows a large sum from his cousin, John Wallingford, giving him a mortgage on Clawbonny as security. Miles and John agree to make wills naming each other as heir, but John seems so interested in the future of the farm that Miles, after the deed has been done, cannot help feeling suspicious about his cousin's intentions. Though Miles insists that he makes the voyage because he loves the sea and needs an occupation, he has actually risked all he holds dear to pursue unneeded wealth.

The course that the action takes during the voyage can be read in a number of ways. From the historical point of view, Miles exposes himself to the depredations that both England and France made on American shipping during the Napoleonic Wars. Seen in these terms, his experience illustrates the fate of a weak America when it confronts the unrestrained power of nations that care for nothing but their own interests. And when Miles escapes from the clutches of the British and French cruisers, the destruction of his ship in the violent gale that rakes the Irish Sea can be read as a sign of how helpless even the most skillful men are before the impersonal forces of nature, a theme developed throughout the novel. Although these interpretations are unquestionably valid, both should be understood as subordinate to a third, one that Cooper presents in all his late fiction. What happens to Miles is more than an illustration of historical injustice or the helplessness of men before overwhelming natural forces. Though Miles's experience does reveal both truths, his fate is ultimately the result of a providential power that transcends both history and nature.

Although the providential doctrine is implicit in much that happens throughout the novel, Cooper makes it a point of emphasis in an episode involving Moses Marble, his first mate on the *Dawn*, a short time before the ill-fated voyage. As an infant, Marble had been left "in a basket on a tombstone in a marble-worker's yard" (MW, p. 32)—hence his name—and he has lived his life alone, without a single known relative or place to call home. Yet when Marble accompanies Miles on a short trip on the Hudson, he discovers a family that he did not know he had in a series of events that the modern reader might call coincidental, but which Cooper interprets as providential. The boat encounters a flood tide and a falling off of the wind that forces Miles to anchor in a cove to await the turn of the tide. The two men go ashore where Marble discovers his origins. He not only finds a mother but even arrives in time to save her farm from a local usurer. To Miles, the episode has but one meaning: "the mother and child [have] been thrown together by the agency of an inscrutable Providence!" (MW, p. 32).

As Miles looks back on his final voyage, he interprets his experience in precisely the same terms. Though he uses ingenuity and skill to escape the British and French cruisers and to save his ship in the violent storm, his own exertions are insufficient to gain his ends. Providence guides the events. This lesson is brought home to him in a most dramatic fashion. By the time he encounters the storm, his crew has been reduced to three men: Diogenes, the black cook; Neb, the slave who has accompanied Miles on all his voyages; and Marble, the first mate. The blacks are washed away when the ship broaches to and a great wave sweeps the deck. It carries Diogenes to his death and drives Neb, who is in the launch at the time, over the side in a small boat. Much of the rigging comes down under the force of the storm, and as Marble tries to clear it from the ship, he is swept away when the wreck breaks free from the vessel. "In this manner," Miles writes, "did it please divine Providence to separate us four, who had already gone through so much in company!" (MW, p.311).

Alone on his sinking ship and surrounded by a vastness of empty ocean, Miles continues to see his experience in religious terms. His friends gone, his cargo lost, his Clawbonny sacrificed to a bid for wealth he did not need, Miles in his solitude begins to pray "to that dread Being, with whom," he writes, "it now appeared to me, I stood alone, in the centre of the universe" (MW, p. 321). Though Miles attempts to save himself by making a raft and stocking it with what he needs to survive, when his ship sinks, he reaches the nadir of his fortunes, and he acquires the deepest sense of his own helplessness. "I cannot describe the sensation that came over me," he recalls, "as I gazed around, and found myself on the broad ocean, floating on a little deck that was only ten feet square, and which was raised less than two feet above the surface of the waters. It was now that I felt the true frailty of my position, and comprehended all its dangers" (MW, p. 326). He is safe enough so long as the weather is calm, but even a moderate breeze could raise a sea that would sweep his few possessions away.

Once Miles has been reduced to this perilous state, his fortunes begin to improve. He awakes next morning to find the launch of the *Dawn* not ten yards from him, "thrown within . . . reach," he believes, "by the mercy of divine Providence!" (MW, p. 332). What is more, Neb and Marble are both in it. Neb had handled the boat so skillfully that he found the wrecked spars and rescued Marble. The two of them had then searched for the *Dawn* and, failing to find it, had concluded that Providence had swept Miles away (MW, p. 331). Providence had, on the contrary, preserved all three, and now that Miles has been shown where his true dependence must lie, he can return to America where additional lessons await him. Thirteen months must pass, however, before he succeeds in reaching home. Picked up by a British frigate bound out to its cruising station, the three remain aboard until they are discovered there by the captain of the frigate they had previously eluded. Taken to his vessel, they are detained for five months before they escape. But even after they find an American vessel to take them home, another five months elapse before they arrive at Philadelphia and make their way to New York.

Here Miles is forced to repeat in a social context the experience he had on the open sea. He is again brought low by forces he cannot control. Because there had been no word from him for so many months, his ship was considered lost and himself presumed dead. At first John Wallingford appeared and assured the people at Clawbonny that no changes would be made, but two months later, the mortgage on Clawbonny was foreclosed and the farm went under a forced sale to a man named Daggett, who acquired it at a fraction of its true value. He dismissed the dependents and laid plans to alter the place completely. Miles soon learns from Daggett's lawyer that John Wallingford has died leaving no will, and the new owner of Clawbonny, who is a cousin of John's on his mother's side, has become the administrator of the estate. A grasping man, Daggett tries to force Miles to surrender his personal effects at less than their true worth as the price for gaining more time to pay off his indebtedness. When Miles refuses to let himself be robbed in this way, he is thrown into jail.

At this low point in his fortunes, Miles learns to still his pride and accept the help of those who come to his aid. Lucy Hardinge and her father hurry at once to the jail, but neither is in a position to stand bail for him. The minister has no money, and Lucy, as a minor, is unable to do so. She makes Miles promise, however, to accept the help of one she will send who can. Miles is surprised when the man who comes to his aid turns out to be Andrew Drewett, to whom he had long believed she was engaged, but he remains true to his word. Drewett then informs him that years before Lucy had refused his offer of marriage, and Miles is relieved of the fear that had troubled him. Freed from jail, he goes to Lucy and the two soon reach an understanding. Miles still perceives her wealth as an obstacle to their marriage, especially now that his own folly has impoverished him, but she makes him put down his pride and accept from her the worldly goods he can no longer command himself. With this agreement, Miles at last achieves the humility that all his recent experience has been designed to teach him.

Once Miles learns this lesson, his material fortunes improve dramatically. Lucy's father arrives with Richard Harison, the well-known lawyer, who informs Miles that his cousin had, as he promised, prepared a will which Harison had not produced only because he did not know of John Wallingford's death. Under its terms, the mortgage is cancelled and the debt forgiven. The forced sale can therefore be set aside and Clawbonny returned to its rightful owner. True to his word, moreover, John Wallingford had named Miles his heir. As a result, the young man comes into a fortune that is even greater than Lucy's, and, with a touch of remaining pride, he is pleased that he will not be forced to live on her money. Miles goes to Genesee County, where his cousin had lived, to settle his affairs, and while he is gone, Mr. Hardinge takes charge of Clawbonny, brings the dependents back to the farm, and restores everything to its proper condition. Though his ship and cargo are irretrievably lost, Miles is now much better off than he was before he sailed on his final voyage. He marries Lucy Hardinge and settles down to a life of contentment on his beloved Clawbonny.

The happy ending must be read as providential, as the final result of a process by which Miles is brought to perceive his true relation to God, his fellow men, and the things of the material world. All three areas of experience—sea, city, and island—were necessary for his education. Though he returns at last to Clawbonny, the point from which he began, his final settlement on the farm does not imply a retreat from the world nor does it invalidate in any way his experience at sea. For Cooper, life afloat is always a proving ground for character, and Miles had to test himself against the sea in order to become a man and develop those qualities of leadership which he demonstrates so ably when he assumes command of the *Crisis*. But his experience at sea also teaches him the awesome power of God and the insufficiency of men to gain their ends by their own exertions. Miles had to become aware of both his abilities and his limitations before he could assume his appropriate position in a rational social order and make proper use of the worldly goods that go with it.

His life ashore includes, moreover, both Clawbonny and New York. Though Miles had been made to feel the false social distinctions that the city fosters, he does not simply withdraw to his island of security and reject New York completely. He and Lucy retain her house on Manhattan, and when commerce drives them away from Wall Street, Miles builds anew, moving uptown as the city grows. Yet the townhouse is merely the place where Miles and Lucy maintain their contact with the world at large.[12] The focus of their life is Clawbonny, for it represents the domestic values on which, in Cooper's view, the health of society depends. Clawbonny is home and fireside; garden, lawn, orchard and tilled fields; the churchyard and the graves of their families. It is their link with the past, the four generations of Wallingfords that have already lived there; the place of domestic happiness where they raise their family; and the basis for a peaceful and productive future when yet another Miles Wallingford will inherit the farm and carry on the tradition. It is, in short, the source of those values which insure both stability and continuity in human life.

Notes

1. James Fenimore Cooper, *Afloat and Ashore: A Sea Tale*, Mohawk ed. (New York, 1896). p. 2. Citations in my text to *Afloat and Ashore* (AA) and *Miles Wallingford* (MW) are to page numbers in the Mohawk edition.

2. John Murray (1737–1808) and William Bayard (1761–1826) may be found in the *DAB*. Archibald Gracie appears in the entry for his grandson, also named Archibald Gracie.

3. "Benjamin Moore (1748–18 16), who was consecrated bishop on 11 September 1801, may be found in the *DAB*.

4. Thomas Barclay (1753–1830) may be found in the *DAB*.

5. Information on Richard Harison (Cooper spelled the name Harrison) may be found in Martha J. Lamb, *History of the City of*

New York: Its Origin, Rise, and Program (New York: 1880). 11, 350, 367,475; *History of the State of New York,* ed. Alexander C. Flick (New York, 1934), V, 32, 52, 53, 189; and Sidney J. Pomerantz, *New York, An American City, 1783–1803: A Study of Urban Life* (New York, 1938), pp. 54, 91, 102, 107, 124, 132–133, 136, 207, 335–336, 375–376, 397.

6. Samuel Bard (1742–182 I), David Hosack (1769–1835), Wright Post (1766–1828), Richard Bayley (1745–1801), and Benjamin Rush (1745–1 813) may all be found in the *DAB.* William Moore appears in the entry for his son, Nathaniel Fish Moore.

7. For Cooper's historical account of the *Ganges* and Captain Richard Dale, see his *History of the Navy of the United States of America,* 3rd ed. (Philadelphia, 1847), p. 155.

8. Although critics have discussed the novel in terms of the contrast between life afloat and life ashore, none have seen this tri-partite division in its geography. See, for example, Thomas Philbrick, *James Fenimore Cooper and the Development of American Sea Fiction* (Cambridge, Mass., 196 I), pp. 161–164; and George Dekker, *James Fenimore Cooper the Novelist* (London, 1967), pp. 206–212.

9. W. H. Auden, *The Enchafed Flood: or, The Romantic Iconography of the Sea* (New York, 1967). pp. 6–25.

10. For Hawthorne's use of the metaphor, see my article, "Romantic Iconography in *The Scarlet Letter* and *The Blithedale Romance,*" in *Ruined Eden of the Present: Hawthorne, POP, and Melville,* Critical Essays in Honor of Darrel Abel, ed. G. R. Thompson and Virgil L. Lokke (West Lafayette, Ind., 1981), pp. 93–107. Auden treats Melville in *the Enchafed Flood.*

11. Clawbonny is thus very much like the Van Tassel farm in Washington Irving's "The Legend of Sleepy Hollow." See *The Sketch Book of Geoffrey Crayon, Gent.,* ed. Haskell Springer (Boston, 1978), pp. 278–279. I discuss this and related passages in my article, "New York and New England: Irving's Criticism of American Society," *American Literature,* 38 (January 1967), 460–462.

12. That society is necessary to the human being is illustrated in an episode in which Moses Marble tries to live alone on a desert island and finds he cannot do it. See **Afloat and Ashore,** pp. 318–33 1, 440–447.

This article originally appeared in the *Hudson Valley Regional Review,* Volume 2.2.

20th Century Leaders

F.D.R., Father Divine, and the "Krum Elbow" Flurry

Thomas W. Casey

In the early years of his Presidency, Franklin D. Roosevelt was busy combating the Great Depression in the nation and the beginnings of World War II abroad. But here at home, in Hyde Park, he was plagued by a minuscule matter that he brought upon himself, revealing perhaps an idiosyncratic side of him few ever knew about.

It was all about a property dispute. The events involved were well chronicled by the local newspapers of the day, as well as by the national press, including *The New York Times, The Washington Post, The Chicago Sun* and *Time* and *Life* magazines.

The broad coverage was due to the prominence of the parties involved. They were Franklin D. Roosevelt, President at the time of these events; Father Divine, a nationally acclaimed Black social and spiritual leader deemed to be God Himself by his followers; and, indirectly, Frederick Vanderbilt of the shipping and railroad family.

In March of 1933, just days after his first Presidential inauguration, Roosevelt wrote to his longtime acquaintance in matters of local history, Helen Wilkinson Reynolds. The letter contained a request that Miss Reynolds trace the property to which the name "Krum Elbow" properly belonged. Probably because of his Dutch ancestry he wanted the name Krum Elbow to refer exclusively to the Roosevelt property. Miss Reynolds's reply later that month informed Roosevelt that her research into the records of both Ulster and Dutchess counties regarding the use of Krum Elbow was inconclusive; she found the name used to designate properties on both sides of the river.

This would explain why F.D.R.'s neighbor directly across the Hudson to the west claimed that his property was rightfully called Krum Elbow.

Not satisfied with Miss Reynolds's findings, Roosevelt proceeded to request that the Board of Geographical Names, a subdivision of the U.S. Department of the Interior, look into the matter and issue a formal decision on the use of the name Krum Elbow.

Not surprisingly, the matter was officially resolved in Roosevelt's favor when on July 23, 1937, George Martin, executive secretary of the Board of Geographical Names, informed F.D.R of the board's findings designating Krum Elbow as "a point on the *East Bank* [emphasis mine] of the Hudson River about 4 1/2 miles above Poughkeepsie, Dutchess County, New York."[1] However, this decision of the Board of Names was not promulgated, possibly because of a report that the board had rendered its decision contrary to certain evidence that supported the claim of neighbor Howland Spencer. *The New York Times* of July 30, 1937, reported:

> Investigation by the geographical board, headed by Dr. W.C. Mendenhall, chief of the Geographic
> Society, and consisting of a score of Government officials and college professors, reliably was reported to

have found that a pre-revolutionary British merchant by the name of Crooks first established what is now Hyde Park and called it "Crooks' Paradise."

Records in Dutchess County were said to bear out the findings of the ownership by Mr. Crooks. The possibility that Mr. Roosevelt and Neighbor Spencer may renew their verbal battle over the name was reported to be the reason Secretary Ickes has been keeping the decision in his safe.

Efforts to get an explanation for the committee shifting the name from the west to the east bank met with little success at Secretary Ickes' department

George Martin, executive secretary of the committee, shuddered when asked about the decision. He said, 'Until decisions are announced, they are subject to change, you know. I never discuss decisions until the Secretary announces them.'

It also was learned that another decision was reached on the Hudson near the disputed Krum Elbow. Hereafter, the name of the four-mile Poughkeepsie boat race course will be called the original name given it by Dutch sailors of many years ago—Lango Baan—meaning 'Long Beach" to US.

Howland Spencer must have been more than amused at the newspaper report that the east bank of the Hudson was originally known as "Crooks' Paradise" since he irreverently referred to the President as "slippery Frank." Incidentally, a small cemetery containing several of the Crooks family can still be seen behind the Morgan estate on the northern border of the Roosevelt property.

The *New York Times* quoted Howland Spencer:

It [the Spencer property] was always known as Krum Elbow. Every map from the early grants up named our point Krum Elbow. Then just before he went into the White House, he claimed Krum Elbow as the name for the Roosevelt estate. . . . And then what happened? In 1938 the geodetic survey—some Washington survey—came along the river and placed brass markers naming it "Spencer Point." The Roosevelt place was called Krum Elbow. Did you ever hear anything like that?[2]

Earlier in the summer of 1938, Howland Spencer, in an apparent move to spite his neighbor Roosevelt, sold his west bank property to the nationally prominent blackcult leader Father Divine. Certainly, Spencer must have known that his sale to Father Divine would command national news coverage. The front page of *The New York Times* of July 29, 1938, contained an article headlined "Father Divine Group Buys 'Krum Elbow' Estate Facing Roosevelt's on the Hudson." The article went on to report that:

It is understood that Father Divine's followers will retain the name of Krum Elbow, which figured in a dispute between President Roosevelt and Mr. Spencer as to whether the original Krum Elbow was on the east or west shore.[3]

Of course, the purchase gained prominent coverage in the local press. Under a front page headline of "Father Divine's Aides Buy Krum Elbow Estate" *The Poughkeepsie Eagle-News* reported the purchase price to be between $40,000 and $50,000 for the 600-acre parcel, including several buildings. It also reported that "the new purchase by the followers of Father Divine increased to nearly thirty the number of estates now owned by them in Ulster County."[4] Indeed, by the early 1930's Divine and his followers owned about 3,000 choice acres in Ulster County. As big a local story as this was, it ran second to the Woodcliff Amusement

Park riot of the previous day. This riot involved local whites and a boatload of black families who had come up the river for the day. The riot was apparently provoked when the local whites attempted to prevent the blacks' entrance to the park. The park was located on what is now the northern portion of the Marist College campus designated "Gartland Commons." Woodcliff Park was eventually closed because of this incident. While the Woodcliff Park incident and the Krum Elbow purchase were not related, both events give some measure of the racial tensions of the time. *Time* magazine, in an article titled "Black Elbow," quoted the gloating Spencer as saying, ". . .this really will annoy Franklin a good deal, won't it?"[5] Aside from abhorring Roosevelt's politics (Spencer was a staunch Republican), we gain a glimpse of his view of Roosevelt's haughty personality in an interview with *The New York Times*. When asked when he last saw the President to chat in a neighborly way Spencer said about two years earlier, but:

> "You can't, you can't, you can't talk to him: he does the talking. Why, he held my hand while I had to listen. If you try to talk he goes like this—"

> Mr. Spencer rose from his chair and thrashed his arms around.

> "That's the way he goes, you can't talk to him." Mr. Spencer likened Roosevelt's manner as "an entire Trinity complex."[6]

M.J. Divine, better known as Father Divine.
Courtesy of the Peace Mission Movement.

A word about Father Divine and his followers, who called themselves "Angels." Whenever asked about his origins Father Divine was vague, evasive and even contradictory. Biographers place his birth at about 1885 in the Deep South. He arrived in New York about 1915. By 1929 the Depression, having hit blacks harder than any other racial group, forged a new militancy. This forced the black clergy to change from positions of spiritual to social leadership. Father Divine made this transition more rapidly than his counterparts and thereby quickly moved from relative obscurity to national prominence as a black social leader. Although frequently referred to as a cult leader whose followers deemed to be God Himself, it is also the case that he was a leader for social reform and fought for desegregation and anti-lynching laws. (He once claimed that he was nearly lynched as many as thirty-two times.) He designated his interracial communities as "Peace Missions" and "Heavens." His followers were predominantly black and about eighty percent female. Estimates of the size of his following ranged from a few thousand to twenty-two million by Divine himself. Dying in 1965, he lived to congratulate President Lyndon Johnson on the passage of the Civil Rights Act of 1964.[7]

From Hyde Park, guests at the Summer White House (center) look out on a curve of the Hudson River which in 1609 Henry Hudson named *Krum Elboge* or Crooked Elbow. Visible opposite is the old home (*in circle*) of Howland Spencer.

For three generations the Spencer estate has been called Crum Elbow. Since 1932 Franklin Roosevelt has called his family estate Krum Elbow. On July 29 Howland Spencer sold Crum Elbow to Harlem's famed evangelist, Father Divine.

After Father Divine bought the property of Howland Spencer, Life magazine ran a two-page photo essay. the essay, which included this photo showing the opposing Krum (Crum) Elbows, appeared Aug. 22, 1938. The headline across the two pages read, "President Roosevelt Gets New Neighbors Across Hudson as Father Divine's 'Angels' Take over Crum Elbow 'Heaven.'"

On August 9, 1938, 2,000 "Angels" assembled with their leader at Krum Elbow to celebrate their recent acquisition. Reports of the actual numbers varied widely. *The New York Times*, 2,500; *The Poughkeepsie Evening Star Enterprise*, 4,000; and *The Poughkeepsie Evening News*, 2,000.

The Poughkeepsie Evening Star and Enterprise of August 10, 1938, ran several photos of the event, including the arrival of Father Divine and reported that:

> The "promised land" of Howland Spencer's Krum Elbow, now Father Divine's chief sub heaven in Ulster County, at the height of the official turnover of the Negro cult yesterday, visited by some four thousand members who came by boat, train, car and foot to get the southern fried chicken and rest in the shade of the big estate.

Eleanor Roosevelt had little to say about the arrival of her new neighbors. *The New York Times* reported that

> Newspaper men who happened later to be crossing the Main Street of Poughkeepsie came upon Mrs. Franklin D. Roosevelt at the wheel of her car waiting for a green light. She had been in New York City all day.

Thomas W. Casey

Main homestead of Father Divine's "Krum (Crum) Elbow" as it appeared in The
*(Poughkeepsie) Evening Star and Enterprise on July 30, 1938. The original caption read
"Krum Elbow, Scene of New 'Father Divine Heaven.'"*

"Father Divine? What estate?" She appeared puzzled. Oh, do you mean that place across the river that has
been sold?

Mrs. Roosevelt laughed and said that she had not witnessed the excursion scene and explained:

"I could not see it anyway because I live in the cottage [Val Kill, about a mile east of the Roosevelt estate]
when my husband is in Washington."[8]

Although most of his followers on that festive day arrived by boat, Father Divine showed his usual flair
for the dramatic when he arrived in his open-top limousine at the tail of a sixty-car cavalcade. He spent the
day inspecting the grounds and buildings, greeting followers and telling the press, "I couldn't have a finer
neighbor, could I?" The same article went on to describe how:

He posed for photographers holding life-preservers labeled "Father Divine." He posed alone, he posed with
groups and he posed with "Blessed," his pretty, young white secretary, a girl with raven black hair, dressed
in a bright blue chiffon dress. [This young Canadian woman would later become Father Divine's second
wife and be known as Mother Divine the Second.][9]

The President issued no comment from the White House on the events of August 9, 1938 but did so when he returned to Hyde Park later that month. Speaking to a small gathering, he welcomed his new neighbors across the river.

> The President thus answered a question that has been in the minds of many Americans since the Negro Evangelist founded his new colony across the Hudson from the Hyde Park Estate—how did he like his new neighbors? After several speakers at the Roosevelt home club's annual reception had referred humorously to the new "Heaven," the President took official notice of the development and said: "I'm confident that the people of the 'heaven' in Ulster County will be good neighbors to us here in Dutchess County."[10]

Earlier in the summer of 1938 Hyde Park lost its wealthiest citizen and largest single employer with the death of Frederick W. Vanderbilt (Vanderbilt died at his Hyde Park mansion on June 28, 1938 at age 86.) His wife had predeceased him and they had no children, so Frederick left the bulk of his estate, including the mansion and grounds, to a niece of Mrs. Vanderbilt, Margaret Louise Van Alen of Newport, RI. Frederick had chosen not to include Vanderbilts in his bequeathment since the family had ostracized him years earlier for marrying a divorcee. At the close of the year 1938 an item buried in the back pages of *The New York Times* indicated that his estate was appraised at $80 million and would be subject to $11 million in inheritance tax.[11]

The summer of 1939 was to be even more eventful than that of '38 for the residents of the Hudson Valley. In early June the young King and Queen of England, George VI and Elizabeth, stopped for an overnight visit with the Roosevelts at Hyde Park. Prior to the Hyde Park visit they went to the New York World's Fair, to Washington, D.C., and on a trip across Canada. It was the first visit by a reigning British monarch to the North American continent and thus their every move received scrutiny and acclaim. One story seized by the national press was the famous "Hot Dog Picnic" the Roosevelts gave for the Britannic Majesties at Top Cottage, the President's recently completed retirement home east of Eleanor's Val-Kill. Elliot Roosevelt, second son of Franklin and Eleanor, later told a story of visiting the Queen Mother in the early 1980's and asking her what was most memorable about her Hyde Park visit. She responded by recalling going to St. James Church for Sunday services and reading a sign outside the church saying, "This is the church of the President of the United States, Franklin Delano Roosevelt" And under it someone had scrawled, "It used to belong to God!"[12]

But back to other events of that summer in the valley that would command national news coverage, as did those of the summer of '38.

A headline of the August 16, 1939, *Poughkeepsie Evening News* read "Hyde Park Heaven" with the subhead, "Father Divine plans to buy Vanderbilt Estate, Roosevelts have no objection to purchase." The article went on to describe Father Divine's plans for the estate. The mansion would become his principal residence, where he would entertain national and world political and religious leaders as well as house some of his "Angels." An editorial of the same day in *The Poughkeepsie Evening Star* seemed supportive of Father Divine's most recent attempt to acquire property in the valley.

> While local citizenry ordinarily view with alarm the arrival of neighbors of the members of any religious cult which does not conform with accepted practices of worship and behavior, reports from across the river indicate that the followers of Father Divine are essentially good neighbors.

Their "heavens" are spotless, the food good, the activities of the followers do not disturb the neighborhood unduly, and scores of people are able to win happiness among pleasant surroundings which they never could have were there no Father Divine.

Opinions of Hyde Parkers generally ran from guarded to negative. But John D. Wicker, sexton of St. James Church, which is directly across the road from the Vanderbilt estate, responded in an interview with *The New York Herald Tribune:*

> Why I don't think they'd disturb anybody . . .I understand Father Divine keeps his followers very orderly and maintains strict discipline. I understand he doesn't even allow them to smoke ...there's plenty of room for them on that place, anyway.[13]

A local real estate broker said, "I'm not sure that when the fireworks have died down the people of Hyde Park won't be glad to have the flock to buy groceries and supplies from them." A bartender asked rhetorically, "Well, how would you feel about it?" And a neighbor adjacent to the property confessed: "I don't like it But I don't know what I can do about it As long as he's [Father Divine] got the money to pay for it, I guess he's got the right to buy it."[14]

About this time Father Divine released some correspondence carried on between himself and Eleanor Roosevelt, and himself and the President, seeking reactions should he attempt to buy the Vanderbilt property. Interestingly, he began his correspondence with Mrs. Roosevelt, presenting his plan, but assuring her that, "I would not for a moment want to embarrass you or your friends in any way."[15] Eleanor replied that she discussed the matter with the President, who had a particular interest in the destiny of the property because it contained such a remarkable collection of rare trees. She said the President for some time had been trying to interest some public body in the acquisition and preservation of the place because of its public value as an arboretum.

The same sentiments were registered by the President through Steve Early, the person designated by the President to respond to correspondence from Father Divine. In each of the President's letters he assured Father Divine that he, like everyone else, had every legal right to acquire the property. It was rumored that Father Divine had offered $80,000 for the property, but Mrs. Van Alen denied ever negotiating with Father Divine or any of his intermediaries. She also denied knowing anything about the correspondence between Father Divine and the Roosevelts.

Franklin Roosevelt had never been a popular figure in his predominantly Republican Hudson Valley. In his four presidential elections he failed to carry Dutchess County or even his native village of Hyde Park. A front page article in the August 16, 1939, *Poughkeepsie Evening Star* on the Divine/Roosevelt negotiations stated the following: "With the tacit approval of President and Mrs. Roosevelt, who offered no objections, the followers of Father Divine, the little Harlem negro called God by his people, today were pushing negotiations for purchase of the Frederick Vanderbilt estate...while Hyde Park villagers *plummeted* [emphasis mine] to fame through the election of President Roosevelt..." But now his fellow citizens of Dutchess County and Hyde Park needed the politically powerful Roosevelt in their hopes of thwarting the designs of Father Divine.

The Dutchess County Realty Board suggested the idea that the Vanderbilt property be used to house the FDR Library. They argued that such a move would avert the cost of erecting a new building for his library.[16] However, this idea gained little support and Roosevelt proceeded to lay the cornerstone for the first Presidential Library three months later on his "Krum Elbow" estate.[17]

The Divine/Vanderbilt story came to an abrupt close when Van Alen announced that she was removing the estate from the market.[18] Hyde Park seemed relieved, but continued to live with the suspense of what the ultimate disposition of the property might be. Their suspense was finally ended when their native son called a White House press conference on February 5, 1940, and announced that the Vanderbilt property would become a national park. Mrs. Van Alen had deeded the estate to the federal government for the sum of one dollar. In July of 1990 the National Park Service celebrated the fiftieth anniversary of the Vanderbilt property as a national park.

Although there is little in the records on exchanges between the President and Mrs. Van Alen regarding the property's final disposition, I think we can assume that Roosevelt played a pivotal role in Mrs. Van Alen's final decision.

If the people of Hyde Park and Dutchess County felt indebted to their native son they never showed it as they continued to repudiate him in two more Presidential elections.

Notes

I would like to acknowledge John Ferris, archivist at the Franklin D. Roosevelt Library, for his assistance and direction in researching this article, as well as my students at Marist College in the History and Culture of the Hudson Valley course. Thanks also to James Kullander for editorial assistance and to Mrs. Myra Witmer for typing services.

1. Decision of the U.S. Board of Geographical Names rendered April 29, 1937, from President's Personal File #273. Geoffrey C. Ward, in his book *A First Class Temperament: The Emergence of Franklin Roosevelt* (Harper and Row, 1989) relates the following: Sara Delano Roosevelt, the President's mother, preferred the name Springwood to Krum Elbow. Her late husband, James, had always referred to it as Springwood. At the time of the dispute Sara, not the contesting Franklin, was the legal owner of the estate. She once corrected a guest who on several occasions used the name Krum Elbow. The guest explained that he was only following the President's lead, to which Sara replied, "Franklin doesn't know *everything*." A three-foot "S" (for Springwood) can still be seen mounted on the southeast and southwest outer field-stone walls of the Roosevelt home. These were added to the original home in 1913 under the direction of Franklin. This raises the question why Franklin in 1915 called the estate Springwood, and 20 years later insisted it be called Krum Elbow. For more information about this, see also F. Kennon Moody's book, *FDR and His Neighbors: a Study in the Relationship between Franklin D. Roosevelt and the Residents of Dutchess County*, pages 164–165.

2. *The New York Times*, Aug. 10, 1938.

3. *The New York Times*, July 29, 1938.

4. *The Poughkeepsie Eagle News*, July 29, 1938.

5. *Time*, Aug. 3, 1938.

6. *The New York Times*, Aug. 10, 1938.

7. Much of the information contained in this paragraph is from a book, *Father Divine and the Struggles for Racial Equality*, by Robert Weisbrot (University of Illinois Press, 1983). Weisbrot puts the purchase price of the estate at $25,000. Although hardly a definitive biography, it is the best work on Father Divine that I could find.

8. The *New York Times*, Aug. 10, 1938.

9. Ibid. *The New Amsterdam News* hailed the purchase as one of the 12 outstanding events in Afro-American history for 1938.

10. The *New York Times*, Aug. 28, 1938.

11. *The New York Times*, Dec. 28, 1938.

12. Told by Elliot Roosevelt on Oct. 11, 1984, at the centenary celebration of his mother's birth.

13. The *New York Herald Tribune*, Aug. 17, 1939.

14. Ibid.

15. The *New York Herald Tribune*, Aug. 17, 1939. The actual letter can be found in the President's Personal File #6170 at the FDR Library.

16. The *Poughkeepsie Eagle News*, Aug. 18, 1939.

17. President's Personal File +6170 reveals that Stephen Early, secretary to the President, replied to Mr. R W. Smith regarding Smith's suggestion that the Vanderbilt estate be used as the FDR Library:

> However, due to the fact that S.J. Resolution 118 "To provide for the establishment and maintenance of the Franklin D. Roosevelt Library and for other purposes." was passed by Congress and approved on July 18, 1939; that the President has already deeded a portion of his Hyde Park property for this purpose, that plans for the library are now complete; and ground-breaking already is under way, I fear it is too late to take advantage of your suggestion.

18. The story was carried by the Associated Press. See *The Washington Post*, Aug. 17, 1939.

This article originally appeared in the *Hudson Valley Regional Review*, Volume 8.1.

John Burroughs and the Hudson Valley

Alfred Marks

Postcard from the collection of Vivian Yess Wadlin, courtesy of Hudson River Valley Heritage.

John Burroughs came to the Hudson Valley to stay in 1873, when he purchased Mauritenz Deyo's farm in West Park, but in a sense he had been here all the time. He was born in Roxbury, just over the ridge, where the Catskills drain not into the Hudson but into the Delaware, and as soon as he could, he moved across into the Hudson watershed for his principal livelihood, returning to Roxbury for summers for much of his life thereafter. Clara Barrus has written that "Home" was the term Burroughs always reserved for Roxbury, but surely his last words, "How far are we from home?" spoken on a train passing through Ohio, referred to the Hudson Valley and West Park. He came over into what we know as the Ashokan Reservoir area to teach when he was seventeen and returned there, to Tongore, for another term in 1855 and 1856. That was not long after he had made his first visit to New York City, followed by his first trip back home on the Hudson River boat to Kingston and the stage from there to Roxbury. He did get away to teach over the winter of 1856–57 in Buffalo Grove, Illinois, but the next summer he was back in High Falls teaching and, that fall, married Ursula North.

From 1858 to 1859 Burroughs taught at East Orange, New Jersey, where he took advantage of the proximity to New York City, as Hudson Valley dwellers will, and as he continued to do for the rest of his life. Then, from 1860 to 1862, he taught at Rosendale and the next year at Buttermilk Falls, near West Point, which had a library he used heavily and, as everybody knows, where he first discovered Audubon's *Birds*.

After the year at Buttermilk Falls—now Highland Falls—he got away for ten years in Washington D.C., a side journey many Americans make and never change home address. They were years not to be belittled, for they were spent in the stimulating intellectual neighborhood of Walt Whitman and some of the brightest minds in the United States—all engrossed in civil war and reconstruction—and they culminated with the publication of *Wake-Robin*. But on December 31, 1872, at thirty-five years of age, he resigned his post with the U.S. Treasury and returned to New York State to look for the home in the Hudson Valley for which he had watched and waited.

Of course the Hudson Valley of 1873 was different from that which we know. Rail transportation was just becoming available between Kingston and Stamford and between New Paltz and Kingston, but from West Park one had to go on foot, horse-power, or boat. The West Shore Railroad was not completed until 1883. There were no bridges across the Hudson. The railroad bridge at Poughkeepsie was not completed until 1888. Ferries from Highland to Poughkeepsie, from Rondout to Rhinecliff, and from Saugerties to Tivoli carried most of the traffic across the Mid-Hudson when the river was not frozen. West Park had no post office. Burroughs first had to go to Elmore's Corners—now known as Esopus—for his mail.

This was long before the advent of the automobile, or the electric light, or the phonograph, or the motion picture, but before he died, forty-eight years later, Burroughs would become involved with each of these inventions in exciting ways.

Much later, in the preface to the 1895 edition of *Wake-Robin*, Burroughs will impart something of what the move to the Hudson Valley meant to him.

> Since I left Washington in 1873, instead of an iron wall in front of my desk, I have had a large iron window that overlooks the Hudson and the wooded heights beyond, and I have exchanged the vault for a vineyard. Probably my mind reacted more vigorously from the former than it does from the latter. The vineyard winds its tendrils around me and detains me, and its loaded trellises are more pleasing to me than the closets of greenbacks.

Neither those Riverby vineyards nor his Slabsides celery will bring him "closets of greenbacks," though they will provide him with cash crop for the New York City market and also, in time, a different kind of produce, for which he will be world famous. Let us make no bones about it—John Burroughs is, without doubt, the Hudson Valley's greatest author. Even in *Wake-Robin*, much of which was written in that lone, though not lonely, ten-year period he spent elsewhere, he keeps referring to the Hudson Valley. And even when his thoughts wander off into transcendental realms, there is no doubt where his feet are rooted. He also carried the spirit and the place markers of the Hudson Valley into the world outside and elicited responses which brought that wide world here to the shores of the river—to Riverby, to Slabsides, and indeed to Roxbury.

Burroughs wrote no fiction. Nothing to rival "The Legend of Sleepy Hollow" and its descriptions of Dutch social life on the shores of the Tappan Zee and the tormenting of the outlander schoolmaster, who just happens to be one of the money-grubbing Connecticut men the Dutch detested. Nothing to rival the mysterious adventures of Dolph Heyliger in the shadow of the Dunderberg or the slumbers of Rip Van Winkle that carried him through the Revolution and into an era that resented his declaring himself "a loyal subject of the King; bless him!" Nothing of the rich humor of *A History of New York* by Diedrich Knickerbocker, with Governor Wilhelm Kieft taking the frustrations of administration out on his dogs in the gubernatorial mansion referred to as misery.

Historic postcard of "Slabsides," Burrough's studio and retreat.
From the collection of Vivian Yess Wadlin, courtesy of Hudson River Valley Heritage.

But, even though Irving settled in Sunnyside and dominated the American literary scene of the first half of the nineteenth century, readers of the *Sketch Tales of a Traveler*, and *Bracebridge Hall*, to say nothing of his books on Spain and Christopher Columbus, know that the Hudson Valley materials, brilliant though they are, represent a minor fraction of Washington Irving's lit-concern.

Burroughs wrote nothing like Melville's "Bartleby the Scrivener," the Manhattan tale worth reading and rereading now that we as well as Manhattan are overwhelmed by people like Bartleby who, for no discernible reason, drop of the workaday world and depend for housing and sustenance on that of sympathetic friends. Burroughs' nothing like Melville's tales of the nearby Berkshire mountains, works like "Cock-A-Doodle-Doo," and "The Lightning Rod Man," and the paired social commentaries "The Paradise of Bachelors and The Tartarus of Maids." He wrote nothing like the Schenectady and Manhattan tragedy, *Pierre*. Burroughs wrote no poetry like that of Whitman's "Crossing Brooklyn Ferry", or "Manhattan," and though he acquired a home on eastern Long Island that still remains a family possession, he wrote nothing as evocative of Long Island's shores as Whitman's "To Paumanok" or the poem that last bore the title "As I Ebbed with the Ocean of Life." And even though Burroughs supplied Whitman with the hermit thrush for "When Lilacs Last in the Dooryard Bloom'd," poetry was not really his idiom. Perhaps his only acclaimed poem, "Waiting," has its place, a place perhaps with William Ernest Henley's "Invictus," but Burroughs himself would not have asked for much more and perhaps not that much. Burroughs' writings could not compare with innumerable Hudson Valley authors writing in their special idiom: the misspelled witticisms of Josh Billings, the wild poetry of Joseph Rodman Drake, the bruited "grace" of Nathaniel Parker Willis, the humor of James Kirke

Paulding. And in the twentieth century, he could have written no novel like Saul Bellow's *Henderson the Rain King*, or John Cheever's *The Wapshot Chronicle*, or T.C. Boyle's already dated *World's End*, or the gently graceful historical essays of Carl Carmer.

But Burroughs was a different kind of essayist than Carl Carmer, and he was by far the most celebrated essayist in the America of his time. He was also an excellent literary critic, and a national celebrity to honor. And though his essays covered a wide geographical range, the ever-recurring center of their discourse and the eye behind their observations was clearly in the Hudson Valley, along some still, yet paradoxically moving, gradient between the Mid-Hudson and the vicinity of Roxbury in the Catskills.

This movement is visible even in Burroughs' first collection, *Wake-Robin*. The first essay is based close to the Hudson, in Buttermilk Falls, and the second essay, "In the Hemlocks" is about the southern Catskills, specifically the Beaverkill Mountains. The essay "Birch Browsings," further on, returns to the southern Catskills, to the Beaverkill area. That essay presents a rather exciting story of bushwhacking in search of a hidden lake. The lake is referred to as Thomas's lake, but the Zen monks of the Dai Bosatsu Zendo, in the Livingston Manor area, are probably correct in believing that this small birch-bound body of water is really their Beecher Lake. The rest of the essays are about other rambles, in the District of Columbia, the Adirondacks, and elsewhere.

One can usually tell where Burroughs is as he writes. He learned much, after all, from Whitman and Thoreau, though he did not have to announce, as Thoreau did, "We commonly do not remember that it is, after all, always the first person that is speaking. I should not talk so much about myself if there were any other person that I knew as well." And he had too much to be concerned about outside himself to bother with the self-obsession of Walt Whitman:

> I celebrate myself, and sing myself,
>
> And what I assume you shall assume,
>
> For every atom belonging to me as good belongs to you.

The concern with his image, however, and the careful recording of himself in photographs, is something Burroughs learned well from, and with, Whitman, and it is one of the legacies he has passed on to us, in countless pictures of his life and movements.

The two volumes after *Wake-Robin*, made up of essays first published before the move to the Hudson Valley or shortly after it, are much more distant from nature. They are, in fact, almost cosmopolitan. The country boy has been caught in what Whitman called "the blab of the pave." The first of the two is *Winter Sunshine*, which is dominated by the long essay "An October Abroad," which is on England, and the shorter essay "Exhilarations of the Road," which begins the volume and is mostly based in the Potomac area. There are, however, the essays "The Snow Walkers," "The Fox," "Autumn Tides" and "The Apple," which are somewhat free from England and the capital district, but which seem to have more research than direct observation in their groundwork.

Next came the volume *Birds and Poets*, first published in 1877, which is more poets than birds, particularly in "The Flight of the Eagle," in which the bird is only a metaphor for Whitman, and the essay entitled simply "Emerson," in which even the metaphors don't fly. There is, however, the essay "A Bird Medley," written in Esopus in 1874, the time when the death of his nephew Channy brought him such grief. In that essay he comes close to prognosticating his future career, when he says "The valley of the Hudson, I find, forms a great highway for the birds. . . ." After a few paragraphs he describes the migration of passenger pigeons:

A year ago last April, the pigeons flew for two or three days up and down the Hudson. In long bowing lines, or else in dense masses, they moved across the sky. It was not the whole army, but I should think at least one corps of it; I had not seen such a flight of pigeons since my boyhood. I went up to the top of the house, the better to behold the winged procession. The day seemed memorable and poetic in which such sights occur.

The note to this passage in the 1895 edition reads: "This proved to be the last flight of the pigeons in the valley of the Hudson. The whole tribe has now been terminated by pot-hunters. The few that still remain appear to be scattered through the Northern States in small, loose flocks."

And there is also in *Birds and Poets* the delightful pastoral eclogue entitled "Our Rural Divinity." Oddly enough, however, the locale for this set of misadventures with the Burroughs family cows is Washington, D.C. Perhaps it should be read at the opening of every session of Congress. At least a passage like this one:

This was during the Arcadian age at the capital, before the easy-going Southern ways had gone out and the prim Northern ways had come in, and when the domestic animals were treated with distinguished consideration and granted the freedom of the city. There was a charm of cattle in the street and upon the commons; goats cropped your rose-bushes through the pickets, and nooned upon your front porch; and pigs dreamed Arcadian dreams under your garden fence, or languidly frescoed it with pigments from the nearest pool. It was a time of peace; it was the poor man's golden age.

In these second and third volumes of the Riverside edition of Burroughs' *Works*, however, we see the first-class literary artist emerge. He has been published time after time in the leading periodicals of the time. He has been to England and visited some of that nation's leading literary figures. He has done the same in his own nation, and he has linked his name with one of America's leading avant-garde poets, Walt Whitman. He gives evidence of having read widely and well in the belles lettres and the scientific literature of his time. He will even demonstrate that somewhere, somehow, he has learned Latin—the badge of intellectual accomplishment. This was no country bumpkin who settled in Esopus in 1873.

Then, in his fourth volume, *Locusts and Wild Honey*, the Burroughs we know best comes forward, and the second essay in the volume, entitled "Sharp Eyes," encapsulates the latest refinement—the career-refinement—in Burroughs' approach to his art. It is partially expressed in this passage:

Nevertheless the habit of observation is the habit of clear and decisive gazing: not by a first casual glance, but by a steady, deliberate aim of the eye are the rare and characteristic things discovered. You must look intently, and hold your eye firmly to the spot, to see more than do the rank and file of mankind. The sharpshooter picks out his man, and knows him with fatal certainty from a stump, or a rock, or a cap on a pole. The phrenologists do well to locate, not only form, color, and weight, in the region of the eye, but also a faculty which they call originality,—that which separates, discriminates, and sees in every object its essential character. This is just as necessary to the naturalist as to the artist or the poet. The sharp eye notes specific points and differences,—it seizes upon and preserves the individuality of the thing.

That volume, *Locusts and Wild Honey*, in its demonstration of the art of observation of natural phenomena, may be the finest collection Burroughs assembled. Besides "Sharp Eyes," there are the essays "The Pastoral Bees," "Strawberries," "Is it Going to Rain?," "Speckled Trout," "Birds and Birds," "A Bed of Boughs," "Birds-Nesting," and "The Halcyon in Canada." This volume combines with the seventh volume, *Signs and*

Seasons, to show John Burroughs in his mature phase as observer of nature. He now has the tools he will use so effectively later, in the "nature fakir" dispute.

Before we leave *Locusts and Wild Honey*, let us look at the essay "A Bed of Boughs," the piece that in many ways, exemplifies best Burroughs' movements about the Riverby-Roxbury axis. It is the record of a trip out of West Park he made with his good friend Aaron Johns, who "came to camp and tramp with me, or, as he wrote, 'to eat locusts and wild honey with me in the wilderness.'" It's discussion about where they should go, they set out for Peekamoose and the upper Rondout valley. They walk along the trails of locust bark peelers, they look at water and rock and tree scenery, they fish, they sleep out on the ground, and once in a while they knock at a door and requisition bread and milk. The image of a bearded, baggy-pantalooned John Burroughs standing at a door just opened by a rustic maiden—reproduced in the Clifton Johnson photograph is so familiar that it could provide the outline for a Burroughs logo.

Before they return home, tired and happy (with Burroughs less tired and happier than Johns, one suspects) they will have followed the east branch of the Neversink and crossed Slide Mountain to the west branch, and finally, after a railroad journey from the area of Biscuit Brook to Kingston, made the last part of the journey on blistering feet over eight downhill miles to West Park. *Signs and Seasons* was published in 1886. Leading it off was the essay "A Sharp Lookout," which had been completed in 1882 under the title that now graced the entire volume, "Signs and Seasons." And that essay begins with words that express one of the principal attitudes toward art, toward science, and toward life that Burroughs imparted, and show the importance to him of his perch on the Hudson:

> One has only to sit down in the woods or the fields, or by the shore of the river or the lake, and nearly everything of interest will come round to him,—the birds, the animals, the insects; and presently, after his eye has got accustomed to the place, and to the light and shade, he will probably see some plant or flower that he has sought in vain, and that is a pleasant surprise to him. So, on a large scale, the student and lover of nature has this advantage over people who gad up and down the world, seeking some novelty or excitement; he has only to stay at home and see the procession pass.

To the literary scholar, most of this is old stuff. The basic attitude can be seen at least as early as Wordsworth or the early William Cullen Bryant. Emerson had much to say in the same vein. But what is different is that Burroughs, in many ways a romantic scientist, is using scientific approaches while sitting still in his backyard by the Hudson, without any scientific apparatus. After a few more sentences in "A Sharp Lookout," he places himself precisely there, sounding much like Thoreau at Walden Pond or Whitman on Long Island.

> I sit here amid the junipers of the Hudson, with purpose to go to Florida, or to the West Indies, or to the Pacific coast, yet the seasons pass and I am still loitering, with a half-defined suspicion, perhaps, that, if I remain quiet and keep a sharp lookout, these countries will come to me.

And those of us who live in the Mid-Hudson Valley know very well the junipers he is talking about, which are almost as commonplace as purple loosestrife in the area, even though many of our neighbors call them "cedars." Incidentally, Burroughs talks at length about the loosestrife in "Among the Wild Flowers," which was reprinted in the *Riverby* volume.

Thus, by the 1880's, Burroughs was ready as he ever would be for the rewards of the bright future he had been busily fashioning. He will continue busily taking himself and the Hudson Valley out into the world

---

Alfred Marks

for thirty-five more years, and for just as long the rest of the world will come to him. In 1895, he will construct the cabin Slabsides where he can entertain in a way consonant with his mythical presence as man of the woods. And there he will receive Theodore Dreiser, John Muir, Elbert Hubbard, Poultney Bigelow and Theodore Roosevelt. Walt Whitman, Oscar Wilde, and many others will be given more refined treatment by his wife at Riverby.

He will publish many more volumes of essays, on literature, on geology, on evolution, and on life in general. In 1903, he will make himself controversial, in the essay "Real and Sham Natural History," published in the March Atlantic. That will not be anything new, however. In "Hasty Observation," which was reprinted in 1894 in the volume entitled *Riverby*, he quietly reports with polite incredulity observations by Boswell, Albertus Magnus, and lesser myopic individuals, and although he says in the Prefatory Note to *Riverby* he believes that will be his "last collection of Out-of-door papers," he will publish at least three more such works.

In 1914, he will he approached by Henry Ford, offering to give him one of his newfangled motorcars, and Burroughs will create headlines as he risks life and limb driving it around local roads. He will go on motor excursions with Ford and mutual friends Thomas Edison and Harvey Firestone, and they will park their tin tizzies in front of Slabsides and make the Roxbury night bright under the light produced by Mr. Edison's portable generators. Some of Burroughs' adventures with these nineteenth-century men who helped make the twentieth century run will even be recorded in motion pictures.

Then, in 1921, not long after his death, Mrs. Henry Ford and a number of other notable friends gathered together at the American Museum of Natural History, in the city Burroughs knew so well, New York, to form the John Burroughs Memorial Association. That organization still functions today and is well known among American authors for its John Burroughs Medal for Natural History Writing. From 1985 to 1989 I was so fortunate as to be present at the ceremony at which the medal was awarded to the author of the outstanding natural history book published in the past year. Every one of those excellent volumes was written in the same spirit of careful observation of natural phenomena that Burroughs exemplified. They were *Cry of the Kalahari*, by Mark and Delia Owens; *Gathering the Desert*, by Gary Paul Nabhan; *Wintergreen*, by Robert Michael Pyle; *On Watching Birds*, by Lawrence Kilham; and *The Control of Nature*, by John McPhee. They are not on the Hudson Valley, but on locales and natural phenomena widely distributed about the United States and even in Africa, but all show the extraordinary heights to which the Burroughs technique of sitting watchfully in one place can be raised.

John Burroughs brought many of the intimate details of the Hudson Valley and his way of catching and dealing with them graphically into the world, and the world replied in full measure. His "Bark Study" still stands in West Park near the river, as does his rustic "Slabsides" a mile inland in the woods, to remind the world of the vantage points he established in the Hudson Valley, the better to catch the world as it shifted by.

This article originally appeared in the *Hudson Valley Regional Review*, Volume 12.2.

Contributors

Rohit T. Aggarwala is director of the New York City Mayor's Office of Long-term Planning and Sustainability. He holds a Ph.D. in History from Columbia University.

Vernon Benjamin, teaches history at Bard College and Marist College and has previously written on the controversial Tawagonshi Hill Agreement between the Dutch traders and Iroquois Indians in 1613. He is presently completing a history of the Hudson River Valley for Overlook Press which will be published later this year.

Claire Brandt is the author of *An American Aristocracy: The Livingstons* (Doubleday). A graduate of Radcliffe, she is a past president of the Friends of Clermont and resident of Rhinebeck, New York.

Mark Carnes is a Professor of History at Barnard College, Columbia University. He served as co-editor for the 24 volume *American National Biography* as well as Executive Secretary of the Society of American Historians.

Thomas W. Casey taught philosophy and local history at Marist College. He founded the Fern Tor History Project, initiated the first "History and Culture of the Hudson Valley" course, and cofounded the arboretum at Marist College.

Firth Haring Fabend has a Ph.D. in American Studies from New York University. Her recent publications include *A Dutch Family in the Middle Colonies 1600–1800* and *Zion on the Hudson: Dutch New York and New Jersey in the Age of Revivals*.

Charles T. Gehring, director of the New Netherland Project, is also a translator and editor of the New Netherland Documents. He has a Ph.D. in Germanic languages from Indiana University.

Michael Groth is an Associate Professor of History at Wells College in Aurora, New York. He holds his Ph.D. in American History from State University of New York (SUNY) at Binghamton.

James M. Johnson, the author of *Militiamen, Rangers, and Redcoats: The Military in Georgia, 1754–1776* (Mercer University Press), is the Military Historian of the Hudson River Valley National Heritage Are and Executive Director of the Hudson River Valley Institute.

Cynthia Kierner earned the Ph.D. in the Corcoran Department of History at the University of Virginia. Her books include *Traders and Gentlefolk: The Livingstons of New York, 1674–1790*. She is currently a Professor of History at George Mason University.

Susan Ingalls Lewis is an Associate Professor of History at at SUNY New Paltz, and the author of *Unexceptional Women: Female Proprietors in Mi-Nineteenth Century Albany, New York* from Ohio State University Press.

Alfred Marks was a member of the Hudson Valley Regional Review board and served many years as Professor of English at SUNY New Paltz. He is currently the Town Historian of New Paltz.

Donald Ringe is Professor Emeritus of English at the University of Kentucky at Lexington. He is the author of *James Fenimore Cooper*, and *American Gothic: Imagination and Reason in Nineteenth-Century Fiction*.

Kenneth Shefsiek is the Executive Director of the Geneva Historical Society. He previously serves as the Museum Curator at the Huguenot Historical Society in New Paltz, New York.

William A. Starna is an adjunct professor Emeritus of Geography at Queens University in Ontario. He was previously Professor Emeritus of Anthropology at SUNY Oneonta and the co-editor of *Iroquois Land Claims*.

Robert M. Toole is a landscape architect practicing in Saratoga, New York. He has been involved over the years with numerous studies of the development of estates on the Hudson River. He was the Principal Consultant for the Management Plan for the mid-Hudson Historic Shorelands Scenic District.

Thomas S. Wermuth is the Vice President for Academic Affairs and Dean of Faculty at Marist College and author of *Rip Van Winkle's Neighbors: The Transformation of Rural Society in the Hudson River Valley*, published by the State University of New York Press.

Patricia West is the Curator for the Martin Van Buren National Historic Site and teaches in the Public History Graduate Program at SUNY Albany. She is the author of *Domesticating History: The Political Origins of American House Museums*, published by Smithsonian Press

Richard C. Wiles was the former editor of the *Hudson Valley Regional Review*. He has a Ph.D. from Clark University and served as the Dean of Academic Affairs at Bard College, where he is currently a Professor Emeritus of Economics.